# LIVING ABROAD LONDON

KAREN WHITE

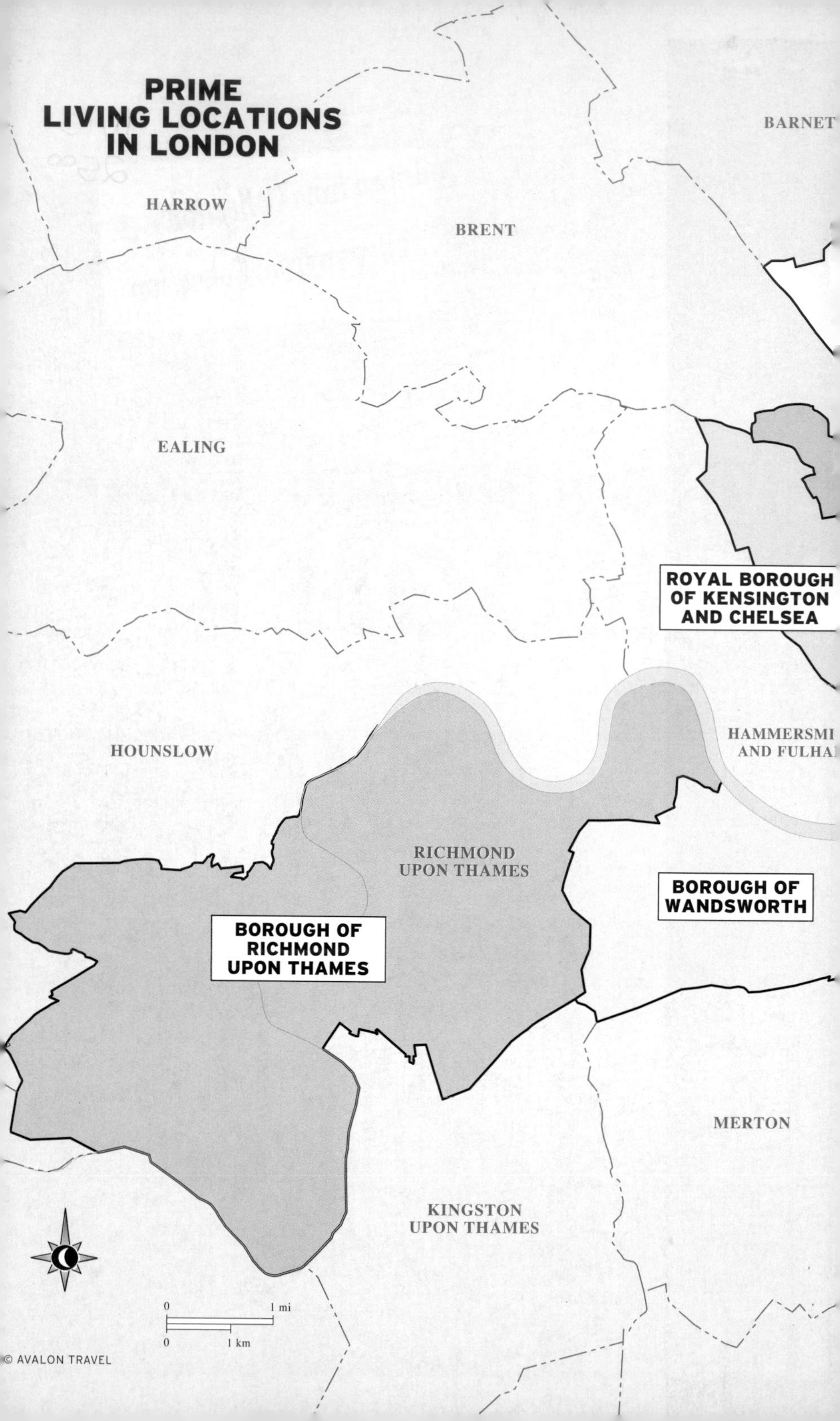
PRIME
LIVING LOCATIONS
IN LONDON
BARNET
HARROW
BRENT
EALING
ROYAL BOROUGH
OF KENSINGTON
AND CHELSEA
HOUNSLOW
HAMMERSMI
AND FULHA
RICHMOND
UPON THAMES
BOROUGH OF
WANDSWORTH
BOROUGH OF
RICHMOND
UPON THAMES
MERTON
KINGSTON
UPON THAMES
0
1 mi
0
1 km
© AVALON TRAVEL

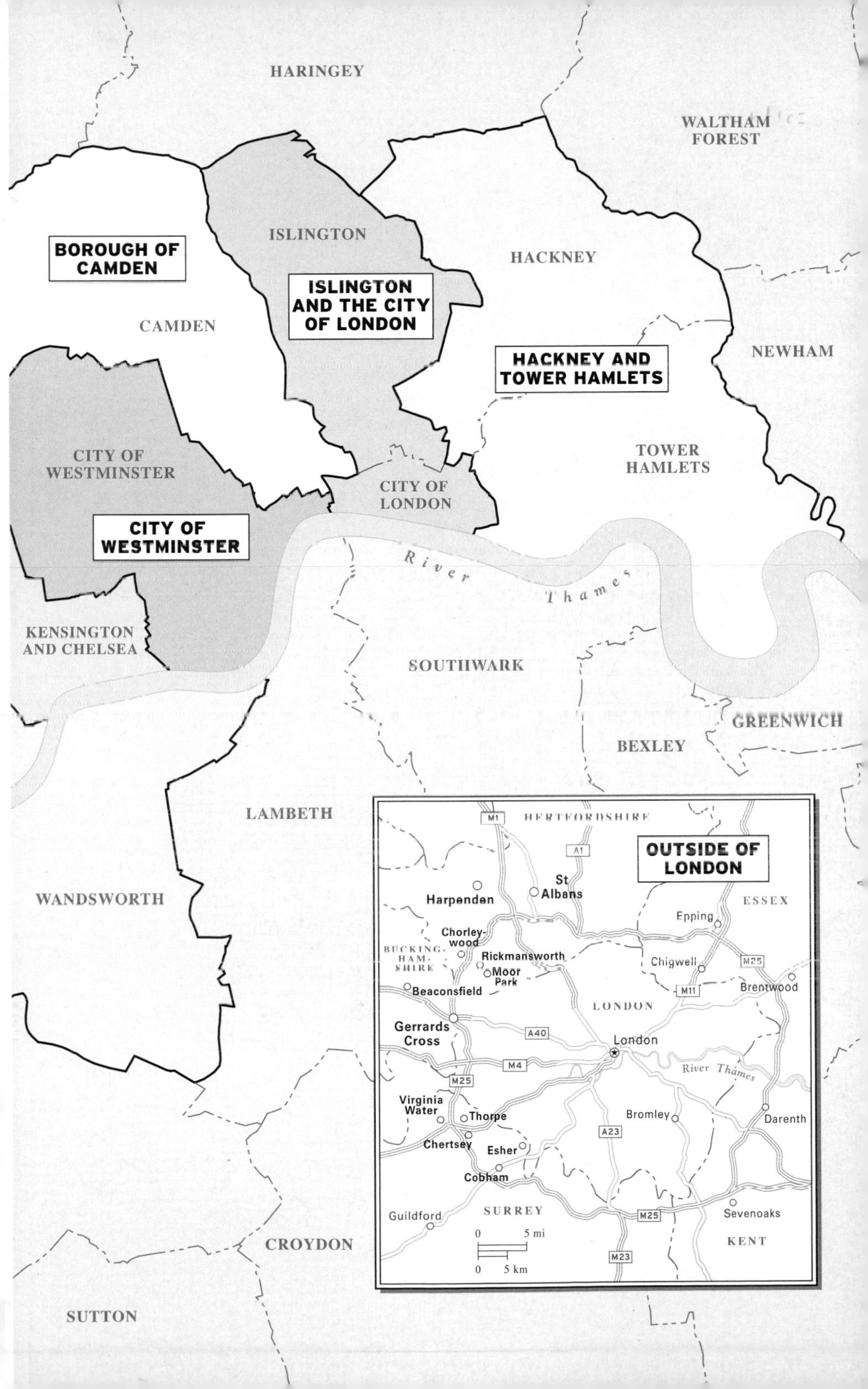
HARINGEY
WALTHAM FOREST
BOROUGH OF CAMDEN
ISLINGTON
HACKNEY
ISLINGTON AND THE CITY OF LONDON
CAMDEN
NEWHAM
HACKNEY AND TOWER HAMLETS
CITY OF WESTMINSTER
TOWER HAMLETS
CITY OF LONDON
CITY OF WESTMINSTER
River Thames
KENSINGTON AND CHELSEA
SOUTHWARK
GREENWICH
BEXLEY
LAMBETH
WANDSWORTH
CROYDON
SUTTON
OUTSIDE OF LONDON
M1
HERTFORDSHIRE
A1
St Albans
Harpenden
ESSEX
Epping
Chorley-wood
BUCKING-HAM-SHIRE
Rickmansworth
Moor Park
Chigwell
M25
M11
Brentwood
Beaconsfield
LONDON
Gerrards Cross
A40
London
M4
River Thames
M25
Virginia Water
Thorpe
Bromley
Dartford
Chertsey
Esher
A23
Cobham
Guildford
SURREY
M25
Sevenoaks
0 5 mi
0 5 km
KENT
M23

# Contents

AT HOME IN

# London

Whether it's due to our shared history and culture, or the fact that we speak the same language (well, almost), many Americans are drawn to London, be it to study, further their careers, or broaden their horizons. While a spell in London can certainly boost your professional standing, it can do much more than that. Living on the other side of the pond offers a view of the world through a new lens.

In many ways, I had it easy when I arrived here. I had previously lived in England, so I had already been through the culture shock. Nevertheless, the prospect of living in such a massive city was daunting. There's no denying that it is a *big* city: The pollution, congestion, noise, and crowds make this perfectly clear. I was afraid that London would be a cold, isolating place, where I would be just one face amongst thousands, lost in the city's vastness.

I needn't have feared. London is not just a city—it's a collection of villages and neighborhoods. My neighbors nod hello, and even the owners of local shops greet me when I pop in for some milk. Many newcomers are amazed by how accessible London feels. There are parks where kids can play, world-class museums can be explored for free, and traveling around by bus is a great, entertaining way to see the city . . . even if the Tube is faster. Those expecting a cold, unfriendly urban center with expensive (and bad) food will find instead a vibrant, engaging city, where kids can quickly make friends playing soccer in the park and the local bistro cooks up a mean *moules marinières*.

Lively and dynamic, London also values its long history and seeks to preserve it—the past is very much part of the city's present. Just take a

look around: The streets are still filled with buildings that look just as they did hundreds of years ago. Sure, there are modern skyscrapers as well, but these tend to be in the financial districts. In Bloomsbury, where I first settled, you'll find Georgian terraced houses with little garden squares in the middle.

Our daily life in London is pretty sweet. My husband has a pleasant walk across the park in the morning to the Tube station where he heads to his job in the City of London. Long workdays are made more palatable by after-work visits to the pub with friends and colleagues. Weekends are filled with visits to farmers markets, retail therapy in the West End, and sunny bike rides along the South Bank (or rainy-day visits to world-renowned museums).

Whatever your reasons might be for "upping sticks" and heading across the Atlantic, the best thing to do is just relax and enjoy the experience. Accept that it isn't just like home. Rejoice in the differences between our countries and let your days in London expand your horizons. You may even find, as I did, that you really don't want to leave.

Pretty sweet, indeed.

## ▸ WHAT I LOVE ABOUT LONDON

- In London you can live in a normal residential street (with backyard and local park) yet be less than two miles from the heart of the city.
- World-renowned museums (such as the British Museum and Tate Modern) are free.
- The shopping is spectacular—whatever you are after you can find it here; you just need to know where to look.
- The numerous green open spaces are a hallmark of the capital. You can walk the dog in the woodlands of Hampstead Heath, ride bikes past wild deer in Richmond Park, or feed the ducks in Hyde Park's Serpentine Lake.
- The extensive system of public transportation (with its mix of the Underground, trains, buses, trams, boats, and even bicycle rentals) is a godsend.
- Here history is on every corner, evident in the capital's streets and architecture, from 18th-century shepherd's cottages to the grand Georgian villas and the occasional medieval churches.
- It's magical to wander around London—especially the City of London and Clerkenwell—on a Sunday, when all the streets are deserted and you can explore its back alleyways without fear of being run over.
- Markets galore: Borough Market is a gourmet's heaven; Portobello Market and Camden Passage are great for antiques; Brick Lane has tasty fast food; Cabbages and Frocks has lovely jewelry and clothing; and don't forget Camden Market, with its overwhelming choice of everything.
- Nothing beats watching the street entertainers on the South Bank and strolling along the southern edge of the River Thames on the weekend.
- There is always something well worth seeing, be it a play, a concert, a gallery, a movie, a museum—the list is endless.
- With just an Oyster card, there is so much you can do that's free.

# WELCOME TO LONDON

© IVAN MATEEV/123RF.COM

# INTRODUCTION

> You find no man, at all intellectual, who is willing to leave London. No, Sir, when a man is tired of London, he is tired of life; for there is in London all that life can afford.
>
> Samuel Johnson, 1777

More than 200 years later Samuel Johnson's words still ring true, with London being one of the world's greatest cities. Whatever you are into—be it Michelin-star restaurants, madcap musicals, or stately homes—you can find it in London.

If the crowds throughout the year are anything to go by, London certainly seems to be a very popular destination for tourists from all four corners of the globe. From the royal pageantry of Buckingham Palace to numerous museums and cultural activities, not to forget one of the world's best-known shopping precincts (Oxford and Regent Streets), London attracts tourists on several different levels with something for everyone. Yet, visiting somewhere for a short vacation isn't the same as living there. Those contemplating a move to London need to realize that they are in it for the long haul and should be prepared for the noise and crowds, the expense, and the inevitable cultural differences that will emerge.

Just as Paris dominates France or New York City used to dominate the rest of the

United States, London is very much the powerhouse of the United Kingdom. For centuries London has been England's commercial, political, and cultural headquarters. Given its size and status, it's not that surprising that the city dominates the rest of England (as well as the United Kingdom for that matter). Undoubtedly, London is the nucleus of the United Kingdom's economy, especially the City of London (a world-class financial center). This dominance means that London and the southeast of England are wealthier than much of the rest of the country. This can be quite noticeable when you travel around the rest of Britain and Northern Ireland, especially the northeast of England, Wales, and Northern Ireland. Of course, London's strong economy doesn't preclude it having its own deprived districts. There are certainly several underprivileged areas in London where both unemployment and crime are high.

Despite London's massive size (with more than eight million inhabitants and around 13 million in its greater metropolitan area), I am often surprised by its strong sense of community, even in busy downtown areas. This is all the more unusual given the wide diversity of people that live in London. There are those whose families originally came from Commonwealth countries (such as India, Pakistan, or Jamaica) as well as numerous European nationals, along with the odd Yank. With such a wide mix of people from such different backgrounds, it's no wonder that London is a hive of activity both socially and culturally.

What draws people here is the vast range of opportunities that are available in London. These are opportunities not just for business or employment, but that also embrace educational, cultural, or leisure possibilities. Most American expats come to London for professional or academic reasons, yet some stay here year after year having fallen for the city and its lifestyle.

## The Lay of the Land

London is in the southeast of England and lies on the River Thames, some 50 miles (80 kilometers) from the coast. It is the European Union's largest city, with the Greater London area measuring over 600 square miles (more than 1,550 square kilometers). Its gargantuan size and density mean that the city can be intimidating at times, especially when you are out of your comfort zone and in an unknown area of town. Yet part of what makes London so exciting is that there are so many hidden treasures well away from the beaten tourist paths just waiting to be explored.

As it is so vast, it should be no surprise that London can be separated and divided on several different levels: north, south, east, and west; central, inner, and outer London; not to forget its boroughs (local municipal governments). Often places are referred to by the nearest Tube station or postcode (the British zip code), both of which are an easy way to refer to specific areas in this massive city. After more than two decades of living in London, I still do not know my way around town completely. There are huge swaths of the city that are a complete blank to me and necessitate the use of the *London A to Z* (a book of street maps) or a GPS navigation system to find my way around.

## CITY DIVISIONS

On a very general level London has a north-south split, with the River Thames acting as the dividing line. For centuries, the river was the lifeblood of the capital as its ports drew in goods imported from all over the globe to be traded and sold. Nowadays the Thames is much less important than in years gone by, though it is still a major feature of London's geography. Certainly getting across the river in rush-hour traffic can be a major headache for commuters who rely on their car or the bus. Traditionally, most business and commerce is based north of the Thames or just along its southern bank, where there is better public transportation, including more Underground lines and stations. This has mistakenly led many people to assume that the better areas of town are all north of the Thames. However, the south of the river is home to some very desirable areas of town, even if much of the public transportation infrastructure is limited to Overground trains and buses.

Historically, the city has also been separated by an east-west divide—the "East End" and "West End." The old Roman part of London (Londinium) was in the part of town now known as the "City of London." As London's population grew, the city became ever more crowded with filth and disease. Wealthier people moved west to avoid the squalor of the city and to be upwind of the stench. This established the West End of London as the more affluent and genteel area of town. At the same time, the slums to the east of the city became home to London's poorer inhabitants. To a certain extent these differences can still be seen today, with West London generally more prosperous than the east of the city. In fact, the West London borough of Kensington and Chelsea is the wealthiest area in both London and the United Kingdom—thanks in part to a few extremely wealthy individuals. As with any city, where you live in London can speak volumes about you and your lifestyle. These days trendy urbanites and artists

the vastness of London, as seen from the London Eye

often flock to Shoreditch (just northeast of the City of London), while the traditional wealthiest areas of London remain in the west, with fashionable Notting Hill and more traditional Chelsea home to some of the city's most expensive properties.

People commonly refer to areas of town as "North London" or "West London" to give a general idea of the area of town they are talking about. They may well combine these so that you get Northwest or Southeast London. In addition, there are inner and outer areas of London, with an even smaller center of town. This is mainly composed of the City of London and the City of Westminster, plus a few neighborhoods from a few of the inner London boroughs. These concentric rings around London are loosely based on transportation routes around the city—be it the Underground's Circle line around the center of town or major roads and highways farther out of town.

## London's Boroughs

As London is such a large city, in the mid-1960s the national government departmentalized the city's administration into smaller municipal governing bodies known as boroughs (pronounced "burruhs"). London has 32 boroughs, plus the City of London (which is considered a separate entity and not officially a borough). Twelve of the boroughs are classed as inner London boroughs, as is the City of London. The remainder are referred to as outer London boroughs. As a generalization, the inner London boroughs have a greater density of population and are more racially mixed, with the outer London boroughs more suburban.

Like most municipal bodies, London's boroughs are responsible for providing local services to its residents, such as state-run schools, road maintenance, street lighting, refuse and recycling collection, and so on. The City of London also functions like a borough, as it is administered by a separate municipal governing body—the Corporation of London. This is the oldest municipal body in England and can be traced all the way back to 1067! The City of London's Court of Common Council formed the basis of the United Kingdom's national Parliament, based in Westminster, and is commonly referred to as the "Grandmother of Parliaments."

In addition to the 32 London boroughs and the Corporation of London, there is a larger city-wide administrative body—the Greater London Authority (GLA). This municipal body oversees the administration of London-wide services and initiatives: everything from public transportation to reducing air pollution and supporting cultural events. The GLA is run by a directly elected mayor and the London Assembly, whose job it is to scrutinize the mayor's policies and to agree with or reject the mayor's annual budget proposals. The boroughs get a certain amount of funding from the central government, and they also raise funds through a local property tax known as the council tax.

## London's Villages and Green Spaces

One of the facts that many visitors to London fail to appreciate is that the city is made up of numerous villages, which centuries ago would have been separated by open rural landscapes. Well-known areas, such as Hampstead or Chelsea, were once rural villages outside of London. Through the centuries, these once-isolated villages have been swallowed up by the giant urban sprawl that is now considered to be London. However, elements of these villages are still very evident today, with a "high street" (similar to our "main street") where you will find banks, the post office, and stores. Some of these old villages have a strong sense of local community and distinctive local character. They certainly help Londoners to partition up the city into smaller, more accessible neighborhoods and communities.

Also helping to make this urban metropolis more palatable are the numerous parks and squares throughout the city, giving Londoners an oasis of green to which they can retreat away from the busy streets. A leisurely stroll (or more energetic run) around any of London's parks is a great way to recharge your batteries. There are five Royal Parks in the center of town, with Hyde Park probably the best known. Centuries ago these parks were used by the monarchy for their entertainment (often for deer hunting), but they gradually turned into public spaces for Londoners as the city became increasingly urbanized. In addition to the Royal Parks you'll find smaller borough-run parks dotted all over town, giving children a place to play and joggers a place to stretch their legs. The Corporation of London owns a great deal of land in the capital, including several parks, such as the ancient woodland of Hampstead Heath.

## Postcodes

As if getting your head around London and its numerous neighborhoods wasn't hard enough, there is yet another way that London has been split up into smaller pieces—its postcodes. A postcode is the United Kingdom's equivalent to America's zip codes. And just like a zip code, a fully extended postcode is a vital element of any address in the United Kingdom. A letter with a complete postcode and house number should be all that the mail carrier needs to sort and deliver the mail.

Thankfully, the Royal Mail in its wisdom decided to base the prefixes for London's

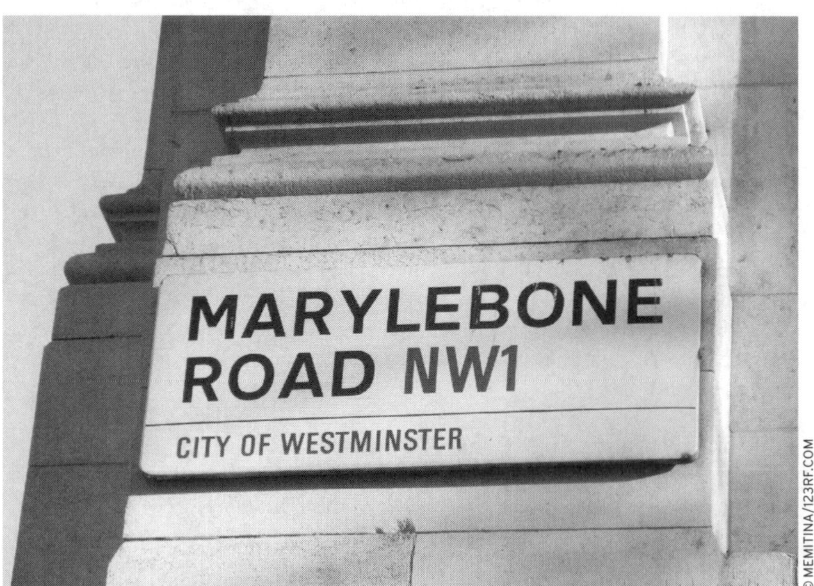


© MEMITINA/123RF.COM

sign indicating postcode NW1

postcodes geographically. So, for example, a postcode starting with W means that it is in the west side of town, while EC1A refers to East Central 1A—part of the City of London. For some reason London does not have any postcode prefixes that start with NE (northeast), although it does make use of NW (northwest), SW (southwest), and SE (southeast). Oddly enough, the postcodes that start with NE are up in the northeast of England, around the city of Newcastle.

Another oddity is that postcodes *do not* run along borough boundaries. This can be an important consideration when you are house hunting. Generally, apartments and houses are listed by postcode. If it is important for you to live in a particular area and borough—perhaps because you want your children to go to a particular school—double-check with the rental agent regarding which borough the property is in if the address is near the border.

### Greater London and Beyond

As with most big cities, the conurbation around London stretches for miles beyond its formal boundaries. Six counties surround the capital: Kent, Surrey, Essex, Hertfordshire, Buckinghamshire, and Berkshire. With London's house prices sky high, many people are forced to commute phenomenal distances to their work in London. Equally, many people want a bit more space and so choose to live in these "home counties" and commute into London for work. This way they can avoid the frenetic atmosphere of the city as well as the close proximity of neighbors and more costly housing. However, this then means that they have a long and expensive commute by train or car to and from work. Like most things in life, living in Greater London or one of the capital's commuter belts is a trade-off between the cost of property and time spent in the daily commute.

## WEATHER AND SEASONS

One of the hardest things I found to get used to when I first moved to the United Kingdom was how London's latitude—51°30' North—affects the daylight. No sooner had the clocks gone back at the end of October than the days suddenly got much shorter, heralding the arrival of winter. By December I found I was leaving home and leaving work in the dark, as the sun didn't rise until around 8am and set before 4pm . . . a bit depressing to say the least! Having come from sunny California, the lack of daylight soon got to me. Likewise, the long days of summer also take some getting used to, as the sun starts to rise at around 4am (with the birds starting at around 3am!). It can be very hard to sleep when the sun is streaming into the bedroom at 5am, not to mention trying to get the children to bed (and asleep) when it is still sunny—in June the sun doesn't set until around 9:20pm. Lovely as it is to have a sunny day, most of us still want and need our eight hours of sleep. To negate the effect of the early morning sun in the summer, many people in the United Kingdom rely on blackout curtains. This curtain lining is a godsend and will provide a bit of thermal insulation in the winter months in addition to keeping the sun out during the summer months.

Given that it is so far north, London and the British Isles are surprisingly temperate. We have the warm Gulf Stream to thank for our relatively mild weather, as it pulls warm water from the Caribbean up to Western Europe, making it warmer than

© KAREN WHITE

a snow-covered bench in Wimbledon Common

it should be given its latitude. This means that London seldom experiences extreme cold in the winter or stifling heat in the summer. The average daytime temperature in January is around 8°C (46°F), with an average high in July of 22°C (73°F). There will of course be some summer days when the temperature climbs above 25°C (77°F) or even 30°C (86°F). Conversely, the temperature in the winter can plummet to around or even below freezing, but most homes have some form of heating to help keep you warm at night.

One fact of London weather that you do need to prepare for is rain, which seems to happen throughout the year. Although the average rainfall isn't actually that high (around 23 inches/58 centimeters a year), rain clouds do seem to descend on the city with great regularity—usually in the form of a drizzle. The easiest solution is to just have a small lightweight umbrella or shower-proof parka on hand. London gets an occasional thunderstorm when rain pours down, but for the most part the rain is fairly light.

Much to the annoyance of London's children, snow is relatively unusual in the city. This is partly because the city generates so much heat from the buildings and cars that it rarely gets cold enough for it to snow (or at least for the snow to settle). Generally, London is several degrees warmer than the neighboring countryside beyond the city. As it is relatively uncommon, when it does snow in London the whole city can come to a standstill, creating misery and chaos. Both the Underground and the train services can be disrupted by freezing weather and snow. Despite what the name implies, London's Underground is generally only underground in the middle of town. As the Tube lines head away from the center of town the trains go aboveground, making them susceptible to snow and ice. Freezing weather and snow can also upset London's train services, with ice on the rails likely to cause cancellations and delays. Yet it is the traffic that seems to suffer the most when snow falls. Just an inch of snow can cause major disruption to London's traffic. This is made worse because so few people are accustomed to driving in snow and ice, and they misjudge the conditions, often with disastrous consequences.

A few years ago I drove to a mall in North London in late afternoon to pick up a gift. As I arrived the snow was just starting to come down, but not really settling. I quickly did my shopping in an attempt to get away before the rush hour, which was bound to be worse because of the snow. Of course I was too late and in just an hour around an inch or two fell. Now, for those of you used to snow in winter two inches is nothing, but in London it can cause major gridlock. That evening it took me more than two hours to get out of the shopping mall's parking lot! The snow had come down too quickly and the local borough didn't grit the roads with sand and salt in time. The whole situation was made worse because the entrance and exit to the mall were on a slight hill. Driver after driver failed to make it up the small incline in the snowy conditions. This, combined with drivers unaccustomed to maneuvering in the snow, meant that accidents and gridlock ensued as people fled the crowded mall. I later found out that some people never made it out of the mall that evening and were forced to spend the night there. So be warned; if it starts to snow London will come to a standstill until the snow thaws.

It is also worth pointing out that Britain's usual weather pattern may be changing. Following more than a decade of extremely mild winters, the past couple of years have brought colder winter temperatures and wetter conditions to the United Kingdom. This increase in more extreme weather conditions may just be part of Northern Europe's long-term weather cycles, or it may be a more worrying sign of climate change. If Britain is indeed experiencing climate change, then London will need to get more organized about dealing with the effects of wet or snowy weather.

At the other end of the scale, London seldom has sweltering summers. About the best we can hope for is a few days in the low 80s (F), when London becomes pleasantly warm and everyone heads to the parks to enjoy the summer sunshine. One thing to bear in mind is that London homes are not usually set up for long hot summers. You are unlikely to find (or need) a house with air-conditioning. I can remember just one unbearably hot summer in all of my 20 years or so of living in London—the summer of 2003. Otherwise we just have the odd spell of hot weather that usually lasts a week or two. For the most part London's summers tend to be fairly damp affairs—as any Wimbledon tennis fan can tell you.

## FLORA AND FAUNA

Centuries ago Britain was covered in deciduous forests of oak, birch, elm, and ash trees. Through the years, the forests were cleared to make arable land for farming and livestock. In London we are lucky enough to have two "wild" parks (Hampstead Heath and Richmond Park), which give Londoners a glimpse of what the region would be like if left to its own devices. One nonnative tree that is commonly planted across the city is the cultivated hybrid of the Oriental plane and American sycamore trees, *Platanus*

## The Myth of Foggy London

*A foggy day in London town*
*Had me low, had me down*

"A Foggy Day (In London Town)," George and Ira Gershwin

Thanks to the Gershwin brothers, it is generally thought that London must be bathed in fog throughout the year. What people don't understand is that the fog in the song referred to smog caused by millions of coal fires being burned in the city.

Much of London's housing stock was built in the Victorian and Edwardian eras (1830s to 1910s). At the time, coal fires were the main source of heating in London's homes and businesses. With so many coal fires burning, heavy thick "fogs" or smogs were a common occurrence in the 19th century through to the first half of the 20th century during the winter months. The smoke from all these chimneys filled the capital with dirty acrid smog, and if there wasn't a breeze to blow the polluted air away, a thick fog would descend on the city.

Although a foggy day may seem romantic, the poor air quality of a heavy and prolonged fog could be deadly. In 1952 a particularly bad fog lasted for four days and is thought to have killed up to 4,000. As a result the government finally acted to improve London's air quality with the introduction of the Clean Air Act and smokeless zones in the city in the mid-1950s. With Londoners no longer able to burn soft coal, the levels of sulphur dioxide fell and the city's air quality began to improve. Finally, London's thick "pea soup fogs" were a thing of the past.

Today there are occasional foggy days in London, but these are usually the result of low temperatures and still winds, which cause the morning dew to condense and create a fog. Thankfully the days of a killer fog are gone, although London's air quality is still pretty poor—certainly the worst in the UK and among the worst in Europe. Today the main culprit as far as air pollution is concerned is the emissions from trucks, buses, and cars, especially particulate matter. Once again the city is taking measures to improve its air quality around busy roads by charging cars to travel around the middle of town during weekdays (known as the congestion charge) and introducing low-emission zones.

*acerifolia*—the London plane. Noted for its unusual peeling bark and dangling seed pods, the London plane is particularly tolerant of air pollution, so it will thrive even where many trees would suffer and die. Don't be surprised if you see London plane trees popping up all over town, even next to very busy streets, bringing some very welcome greenery to an otherwise gray skyline.

One visitor to a London street that you may not expect to see is the urban red fox. Incredibly versatile and adaptable, the red fox has made a very comfortable home for itself in the metropolis. The numerous garbage cans full of leftover food provide easy pickings for these sneaky canines. Generally, foxes aren't a risk to either humans or pets, but you'd be advised to just leave your bags of garbage in a covered outdoor garbage can. Otherwise you'll be picking up the remains from all over the front yard.

# Social Climate

For centuries Britain dominated much of the world through its massive empire. Although it has relinquished the empire and given independence to many nations, these Commonwealth countries still have a close affinity with Britain and its monarchy. People from all parts of the Commonwealth have moved to London and made it their home. As you'd expect, there is a strong presence from the Indian subcontinent and the West Indies, as well as parts of Africa. With there being a better standard of living in Europe, many immigrants from around the world are drawn to live here, and many prefer to live in the United Kingdom. Whether they come illegally or with a visa, countless migrants end up in London. The city also attracts people from the 28 member states in the European Union (EU). The result is that London is very much the melting pot of people from a wide variety of countries, although the British do not always relish this cultural diversity. And this sometimes leads to tension between certain communities, especially in poorer areas of town, where people are vying for social housing and jobs. In the past there have been tensions between the capital's different communities, be it whites and non-whites, those from different Indian subcontinent communities, or West Indians and Africans, but these were mainly confined to just certain areas of town.

Many Europeans have also moved to London, either for the greater job opportunities or because they have been transferred here with work. One of the benefits of being a European Union member state is that their citizens can migrate around the European Union, following jobs and opportunities. It is thought that EU nationals account for

© KAREN WHITE

a busy London corner

## Comfort in a Cup of Tea

© LES SMITHSON

It is odd how some stereotypes never really ring true to form, and yet others are spot on. Certainly the stereotype of the British loving tea is very apt. Nearly everyone here drinks black tea, and for some it can be an important ritual requiring the teapot to be preheated and putting the milk in first (never the other way around). In times of crisis or sorrow, the British often seek some solace in a cup of tea. The comforting rituals of filling the kettle and finding the mugs, as well as the resulting warm mugs to grasp, somehow help to calm frayed nerves and console both the maker and the recipient.

What I find fascinating about the British affinity with a cup of tea is that it is so

4 in every 10 long-term migrants to the United Kingdom, and this trend may increase while the eurozone remains in recession. Citizens from the eastern side of the European Union (such as Poland) have moved to London and the United Kingdom in large numbers in the past few years and now seem to dominate the building profession.

As is the case in countries around the world, the recent economic downturn has made unemployment an issue. As a result, the United Kingdom is trying to protect its own workforce and limit immigration—especially for unskilled workers. While it won't be easy to control the number of European Union citizens that move to London, they are taking steps to control non-EU immigration. The government definitely seems to think that immigration has gotten out of hand in the United Kingdom, hence its tightening of quotas and new regulations that require greater assimilation for those who plan to live here for more than a few years.

## LONDON AND FOREIGNERS

For the most part Londoners are generally tolerant of visiting foreigners, perhaps because there have been so many waves of them moving to these shores—from the Huguenots in the 16th century to more recent immigrants from war-torn nations

pervasive: You immediately offer it to visiting friends if it's during the day (a glass of something stronger may be more appropriate in the evening). Tea isn't just for social visits—even contractors that have come to do some building work are offered a cup of tea (they usually take "builder's tea," a strong tea with several sugars). As you'd expect there are numerous nicknames for a mug of tea, with a "cuppa" (which sounds like "cupper") probably the most common, though it is also referred to as a "brew" or "brew up." The London slang for tea is "Rosie" or "Rosie Lee," so you have a "nice cup of Rosie."

Wherever you are, be it shopping or at a gallery, even at work or a university, come 3pm-3:30pm people may well disappear to get a quick cup of tea and snack before returning to their tasks. These days they may well be drinking a latte or herbal tea rather than black tea, but they will still take a short afternoon break with a warm drink for refreshment. This is most evident when you are out shopping, for example, and suddenly see the lines at coffee shops dramatically increase.

You should also be aware that the word "tea" can also imply a meal. In particular, people from the north of England use the term "tea" or "teatime" to refer to their main evening meal. My ignorance about "tea" being used to refer to an early evening meal caused me no end of confusion when my children were young and visiting friends. They would be invited around for a play-date and "tea," which I assumed meant I'd be offered a cup of tea when I arrived to pick them up. In fact, my children had been given their dinner as part of the visit, making the one I had planned at home redundant. The best advice is to listen closely to see if the invitation is for "a cup of tea" or "tea," and just ask if you are confused (after all, you are a foreigner).

Adding to the confusion of "tea" as a meal are the numerous cream teas (with jam, clotted cream, and scones) and afternoon teas (with cakes and light sandwiches) that are offered at hotels, cafes, and restaurants all around Britain. Going for afternoon tea has gained in popularity in recent years as both business meetings and social get-togethers are sometimes held over a pot of tea and some cake.

around the world. However, it also has to be said that there are those on the political right in the United Kingdom (with a noticeable increase in following around the UK) that are opposed to the UK's membership of the EU and have a staunchly anti-immigration policy, conveniently forgetting that a fair number of "Brits" live in countries such as Spain. And London does have a history of race riots (though more recent unrest, such as the riots in 2011, were concerned primarily with social inequality). Given the current state of affairs in the world, Muslims (even British ones) probably encounter the most prejudice at the moment.

For the most part, Londoners are welcoming of Americans who live here. Certainly the fact that we share a common language makes it relatively easy for Americans to adapt to the British way of life. Of course the notorious British reserve can make people here seem standoffish and a bit unfriendly to many Americans. Unfortunately, this trait is even more pronounced when it is mixed with the general London manner of "keeping oneself to oneself." Yet in such a crowded and frenetic city, you sometimes need to close yourself off to others to maintain a bit of sanity. That said, you will no doubt at some point be required (or want) to strike up a conversation with perhaps a colleague, neighbor, or fellow parent at school. The best way to do this is to mention the weather, a subject the British will usually talk about (sometimes at length). Given that the weather changes fairly regularly in Britain, mentioning it is an easy way to break that awkward silence.

As you'd expect anytime you are out of the United States, you can encounter people who disagree with American politics or its foreign policy, though most people are too polite to criticize your country in your presence. In my experience people here tend to judge you by what you say and do, not necessarily what your country does. Certainly, these days Britain and the United States are strong allies, with both countries concerned and on occasion militarily active against the same antagonists around the world.

If Americans moving to London are constantly expecting it to be just like home (only more expensive), they may be in for a tough time of it. Adopting an "us and them" mindset will not aid their transition into life here. But providing that they are accepting of the British with their reserved nature and sarcastic wit, and rejoice in the fact that they have an opportunity to view the world in a different light, they should get along just fine here.

# HISTORY, GOVERNMENT, AND ECONOMY

As they are all on an island, you would expect England, Scotland, and Wales to have a fairly homogeneous history and economy. However, Britain is very much three different countries, brought together through England's success as conqueror of its neighbors. Its ancient and medieval history was shaped by waves of conquering invaders, from the Romans to the Anglo-Saxons and the Normans. In time Britain also became a conqueror of much of the world, resulting in the British Empire. Inevitably empires fall, and after the end of World War II, Britain relinquished its power over the colonies and granted them self-rule. Although London has become an economic powerhouse and a global financial center, the rest of Britain has been less fortunate—especially following the decline in manufacturing here. The economic boom years of the 1990s collapsed with the 2008 banking crises and subsequent economic downturn. Today, despite being heavily in debit, the UK's economy has returned to growth, yet it still has a ways to go before the economy is booming.

# History

## ANCIENT BRITAIN AND LONDON

Although evidence for Britain's prehistoric background is well known (such as Stonehenge in Wiltshire), there is little evidence of prehistoric settlements in London. Although there most likely were the occasional settlements along the River Thames, it was the establishment of Londinium by the Romans a few years after their successful conquest of southern England in AD 43 that put London on the map. For the next 400 years the Romans ruled much of England and Wales. During the 2nd century, London became the capital of Roman Britain. During this time its population swelled to nearly 60,000, making it the largest conurbation in England at the time. Roman London was mainly in the old heart of the city, in what is now called the City of London. The Romans built a bridge across the River Thames and a stone wall around the city (bits of this are still visible at the Museum of London and elsewhere) to protect it from invaders. Londinium had a forum, bath houses, an amphitheater, and a temple, with its port an important link for trade with the rest of the Roman Empire. By 407 the Romans had left London and England, and it swiftly went into decline.

## ANGLO-SAXON LONDON

With the departure of the Romans, the Anglo-Saxons were the next foreign force to invade and conquer England. By AD 600 Christianity had been brought to the island, and England as we now know it was made up of several smaller Anglo-Saxon kingdoms. In the mid-9th century the Vikings began to invade along the eastern coast, including London. The Danes were successful in capturing territory along the eastern half of the island. By the end of the century England had been split in two, with the Vikings controlling the east of England and the Anglo-Saxons preserving the south and west. Originally, London was controlled by the Vikings but was recaptured by the Anglo-Saxons in 886, with the Anglo-Saxon king Alfred the Great, King of Wessex, finally pushing the Vikings out of England and unifying the country. At this point Londoners began to return to the walled Roman city for protection. Prior to this, they had lived outside the old Roman city (around what is now known as the Strand and Aldwych). Around this time London began to develop its own local government. Although at the time London was the wealthiest and largest city in Britain, the royal capital was to the west in Winchester. It wasn't until Edward the Confessor came to the throne in 1042 and his building of an abbey in Westminster that London became home to royalty. During his reign, Edward the Confessor gave London some autonomy and the right to run its own affairs. Edward the Confessor died in early 1066 and was succeeded by Harold II, who was the last Anglo-Saxon king of England.

## MEDIEVAL LONDON

William the Duke of Normandy believed himself to be Edward's rightful successor, and in support of his claim to the throne, he invaded England in the fall of

sculpture depicting the Roman Emperor Trajan, located in front of a section of the London Wall

1066. King Harold II and his men fought William's forces at the Battle of Hastings but failed to prevent the Norman Conquest, and thus a new French king took the throne of England. To create a dominant presence and quell any possible uprisings in London, William ordered that a great stone fort—the Tower of London—should be built just beyond the eastern edge of London. At the same time, he also promised to recognize the special status and privileges that Edward the Confessor had granted London. Under William the Conqueror's reign, the commune of London was made a county, thereby responsible for its own administration. Elsewhere in England, the Normans introduced a feudal system, and the king was advised by landowners and clergy before making laws.

The first mayor of London was appointed (with the king's consent) in 1189. King John extended London's self-rule in 1215 and allowed it to elect its own mayor. It is worth noting that then (as now) London was a powerful center for trade and commerce, and its size and wealth meant that it was able to gain concessions of liberties from royals who came to rely upon it for the funding of their policies at home and overseas. Also in 1215, King John was forced to sign the Magna Carta, which meant that the country could not go to war without the landowners' consent and ultimately laid the foundations for the English Parliament.

By the start of the 14th century, the population of London had risen to around 80,000, spurred on by economic growth in the city. Trade in London was separated into different guilds, which effectively ran the city and controlled commerce. The guilds would elect the Lord Mayor of the City of London. Like other big cities during the medieval period, London suffered from epidemics of bubonic plague.

## TUDOR LONDON

While London was prospering in the 1400s, politically the country was unstable. It was reeling from the loss of the Hundred Years War (in support of the House of Plantagenet's claim to the French throne) and Henry VI's failure to prevent civil war between Yorkshire and Lancaster in the War of the Roses. Henry Tudor (from the House of Lancaster) finally ended this conflict when he succeeded in killing Richard III (from the House of York) at the Battle of Bosworth Field in 1485. Henry VII continued to reign until his death in 1509, and his son Henry VIII took the throne. Little did Henry VIII realize that his decision to secede from the Catholic Church so that he could divorce his wife Catherine of Aragon would have such profound repercussions for the British Isles for several centuries.

Built in 1597, 41 Cloth Fair is the oldest house in London.

The English Reformation, especially the Dissolution of the Monasteries (the dismantling of the churches' property and wealth), was yet another financial opportunity for Londoners. It is thought that the Catholic Church may have owned up to a quarter of the land in London, and following the dissolution this property was now available for development. The extra land was sorely needed, as by the middle of the 16th century, London's population had swollen to around 80,000—doubling again by the end of the century.

At the beginning of the 1600s, wealthy Londoners had begun to move west along the Strand, with the spillover from the City of London butting up to the City of Westminster. London (and England) thrived under the steady rule of Elizabeth I, with the city becoming an important commercial center not just in Britain, but in Europe as well. London also prospered culturally with the likes of poets and playwrights such as William Shakespeare and Christopher Marlowe. The Globe Theatre, associated with Shakespeare, was constructed on the south bank of the River Thames.

## THE 17TH CENTURY AND THE ENGLISH CIVIL WAR

In 1642 the Civil War began between King Charles I and Parliament. Charles, like his father before him, believed in the divine right of kings to rule and was uneasy with the financial power and influence that Parliament had gained through the centuries. Charles I's reign was characterized by jostling between the king and Parliament for power to rule the country and its foreign affairs. Things came to a head between the Parliamentarians and the king in 1642, when civil war broke out. The war ended a few years later at the Battle of Naseby in June 1645, when the royal forces were effectively destroyed. The king surrendered to the Scottish and was eventually handed

© LES SMITHSON
Sir Christopher Wren's Monument to the Great Fire of London in 1666

over to the English Parliament in 1647. However, he escaped and started a second English Civil War, although this was short lived. In 1649 he was finally captured and beheaded in London, turning England into a republic. Oliver Cromwell was made Lord Protector in 1653 and ruled the Commonwealth of England between 1649 and 1658, with his son succeeding him until 1660. Cromwell's Puritan government was deeply unpopular with the people, and when Charles II returned to London from his exile in France (following the death of Richard Cromwell), he was greeted with open arms. However, the restoration of the monarchy to the English throne came at a price to the royalty. It established Britain as a constitutional monarchy, with the royalty as merely the head of state and the Parliament as the main ruling body—a framework that continues even to this day.

While the rest of England was recovering from the Civil War and 10 years of Commonwealth rule, London had its own problems to contend with. In 1665 bubonic plague hit the city yet again, and in the overcrowded city it soon spread rampantly. The Great Plague, as it came to be known, is thought to have killed around 60,000 people. Yet this wasn't all that London had to cope with. In September 1666 another tragedy was to befall London—one that was to shape its infrastructure for years to come. For three days a great fire swept through London, destroying much of the medieval center of the old city within the Roman walls. The fire was caused by a fire at a bakery on Pudding Lane, which rapidly spread through London's tiny alleys and medieval wooden buildings, aided by strong winds. Although most of the city was razed to the ground by the fire, the fierce heat and destruction finally put a stop to the plague epidemic. Another consequence of the Great Fire of London was that from the post-fire reconstruction of the city, some of its greatest architectural masterpieces were built, such as Christopher Wren's St. Paul's Cathedral.

## Guy Fawkes Day

*Remember, remember the 5th of November*
*The Gunpowder treason and plot.*

This is the opening of a popular nursery rhyme, which oddly enough harks back to a murderous plot to blow up the Houses of Parliament and in doing so kill the Protestant King James I of England (who was also James VI of Scotland). The story goes that in 1605, Guy Fawkes, backed by a group of likeminded recusant Catholics, tried to blow up the Palace of Westminster. The group's aim was to kill the Protestant king along with most of the aristocracy that controlled both England and Scotland at the time. Fawkes and his conspirators would then bring to the throne the king's nine-year-old daughter, Princess Elizabeth, as a Catholic monarch. The group had decided to undertake such a daring plot after it become clear that the king and Parliament would continue to persecute Catholics.

On November 5, 1605, King James was to be at Westminster Palace (home to both parts of the British Parliament) to open the Houses of Parliament. Just after midnight on this day, Guy Fawkes was found with 36 barrels of gunpowder in the cellars under Westminster Palace. This was more than enough to destroy the building and kill most of its occupants. Luckily, the authorities had been given an anonymous tip off about the Gunpowder Plot and were able to prevent the act of terrorism. Subsequently, Guy Fawkes and his co-conspirators were tried as traitors and sentenced to death. They were given not just any death sentence, but were hanged, drawn, and quartered—a gruesome practice to say the least. Unfortunately, the acts of these individuals only made things worse for British Catholics, and laws were passed that further diminished their religious freedom.

The following year the king and Parliament decided to hold a special service to mark November 5 and give thanks that the plot was thwarted. This became an annual tradition to ensure that the event is never forgotten. The nursery rhyme has evolved to ensure that each new generation knows about the Gunpowder Plot.

To this day, the English, Welsh, and Scottish celebrate the saving of the Protestant king and Parliament on November 5, usually with firework displays and a bonfire. In years gone by an effigy of Guy Fawkes ("The Guy") would have been burnt on the bonfire, but these days people are more aware that this could offend Catholics, as well as scare the children. Nevertheless, don't be surprised if neighbors set off fireworks in their backyard or a park has a professional fireworks display around November 5—it's all good fun, if a somewhat vindictive commemoration of the event.

## THE 18TH AND 19TH CENTURIES

Although the British first started their quest for colonies back in the late 16th century, it wasn't until 1607 in Jamestown, Virginia, that they succeeded in establishing a permanent English settlement. This led to the establishment of the North American colonies in what is now the United States, Canada, and parts of the Caribbean. These colonies created ample wealth for England. Of course in time the American colonies rebelled, and by 1783 had gained self-rule following the War of Independence.

Naval success at the Battle of Trafalgar in 1805 during the Napoleonic Wars established Britain's superiority at sea and paved the way for further colonial expansion. Britain's defeat of the French in 1815 at the Battle of Waterloo ended Napoleon's rule as emperor and established Britain as the dominant force in Europe in the 1800s.

Britain moved on to create colonies all around the world, including the Indian subcontinent, parts of Africa, and Australasia. Also during this period, Britain began to mechanize manufacturing, agriculture, and transport following the discovery of how to harness steam power, resulting in the Industrial Revolution. During Queen Victoria's reign, Britain and London were to gain great wealth from both the empire and industrialization.

### THE 20TH CENTURY TO THE PRESENT

To a large extent, Britain's recent history has been shaped by the two world wars and the "Troubles" in Northern Ireland. While World War I decimated a generation of British (and European) men, the ramifications of World War II were perhaps more profound. The high cost of fighting World War II crippled the United Kingdom's economy for years and quickened the dismantling of the empire. While London had grown and prospered during the first few decades of the 20th century, during World War II it (and other British cities) faced relentless German air raids that destroyed much of the city. Even today, you can make out where the bombs fell. Wandering through the streets, you'll occasionally see a row of terraced Victorian houses that are abruptly separated by a 1960s apartment building. The chances are (especially if the street is near a railway line) that the apartment building marks the place where a bomb fell and destroyed the Victorian houses. The other dominant issue in recent British history has been the terrorist attacks from the Irish Republican Army (IRA) from the 1970s until the mid-1990s, when a peace deal was brokered. London has also been the target of Al Qaeda-backed attacks; in the summer of 2005 several bombs were set off on the London Underground and a double-decker bus, killing more than 50 people.

In 1948, while Europe was recovering from World War II, the Summer Olympics were successfully held in London. Sixty-four years later, the Olympics returned to the capital when London hosted the 2012 Summer Olympics and Paralympics. The London Olympic Park was built in Stratford in East London and includes the 80,000-seat London Olympic Stadium along with several other venues. Although the games are just a memory, their legacy continues at the Queen Elizabeth Olympic Park—one of the largest urban parks in Europe. Many of the venues are open to the public for all to enjoy, and the Olympic village (where the athletes stay) has provided much-needed housing for Londoners. In 2016, West Ham United Football Club will move into the Olympic Stadium, which will remain a venue for athletics as well as soccer.

## Government

Like many countries in Europe (such as Spain, Norway, and the Netherlands), the United Kingdom is a constitutional monarchy. This means that the monarchy acts as the head of state, participating mainly in ceremonial duties. The democratically elected Parliament is responsible for running the affairs of state. It is important to remember that the United Kingdom is made up of four countries: England, Wales, Scotland, and Northern Ireland. Since the late 1990s the UK Parliament has devolved some of its powers to national parliaments or assemblies in Scotland, Wales, and Northern Ireland. London too has been given a greater say over the running of the city and has its own democratically elected assembly and a directly elected mayor.

## The Blitz

During World War II, once France had fallen to the Germans in 1940, Hitler then turned his attention toward invading Britain. But first, he had to cripple its air defenses. To achieve this, his Luftwaffe had to gain air superiority over the Royal Air Force. This involved sending wave after wave of fighter planes to engage and destroy the British air force, as well as destroying important military targets on the ground. This primarily aerial battle is known as the Battle of Britain. During one such raid, a German aircraft strayed over London, dropping bombs in the east and northeast of town. This event prompted Britain to retaliate on Berlin, and started a new and tragic phase of the war. Hitler was said to be furious about the attack on Berlin and ordered the purposeful targeting of populated city areas (including London) and Britain's air defenses around the clock. His aim was to destroy the British morale and undermine the support for the war.

one of London's memorials to victims of the Blitz

From September 1940 to May 1941, Britain and its population had to endure sustained bombing by the Germans—an event that is referred to as "the Blitz" (German for "lightning"). Several British cities were targeted by the Luftwaffe during this period, including Coventry, Birmingham, Edinburgh, Belfast, and Portsmouth (to name but a few). However, it was perhaps London that felt the terrible effects of Hitler's bombing raids the most, having to sustain 76 consecutive nights of attack.

To escape the bombing Londoners would take to the Underground, where they would crowd into the stations. Outside of the center of town, those who had a backyard were encouraged to build an "Anderson Shelter" where they could seek safety during an attack. Although the government initially tried to stop Londoners from using the Underground as a bomb shelter, it soon had to change its thinking as there simply wasn't any other place safe enough to accommodate everyone in the middle of town. The hastily constructed concrete air raid shelters that the government had built simply weren't up to the job. It is thought that during the height of the London Blitz as many as 177,000 people would assemble in London's Underground stations, during daytime air raids and at night.

By the end of the Blitz as many as 60,000 British civilians had been killed during the air raids—half of which were in London—with around 87,000 people seriously injured. More than two million homes were lost in the Blitz (60 percent of which were in London). This had a lasting effect on London's post-war housing, prompting the rapid development of new towns outside the city. In town, you can still see the scars of where the bombs fell, knocking out a few houses in a terrace of older properties. These have usually been replaced with 1950s or '60s buildings, which are not always sympathetic with the surrounding architecture. The occasional unexploded bomb is still being found, forcing nearby residents and workers to evacuate the area while the bomb squad deals with the device.

## THE UK PARLIAMENT

It took me a while to get my head around how the UK Parliament works, as the system is so different from America's separate bodies of the executive, legislative, and judiciary branches. It also doesn't have a written constitution or bill of rights; instead it governs according to statutes, common laws, and established "traditional rights."

In fact, it is quite a straightforward system of government without all the checks and balances that characterize American politics. In the UK, people vote for a Member of Parliament to represent their constituency. The party that wins the most seats in a national election (referred to as a "general election") takes control of the Parliament and is responsible for running the country, with the party's leader becoming the prime minister. If there isn't an outright winner, then a coalition government is formed made up from two or more parties. The winning party (or coalition) should govern according to the pledges that they have made in their election manifesto, and, as in America, if promised changes prove too controversial or expensive they will simply be placed on the back burner.

Since World War II, the two main political parties in the United Kingdom have been the right-of-center Conservatives (also called Tories) and the left-of-center Labour party, with the social-liberal party, the Liberal Democrat, the other main national party. There are also a handful of small parties whose policies tend to be dominated by a single or regional issue.

The UK Parliament is made up of the House of Commons and the House of Lords. Only the House of Commons is elected. The House of Lords, on the other hand, comprises hereditary and appointed peers, as well as senior bishops in the Church of England. The House of Lords is meant to have a moderating influence on the House of Commons, with the Lords scrutinizing and suggesting amendments to the legislation

© IVAN KRYCHKOVSKYI/123RF.COM

the Palace of Westminster, home to both houses of Parliament

proposed in the Commons. Of course, a member of the House of Lords could table legislation, but convention dictates that legislative changes should come from the Commons. If the proposed legislation makes it into the statute books, the proposal has to get through the Commons, and so it may as well emanate from there. Importantly, both houses have to agree on the wording of a law before it can be introduced.

As of 2009, there has been a Supreme Court of the United Kingdom. Prior to this, the House of Lords performed the United Kingdom's judiciary functions. However, the Supreme Court of the United Kingdom does not have the constitutional powers of the American Supreme Court and cannot overturn primary legislation. Sovereignty lies with Parliament, which is the supreme lawmaker, and it can make laws about anything, though no Parliament can pass laws that cannot be undone in the future. Parliamentary sovereignty is a key tenet of the laws and statutes that combine to create the United Kingdom's constitution. One important aspect of parliamentary sovereignty is that no valid act of Parliament can be overturned by the courts. When it comes to European laws, however, the Supreme Court can act to ensure that domestic laws are consistent with applicable European Union laws and the European Convention on Human Rights.

Although you may be just be a visitor to these isles and so not really able to get involved with politics, it is worthwhile keeping an eye on events at the Palace of Westminster (home to Parliament). No doubt legislation will be passed that will affect you while you are living in London, be it an increase in sales tax, a new consumer law, or even a change to immigration policy. And to be honest with you, unless you completely avoid all British news, you will find it difficult to not know about major changes in legislation and policy—the TV and newspapers will be full of it.

## THE MONARCHY

Ever since some barons forced King John to sign the Magna Carta in 1215, the absolute powers of the English monarch have been held slightly in check. They were limited still further after the English Civil War (1642-1651) and the brief period of the Commonwealth of England, Scotland, and Ireland (1649-1660) that followed Oliver Cromwell's victory over Charles I. With the monarchy's reinstallation with Charles II, its power to rule had been severely curtailed, with Parliament established as the main ruling body. The role of the king was now that of a constitutional monarch, with limited executive authority.

The current monarch is Elizabeth II, who acceded to the throne in 1952. As the head of state, the queen must be involved with state functions in Britain. These include the opening of Parliament, signing into law the Acts of Parliament, and holding regular weekly meetings with the serving prime minister—not to forget her tea parties, where she acknowledges people for their hard work for charities, the arts, or the nation. The queen also acts as a host for formal events, such as entertaining foreign heads of state, and supports the interests of Britain (and other Commonwealth countries) diplomatically and economically on her overseas visits.

All of the pageantry that comes with having royalty is also a big draw for tourists and gossipy publications alike. News about the royals fills column after column in newspapers and magazines the world over, helping to boost their sales. In popular tourist locations in London, you'll also find stalls selling a wide variety of tourist paraphernalia, such as mugs with a picture of the queen or the royal seal. Having such a high-profile royalty does seem to be a bit of a money spinner.

## THE EUROPEAN UNION

Although the United Kingdom in general is less enthusiastic about the European Union (EU) than some of the other 28 countries in this political and economic union, it is still a member. As such, the United Kingdom is affected by the laws and regulations established by the European Union (these can range from using metric measurements when buying food to equal access for people with disabilities and human rights legislation). Perhaps it is because they have an island mentality (part of Europe, yet slightly aloof), but the British tend to be a bit disdainful about the European Union, with some of the press here very quick to criticize it. Yet it is Britain's largest trading partner, and having a common market amongst its member states has served the United Kingdom well.

The recent decline of the euro and perilous economic state of some EU members has helped to reinforce Britain's skepticism. Interestingly, the anti-European Union party, the UK Independence Party, has gained in popularity, forcing mainstream parties to rethink their stance on Europe.

## LOCAL GOVERNMENT IN LONDON

For those living in London there is one more layer of government: the Greater London Authority (GLA) and London's 32 boroughs and the Corporation of London. The boroughs are the local municipal bodies in London and are responsible for providing local services to its residents, including education, local planning, and refuse/recycling collection, as well as sports and leisure facilities. The Greater London Authority is London's city-wide administrative body, created in 2000 and run by an elected

Buckingham Palace gates

assembly and a directly elected mayor for all of the capital (this was in fact the country's first directly elected mayor). The GLA is responsible for providing London-wide services, such as public transportation, the police, and the fire service (called the "fire brigade"). It is also responsible for improving London's environment (including reducing air pollution), promoting art and culture in the city, and championing London in the United Kingdom and abroad.

the London Assembly building on the South Bank

© KAREN WHITE

As with most municipal bodies, London's boroughs are able to raise taxes to supplement the basic funding that they get from the national government. This is done through the council tax, a property-related tax charged to all local residents. The amount of council tax that residents have to pay is determined by the tax bands of the property where they reside. In England the tax bands are based on the value of the property in 1991. It is important to note that all residents—be they the property owner or a renter—are usually expected to pay council tax and will be required to register for it when they move in. The GLA is funded partly by the national government and partly by a levy on the council tax charged by the boroughs.

# Economy

During the heady days of the British Empire, the British economy soared as it took in goods from the colonies and sold them on, making a hefty profit along the way. Britain prospered from sugar plantations in the Caribbean and cotton plantations in the North American colonies, on the back of the slave trade that supported these industries. Although it saddens me to say it, the slave trade from western Africa was a source of great wealth in Britain, especially for the cities of Liverpool and Bristol. The "jewel in the crown" of Britain's empire was India, which gave it cotton, tea, and spices. At the same time, the Industrial Revolution (first seen in Britain) mechanized manufacturing, agriculture, and transportation and made Britain the industrial powerhouse of the world. Although the empire and Britain's strong manufacturing-based economy didn't survive through two world wars, the United Kingdom can still lay claim to having one of the largest economies in the world and is a member of the G8.

The United Kingdom was one of the first large economies to recover from the global financial crisis of 2008-2009 and the resulting recession. Yet high levels of national debt remain an issue. In response, the government is implementing cost-cutting measures to bring borrowing under control. So although growth has returned to the UK economy, it is precarious—uncertain times will be around for a while.

## LONDON'S ECONOMY

London's position as the most important city in England started when William the Conqueror established it as his capital in England. William let London keep the rights, privileges, and laws that it had held under Edward the Confessor, before the Norman invasion. These gave London exceptional status and privilege, making it protected by and answerable to the king—not local aristocracy. It also meant that the city was granted electoral rights and some self-governance. More importantly, the royal charters that granted this special status laid the foundation for a strong, independent commercial center: the Corporation of London. The city continued to thrive during Tudor times, especially during the reign of Elizabeth I. In the 17th century the Great Plague and Great Fire of London devastated the city. By the 19th century both the Industrial Revolution and the British Empire fueled further economic activity in London. By now the city was at the heart of Britain commercially, thanks in part to mercantilism and the exploitation of the colonies and the city's ports. Britain and London prospered during the first half of the 20th century, escaping the depression that plagued America at that time. However, World War II devastated London, both economically and physically, with the destruction caused by the German air raids—the Blitz.

Since the end of the World War II, London has established itself as primarily a service-based economy, returning once again to its roots as a center for commerce. Today it is one of the (if not *the*) largest financial centers in the world (there seems to be some debate as to whether this honor should belong to New York City or London). Whichever is correct, there is no doubt that London is a dominant player in global financial markets.

A number of factors have helped London to establish itself as a service-based financial center. Certainly as the capital of the British Empire, London has a long history of trading globally. It is also an English-speaking member of the European Union, English being the dominant language used in business. Its influence from its colonial days has helped it to establish close ties with Asia and America. The fact that it is on Greenwich mean time—so halfway between the Far East and North America—means it can easily do business with those to the east or the west. Unsurprisingly, the largest business sector in London is the finance sector, home to foreign exchange markets, banks, brokerages, asset managers, hedge funds, private equity firms, insurance companies, and reinsurance markets. Other popular business sectors include professional services with scientific and technology industries, which are becoming increasingly important (it is Europe's top startup center). Tourism is also big business in London, with millions of people visiting the capital each year.

London's economy dominates that of the United Kingdom and contributes more than 20 percent to the United Kingdom's total GDP. It also has the largest city GDP of anywhere in Europe, and is home to several of Europe's largest companies. Quite a few American businesses have a presence in London, including several well-known financial institutions and banks. The City of London is home to both the Bank of England and the London Stock Exchange.

# PEOPLE AND CULTURE

From a Londoner's perspective, there tends to be an "us" (in London) and "them" (non-London) sentiment. The rest of the United Kingdom, meanwhile, tends to view Londoners as a bit arrogant and rude, with Londoners having a faster pace and being less polite—a bit like the stereotype of a New Yorker. But the truth is that the United Kingdom (even though it is made out of four different countries) is more homogeneous than you might expect. Sure, there are regional variations, as the 2014 Scottish referendum on independence may attest; however, the overwhelming majority voted to remain in the UK, which shows that the Brits are strongly bound together and more alike than different.

While the British are more similar than they want to admit to, certainly here in London we are a very mixed bag culturally. People from all four corners of the globe and all walks of life call London home, making it one of the most culturally diverse cities in the world. This rich mixture of cultures, nationalities, religions, and traditions has established London and the southeast of England as the most liberal area in the United Kingdom—generally accepting of people regardless of their ethnicity, religion, gender, or sexual orientation.

© LES SMITHSON

# Ethnicity and Class

Americans moving to London may well be a bit shocked by the immense range of cultures, religions, nationalities, and people that you get in a large city like London. It is thought that around a third of London's population is made up from ethnic minorities. As well as people from all over the British Isles, there are numerous European nationalities represented in London. Some groups even have their own little "ghetto," usually based near their national school, such as the French and the Lycée Français Charles de Gaulle in South Kensington or the Spanish and the Instituto Español Vicente Cañada Blanch in North Kensington. Golders Green and Stanford Hill in North London both have large Jewish populations, while to the west of London you'll find a large population of people from an Asian background, such as those whose family originated in India or Pakistan.

Even though there may be areas of town that are popular with certain groups, they are by no means exclusive, and people from a wide background can live almost anywhere in town. On my street alone there are people from or whose heritage is from: England (London and elsewhere), Wales, Ireland, Germany, Spain, Belgium, India, Jamaica, Greece, and, of course, the United States—and these are just the ones I know.

The amazing range of people and cultures in London is exemplified by a visit I made to my local hospital's emergency department. I wasn't badly injured, but had been advised to go to a hospital to get it sorted out. While I was there an older man was brought into the department. He had collapsed inside his apartment building, and a neighbor found him. Although the neighbor didn't know the ill man, he could tell that he was

London's population is extremely diverse.

seriously ill and needed to get to a hospital. Unfortunately the ill man did not speak any English, so no one could work out what was wrong. The ill man looked North African, so doctors addressed him in French, but to no avail. An Israeli tourist tried speaking to him in Arabic and Hebrew, as did the neighbor—again nothing. Person after person tried to address the poor man in different languages and dialects, but he simply became more withdrawn, confused, and frightened. Finally, a young translator arrived, and she was able to communicate with him through a shared Eritrean dialect. The patient and translator were then whisked off so that he could be diagnosed and treated. To think that on an average night in a large London hospital you could get a handful of different people able to speak such a range of languages shows you the extent of London's cultural diversity.

It is also worth mentioning that although they are a small minority, there are those who are not as accepting of other races, religions, or sexual orientations. The far-right jingoistic British National Party (BNP) does have a bit of a following in parts of London's East End (and elsewhere in the country). I hasten to add that the BNP is very much out in the political wilderness, with its extreme views a cause for concern by many. More mainstream politically, but with a strong anti-immigration/anti-European Union sentiment, the UK Independence Party has seen an increase in popularity and is forcing other political parties to rethink their stance on immigration and Europe.

### CLASS DIVISIONS

Social immobility in the United Kingdom has a long history and to a certain extent can be deeply ingrained, with people from the lower class encountering real obstacles to their climb up the social ladder. Some of these are external restraints from society and family (a "don't try to get above your station" attitude), and some of it may be a self-limiting belief that they are incapable of getting ahead—that is, of course, unless they are the next David Beckham. That strong American sentiment that "with hard work you can achieve your goals" doesn't always ring true here. Even to this day, you have a distinct advantage if you have a "posh" non-regional, non-working class accent. Thankfully, this is less prevalent than it was 50 or even 20 years ago, but the barriers to social class are still noticeable at times.

## Customs and Etiquette

While Americans are generally regarded as being forthright (especially about complaints) and on the loud side, the British are known quite rightly for their steely reserve, as well as their ironic and sarcastic sense of humor. So while we may share a similar Anglo-Saxon ideology, background, and language, there are distinct differences between us and how we interact with our fellow humans. For example, as an American, I find it difficult to accept the poor customer service that is often handed out, expecting much more from the food server or sales assistant. Yet I have come to realize that making a big fuss won't necessarily get me anywhere and I will be dubbed a pushy American

Don't even think about jumping the queue.

and duly ignored. However, a polite, yet direct, request that they do something (such as checking the stockroom) may be the best approach. Thankfully, some retailers (albeit the more expensive ones) have finally realized that customers do value good service, and there has been a marked change to improve their customer service.

The most noticeable difference between the British and any other nationality is their tendency to "queue" (line up) and their deep indignation if someone "jumps the queue" and pushes in front of the line. Likewise, "cutting someone up" (when a driver purposely gets into the wrong lane at a traffic light or line of traffic and then darts into the right lane at the last minute, thereby avoiding the line of traffic) can easily lead to road rage. Even in crowded London, people patiently queue for a bus. The more polite members of society will ask anyone even remotely near a queue, such as at a sales till, whether they are in a queue before stepping toward the line. And if I am completely honest with you, on more than one occasion I have stood behind someone believing them to be in a queue, only to realize that they weren't when the sales till became empty and they didn't move forward.

Another major difference between the British and many other nationalities comes from their driving habits. So, not only do you drive on the left, with oncoming traffic to your right, but often people will adopt the same approach when walking down the sidewalk (referred to as "pavement" here). Of course this depends on how crowded the sidewalk is, but generally people naturally keep oncoming traffic to their right, whereas Americans naturally keep oncoming traffic to their left. Don't be surprised when you first arrive and you have a few odd little dances with people, as you both sidestep the same way to avoid bumping into each other, or someone makes an embarrassingly large maneuver to ensure that they pass you on their right.

On the whole there is more day-to-day formality in Britain, such as men holding or opening doors for women or removing their hats when they are inside. Sometimes a man will give up his seat on a train for a woman or someone younger will give their seat to someone older. Generally, people will shake hands when they are introduced, with the younger generation making do with a nod of the head and greeting of "hi" or "all right?" although handshakes are common in the workplace. The French custom of air-kisses on both cheeks is fairly widespread in some circles, although it is a considered by some to be a bit bourgeois.

## Drinking Etiquette

© SUNG KUK KIM/123RF.COM

The one exception (and it's a *big* one) to the British obsession with queuing is in the pub (short for "public house"). There is no table service at pubs, so getting a drink is a free-for-all at the bar. Drinking with friends in pubs is usually done in "rounds," with each person (or couple) taking it in turns to get drinks from the bar for the whole group of friends. It is considered very poor form if you are in a round and have been bought drinks, to leave before you have returned the favor and gotten a round in (or at least offered to get one). If it's a really big group—of say 10 or more people—the group may be split into smaller groups so that the "buying round" isn't too expensive. If you are unsure if people want to drink in rounds (or one big round), ask for a consensus before the drinks are ordered. If it's your turn to buy a round and someone in the group is finished or nearly finished, you need to get the round in, even though you are not ready. It is considered ill-mannered to keep them waiting for you to catch up. This can be difficult if someone drinks like a fish and you do not. The best solution is to try to go to the pub with those who imbibe at a similar rate to yourself, though this is not always easy.

Men tend to drink pints of beer, while women may stick to "halves" (a half pint)—though younger drinkers may all drink pints regardless of their gender. It is worth noting that a British pint is 20 ounces, not the standard American 16, so be sure to pace yourself. Spirits such as whiskey, vodka, or gin are referred to as "short."

If you want to try British beer, ask for "bitter," which is served at room temperature and has a stronger, slightly sour taste and dark amber color. Traditional beers and ales are not carbonated and are served using traditional hand-pulls that suck the beer from the cask in the cellar. The pale cold fizzy beer served in the States is called lager. Craft beers and breweries have undergone a renaissance in London and the UK, so look out for these artisan beers when you are in a pub.

Another traditional British drink is cider, which is made from fermented apples. This has become increasingly popular in recent years—especially among the young, as it can be strong and sweet to drink. Similar to cider, perry is made from pears and is deliciously refreshing on a hot summer's day.

The latest trend in drinking in the capital has seen the return of the cocktail. You'll find trendy bars, restaurants, and cocktail clubs in nightlife hot spots offering a wide variety of mixed beverages—be it a mojito, cosmopolitan, or something more imaginative . . . truffle martini, anyone?

# Gender Roles

The gender roles in the United Kingdom tend to fall along traditional lines, with the running of the home and the majority of the child care carried out by women—this is despite many of them being in full-time employment. The integration of women and some ethnic minorities into certain professions has been relatively slow. The Anglican Church faced controversy when it allowed the ordination of women; it took another 20 years before it allowed female bishops. Equally, the use of a female official at a professional soccer game can still raise a few eyebrows and has been known to prompt a few sexist comments by TV pundits. At least nowadays such actions are seen as unacceptable, with the perpetrators losing their jobs.

## WOMEN AND EQUALITY

Gaining equal rights for women in Britain has been a long and sometimes torturous affair, starting with enlightened thinkers such as Jeremy Bentham and John Stuart Mills calling for women's suffrage in the mid-1800s, followed by women activists turning to civil disobedience, criminal damage, and even arson to express their frustration at such iniquitous treatment. Generally, women didn't get the right to vote until after World War I, although some women aged 30 (or more) were able to vote during the war, provided they were members of a local council or married to a member. Finally, in 1928, after nearly a century of campaigning, all women aged 21 or older were given the right to vote. This milestone, important as it is, did not in and of itself bring gender equality to Britain. Gaining equal opportunity to employment and pay, while enshrined in law, continues to elude women. They still lag behind men on pay, receiving about 15 percent less hourly pay than males—making gender inequality in the United Kingdom among the worst in Europe.

This continued inequality is perhaps evidence that society still has yet to fully accept gender equality. For the most part women in the United Kingdom abandon their maiden names and adopt their husband's. When filling in a form, women may well be asked if they are a Miss or Mrs; my reply of "either . . . I'm married but use my maiden name" tends to confuse and embarrass people, who hastily reply, "I'll tick the Ms box then, shall I?"

Some sections of society persevere with a cultural mindset that is very rigid with regard to the role of women. Forced marriages still occur within some communities in London and the United Kingdom, even though it is illegal, and one occasionally hears of honor killings of women and girls because they have brought dishonor upon the family, usually for being sexually active and not married or involved with the "wrong" type.

## GAY AND LESBIAN CULTURE

The United Kingdom has allowed a "civil partnership" between same-sex couples since 2005; in England and Wales, same-sex marriage was introduced in 2014. The public is generally very accepting of gay men and women, and there are even high-powered openly gay politicians in Parliament—in all the main political parties. The gay population in London is certainly thriving, although the gay capital of the United Kingdom is

London's exuberant Pride Parade



on the south coast in Brighton (some 40 miles/65 kilometers from London and easily within the commuter belt). In the central London area, you'll find lots of clubs, pubs, and restaurants geared toward gay clientele. The London Pride Festival is the largest such event in the United Kingdom, attracting people from all over the world to come and join in the celebrations and promote equality for LGBT people. As a nation, the British aren't given toward displaying affection in public (unless all the parties are so drunk that they abandon their natural reserved composure). So while passionate expressions of affection between same-sex couples (like those between heterosexual couples) will probably be tolerated, they will be viewed a bit disdainfully—such activity is "best left indoors."

## Religion

According to a recent census, the United Kingdom as a whole is a fairly religious place, with believers outnumbering nonbelievers. This may come as a bit of a surprise to many, as attendance at churches and other places of worship is in a downward cycle. People must still be holding on to the spiritual faith even if they don't make it to church on Sunday. The dominant religion in the United Kingdom and London is Christianity, with the Protestant Church of England (also known as the Anglican Church) the most common. The senior bishop and principal leader of the Anglican Church is the Archbishop of Canterbury, and his official residency is Lambeth Palace,

© KAREN WHITE
St. Paul's Cathedral in the City of London

next to Southwark Cathedral on London's South Bank. The queen is the figurehead of the Church of England, and part of her role is to act as the Defender of the Faith and Supreme Governor of the Church of England, with responsibility for maintaining the church and opening the General Synod (the legislative body of the Anglican Church). Although many of London's oldest churches didn't survive either the Great Fire of 1666 or the Blitz in World War II, nevertheless some magnificent churches and cathedrals can still be found in the City of London and its westerly neighbor the City of Westminster. Two architecturally significant Anglican churches that you may want to attend for a service are Westminster Abbey and St. Paul's Cathedral.

Despite centuries of persecution, there are still many Roman Catholics in London. The head of the Roman Catholic Church in England and Wales is the Archbishop of Westminster, with Westminster Cathedral, near Victoria station, the most prominent Roman Catholic Church in London. As you would expect in a large cosmopolitan city, there are numerous other Christian faiths represented in London—from Eastern Orthodox to several other Protestant faiths (including Methodist, Baptist, and Presbyterian) and even an Egyptian Coptic Church.

Another significant religion in London is Islam; around 12 percent of the capital's population are Muslim. The London Central Mosque, on the borders of Regent's Park, is probably the best-known mosque in the London, although there are others dotted all around the city. Sometimes abandoned churches and synagogues have been turned into mosques, with this change in religion representing a shift in the religious and ethnic background of local residents. The Baitul Futuh Mosque, one of the largest mosques in Western Europe, is in Morden, Surrey, in Greater London.

With such a large percentage of the population having their ethnic roots in India, it should be no surprise that eastern religions such as Hinduism, Buddhism, and Sikhism are practiced here. London is home to the vast majority of the United Kingdom's Hindu worshippers. The Shri Swaminarayan Mandir Hindu temple in northwest London is the largest Hindu temple in Europe.

Jews have been worshipping in England for centuries, and they have been mentioned in documents dating from the time of William the Conqueror, although they may have been here as early as Roman times. Built in 1701, London's Bevis Marks Synagogue is the United Kingdom's oldest synagogue still in use today. Most of Britain's Jews live in London, and there are several areas in North London with large Jewish populations. There are four eruvin in North or Northwest London: the North West London Eruv (covering parts of Golders Green and Hendon), Edgware, Elstree and Borehamwood, and Stanmore.

# The Arts

London is known the world over for having an eminence, variety, and exceptional quality of art in all forms. It is certainly the cultural heart of the United Kingdom, offering an amazing number of theaters, cinemas, music venues, galleries, and museums. There is little doubt in my mind that being able to enjoy such a wide variety of art in London is definitely part of what makes living here so special. If you want to see a play, attend a concert, or roam around galleries, it's all very easily done here.

## LITERATURE

Britain's literary heritage is unrivaled, with literary credentials from *Beowulf* and Geoffrey Chaucer's *Canterbury Tales* to the works of William Shakespeare and Charles Dickens, and more recently the immensely popular J. K. Rowling. London has played host to many of Britain's best-loved writers and set the scene for many British literary works of art, from Chaucer's pilgrims setting off for Canterbury from Southwark to Arthur Conan Doyle's hero Sherlock Holmes at 221B Baker Street.

In Westminster Abbey's Poets' Corner, numerous literary giants, from Chaucer to Dickens to Rudyard Kipling (to name but a few), have been laid to rest. Elsewhere in the city, you'll find commemorative plaques and statues of famous authors, poets, and playwrights, often marking where they lived or a spot mentioned in their works. In 1997 a replica of Shakespeare's Globe Theatre was built near its original site on London's South Bank. Nowadays visitors can watch the Bard's works in authentic surroundings.

## THE PERFORMING ARTS

Ask any American tourist what they associate with London and they are quite likely to reply its theater. The range of plays and musicals on offer here is awe-inspiring. There are around 150 theaters across London (with around 50 in just the West End), showing a range of classical works, such as those by Shakespeare, to the long running *Mousetrap* by Agatha Christie to musicals such as *Les Misérables* or modern works such

the National Portrait Gallery

as Michael Morpurgo's *War Horse.* For those who prefer something more out of the ordinary, there are numerous fringe theaters.

Opera fans will be overjoyed to learn that London is home to 12 opera companies, including the Royal Opera Company in Covent Garden. Several of Britain's dance companies are also based in the capital, such as the Royal Ballet Company and the English National Ballet, with the Saddler's Wells being London's main modern dance company.

As you'd expect in a city the size of London, the music scene here thrives right across a wide range of musical genres. Venues can range from the massive O2 Arena in Greenwich to pubs, such as the Barfly in Camden, and everything in between. And although Britain can't match the classical musical prowess of countries such as Germany or Italy, its modern musical performers and bands are some of the world's most popular.

## FINE ART

London has a well-deserved reputation for the quality of its numerous galleries and museums of art, laying claim to some of the best works of art and antiquities of anywhere in the world. Best of all, many of these galleries and museums are free to visit, although there may be a charge for special exhibits and collections. Well worth visiting are the National Gallery and the National Portrait Gallery, as well as both the Tate Britain and Tate Modern. Although in the 20th and 21st centuries British artists have established a reputation for themselves, historically British artists have struggled to gain international acclaim, excepting perhaps Gainsborough, Hogarth, and Turner.

# Sports

Having invented many of the most popular ball games that are played today—such as soccer ("football"), rugby, and even baseball—it should be no surprise that the English are big sporting fans. Certainly the main sporting passion is soccer, and here in London there are several of the world's best teams, each with a loyal following. Whether it is Chelsea in West London or Arsenal in North London, Londoners are passionate about their soccer team—a passion that has in the past led to fighting between rival fans.

The national venues for sports such as rugby (Twickenham), tennis (Wimbledon), and cricket (Lord's) are all in London. Whatever the time of year there's bound to be a sporting event to tempt you out of your armchair and into the stands.

In 2012, London successfully hosted the Olympic and Para-Olympic Summer Games. While it has taken several years for the venues to be adapted for use by the general public, the games helped transform a derelict corner of east London with new housing and infrastructure. Certainly the Queen Elizabeth Olympic Park is well worth a visit, even if it is just to see the park from the massive ArcelorMittal Orbit.

# PLANNING YOUR FACT-FINDING TRIP

Moving across the Atlantic to settle in London is a big step and not one that should be taken lightly. Most people find it useful to make at least one short trip to the capital before they make the big move so they can become acquainted with the city. Even those people who have visited London before can find a pre-relocation visit worthwhile, as it gives them a chance to look at the city through a different perspective—not as a tourist, but as a potential resident.

The itineraries shown in this chapter should be used as a general guide to visiting London with a view to moving here. It will pay dividends if you do a bit of online research on the neighborhoods that you think you will like (especially the rental prices) before your visit. There is little point in setting your heart on Notting Hill Gate if you simply can't afford to live there. Try to take your time and really explore an area of town, checking out local shops, supermarkets, cafés, and restaurants as well as walking around the residential streets. Stop by some realtors (called "estate agents" here) to get a sense of current rental prices. Don't be afraid to go in and speak to them about the market—they may even show you a few places.

If you have children it would be a good idea to organize a few viewings of some

© ROBERT JENKIN/123RF.COM

private schools to see if they are a good fit for your children's needs (state schools are less accommodating about one-off visits). It is helpful if you can bring your children's most recent report cards so that the school can get an idea about their academic level. Be sure to ask about application deadlines because most schools want you to apply by a certain date for the following September. Bear in mind that your chosen school may ask that your child attends for a few hours and/or does a written test (and perhaps an interview) to make sure that he or she has the right social and academic background. If your child is not traveling with you, the school may ask the child's current school to supervise its entrance exam.

If your employer has organized a relocation company for you, let them know that you are planning a fact-finding trip and ask if they can organize an orientation day to show you around a few neighborhoods. There are meet-up groups in London (www.meetup.com/americansabroad) if this takes your fancy, and it would be a way to meet Americans already based in London. Or you could contact one of the women's clubs to see if they are having a get-together while you are in town.

It is also important to enjoy your visit, so the itineraries also include a few ideas for some fun activities to spice up your fact-finding trip to London.

# Preparing to Leave

London is a large and varied city, and you certainly would not become intimately acquainted with all of it in just a few days—I've been here more than 20 years and still don't know the entire city. Instead, think about your requirements—in terms of transportation, accommodations, and education—and select a few areas that may fit the bill. I suggest staying in a hotel that is centrally located to make it easier to get around town with public transport. However, if you think that you'd prefer to live outside London and commute to the city, I recommend that you stay in your chosen town in Greater London for a few days and do the commute in rush hour so that you know what you are taking on.

## WHAT TO BRING

### Passports and Credit/Debit Cards

If you are coming to the United Kingdom and London as a general visitor, you may be able to stay for up to six months. US citizens do not need to apply for a general visitor's visa or business visit visa before they arrive in the United Kingdom; this visa will be stamped in their passport when they pass through Border Control. However, you should bring with you all the documentation that is needed to apply for a visitor's visa. This includes a valid passport, a round-trip ticket back to the United States, evidence of where you will be staying and what you will be doing while in the UK, as well as some proof that you have enough funds to cover your expenses while in London. You may also be asked to provide proof of your employment or financial information, as well as a passport-size photograph. You will find more information on visas on the United Kingdom Government's website under Visas and Immigration.

If you plan on renting a car while you are here, you will need a valid driver's license.

It is also a good idea to keep a photocopy of your passport, airline tickets, and insurance documents, and take note of your card numbers just in case yours get lost or stolen.

Credit and debit cards are accepted by most retailers and restaurants in the United Kingdom, and they can be used to get cash out of an ATM. American Express is not usually accepted in the United Kingdom, so you may not want to bring it along. Let your bank know that you will be using your card in the United Kingdom, so they don't think that it has been stolen. You should also ask about charges for international transactions and your maximum limit before you leave.

The chip and PIN (personal identification number) system is used to authorize card payments in the United Kingdom and is similar to entering a PIN with a debit card at the checkout in the States. What is different about the UK's system is that both credit and debit cards are "smartcards," which means that they have an integrated circuit board embedded in them. Using a smartcard and PIN is considered to be more secure than using just a magnetic strip on the back of a card and a signature for payment authorization, which is why this system is used across Europe. Don't be surprised if you are asked for your passport for proof of ID when you are using your credit card, and they may also call up to get authorization on the card, even for fairly small amounts. I have also found that some places are reluctant to take my US card as it does not use chip and PIN. If your debit or credit card doesn't have a chip and PIN, you won't be able to buy a ticket (such as an Underground ticket) from a machine with that card.

Card fraud is an issue here in the United Kingdom, especially in London, so it is a good idea to take a few precautions when using your cards. Always keep an eye on them, and *don't* use them at ATMs that look unusual (I tend to use the ones inside a bank). Always cover the keypad when you type in your PIN. Also, keep an eye on who is around you at the ATM—better to be safe than sorry. On the same note, be sure to have a backup card or another way of getting money if your card is lost, damaged, or stolen.

## Medical and Travel Insurance

Before you head off to London be sure that you have adequate medical and travel insurance. Contact your medical insurance provider to see if you are covered while you are overseas and find out about the claiming process. The United Kingdom has a National Health Service, which provides free medical care at the point of use for qualifying UK residents. As non-European Union citizens, Americans will only be given free emergency care, and will need to pay for any follow-up treatment. Even if you get some medical coverage while overseas with your policy, you may want to take out some travel insurance for your trip. This can be a big help if your flight gets delayed or canceled, or if your valuables get lost or stolen, as well as providing medical coverage.

If you need prescription medication be sure to bring enough medicine for your entire trip; a US prescription will not be valid here in the United Kingdom. Remember that some conditions may flare up while you are traveling, so be sure to bring any medication for these conditions, too. Likewise, if you wear glasses or contact lenses, you may want to bring a spare pair of glasses/lenses, just in case you lose your regular pair. The United Kingdom is pretty good when it comes to getting over-the-counter treatments for common ailments. If you have a non-emergency medical problem or fall ill, stop by a drugstore (called "chemist" here) and speak to the pharmacist to see what they recommend. They may be able to give you something that will help, without having to go to the doctor. Equally, if a doctor is called for they will let you know, and can tell you which hospital to go to.

## Clothing

It is said that you can get all four seasons in a single day in Britain, and certainly London is no exception. It's easiest to dress in layers, so you can build them up or take them off to suit the ambient temperature. As a rule, Londoners tend to dress more formally than many Americans. That said, people are much more relaxed about what they wear these days, even at some offices. In a trend-setting fashion capital of the world, Londoners can get very creative with their attire, so don't be afraid to get inventive with your look (assuming it is all age-appropriate).

Pack with ease and comfort in mind. Simple versatile clothes that don't require ironing and can be dressed up or down are ideal. As you will be on your feet for much of the day, be sure to take comfortable shoes that you can walk long distances in. Something to keep in mind when packing is that you may have an occasion to dress more formally, be it a business meeting, school interview, meal at a top restaurant, or visit to the theater. Just be sure to include clothes and footwear to cover all occasions.

One item that you will not want to be without is a waterproof jacket or coat. It rains with tedious regularity here in London, and while it is unlikely to be a full-blown monsoon, if you are out and about in the drizzle all day, you'll be glad that you had a waterproof coat. If you are traveling in the late fall or winter, then you may need some gloves or a scarf. The United Kingdom is noted for its woolen and cashmere knits, so you could always pick up a sweater or scarf while you are in London if the weather suddenly gets much colder.

## Electronics

If you are bringing rechargeable items such as a cell phone, iPod/MP3 player, laptop, or games console, be sure to check whether its charger will work with 240 volts (the standard current in Britain). You'll also need to get an adapter for US to UK plugs. Try to get an adapter before you leave. If not, you may find that your hotel can provide one. Or, you could pick one up in a hardware shop, large drugstore, or department store in town. Most hotels these days have a hair dryer in the room or will let you borrow one, so you shouldn't need to bring one. Contact your cell phone network provider to find out about international calls, texts, and data-roaming fees and deals. If you don't, you may be in for a nasty shock when you get your next bill after your trip.

## Currency

The currency used in the United Kingdom is pounds sterling (£). Bills (referred to as "banknotes") come in £5, £10, £20, and £50 denominations, with 1p, 2p, 5p, 10p, 20p, 50p, £1, and £2 coins available. Compared to American change, British coins are large and heavy. Ideally you should arrive with some British currency, to cover the cost of a train/Underground ticket or taxi from the airport to your hotel, and any other small costs, such as a snack or coffee. This way, you can avoid the long lines at the airport's ATMs or currency exchange counter (bureau de change). You should be able to buy some currency from your US bank before you leave or at the airport before you depart.

Your bank will probably charge a transaction fee for each withdrawal using your debit card. The exchange rate may not be the best, but an ATM is usually the best option for changing money. Avoid using your credit cards to withdraw cash; the fees and high interest rate make this an expensive option—only do this in an emergency. Save your credit cards for large expenses, such as hotel bills or car rentals. As well as at many UK banks and ATMs, you can withdraw money from your cards at many central London post offices, and they don't charge commission.

Travelers checks are not taken by businesses, but you should be able to cash them at banks or a bureau de change. Once again, you may have to pay some commission fees, but they could be a good backup option for your credit cards.

## Security

London is a fairly safe city, providing you exercise common sense with your possessions. As a visitor your main security risk will be petty theft in the guise of pickpocketing or purse snatching, so be careful with your possessions, and never let them out of your sight. Cell phones are a common target for pickpockets, so be discreet about when and where you take your phone out, especially if it's an expensive brand. Men should put their wallet in their front trouser pocket instead of their back one. Women should always keep an eye on their purse, and make sure to use one that closes completely. If it is a shoulder bag tuck it under your arm or wear it diagonally across your body and have the flap facing your body when you are in crowds (such as in the Underground or a market). When I am in a café or coffee shop I *never* put my purse on the back of my seat; I know too many people who have lost it this way. Instead I put it on my lap or on the floor between my feet. In a crowd, a talented pickpocket can easily get into the front pockets of a backpack, so don't put anything of value in these. A zipped closed pocket inside a bigger pocket will be more secure. Remember, pickpockets may work in pairs or as a group, with one element distracting you while the other steals your wallet.

Always, always, always keep an eye on your stuff and never leave it unattended. Besides the obvious worry of your bags being taken, unattended bags are a real security issue. Ever since the mid-1800s when Irish Republicans started to bomb the capital, Londoners have developed a watchful eye for any unattended bags that could be bombs. While this may sound apocryphal, I have one friend who after a night out in the pub with some colleagues managed to cause a bomb scare just by forgetting his briefcase. He remembered it a little bit later and returned to the pub to get it only to find that the pub had been evacuated and was surrounded by police. Profuse apologies and red faces followed. So be warned; always keep an eye on your possessions and never leave them unattended.

Leaving some of your more valuable items in your hotel spreads the risk of losing everything in one fell swoop. Ask if the hotel offers a safe or if there is a way to secure items in the room. Hotels at the lower end of the market or hostels may not be that secure, so take your valuables with you when you go out for the day. If you are taking a laptop invest in a lock for your laptop bag. Sometimes making it awkward is all that is needed to deter a thief.

If you are unfortunate enough to have something stolen report it to the police (although it is unlikely that you will get anything of value back). If it is an emergency, call 999 or 112—it's the same phone number for both fixed lines and cell phones.

There are police stations throughout the city; the non-emergency telephone number is 101, or you can call the Metropolitan Police Service (020/7230 1212) and the City of London police (020/7601 2222). Until 2017, the US Embassy will be based at 24 Grosvenor Square, W1A 2LQ (tel. 020/7499 9000).

## WHEN TO GO

### Spring and Fall

Both spring and fall can be ideal times to visit London. For the most part the hordes of summertime tourists should be gone, making it easier to enjoy the sights of London. While you can't expect warm balmy days and nights, you may be lucky with the weather and get a few fine days, but don't be surprised if it rains a bit. There are no national holidays in the fall in the United Kingdom, so you won't need to worry about offices being closed if you travel at this time of year. Of course, Easter falls in the spring (both Good Friday and the Monday after Easter Sunday are national holidays here), and there are two national holidays in May (usually the first and last Mondays of the month).

If you want to visit schools, plan your fact-finding trip in the fall. Arrange visits to any private schools that you are interested in before you travel. State schools usually hold an open day in September or October, though whether you will get a place once you've moved is another question. In springtime, the long Easter vacation between school terms—this can be as much as three weeks—can make school visits difficult.

### Summer

London in the summer has some definite advantages—the weather is nicer so you can enjoy eating outdoors at cafés or strolling around the parks and along the river. The downside is that prices will be up and it will be crowded at the museums and other

Regent's Park

attractions, and hot on the Tube. Schools are shut in July and August, so you won't be able to visit them. However, the school year doesn't end until early July, so you could visit schools here in June—taking advantage of the United States' summer break but avoiding the United Kingdom's.

### Winter

London is very much a year-round city, and all of the main tourist attractions in town remain open in the winter. Often tourism picks up around December as many Europeans come to London for a weekend break and a bit of Christmas shopping. There are also several Christmassy events here, such as open-air ice-skating at the Tower of London or the Winter Wonderland at Hyde Park. Flights and hotel prices tend to fall a bit in the winter, making this a slightly more affordable time of year to visit London (excluding the immediate period around Christmas). If you are a bargain-hunter then the post-Christmas sales are worth bearing in mind—it can be a great time to get a woolen sweater.

# Arriving in London

Flights from North America land at two London airports: Gatwick to the south of the city and Heathrow to the west. Of these two, Heathrow is by far the easiest to get to and from by public transport. A flight from elsewhere in Europe may land at one of London's three other airports: Stansted, Luton, or City Airport. Wherever you land you will pass through customs and immigration at the airport. As a short-term visitor this should be little more than a quick glance through your passport and a stamp. Your next step is to collect your bags and head to a taxi rank or the Tube/train station.

## IMMIGRATION AND CUSTOMS AND EXCISE

Getting through Border Control at the airport should be very straightforward. Non-European Union citizens are required to fill in a landing card before their arrival in the United Kingdom. This is just a simple form asking for some basic information about you, including where you are staying in the United Kingdom. You should be able to get a visitor's visa as you pass through immigration, providing you have a valid passport and have brought the relevant information and funds to support your application.

Before you enter the arrival hall you pass through Customs and Excise. You can go through three different channels. Red is only for those who are bringing in more than the duty-free allowance. Blue is for those arriving from an EU country (regardless of which passport they hold). Finally, the green channel is for those with nothing to declare. Just as in the States, you cannot bring meat and dairy from a non-EU source into the United Kingdom. Customs agents can stop you and ask to search inside your bags (and even do a body search) if they suspect that something is awry.

## TRANSPORTATION

### Getting to and from the Airport

Generally speaking, Heathrow is easier to get to and from the center of town than

## Public Holidays

Christmas lights on Regent Street



Most businesses and nonessential services are closed on public holidays, although large retail businesses may remain open for some part of the day (with the exception of Easter Sunday and Christmas Day). Public holidays are often referred to as "bank holidays," which simply means that banks—and therefore most businesses—are closed. The following are standard public holidays:

- New Year's Day (January 1)
- Good Friday (Varies)
- Easter Monday (Varies)
- May Day Bank Holiday (First Monday in May)
- Spring Bank Holiday (Last Monday in May)
- Late Summer Bank Holiday (Last Monday in August)
- Christmas Day (December 25)
- Boxing Day (December 26, if this date is not a Sunday)
- December 27 (This is a public holiday if Christmas Day falls on a Saturday or Sunday.)
- December 28 (This is a public holiday if Boxing Day falls on a Saturday or Sunday.)

### PERIODIC PUBLIC HOLIDAYS

Occasionally, important royal celebrations, such as a royal wedding or an important anniversary of the monarch's realm, will prompt the introduction of a one-off national holiday.

Gatwick, mainly because the Piccadilly Tube line goes all the way out there. Cash tickets from Heathrow airport to central London cost £5.70; that drops to £5 with an Oyster travel card, which you can buy at the Travel Information Centre or at the Tube station at Heathrow. A fast overground train—the Heathrow Express—from Paddington train station costs £21 (£10.50 for a child) one way and makes getting to and from Heathrow airport a breeze. The Heathrow Connect (£9.90 one way) from Paddington isn't as quick as the Express but will also get you in and out of Heathrow. A bus service runs between Victoria bus station and Heathrow; one-way tickets start at £6 (plus a £1 booking fee).

Gatwick Airport isn't serviced by the Tube; instead, take the Gatwick Express train from Victoria train station (£17.90). Alternatively, the Thameslink from London Bridge, Blackfriars, Farringdon, or St. Pancras train station also goes to Gatwick and costs from £10 one way. Southern Railway trains also run between London Bridge and Victoria stations to Gatwick Airport and cost £13.30. Just remember that Underground and train fares rise annually and the prices given here should just be used as a guide.

At both airports you can take a black taxi to your hotel—just be prepared for a long line at the taxi rank. Although it may be a luxury, if you are tired and jet-lagged, just falling into a black cab and telling the driver your hotel can make life much easier. Just make sure you have enough cash on hand to pay (currently running £45-85). Use only a black cab from an authorized taxi rank or a reputable minicab from an approved taxi desk at the airport, and *never* use unauthorized drivers or taxis.

## Getting Around

By far the easiest way to get around town is on the Underground. Get an Oyster card or a travel pass for your visit so that you can use London's public transportation,

arriving at Heathrow

especially as the fares using an Oyster or Travel card are cheaper. Sometimes it is faster to walk to different areas, rather than take the Underground, so get a good street map.

# Accommodations and Food

## ACCOMMODATIONS

There are numerous accommodation choices in London, from five-star hotels to simple hostels, and everything in between. Generally prices are on the high side—London is one of the world's most expensive cities. If you plan on staying in town for a while, think about renting an apartment for your stay. This will give you a much more realistic idea of what living in London is like, although it can be pricey. Whatever type of accommodation you go for, you need to pre-book it, as London is a top tourist destination. If you find the hotel of your choice is dire, by all means look into changing, but you'd be foolish to arrive with no idea of where you are going to stay that night.

Hotels are the most common type of accommodation in London, with prices and quality varying immensely. When you book be sure to check what is included with the room and what isn't—including breakfast. Often, online travel-booking websites can get you a real deal on your London accommodations, so be sure to shop around. Unfortunately, traditional bed-and-breakfasts (B&B) are rare these days in London. Most of the big international hotel chains have a strong presence in London, alongside the usual British chains. Budget hotels do exist in London, although the rooms may not be big enough to swing a cat or are miles away from the center of town. There are also some low-cost hotels and hostels specifically aimed at students traveling around Europe. One of these may be a short-term idea for students who need a place to stay while they try to sort out their long-term accommodations.

## FOOD

British food has a terrible reputation, probably because it is not as important to the British as it is to the French or Italians. However, these days food and eating out are high on the agenda of many Londoners. Throughout London you'll find cafés, bistros, and numerous restaurants serving a wide variety of food, reflecting London's multicultural makeup. Special diets, such as kosher, halal, and vegan, are also catered to, although you may have to travel to the right area of town. As far as British food goes, there is the traditional British "fry up" breakfast, including eggs, bacon, grilled tomato, baked beans (*not* the American barbecued variety), and toast. Other traditional British fare includes meat pies, sausages, and, of course, deep-fried fish and "chips" (french fries). It's well worth trying a meal in a new dining trend in London, the gastropub, where the food is just as important as the beer—if not more so.

### Meal Times

Meal times are pretty much the same as in the United States, although the evening meal may be taken slightly later—closer to 8pm rather than 6pm. Lunch runs from noon to 2pm, and for most people tends to be a quick sandwich or light meal, though

© MEMITINA/123RF.COM

Many London eateries serve a variety of food.

Sunday lunch is the exception. Traditionally, people would have a Sunday roast (after a visit to church) served in the early afternoon, having a lighter meal later on in the evening or a snack before heading off to bed. Nowadays people tend to reserve Sunday lunch just for entertaining, reverting back to the normal evening meal time when they don't have guests.

## Sample Itineraries

If you have a fair idea of where you'll want to live in London, then try to find accommodations in that area of town. Or, you could stay more centrally, say in Westminster or Kensington and Chelsea, where there are numerous hotels to choose from. You can then use the Underground, a train, or a bus to get to the area of town that you want to explore. If you are unsure where you want to live, I suggest that you stay centrally. When you explore an area, you should plan to spend at least a few hours there. Use your time to wander down the high street, stop for a coffee or lunch—even find the nearest supermarket and see what it is like. You should also walk around the residential streets to see what type of accommodation is available.

### ONE WEEK OR LESS

You will probably be exhausted after your flight to London, so take it fairly easy on the first day. Once you're settled into your hotel and refreshed, try a bit of easy sightseeing, perhaps by taking one of the tour buses that let you get on and off, so you

## Tipping in London

When you first come to another country, it is difficult to know when, who, or how much you should tip the service provider. Certainly here in the United Kingdom there isn't the strong tipping culture that you get in the United States, where tips are considered part of a service provider's pay. With this ambiguity in mind, here is a quick guide to tipping in London.

### TIPPING IN RESTAURANTS

Unfortunately we are off to a bad start here with regards to tipping, as there are no hard-and-fast rules about tipping and service charges in London's restaurants. Some restaurants add a discretionary 10 or 12.5 percent to the bill as a service charge. If this is included, it should be shown on your bill (and in the menu), and you don't have to leave an additional tip. However, not all employers are good about passing on the gratuities to their staff, so you may want to leave a cash tip instead of the service charge. This way the person who served you gets the gratuity, not the restaurant owner.

If there isn't a service charge, then the normal amount for the tip should be between 10 to 15 percent and can be left on the table. If you are paying by credit card, there will be a chance to include a tip with the credit card transaction, though most wait staff prefer a cash tip. Generally, in sandwich bars, coffee shops, and cafés staff do not expect a tip, although there may be a jar by the checkout where you can leave some change in appreciation of the service.

### TIPPING IN PUBS

As a general rule, you do not tip in pubs—not even if you have ordered food (although once again there may be a jar on the bar for tips). Of course, if it is a pub that has a restaurant attached, then the rules for tipping in a restaurant apply. If you want to show your appreciation to the bar staff or publican you can always offer to buy them a drink. However, this is a bit uncommon in pubs, unless you are a well-known regular.

### OTHER TIPS

It is not required to tip taxi drivers, but they appreciate it. Most people just round the fare up to the nearest pound if it is a straightforward fare. If they've helped you with your bags, give them a bit more—say a pound per bag. If the cabbie has given you a bit of a tour around town or been a real help, feel free to leave up to 10 percent. If a bellhop has carried your luggage to your room, give them a pound or so. It is up to you whether you want to tip a hairdresser or barber, though most appreciate being given a few pounds.

can explore London at your own pace. You may also want to take the opportunity to wander around the area near your hotel to help you get your bearings, and explore nearby attractions.

The next day get down to business and visit possible living locations. For central upmarket urban living, it's hard to beat Marylebone Village; the nearest Underground stations are Baker Street (to the north) and Bond Street (to the south). For a bit of sightseeing, jump on the Jubilee line at Bond Street station, go to Green Park, then walk across the park to Buckingham Palace. If you want to see the Changing of the Guard, be there by 11:15am.

If you are going to be based in central London for work—be it the financial district in the City of London or in the West End—spend some time exploring Clerkenwell (the nearest Underground station is Barbican or Farringdon Station) or the City itself. Slightly north is another fairly central urban location, Upper Street in Islington

© KAREN WHITE

Take in all of the major sights in London on a tour bus.

(nearest Underground station is Angel). If you want to live somewhere that offers a trendy, edgy feel, then check out Shoreditch (nearest Tube station is Old Street). While in this part of town, visit the Tower of London, if you haven't had a chance yet. Even Canary Wharf in Docklands (on the Docklands Light Railway or Jubilee line) could be worth a visit.

Families may prefer the quieter residential areas of St. John's Wood (St. John's Wood Tube station) or Maida Vale (Warwick Avenue or Maida Vale station), which border each other. The American School in London is based in St. John's Wood, so this would be an ideal time to visit the school (be sure to pre-book a visit).

The next day you could combine a bit of sightseeing and location scouting, by visiting the parts of Kensington and Chelsea nearest South Kensington Tube station, followed by a trip to one or more of the South Kensington museums. If you think Chelsea may be to your liking, start at South Kensington Tube station and walk down Pelham Street and Sloane Avenue until you get to Kings Road, or you can take the number 49 bus. Don't be afraid to wander down some of the side streets and check out both north and south of Kings Road. Once you are finished exploring this area of Chelsea, head back on the 49 bus to South Kensington, where you can visit the Natural History Museum, the Science Museum, or Victoria and Albert Museum (or all three if you are a museum buff).

The next day give yourself a break from location hunting and just enjoy London. If you like walking you could go to Parliament Square (Westminster Tube station). Here you'll find the Houses of Parliament, including the bell tower that holds Big Ben, as well as Westminster Abbey. Then walk across Westminster Bridge and take a trip on the London Eye (you can pre-book online). Next you can walk up the river's edge along the South Bank to the Globe Theatre and take in a play, or continue on until the Tate

Modern. If you still have energy you can walk across the Millennium Bridge and up to Queen Victoria Street, where you turn right to get to Mansion House Tube station and hop on the Circle or District line to Tower Bridge to see the Tower of London. If you are tired, you can leave this to another day.

If you'd prefer a predominantly residential area near a large park, check out Hampstead, Belsize Park, or Highgate on the Northern line on your fourth day in London. Hampstead (in the borough of Camden) is packed with good independent schools, so build any Hampstead school visits into this day. You could then take the Northern line down to Tottenham Court Road to visit the British Museum and explore Bloomsbury.

One last area I'd suggest that you visit would be around High Street Kensington and Notting Hill. Both neighborhoods offer a good mix of different accommodations in a fairly central location, but aren't as busy as some of the central areas of Westminster and Islington. If you are a tennis fan, then a trip to Wimbledon to do a tour of the grounds may be in the cards; just be sure to pre-book your tour. While there, you could explore the streets toward Wimbledon Common to see if it may work for you as a place to live. On the way back you could take the train to Clapham Junction and walk around Battersea and Northcote Road or take the District line train and get off in East Putney to quickly check out this neighborhood.

If suburbia calls, head south of the river to the borough of Richmond, by taking the District line to Kew Gardens (at the station, follow the signs to Kew Gardens and then walk down Lichfield Road to get to the gardens themselves). Afterwards you can go into Richmond and have a wander around its pretty town center before heading to the river and taking a boat ride from Richmond back to Westminster Pier. For a distinctly rural flavor, take the river boat from Westminster Pier to Hampton Court and spend some time touring this palace. Many of the towns and villages that are popular with Americans in Surrey are within 20 miles (32 kilometers) of here. By taking the train back to Surbiton and changing lines you could pay a visit to Esher, Cobham (via Cobham and Stoke d'Abernon station), or even Virginia Water. Unfortunately they are all on different train lines, but you could visit at least one of them.

If you think you and your family would prefer to live outside of London, rent a car and spend at least a day out of town and skip some of the areas in London. This would be a good time to check out Surrey (around Cobham and Thorpe) or parts of Buckinghamshire or Hertfordshire. If you have kids under the age of seven, then you may want to visit the Bekonscot Model Village and Railway (www.bekonscot.co.uk), which is in Beaconsfield, Buckinghamshire, and around five miles (eight kilometers) away from Gerrards Cross. If your kids are too old for this, there is an amusement park in Chertsey (Thorpe Park, www.thorpepark.com) that they may enjoy. There are also several stately homes (such as Hughenden Manor or Cliveden House) in this part of Buckinghamshire, or you can visit Runnymeade, where the Magna Carta was signed. For more information see the National Trust website (www.nationaltrust.org.uk). North of London in Hertfordshire the grand stately Hatfield House was built in 1611, and part of an early palace (home to Elizabeth I in her childhood) can still be seen. Hatfield House is less than 10 miles (16 kilometers) away from both Harpenden and St. Albans, so explore these areas while you are up this way with the car. St. Albans was an old Roman town (called Verulamium), and the Verulamium Museum has some wonderful Roman artifacts.

## MORE THAN A WEEK

If you can afford a two-week fact-finding trip to London you will be much more able to really explore the capital's various neighborhoods, as well as its suburbs. Think about renting a short stay or serviced apartment. You could also look into doing a house swap with some Londoners, as a more affordable solution. Either would give you the chance to really experience what it is like to live in London.

You can do all of the activities listed in the one-week itinerary, but at a much slower pace. Fill in your time by exploring more of London's museums, art galleries, parks, shops, markets, sights—whatever takes your fancy. As well as staying in town, you could spend a few days (and nights) out in the suburbs of Surrey, Buckinghamshire, Hertfordshire, or elsewhere, which would give you a chance to visit a school or two. If you are thinking of living outside the city, whoever will be working in town should experience the commute in rush hour so that they know what they are taking on.

As you'll be in town over a weekend you may want to visit some of London's markets, such as the Saturday Portobello Market (Notting Hill Gate Tube station) or Borough Market (London Bridge Tube station)—gourmet heaven. Camden Town Market (Camden Town Tube station) runs on both Saturday and Sunday and is great for students. The Greenwich Market (take the Docklands Light Railway to Cutty Sark station) is also open on the weekends. While you are there you can visit the Observatory, stroll through the park, or visit the National Maritime Museum. A fun way to get back to Westminster is by river boat under the Tower Bridge.

A longer trip to London enables you to have a few day trips, such as going on the

pastries for sale at Borough Market

train to Bath to see the Roman Baths or heading to the seaside in Brighton to see the splendid Brighton Pavilion. If you have kids, Legoland in Windsor would be a real treat, perhaps as a reward for trudging around town looking at places to live, or you could pay a visit to Windsor Castle. You could also use some of your time to explore farther afield for a few days, be it north to the Lake District and Scotland or west to Cornwall and the Cotswolds. You could even take the Eurostar train to Paris for a short break to experience the delights of that city.

# Practicalities

With around 10,000 hotels to choose from there are numerous options when staying in London. Following are a few suggestions.

Always book your accommodations in advance; you will be jet-lagged and tired and will just want a place to crash before hitting the city streets. The cost of staying in a London hotel is on the rise, and increased nearly 10 percent between 2013 and 2014, boosting the average hotel room to more than £125 per night. Prices for some central London hotels will be even more expensive. Many hotels offer midweek specials or out-of-season or advanced booking discounts, so it makes sense to plan ahead and shop around. Many of the large international hotel chains have locations across London and may offer a deal on rates. You may also be able to find accommodation bargains online at www.lastminute.com, www.hotel.com, and www.expedia.co.uk; or try property-sharing services, such as Airbnb (www.airbnb.co.uk).

Although these aren't in a prime living location, students and those on a tight budget could try one of the five **St. Christopher's Inns hostels** (www.st-christophers.co.uk) across London, which offer dorm rooms from £21 and private rooms from £44. Another low-cost option is the budget Asian chain Tune Hotel, with five London locations; prices at the **Tune Hotel-Kings Cross** (324 Gray's Inn Rd., London WC1X 8BU, tel. 020/7713 2050, www.tunehotels.com) start from £40.

## ACCOMMODATIONS

### Kensington and Chelsea

In South Kensington there is the chic, feng shui-ed 45-room **Myhotel Chelsea** (35 Ixworth Place, SW3 3QX, tel. 020/7225 7500, www.myhotels.com, from £150), one of the area's hippest hotels. Myhotel Chelsea is part of a small group of boutique hotels in London and Brighton, and it has a sister hotel in Bloomsbury. Set in a Grade II-listed Georgian townhouse just minutes from Chelsea's fashionable Kings Road, the 21 rooms offered by **The Sydney House** (9-11 Sydney St., SW3 6PU, tel. 020/7376 7711, www.sydneyhousechelsea.co.uk, from £255) provide maximum comfort in luxurious surroundings.

**The Aster House** (3 Sumner Place, SW7 3EE, tel. 020/7581 5888, www.asterhouse.com, from £200) is one of London's best-known bed-and-breakfast establishments. It offers traditional B&B accommodations in its 13 comfortable rooms in a large 1850 Victorian townhouse just minutes from the museums in South Kensington. If you're after a bohemian atmosphere, **The Portobello Hotel** (22 Stanley Gardens, W11 2NG,

© KAREN WHITE

The Sydney House hotel is well positioned between Chelsea's Kings Road and South Kensington.

tel. 020/7727 2777, www.portobellohotel.com, from £255) in Notting Hill won't disappoint. Since the early 1970s, this place has hosted legends from the world of music, fashion, and show business. The rooms at The Portobello have been individually decorated to provide sumptuous surroundings, including the odd four-poster bed.

## Westminster

Near Oxford Street and Marylebone is the **Hart House Hotel** (51 Gloucester Place, Portman Square, W1U 8JF, tel. 020/7935 2288, www.harthouse.co.uk, from £140), a small hotel in a charming Georgian townhouse in the heart of Marylebone. If you'd prefer a small cozy hotel in Marylebone try the **Montagu Place Hotel** (2-3 Montagu Place, W1H 2ER tel. 020/7467 2777, www.montagu-place.co.uk, from £149). Contained in a five-story Victorian townhouse, this very small hotel doesn't have an elevator, so if climbing stairs is an issue for you, be sure to request a room on the ground floor.

For a luxury bed-and-breakfast in an 1820s building near Marble Arch, try a stay at **The Sumner** (54 Upper Berkeley St., W1H 7QR, tel. 020/7723 2244, www.thesumner.com, from £140), which has 20 comfortable rooms to choose from. For a modern, stylish take on bed-and-breakfast accommodations, try the **B&B Belgravia** (64-66 Ebury St., SW1W 9QD, tel. 020/7259 8570, www.bb-belgravia.com, from £160), which also offers studio apartments. In Covent Garden you may like the 25-room **Fielding Hotel** (4 Broad Court, Bow St., WC2B 5QZ, tel. 020/7836 8305, www.thefieldinghotel.co.uk, from £140), which is just opposite the Royal Opera House, making it very well placed for all the theaters in the area. For ideas in a more residential part of town in St. John's Wood there is **The New Inn Public House** (2 Allitsen Rd., NW8 6LA, tel.

020/7722 0726, www.newinnlondon.co.uk, from £100), which is a gastropub/B&B inn with just five en-suite rooms. If you are looking for something a bit quirky try the **Pavilion "Rock & Roll" Hotel** (34-36 Sussex Gardens, W2 1UL, tel. 020/7262 0905, www.pavilionhoteluk.com, from £110). As the name implies, each of the 30 rooms at the Pavilion Hotel is themed around a funky and glamorous image—a definite must for style gurus.

## Camden

If you want to stay in Bloomsbury, near the British Museum and University of London, you could try the **Ridgemount Hotel** (65-67 Gower St., WC1E 6HJ, tel. 020/7636 1141, www.ridgemounthotel.co.uk, from £102), which has 32 rooms, though only half of them come with an en-suite bathroom, so be sure to ask for one. Just up the street is **The Academy Hotel** (21 Gower St., WC1E 6HG, tel. 020/7631 4115, www.theacademyhotel.co.uk, from £129). Made up from five restored Georgian townhouses, this charming hotel in the heart of Bloomsbury offers 49 rooms, as well as a library and a conservatory. Heading up the luxury ladder is the four-star **Radisson Edwardian Bloomsbury Street Hotel** (9-13 Bloomsbury St., WC1B 3QD, tel. 020/7636 5601, US toll-free tel. 800/967 9033, www.radissonedwardian.com, from £215), which is part of a small luxury chain of central London hotels. This hotel has 174 rooms, including three suites and 87 deluxe rooms.

Conveniently located near Hampstead Primrose Hill and Camden Town is the **Haverstock Hotel** (154 Haverstock Hill, NW3 2AY, tel. 020/7722 5097, www.haverstockhotel.co.uk) in Belsize Park. This former pub has been transformed in a sleek modern hotel with rooms from £139. For something more homey, there is **La Gaffe** (107-111 Heath St., NW3 6SS, tel. 020/7435 8965, www.lagaffe.co.uk, from £99 for a double room), which is right in Hampstead village and has been praised for both its food and well-priced cozy rooms. The accommodations here are above the Italian restaurant below, so there are just a handful of rooms, though all come with a bathroom.

## Islington and the City of London

Part of London's charm is its history, and Clerkenwell in Islington has buckets full of it. If you want to stay in a small four-star hotel full of antiquated, period charm there is the **Rookery Hotel** (12 Peter's Lane, Cowcross St., EC1M 6DS, tel. 020/7336 0931, www.rookeryhotel.com, from £288) near Farringdon. It offers 33 rooms, each individually decorated and well-equipped. Another boutique hotel in Clerkenwell is **The Zetter** (St. John's Square, 86-88 Clerkenwell Rd., EC1M 5RJ, tel. 020/7324 4567, www.thezetter.com, from £155), with its eclectic mix of vintage-modern interiors and 59 individually designed rooms. The owners also have an ultra-luxurious 13-room hotel in a Georgian townhouse just a few doors away, **The Zetter Townhouse** (49-50 St. John's Square, EC1V 4JJ, tel. 020/7324 4545, www.thezettertownhouse.com, from £246), offering similarly styled accommodations and cutting-edge in-room entertainment.

In the City of London try the more reasonably priced **Club Quarters St. Paul** (24 Ludgate Hill, EC4M 7DR, tel. 020/7651 2200, www.clubquarters.com, £140 for nonmembers), which offers a range of affordable accommodations—everything from single rooms to two-bedroom apartments. Of course, members of the Club Quarters organization, which offers business travelers member-only, full-service hotels in downtown locations in the United States and London, get a much better deal depending on the type of membership. Club Quarters also has a hotel in the West End near Trafalgar Square. For a more luxurious option there is the **Threadneedles Hotel** (5 Threadneedle St., London EC2R 8AY, tel. 020/7657 8080, www.theetoncollection.co.uk, from £179). Part of the Marriott's Autograph Collection of boutique hotels, the establishment has 70 spacious, well-equipped rooms.

## Hackney and Tower Hamlets (including Docklands)

To check out London's coolest location head to Shoreditch and the **Hoxton Hotel** (81 Great Eastern St., EC2A 3HU, tel. 020/7550 1000, www.hoxtonhotel.com, from £89). Near the border with Islington, this hotel offers stylish modern decor with exposed brick interiors and leather furniture. Plus, it offers an annual sale of 500 rooms for just £1, but you need to be quick as they can sell out in just 15 minutes; check the website for more information. Equally trendy would be a room at **Shoreditch House** (Ebor St., E1 6AW, tel. 020/7739 5040, www.shoreditchhouse.com), part of the SoHo House private club. This hotel is also open to nonmembers, and a stay in one of the 26 bedrooms in this former East London pub and lodging house starts at £125. For an affordable option in East London there is **The Shoreditch Inn** (1 Austin St., E2 7NS, tel. 020/3327 3910, www.shoreditchinn.com, from £119), conveniently located for access to Spitalfields Market and Brick Lane, as well as the legendary nightlife of Shoreditch.

Out in Docklands there is the massive 442-room modern **Britannia International Hotel** (163 Marsh Wall, E14 9SJ, tel. 0871/222 0042, www.britanniahotels.com, from £220), part of the Britannia Hotel chain; discounts are sometimes available.

## Wandsworth

One of London's leading brewers is Young's, which is based in Wandsworth. In the past few years, this company has started going back to its original roots establishing inns, where people can have a drink, a meal, and/or stay the night. One of its hotels is the 16-room **Brewers Inn** (147 East Hill, SW18 2QB, tel. 020/8874 4128, www.brewersinn.co.uk, from £110) in Wandsworth. This establishment has just 16 comfortable and well-equipped en-suite rooms. The same chain also has a hotel in Clapham, **The Windmill** (Windmill Dr., Clapham Common South Side, SW4 9DE, tel. 020/8673 4578, www.windmillclapham.co.uk, from £149), which offers up to 29 well-equipped bedrooms in the three floors over the pub; the nearest Tube station is Clapham Common on the Northern line.

If you'd like to stay out in Wimbledon, then you could try the very grand **Cannizaro House** (West Side Common, SW19 4UE, tel. 020/8879 1464, www.cannizarohouse.com, from £195), based in an 18th-century manor house offering 46 elegant rooms (each has its own signature wallpaper) and a wonderful restaurant. If you'd prefer something more basic try the **Antoinette Hotel** (The Broadway, SW19 1SD, tel. 020/8546 1044, www.antoinettehotel.com, from £104). This simple hotel has just 50 rooms, all with en-suite bathrooms, and the better ones have a balcony. This place is ideally situated for access to the town center, the station, and the Wimbledon Lawn Tennis Club.

## Richmond

Just on the edge of rural London, at the end of the District Underground line is

Richmond. For a luxury hotel in this part of town try the **Richmond Hill Hotel** (144-150 Richmond Hill, TW10 6RW, tel. 020/8940 2247, www.richmondhill-hotel.co.uk, from £150). The Grade II-listed building was once a manor house dating from 1726, and it has wonderful views of the Thames. Right beside the river in Richmond is the utterly enchanting **Bingham Hotel and Restaurant** (61-63 Petersham Road, TW10 6UT, tel. 020/8940 0902, www.thebingham.co.uk, from £210). Set in two Georgian townhouses with 15 elegantly designed bedrooms and a Michelin-starred restaurant, this place exudes luxury. Another one of the Young's chain of hotels/inns is the **Coach & Horses** (8 Kew Green, TW9 3BH, tel. 020/8940 1208, www.coachhotelkew.co.uk, from £140) in Kew. With 31 rooms above the pub/restaurant below, this place is ideally located for access to the Kew Gardens and Richmond.

### Outside of London

In Cobham there is the **Woodlands Park Hotel** (Woodlands Lane, Stoke d'Abernon, Cobham, Surrey KT11 3QB, tel. 01372/843933, www.handpickedhotels.co.uk/hotels/woodlands-park, from £126) or **Cobham Lodge** (46 Portsmouth Rd., Cobham, Surrey, KT11 1HY, tel. 01932/589948, www.cobhamlodge.co.uk, from £68). The Young's chain of hotels has stretched into Surrey with **The Bear** (71 High St., Esher, Surrey KT10 9RQ, tel. 01372/469786, http://bearesher.co.uk, from £130) in Esher. This traditional inn has just seven rooms, but they are all well appointed and comfortable. Opulent and historic, the 15th-century coaching inn **The Crazy Bear Beaconsfield** (75 Wycombe End, Old Town, Beaconsfield, Buckinghamshire, HP9 1LX, tel. 01494/673086, www.crazybeargroup.co.uk/beaconsfield, from £290) offers 19 individually designed luxurious bedrooms and has an English and Thai restaurant. For a more affordable hotel try the **Travelodge Hotel** (Aylesbury End, Beaconsfield, Buckinghamshire HP9 1LW, tel. 0871/559 1803, www.travelodge.co.uk, from £45). In Gerrards Cross, try the **Bull Hotel** (Oxford Road, Gerrards Cross, Buckinghamshire, SL9 7PA, tel. 1753/885995, www.sarova-bullhotel.com, from £104). Although this establishment originally opened as a coaching inn back in 1688, it is now a 150-room hotel offering modern, comfortable accommodations and dining.

In St. Albans try **Ardmore House Hotel** (54 Lemsford Rd., St. Albans, Hertfordshire, AL1 3PR, US tel. 866/332 3590, www.ardmorehousehotelstalbans.com, from £85). This converted Edwardian property has a wide range of well-appointed rooms available, including some with four-poster beds. If you think leafy Kent is more to your liking then you could try the **Royal Oak Hotel** (5 Upper High St., Sevenoaks, Kent, TN13 1HY, tel. 01732/451109, www.rosevenoaks.co.uk, from £105). With just 18 rooms and a popular restaurant, this three-star hotel started life in the 18th century as a coaching inn.

## FOOD

### Kensington and Chelsea

A gastropub in West London that you may want to visit is the **Harwood Arms** (27 Walham Grove, SW6 1QP, tel. 020/7386 1847, www.harwoodarms.com); London's first Michelin-starred pub is in Fulham and has gained a reputation for its clever twist on British food. For something a bit special I'd try **The Ledbury** (127 Ledbury Rd., W11 2AQ, tel. 020/7792 9090, www.theledbury.com)—another Michelin-starred

## Historic Public Houses

A trip to London wouldn't be complete without a visit to a historic pub. Some famous old London pubs that you may want to visit for a pint or two include the last surviving example of a 17th-century galleried coaching inn—**The George Inn** (77 Borough High St., SE1, tel. 020/7407 2056), just a few minutes' walk from London Bridge station. This pub is on the tour bus circuit, so don't be surprised if busloads of people suddenly descend upon the pub. Hidden down a tiny alleyway in the City of London is **Ye Olde Mitre** (1 Ely Court, Ely Place, EC1, tel. 020/7405 4751, http://yeoldemitreholborn.co.uk), which was originally built as a hostelry back in 1546 and is a great place to get a pint of Fuller's London Pride (a local London beer).

©KAREN WHITE

The George Inn

For Victorian splendor I like **The Audley** (41-43 Mount St., London W1K 2RX, tel. 020/7499 1843) in Mayfair. Up in Hampstead is the **Holly Bush** (22 Holly Mount, NW3 6SG, tel. 020/7435 2892), where you can enjoy a pint in front of a warming fire—the perfect way to warm up after a walk on nearby Hampstead Heath in the winter months.

Not far from Bloomsbury there is **The Lamb** (94 Lambs Conduit St., WC1N 3LZ, tel. 020/7405 0713, www.youngs.co.uk/pubs/lamb), which is another favorite of mine. I find it charming that this place still has Victorian-era snob screens (rotating etched glass screens used in the public bar so that the staff couldn't see who they were serving), even if it can make it a bit awkward to order a drink at the bar sometimes.

restaurant. The Ledbury is in Notting Hill and offers outstanding French cuisine with an emphasis on seasonal food; table reservations are a must. For traditional British cuisine brought bang up-to-date, try the **Launceston Place** (1A Launceston Place, W8 5RL, tel. 020/7937 6912, www.launcestonplace-restaurant.co.uk). It's conveniently located for the museums in South Kensington, the Royal Albert Hall, and the shopping on High Street Kensington, though you will need to reserve a table in advance.

### Westminster

For a reasonably priced meal it is hard to beat the well-established **Stockpot** (18 Old Compton St., W1D 4TN, tel. 020/7287 1066), which still serves traditional English food from a menu that has barely changed since the 1960s. With its exceptional fish and chips, the **Sea Shell** (49-51 Lisson Grove, NW1 6UH, tel. 020/7224 9000, www.seashellrestaurant.co.uk) is a good place to try this staple of British cuisine, even if it is a bit out of the way tucked behind Marylebone station. If you are a bit homesick and feel like a Mexican meal, try **Wahaca** (80 Wardour St., W1F 0TF, tel. 020/7734 0195, www.wahaca.co.uk), with 13 locations spread across town. If you just want a burrito,

**Poncho 8** (12 Sheldon Sq.,W2 6EZ, tel. 020/7121 0325, www.poncho8.com, with five other London locations) is tough to beat . . . at least on this side of the Atlantic.

Indian food is excellent in London and good value. It is certainly well worth trying if you are unfamiliar with it. I'd recommend **Dishoom** (12 Upper St. Martin's Ln., WC2H 9FB, tel. 020/7420 9320, http://dishoom.com), which models itself on a Bombay café (with café prices), or **Imli** (167-169 Wardour St., W1F 8WR, tel. 020/7287 4243, www.imli.com), which also aims to provide well-prepared food in a stylish surrounding, all for a moderate price.

Not far from Piccadilly Circus is **Hix** (66-70 Brewer St., W1F 9UP, tel. 020/7292 3518, www.hixsoho.co.uk), thought to be one of the best restaurants for traditional British fare. It's well located for the nearby theaters and a good place to dine before you head off to watch a show. Be sure to pre-book. An evening at the well-known **Locanda Locatelli** (8 Seymour St., W1H 7JZ, tel. 020/7935 9088, www.locandalocatelli.com) Italian restaurant would be ideal if you want to celebrate something special, though you'll need to book a table in advance. In St. John's Wood the French **L'Aventure** (3 Blenheim Terrace, NW8 0EH, tel. 020/7624 6232, www.laventure.co.uk) is a hidden neighborhood gem, offering classical French cuisine in a friendly cozy atmosphere—you may think you've been transported across the channel.

## Camden

In Hampstead I recommend the **Horseshoe** pub (28 Heath St., NW3 6TE, tel. 020/7431 7206, www.thehorseshoehampstead.com), where you can try something from its seasonal menu and enjoy a pint of its home-brewed ale—a great place for a Sunday roast followed by a walk on the Heath. Also in Hampstead is **Villa Bianca** (1 Perrins Court, NW3 1QS, tel. 020/7435 3131, www. villabiancagroup.co.uk), a staple of NW3 for the past 30 years. This restaurant is tucked up a small alleyway off of High Street and serves wonderful traditional Italian cuisine. The same establishment also owns the quaint **Coffee Cup** café (74 Hampstead High St., tel. 020/7435 7565, www.villabiancagroup.co.uk), with its lovely wood paneling. It's a great place for breakfast, though it also does traditional simple Italian lunches and dinners as well. This place is a popular meeting place for local moms for a morning coffee and croissant. A good gastropub by Regent's Park is the **Queen's Head & Artichoke** (30-32 Albany St., NW1 4EA, tel. 020/7916 6206, www.theartichoke.net), located in a restored classic Victorian pub. The building originally dates back to the 16th century, when it was a royal hunting lodge. The tapas are a real treat, but downstairs can be crowded, so reserve a table upstairs. For classical French cuisine in Bloomsbury, there is the Michelin two-star **Pied-à-Terre** (34 Charlotte St., W1T 2NH, tel. 020/7636 1178, www.pied-a-terre.co.uk). Its two-course lunch for £27.50 is a steal and they also offer pre-theater dining. Be sure to reserve a table. If you are meeting a group of people and want a meal that you can all share, then Spanish tapas may be the answer—I particularly like **Navarro's** (67 Charlotte St., W1T 4PH, tel. 020/7637 7713, www.navarros-tapas-london.co.uk). The set price menus are a great way to share and are quite generous, so build up an appetite sightseeing before your visit.

© KAREN WHITE

The Coffee Cup on Hampstead High Street is a great place for breakfast or a cup of tea and a cake.

### Islington and the City of London

One of Islington's more popular eateries is the **Almeida Restaurant** (30 Almeida St., N1 1AD, tel. 020/7354 4777, www.almeida-restaurant.co.uk), offering mainly modern French cuisine with an emphasis on seasonal produce. Its pre- or post-theater set dinner menu is good value at £17 for two courses and £20 for three courses. It is opposite the Almeida Theater, so be sure to reserve a table first. A place to eat lunch (or dinner) on Upper Street is **Ottolenghi** (287 Upper St., N1 2TZ, tel. 020/7288 1454, www.ottolenghi.co.uk)—one of its four locations in London. Not far from Farringdon Tube station is the gastropub **The Eagle** (159 Farringdon Rd., EC1R 3AL, tel. 020/7837 1353, www.theeaglefarringdon.co.uk), which is credited with launching the dining trend of serving top quality food in a pub. The blackboard menu changes daily at this well-loved gastropub.

Confirmed carnivores may want to try the **Grill on the Market** (2-3 West Smithfield, EC1A 9JX, tel. 020/7246 0900, www.blackhouse.uk.com/london, closed Sun.) for a hunk of rib-eye steak or Kobe beef burger, though those preferring fish are also catered to here. For traditional fish and chips try **Sweetings** (39 Queen Victoria St., EC4N 4SA, tel. 020/7248 3062), a lunchtime institution with workers since 1889. If you want to eat in one of the City's historic buildings, the Royal Exchange's **Grand Café** (Royal Exchange Building, corner of Threadneedle Street and Cornhill, www.theroyalexchange.com) serves traditional breakfasts and modern European cuisine for lunch and dinner—or you could stop by for afternoon tea. Voted London's best Mexican restaurant, **Chilango** (27 Upper St., N1 0PN, tel. 020/7704 2123, www.chilango.co.uk) serves freshly prepared tacos, burritos, and salads with a choice of fillings. It has five branches across the City of London, as well as in Spitalfields and by Angel station.

### Hackney and Tower Hamlets (including Docklands)

One of London's most celebrated restaurants is **Fifteen** (15 Westland Place, N1 7LP, tel. 020/3375 1515, www.fifteen.net), by Old Street on the Hoxton/Shoreditch border, serving modern Italian-led dishes. What makes this place special is that it takes young unemployed people and offers them a one-year intensive apprenticeship teaching them about food and its preparation, helping them to turn their lives around. You'll need to reserve a table. For a classic American burger try the **Hoxton Grill** (81 Great Eastern St. EC2A 3HU, tel. 020/7739 9111, www.hoxtongrill.com) in Shoreditch.

If you fancy pizza try **Pizza East** (56 Shoreditch High St, E1 6JJ, tel. 020/7729 1888, www.pizzaeast.com). Housed in a former tea warehouse, this isn't your standard pizzeria, but it offers a fresh take on the humble pizza using fresh seasonal ingredients. Also well worth a visit is the **Princess of Shoreditch** (76-78 Paul St., EC2A 4NE, tel. 020/7729 9270, www.theprincessofshoreditch.com), which is just as popular for its beer as its superb food. For great Chinese at affordable prices try **My Old Place** (88 Middlesex St., E1 7EZ, tel. 020/7247 2200) in Spitalfields. The service can be trying, but boy is the food great! A wonderful, but slightly more expensive Indian meal can be had at **Café Spice Namasté** (16 Prescot St., E1 8AZ, tel. 020/7488 9242, http://cafespice.co.uk).

### Wandsworth

For some Italian food south of the river there is the family-run **Enoteca Turi** (28 Putney High St., SW15 1SQ, tel. 020/8785 4449, www.enotecaturi.com) in Putney, offering authentic regional cuisine and an amazing wine list; be sure to reserve a table. For a special evening you could try the Michelin-starred **Chez Bruce** (2 Bellevue Rd., Wandsworth, SW17 7EG, tel. 020/8672 0114, www.chezbruce.co.uk), where the food has a French/Mediterranean feel and the cheese board takes pride of place. The menu changes according to what's in season; be sure to reserve a table. If you are a fan of tasting menus and enjoy modern French cuisine then you may be impressed by **The Trinity** (4 The Polygon, Clapham Old Town, SW4 0JG, tel. 020/7622 1199, www.trinityrestaurant.co.uk); just be sure that you book the bespoke tasting menu well in advance. Down in Wimbledon, **The Light House** (75-77 Ridgway, Wimbledon, SW19 4ST, tel. 020/8944 6338, www.lighthousewimbledon.com), with its relaxed friendly atmosphere and modern European menu, is a perennial favorite with locals. It also offers a very reasonably priced early evening set menu; reservations are advised, especially during the tennis tournament.

### Richmond

For an Italian meal try the **Riva** (169 Church Rd., SW13 9HR, tel. 020/8748 0434) in Barnes. The food is mainly northern Italian and the seafood is well worth trying. Another option in Barnes would be **Annie's** (36-38 White Hart Ln., SW13 0PZ, tel. 020/8878 2020, www.anniesrestaurant.co.uk), specializing in tasty, seasonal comfort food for breakfast, lunch, and dinner, which they refer to as "modern Brit-erranean."

All I know is that the warm goat cheese salad is perfect for lunch. For a special meal in Chiswick try the French-inspired **La Trompette** restaurant (3-7 Devonshire Rd., W4 2EU, tel. 020/8747 1836, www.latrompette.co.uk)—book ahead.

## Outside of London

Situated in a rustic riverside barn in Cobham, the Italian restaurant **La Capanna** (48 High St., Cobham, Surrey KT11 3EF, tel. 01932/862121, www.lacapanna.co.uk) serves up traditional Italian fare. And in nearby Esher you can try traditional British dishes at **The Bear** (71 High St., Esher, Surrey KT10 9RQ, tel. 01372/469786, http://bearesher.co.uk). For a special meal there is a Michelin two star gastropub in Marlow, Buckinghamshire: **The Hand and Flowers** (126 West St., Marlow SL7 2BP, tel. 01628/482277, http://thehandandflowers.co.uk). The menu is a mix of modern British fare and rustic French dishes, with an emphasis on fresh seasonal ingredients—definitely a winning combination. In many of the larger towns in the London suburbs you'll find perfectly acceptable national chain restaurants—be it the ubiquitous **Pizza Express** (www.pizzaexpress.com) to keep the kids happy, the traditional Italian **Carluccio's Café** (www.carluccios.com), or a classic French bistro meal at **Café Rouge** (www.caferouge.co.uk).

# DAILY LIFE

# MAKING THE MOVE

So now that you've visited London and fallen for the place, the question arises: What can you do to make your dream a reality? Unfortunately, you can't just up and move to London and expect to get a job (unless you are lucky enough to have dual nationality). Instead you must get a visa that allows you to live and work in London, which means coming to grips with UK immigration, its rules and regulations, as well as the job market. UK immigration law is among the most complex in the world, with different rules for European Economic Area (EEA) and Swiss nationals, as well as Commonwealth nations. Further complicating the issue is the fact that some nationalities are considered to be non-visa nationals (such as Americans), whereas others are visa nationals. Basically, non-visa nationals do not normally need a visa to come to the United Kingdom if they are just coming for a short trip, whereas visa nationals need a visa even if they are only here for a day or two. If you are not moving here through your employer, get some professional advice about immigrating to the United Kingdom.

Remember, getting the visa sorted is just your first "moving to London" hurdle; you will also need to sort out a shipping company and decide what to take and what to leave behind. There is also the family pet to consider, as the United Kingdom has strict controls in place to prevent infectious animal diseases, such as rabies.

# Immigration and Visas

The first step to take before you can move to London is to tackle the visa process. Usually, getting a visa to live in the United Kingdom will be linked with either a job offer, an intra-company transfer, or being accepted to study at an institution of higher education (for example, a college or university). One consequence of the 2008 credit crunch and subsequent global economic downturn is that countries across the globe will hire only skilled individuals that they really need. Like the United States, the United Kingdom has dramatically tightened its immigration policy for non-European Union (EU) citizens and is pushing to restrict EU citizens as well. Nevertheless, London is one of the world's leading financial centers, and many multinational corporations and American firms have offices here. By far the easiest way to get a visa to live and work in London is through an intra-company transfer with an American firm, so think about getting a job with one of these companies in a role where you could qualify for a transfer. Of course you could also try studying or doing research here, or applying directly for a job, assuming you are in the right profession.

Do not make the mistake of trying to move to the United Kingdom without a visa. If you plan to be here for more than six months, you must have your visa organized before you arrive. It can take some time for both points-based or non-points-based visas to be processed—anything from less than a week up to four months or more. However, most visas are processed within a month to six weeks, with settlement visas usually taking up to three months. Remember that if you don't have the right visa when you get here, you may be denied entry.

Once you know how you are going to qualify for your visa, you can get down to the nitty-gritty and start your visa application rolling. Thankfully, the UK government offers most of its application forms online—including those for visas. This dramatically cuts down the bureaucratic elements of applying for a visa, although you need to ensure that you have all the necessary paperwork before starting. In fact, the only way you can apply for a visa from the United States is online, although you may need to support your application with a biometric finger scan from one of the Application Support Centers in the United States. Don't forget that you (or your employer) also need to pay a fee for your visa application. How much this is depends on the type of visa you are applying for. It is also worth remembering that getting a visa of any sort may take a while—up to several months—so you *should not* make travel arrangements until your visa comes through, unless they are flexible.

There are two types of visas for the United Kingdom: non-points visas (such as the standard tourist visa) and points-based visas (which include sponsored work visas). For more detailed information on all aspects of UK immigration, visit the UK Visas and Immigration website (www.gov.uk/government/organisations/uk-visas-and-immigration).

## NON-POINTS-BASED VISAS

You can, of course, visit London with a general visitor's visa for up to six months, though it is illegal to work with this visa. This may be extended for up to 12 months

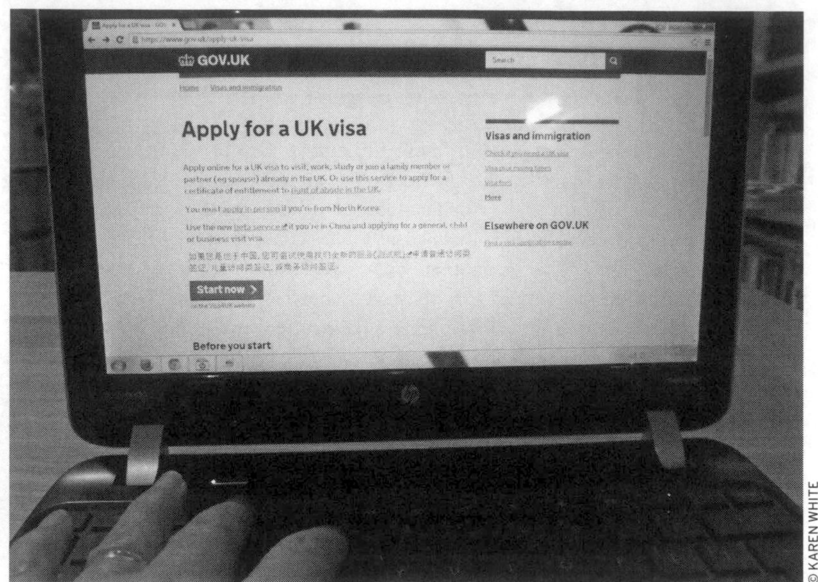




If you can, apply for your UK visa online.

if you are an academic visiting the United Kingdom. Individuals who come to the United Kingdom for a few weeks or months as part of their work, and are not paid by a UK company, can come on what is known as a general business visa. This visa is designed for employees who need to move around a lot as part of their job, such as journalists, media, and film crews, or even corporate trouble-shooters who provide specialist support. If you are the sole representative of a non-UK company in Britain or an employee of a US newspaper, news agency, or broadcasting organization you may qualify for a non-points-based visa.

Students who are planning to study in the United Kingdom for less than six months can apply to enter through a non-points visa known as the student visitor visa. If you are American and planning on entering the United Kingdom with this visa you don't have to organize it before you arrive. When you arrive in the United Kingdom, however, you will need to show documentation that you have been accepted or enrolled in a course at an approved and accredited educational institution and that you have enough funds to support yourself. You can't work with this type of visa.

Of course, if your mother or father is British, then you can move to London through your British passport. If you don't have a British passport you can apply to become British and get one. Another option would be to apply to live in the United Kingdom through your Right of Abode. All British citizens have the right to abode in the United Kingdom. So do some Commonwealth citizens, depending on their age and country of origin. If you aren't or don't want to be a UK passport holder, you can apply for a Certificate of Entitlement to Right of Abode at your nearest British Consulate. Just remember that there will be a fee for this application, and it can take up to six months or more to process. There is also a fee to become British and get a passport, and again this usually takes up to six months.

If you are a citizen from a country in the European Economic Area (EEA) or Switzerland, as well as American, you can live and work in the United Kingdom through your European nationality. You may find it easier to move to the United Kingdom through your EEA or Swiss nationality if you apply for a registration certificate, though under European law this is not required. However, a registration certificate will confirm your right of residence in the United Kingdom under European law. You can download this application form via the UK Visas and Immigration website, and it should take less than six months to process.

EU immigration to the United Kingdom has increased in recent years, and the British government is exploring whether to cap EU immigration. Before using a European passport to move to London, confirm that there is still free movement between all EU countries.



## POINTS-BASED VISAS

The United Kingdom uses a five-tier system for its visa system for non-European nationals. For most Americans this will mean entering the United Kingdom under a Tier 1 (highly skilled), Tier 2 (skilled), or Tier 4 (student) visa. Unless you have dual nationality with Britain, a European Economic Area country, or Switzerland, you need to get a points-based visa to live, work, or study in London. As the name implies, these types of visas are awarded according to a points-based system with factors such as occupations, skills and experience, salaries, and levels of education awarded a certain number of points. To qualify for a visa through this system you must achieve a certain number of points from the relevant criteria. In most circumstances, you can also apply to bring your family with you through these points-based visas, provided you have adequate funds to support your dependents. Students may be able to bring their partner and children if on a government-sponsored course (which is six months or longer) or if studying for a doctorate, and if you are able to provide support yourself. One advantage for Americans trying to get a visa is that you get more points if you speak English well, so as a native English-speaker this is one element of the points system that you shouldn't have to worry about. For a points-based calculator tool, visit www.points.homeoffice.gov.uk. The United Kingdom has clamped down on the number of work visas given to non-EU nationals in order to reduce net immigration. A priority of this immigration regime is to reduce the overall numbers of visas awarded each year—so requirements and rules seem to be getting stricter.

### Tier 1 Visas

There are three main categories of Tier 1 visas: Exceptionally Talented, Entrepreneur, and Investor. The first Tier 1 visa is for exceptionally talented or world-renowned experts in fields such as the sciences, engineering, medicine, humanities, and the arts. It allows the holder to work in the United Kingdom for three years. For this visa, you must apply to the UK government's Home Office for endorsement as a leader in your particular field. If you want to set up a business in the UK and have at least £500,000 to invest, then you may be able to get a Tier 1 Entrepreneur visa, which entitles you to live and work in the United Kingdom for up to three years and four months. If you are able to invest at least £2 million or more of disposable personal income in a UK business, then you may be able to get a Tier 1 Investor visa; the number of Investor visas awarded annually is limited to 1,000. A Tier 1 Graduate Entrepreneur visa is available if you are endorsed by the UK Trade and Investment body (as part of the elite global graduate entrepreneur program) or your current UK higher educational institution, providing it is an authorized endorsing body. This visa entitles you to stay for one year, but you can extend it for a further year.

## Tier 2 Visas

With the tight restrictions on the Tier 1 visa, the vast majority of Americans moving to London for work will use the Tier 2 visa. It too is points-based and is for skilled workers. It usually requires at least an undergraduate degree, but the higher the academic qualifications the better. The Tier 2 visa requires an employer to sponsor your application, so you need to have a job (or job offer), and the company must apply for the work visa on your behalf. The work permit is tied to the position, so if you decide to change jobs you will need a new visa to go with the new job. The length of time a Tier 2 visa gives you depends on the subcategory for the visa, but at the moment it is five years, or the time given on your certificate of sponsorship plus one month, whichever is shorter. If you work in certain fields, such as health care or engineering—two professions that the United Kingdom is always crying out for—then you have a chance of being awarded a Tier 2 visa. To sponsor a non-EU national for a Tier 2 visa the employer must prove that they can't find a UK resident who can do the job, and they must pay the sponsored employee a specified minimum salary at the very least. If you work in a field where there isn't a shortage of highly skilled workers, then the employer will find it difficult to meet sponsorship requirements, and it is unlikely that your visa will be granted. The UK government has a Tier 2 Shortage Occupation List, and if you are lucky enough to work in one of these professions, then your potential employer may be willing to take on all the paperwork required to prove that they can't find a Brit or EU national to do this role and therefore need you. It is also worth noting that the current annual limit for Tier 2 visas is 20,700.

Another Tier 2 visa that Americans can use if they want to live and work in London is an intra-company transfer. And the really good news is that intra-company transfers are exempt from the annual limits for Tier 2 visas (at least for the moment). There are four different types of this visa: long-term for stays more than a year; short-term for stays of less than 12 months; graduate trainee; and skills transfer. This visa usually requires you to have worked for your employer for more than a year, or for three months in the case of a graduate trainee. Depending on the type of intra-company transfer visa you have, you may be able to stay in the United Kingdom between six months up to five years for long-term staff. Given the United Kingdom's current immigration restrictions, most Americans who come to live and work in London will do so through an intra-company transfer. There is also a sponsored Tier 2 visa for ministers who have been offered a role within a faith community. If you are an elite sportsperson or coach, you may be able to get a Tier 2 visa.

## Tier 3 Visas

The Tier 3 visa was a temporary visa for low-skilled workers such as farm workers and laborers. It is currently suspended and unlikely to return anytime soon, as much of this work is now being carried out by EU citizens.

### Tier 4 Visas

This is the student visa, and it can be broken down into two subsections, with both of them requiring sponsorship from a school or college/university. Firstly, there is a child Tier 4 visa for children aged 4-17 who are attending boarding school in the United Kingdom. Once students have reached the age of 16, they can apply for an adult student visa, assuming they are studying at an approved and accredited institution. Most American undergraduate, master's, or doctorate students will need a Tier 4 visa to study at one of London's colleges or universities if they plan to study here for more than six months. To apply for this visa you must be accepted to study at a qualified British college or university, and be able to prove that you have enough funds to cover the university/college fees and to support yourself while you are a student (or get a full scholarship and maintenance grant). At the moment, to study in London, you need to prove that you will have at least £1,020 (US$1,632) per calendar month of your course to cover your living expenses, in addition to course fees.

The good news, though, and a real change from when I was a grad student, is that degree-course students can work (for example, on the weekends) during term time or on weekdays if the job is part of a required work-placement. This should help to ease some of the high cost of living in the capital. For more information, check out the UK Visas and Immigration website.



### Tier 5 Visas (for Temporary Workers)

This visa is for temporary workers, such as athletes, people in a creative/entertainment field, religious workers, and diplomats or other government officials. These visas must be sponsored by an employer and are awarded according to a points-based assessment. They allow the worker to stay in the United Kingdom for up to 12 months, and can be extended. Canadians between ages 18 and 30 years old who have recently graduated can apply for a Tier 5 (Youth Mobility Scheme) visa. This allows them to work in the United Kingdom for up to two years. Other countries participating in the Youth Mobility Scheme include Japan, Australia, and New Zealand.

## SETTLEMENT

A settlement visa is for individuals who want permanent residence in the United Kingdom, usually due to family ties with a resident in the United Kingdom or because they have lived and worked in the United Kingdom for several years. A settlement visa will give you "indefinite leave to remain," and there will no longer be any restrictions on working or staying in the United Kingdom. These visas are used for those who have married, have an unmarried or same sex partner, or are in a civil partnership with someone who is British and resides in the United Kingdom. To qualify for a settlement visa you will need to have been in a proven relationship with a British national for at least two years and he or she is settled in the United Kingdom, or you are both moving to the UK to make it your shared home. Children of a British resident can also be granted permanent residency in the United Kingdom. If your fiancé, fiancée, or proposed civil partner has residency within the United Kingdom, then you can get a visa to stay in the United Kingdom for six months before the ceremony; however, you must both be age 18 or older. If you have lived and worked in the United Kingdom for at least five years through a Tier 1 or Tier 2 visa, then you may be able to apply

## A National Insurance Number

The United Kingdom's National Insurance Scheme is a fund that was created to provide benefits, such as the National Health Service, unemployment benefits, and the United Kingdom's state pension. All workers in the United Kingdom who have a certain level of earnings must pay a National Insurance contribution, and those with the greatest earnings also make the largest National Insurance contributions. But to make these contributions you first need your National Insurance number.

The whole National Insurance scheme is administered by the United Kingdom's tax office—HMRC (Her Majesty's Revenue and Customs). Non-UK citizens who come to the United Kingdom to work need to get their National Insurance number as soon as possible. To get a National Insurance number you must have the right to work in the UK and must be in the country. Once you have a visa giving you permission to work here your next bureaucratic hurdle will be to get a National Insurance (NI) number. If you're a student and plan to get a part-time job, you will also need to get a National Insurance number.

### GETTING A NATIONAL INSURANCE NUMBER

To apply for a National Insurance number you need proof of your identity, proof of your postal address, and evidence that you are permitted to work in the United Kingdom. You don't have to have an NI number to start work, but you should get one as soon as possible so your tax situation is correctly sorted out. Your first step in this process will be to call the Jobcentre Plus National Insurance number allocation service (tel. 0345/600 0643). The service is open 8am-6pm Monday-Friday. The Jobcentre Plus will either arrange an "evidence of identity" interview for you or it will mail you an application form.

If you are asked to attend an interview be sure to bring the items of identification requested in the letter telling you to attend an interview, be it your passport, residence permit, driver's license, or your birth or marriage certificate (if relevant). At the interview you will be asked a few questions about your circumstances, background, and why you need a National Insurance number. You will also be asked to fill in and sign a National Insurance application form. If you are not asked to attend an interview you will just be sent the application form to complete and return, along with any requested documentation. Assuming all goes well, you should receive a National Insurance card with your number on it within 12 weeks. Just be sure to tell your employer your NI number as soon as you get it.

### CONTINUING WITH SOCIAL SECURITY CONTRIBUTIONS

The United Kingdom and the United States have a reciprocal agreement on Social Security, which means that as an American you can continue with your Society Security taxes rather than pay NI contributions. You have to pay for one, but which one is up to you. To do this, you need to get a certificate showing that you are exempt from National Insurance contributions under these rules. Usually your US employer will issue one of these certificates as part of the intra-company transfer process. If you don't have an exemption certificate from the United States, you will be required to register for a National Insurance number and pay National Insurance contributions, just like everyone else.

You'll find more information about National Insurance for people coming to the United Kingdom at the HMRC website (www.hmrc.gov.uk).

© KAREN WHITE

Do not forget to bring all of your passports.



for permanent residency in the United Kingdom. In all instances of settlement visas, applicants must demonstrate that they have met the knowledge of language and life requirements for settlement. For most Americans this means passing the *Life in the UK* exam to show that they know about life in the UK and speak English well. The *Life in the UK* exam may be harder than you would imagine, and consists of a written test covering UK society and immigration, the United Kingdom's regions and government, and everyday knowledge about life in the United Kingdom, including education, housing, and employment. These tests are taken at exam centers spread across the United Kingdom and currently cost £50. You'd be well advised to pre-book your exam (you can do this online) and prepare for it.

## GETTING BRITISH CITIZENSHIP

If you have been married to a Brit for three years or living in the United Kingdom for at least five years, you can go whole hog and apply to become a British citizen. Once again you'll need to prove that you speak English and pass the *Life in the UK* test, as well as be over 18. Unlike permanent residency, becoming a naturalized British citizen means that you won't have to fill in landing cards or be stamped in and out of the country when you take a vacation abroad. It also means that you won't need to get your visa transferred to a new US passport. Believe me, dealing with American bureaucracy to get a new passport is trying enough, without the added misery (and further expense) of getting your visa transferred into your new passport or carrying around your old passport with the visa in it every time you go in and out of the country. Another advantage of being British is that you can vote, as well as live and work elsewhere in the European Economic Area. You will also receive a British passport and be able to enjoy all the same benefits as the British.

Contrary to popular misconception, the United States *does* allow its citizens to have dual nationality with another country. There is no need to give up one in favor of the other—you can simply be a citizen of both the United States and the United Kingdom. Just be sure to use the right passport when traveling to and from the United States (or to and from the United Kingdom) and remember that you must obey the laws for both countries.

### WORKING ILLEGALLY

The British government is really cracking down on illegal immigrants and the people who employ them. There are very severe penalties if you illegally employ someone and don't check their credentials properly—a member of the House of Lords was caught doing this and her political career never really recovered. Most online job sites and job applications ask if you are legally able to work in the United Kingdom. If your answer is no, then I wouldn't hold my breath about getting the job (unless you work in a few highly desirable professions, and even then it may be tough). Don't think that you can lie about being able to work here, especially as employers and employment agencies are requiring proof before they take your application forward.



If you are still determined to live and work in London, you may think it worthwhile to do it illegally with a cash-in-hand casual job. Just don't expect to get anything like a living wage for London or to have any worker's rights. There are already massive numbers of illegal workers in London, not to mention cheap labor from legal EU nationals. It is also worth noting that Americans are number six on the United Kingdom's list of nationalities that are most commonly deported. So the real question is—do you really want to live with one eye always looking over your shoulder, knowing that if you are caught you will be deported? Believe me, it would be much better to find a legal way to live and work in London, and you are less likely to be exploited as a worker.

## Moving with Children

If you are moving to London with a visa from the points-based system, then your partner and children (18 or younger) should be able to join you as dependents. The same is true for people using a non-points-based visa. However, you will need to prove that you can afford to support your dependents. You should apply for their visas at the same time as you apply for your own. This way the UK Visas and Immigration department knows that you are a family and that the applications should be looked at together. Visa applications for dependent children are usually dealt with within six weeks, though delays can happen. Normally, children moving to the United Kingdom with their family as part of a limited leave-to-remain visa (such as a Tier 2 visa) will be allowed to stay in the United Kingdom for the same length of time as their parents. Unless the person moving to London has sole responsibility for the children (or there are serious reasons why these children must be allowed to come to the United Kingdom), they will not be allowed to come and live here unless both parents are also immigrating. If you are not traveling as a family to the United Kingdom (perhaps due to work obligations), the parent traveling with the child may find it easier if they have

© PAWEŁ OPASKA/123RF.COM

Make sure your children are settled and happy.

written permission from the other parent that the child is free to travel.

Having seen several families move to London from the States, I'd say that getting a visa for your dependents is simple compared to settling children into a new school, establishing friendships, and getting used to life in London. And by all accounts, it is equally traumatic moving back to the United States. When I ask my expat friends what jewels of advice would they pass on to would-be American expats in London, their first reply is "make sure the kids are settled and happy."

Luckily, moving to London doesn't require that the whole family learn a new language—though they will need to get used to the London accent. And don't be too surprised if your children are teased (sometimes quite mercilessly) about their American accent. Just like many children elsewhere in the world, British kids can be ruthlessly critical of children who are different in some way. The key to the successful relocation of your family in London will be to find a school and social network where your children are comfortable and feel welcome.



# Moving with Pets

There is little doubt that uprooting your family and moving across the Atlantic can be a difficult time for everyone concerned. However, for furry members of the family, moving to London can be fraught with difficulties. As a rabies-free country, the United Kingdom is very particular about the movements of rabies-prone animals into the United Kingdom—including household pets such as cats, dogs, and ferrets. And believe you me, moving a pet from the United States to the United Kingdom will be expensive and require carefully prepared paperwork. However, moving to London with a pet is much easier than it used to be; pets are no longer required to go into quarantine for six months. You still must meet the rules of the Pet Travel Scheme, so be sure to organize the arrival of your family's furry friend in the United Kingdom in advance. If you decide to bring your pet with you to London, use a pet relocation specialist to help guide you through this process.

## PET TRAVEL SCHEME

In 2001 the European Union introduced a Pet Travel Scheme to allow family pets to move around the EU with a pet passport. In 2004 the Pet Travel Scheme was expanded

© IRSTONE/123RF.COM

Although it's expensive and requires extensive paperwork, it is possible to bring your dogs to London.

to cover a few non-European countries, including the mainland United States and Canada. Under this scheme, domestic pets must be fitted with an international microchip (such as ISO Standard 11784) and then vaccinated against rabies (with any necessary boosters given). I'm afraid there is no exemption to this requirement, even if your pet has already been vaccinated against rabies. Once the pet has been vaccinated, owners can then get their pet's passport (if in the EU) or their Third Country Official Veterinary Certificate (if they are in a listed non-EU country such as the mainland US or Canada). However, you must wait for at least 21 days after this vaccination (or the second vaccination if this is being done in two vaccinations) before your pet can enter the United Kingdom. In addition, your dog will be required to be treated for tapeworm before traveling to the United Kingdom. Once you have your pet's passport/certificate, you must make sure that you keep your pet's rabies booster up-to-date. For the latest information on these requirements be sure to check the UK government website (www.gov.uk/bringing-food-animals-plants-into-uk) before your pet travels.

## THIRD COUNTRY OFFICIAL VETERINARY CERTIFICATE

To bring your pets to the United Kingdom when you move to London you must carry out all of the requirements for the Pet Travel Scheme, including getting them microchipped and vaccinated for rabies, and waiting for the prescribed period. Dogs need to be treated for tapeworm by a vet. You'll need a Third Country Official Veterinary Certificate from an authorized vet in the United States to verify these requirements. Once you have your certificate, your pet can travel to the United Kingdom under the Pet Travel Scheme. Traveling with a dog requires careful planning; although the certificate is valid four months, your dog must arrive in the United Kingdom no less than

24 hours and no more than 120 hours after the tapeworm treatment—it is essential to get your timing right. The Pet Travel Scheme requires your pet to travel on certain prescribed routes and with authorized carriers; check with your chosen carrier to see if it has any further health requirements or regulations.

# What to Take

Deciding what to take when you are packing is never easy, and I always seem to be one of those who take everything . . . including the kitchen sink. Yet moving overseas is expensive and you may want to be a bit more discerning with your packing. It would be a good idea to pare down the possessions you bring to London to just the necessities, with a few sentimental nice-to-haves.

Unlike in the United States, here in London it is fairly easy to find furnished apartments and houses. While the decor and furniture may not be exactly to your taste, if you are only in London for a few months or a year, then you may want to store most of your possessions in the United States and just go with furnished accommodations in London. You can always personalize them once you are here, picking up some soft furnishings or cookware at a sale. If you go for this option then you will just need some clothes and whatever other personal items you can't live without. Although I am a notorious clotheshorse, when I first arrived as a student here in London, I came with just two pieces of luggage and a carry-on. Later on I had my dad ship me a box of books that I needed, and that was it. I either bought it here or did without. The next time I moved from the States to London, it was clear that London was to be our home from now on, so I shipped any furniture that I wanted to keep and many other items.

Just how much you think you will need depends on your circumstances. Students (like myself many moons ago) and young single executives should be able to get by with just the luggage allowance on their flight. Corporate relocations of families will probably be given more money for their move, so they can afford to ship over more personal possessions. Just bear in mind how much room you will have in your London home. Older British properties are notorious for their lack of storage facilities. If you plan on having a car here in London, I strongly suggest that you buy or rent one here—don't even think about bringing your car from the States. Remember that

© KAREN WHITE

Deciding what to pack can be a major headache.

the steering wheel will be on the wrong side of the car, making it much more difficult to drive around, and getting insurance (which is required) is more difficult and costly.

## ELECTRICAL ITEMS

Britain uses a different level of voltage—240 volts, which is more than double the American 110 voltage. Many of your American electrical items will not work here, let alone fit the United Kingdom's odd three-prong plug. Leave most of your electrical items in the States, except those that you know can adapt to 240 volts (just be sure to double-check before you pack them). Get an adapter so that these items can be plugged in to a British socket, or buy a British USB or micro USB charger. Plan on getting the rest of your electrical items when you are here—be it a hair dryer, toaster, or TV. If you don't mind second-hand goods, you may be able to buy some of these electrical items through the US expat forums or classified ads portals such as Gumtree (www.gumtree.com). These can also be good places to sell your goods when it is time for the return trip home.



## SHIPPING OPTIONS

If your employer is offering relocation assistance as part of your move to London, then this company should help organize the packing and shipping of your possessions. If you are doing it off your own back, then you need an international removal company. Try searching online or ask around for a recommendation—just be sure that the company you are using is a member of the International Federation of International Removals (FIDI). Some firms even offer a specialist service for students or families. Just remember that shipping things overseas is very expensive, so you should really only take what you know you can't live without—don't forget that you will have to

© KAREN WHITE

Organizing the delivery of your shipment to the UK will take careful planning.

## UK Measurements

One aspect of everyday living that you will need to become accustomed to once you start living in London is how the British use measurements. Unfortunately, these can be a little bit confusing as they use a mixture of metric and Imperial, and some British Imperial measurements are different from those used in the United States.

One reason why the United Kingdom uses a variety of measurements stems from a 1978 European Union law that requires that goods in the EU should be sold using the metric system. This was gradually introduced during the next 12 years, though there was a lot of opposition to the change and the British public tenaciously clung on to their Imperial measurements. In 2007 the European Union finally agreed that the Imperial measurements may be shown alongside metric measurements in the United Kingdom. So, when out shopping, you may see loose items advertised as per kilo and per pound, while prepackaged items may show the weight of the contents in metric and possibly in Imperial units.

Using both metric and Imperial seems to be common practice for most things these days, though there are some notable exceptions. Just how long the United Kingdom can cling on to its Imperial measurements, however, is uncertain. Most British schools teach measurements using the metric system, with just a passing reference to Imperial units. Certainly my kids don't really know their Imperial measurements and have just a general understanding that a yard is smaller than a meter and that an inch is around two centimeters—and making sense of Fahrenheit is definitely a dark art. Given that schoolchildren don't know Imperial units, I would imagine that measurements in the United Kingdom will become more or less metric within a few decades.

### COMMON IMPERIAL MEASUREMENTS

One example of an Imperial unit that is still used here is evident on road signs—distances are given in miles and speed limits are in miles per hour. Of course, pints of beer or cider are still sold in pubs and restaurants, but remember that a British pint is 20 ounces (not 16). You may also hear someone talk about their weight in "stones." A stone equals 14 pounds and is based on an old Anglo-Saxon measurement. However, they are just as likely to mention their weight in kilos. Height seems to be one area where the British favor Imperial (at least in conversation), although a doctor or nurse will measure and refer to height using the metric system. The same will be true of your weight, though they should understand stones and even just pounds.

### COMMON METRIC MEASUREMENTS

Temperature is usually referred to in degrees Celsius. The easiest way to convert to Fahrenheit is to multiply the number in Celsius by 1.8, and then add 32. An exception to goods being sold in both metric and Imperial units is gas (called "petrol" here), which is always sold by the liter.

### COOKING MEASUREMENTS

When it comes to cooking, the British do not use measuring cups to measure quantities. Instead they generally use weight or fluid measurements, with recipes showing amounts in metric and Imperial. However, smaller measurements such as tablespoons and teaspoons are used in the United Kingdom. If you are a keen cook, be sure to bring your measuring cups for your American recipes and then buy scales once you are here for any UK recipes.

### 24-HOUR CLOCK

Although the United Kingdom still tends to use am and pm, you should also become familiar with the 24-hour clock, as this is seen regularly here. I have to admit that I still struggle with this clock and mentally have to translate these times back to the 12-hour clock for a time to make sense, but it is getting easier.

schlep it all back home again. Make sure that the shippers know what you want them to do and what you are willing to do, make a detailed list of everything you are shipping and its value, and read your contract carefully before you sign it. Make sure that all the customs requirements have been carried out before your goods arrive, though a good shipping company should help with this. Given how stressful moving can be, especially overseas, it may be worth it to pay a bit more for a more reliable and full-service removal company.

# Getting Involved



One thing that I've noticed during my long tenure as an expat is that, once people have settled in a bit and have a normal routine going, they often want to reach out to the community and get involved in something. This seems especially true for the full-time parent of school-age children whose partner has started working in their company's London office—a "training spouse." Certainly joining in with something, be it the school's PTA, a social organization, an adult education class, a sports club or gym, or even volunteering somewhere, can be a great way to create a network of buddies. I strongly recommend that people do try to connect with others (be it other expats or their local community) so that they don't feel so isolated. The advantages of having a shared language and culture as well as the wide range of activities in London should make settling into life here a bit easier for Americans.

## MEETING OTHER EXPATS

Perhaps it is because I married a Brit and merged into the British community quite readily, but it wasn't until I had kids that I began to interact with other Americans in London. Around this time, I think that there was a bit of a sea change with the expat community, as suddenly there seemed to be lots more of us in London. I imagine this was due to London's emergence as a dominant player in the global financial markets. In any case, there are now numerous ways to meet up with other Americans living in the capital. You will find an exhaustive list of American organizations on the US Citizen Services pages of the US Embassy in London's website and its *Guidebook to Living and Traveling in the United Kingdom.* There are also numerous forums and meet-up groups listed online, as well as several women's clubs, such as the American Women's Club or similar local organizations in different parts of town.

Those of you with children should find a natural community to become involved with through your children's school. If your children are at one of the international schools, then there will be expats galore and you should soon find like-minded friends. But don't feel that you'll only find other Americans at an international school—in my experience there are usually a few expat families at most good private schools in London.

I would also warn against just immersing yourself within the American community here in London. So much of the joy of living here is to be involved in London's culture, and it would be a shame to not get involved in your local community at least a bit, be it by helping at your church, volunteering or fundraising for a charity, joining the local running club, or taking an evening wine-tasting course. It will be up to you to decide what type of involvement works best for you based on your interests, but you will settle in better if you do make the effort to get out there and interact.

## COMMUNITY SERVICE

One of the dominant features of many of the social organizations that many Americans get involved with is that they have a philanthropic element to them, helping to raise funds for worthwhile charities. A classic example is the annual "lightly used" second-hand clothes sale organized by the Hampstead Women's Organization. The Junior League of London is another women's organization that works on several different levels to help ease the plight of disadvantaged or disenfranchised children and teenagers in London. I also know a fair few Americans who volunteer some of their time—be it at their children's school, their church, a museum, a charity store, or an organization or local event, such as a Christmas fair or Summer Fete. I know others who raise money for their favorite charity by being sponsored to run the London marathon or in one of the annual Race for Life events in aid of cancer research. So, if you have the time and the inclination, there are many ways you can link up with your local community and help others in the process. You can get an idea of which organizations are looking for volunteers at www.do-it.org.uk.

# HOUSING CONSIDERATIONS

There are numerous types of properties available in London, and the range is staggering: from converted lofts to terraced houses to apartment blocks—with everything in between. Much of the housing stock here is old (Victorian or Edwardian) and has been modernized to provide fundamentals such as electricity and plumbing. London is a crowded city, and often old buildings whose original purpose is no longer needed have been turned into homes, such as loft apartments in converted warehouses or mews houses. Of course, not all property is old—there are modern apartment buildings and new housing estates also available. Just what type of accommodation you opt for depends on where you want to live and your budget.

As you'd expect, you can rent a place for either a short or long term, depending on your needs. If you have enough capital floating around you could look into buying property in London. The whole process of finding accommodation in London (especially a home purchase) is very different from the procedure used in the United States, so be prepared for a bit of a roller-coaster ride when trying to rent or buy a home in London.

A word of advice: Before you sign a contract you should visit the area at different times of day and night, both during the weekday and on the weekend. Will you feel

safe in that neighborhood walking around at night? Will that pub up the road be noisy? Does the local Saturday market spill over to your street? Sometimes what seems like an idyllic location or property is anything but that at certain times of day or night.

# Renting or Buying

Whether to buy or rent property is a question that plagues most American expats who have been in London for a while. It seems silly to keep on shelling out vast sums of money for rent and not see any appreciation on this expense, which a mortgage and home ownership could potentially give them. Yet most expats I know continue to rent their homes. Perhaps this is due to the high cost of buying property in London, or maybe it's because of their uncertain future as expats. I am sure that the long and tedious process of buying property in London must also contribute a bit to their hesitancy to buy a home, even though I know that many of them aren't happy renting year after year.

Generally, most expats don't buy property in London until they have lived in the city for a while—perhaps several years. Even then, they may not buy unless they get their settlement visa (for indefinite leave to remain) or British citizenship. It's not that they have to wait until then, it's just that house buying can take so long (six months or more) that they often wait until they know they want to remain in London before they take the plunge and buy a home. Certainly, I wouldn't recommend buying in London unless you already know the city very well. Even then you will need to rent for at least several months while the legal paperwork is processed.

It should also be pointed out that both buying and renting in London is expensive due to there being more demand than supply, and prices always seems to be on an upward spiral. Plus, many expats choose to live in expensive areas of town, where the cost of buying can be astronomical. True, it is cheaper to buy or rent farther out of town, but then you need to factor in the high cost (and time) of a daily rail and Underground commute into work.

There are advantages and disadvantages to either renting or buying. In the end, whether you favor one over the other will depend on your finances, patience, and how long you are likely to be staying here. If you are used to owning your own home, then renting can be very frustrating. On the other hand, not being responsible for the upkeep and maintenance of a property can be very liberating—you just call the landlord and they have to deal with it. Whatever you decide, you should rent for a little bit while you search for your London home and wait for the long home-buying process to finish.

## RENTING

Unfortunately, finding a place to rent in London isn't always easy, and can be fraught with problems. First you need to decide where you want to live. Then you need to find a place that you can afford and meets your requirements (or at least comes close). Once you've found your chosen home, you need to provide your references and pay the fees, first month's rent, and security deposit, all of which needs to be done before you can move in. If you are lucky it will be a case of looking at a few places, deciding

## The Past Is Never Far Away

Several years ago I stayed at a stately house-turned-hotel in Pennsylvania. Every inch of the house looked to be a grand Georgian villa, so you can imagine my astonishment when the proprietor proudly told me that the house was nearly 80 years old. Unfortunately, my surprised response that my ordinary late Victorian house in London was several decades older than her replica 18th-century manor instantly deflated her pride, creating one of those very awkward moments of silence that seem to go on and on. What this exchange made crystal clear to me was that what is considered "old" in the United States is nothing out of the ordinary in the United Kingdom. In fact, residential property in London that is less than 20 years old is much more of a novelty than something built in the 19th century.

America is still a very young country by European standards. Whenever British friends of mine visit the United States, they always remark on the wide streets and grid-like layout of the cities—both of which make driving around town so easy. By contrast London can be a confusing maze of small medieval streets, whose names seem to change every few blocks. Many of the roads that remain in London were designed for walking, a horse and cart, or a carriage—not cars. A house with a garage (or even a driveway) is unusual in a central location in London, as car ownership didn't really become affordable to the average UK family until the 1950s and '60s. They were very much a luxury item before then.

Of course, London has had to give way to the modern world, leveling a few areas to make way for large thoroughfares and main roads. Yet it tends to cling to its ancient origins, preferring to preserve that past as much as possible. Although many of its oldest buildings were destroyed in the Great Fire of London in 1666, those that remain are cherished. These days, older buildings are subject to historic preservation controls or are in a historic conservation area so that the character of London's older architecture is retained. As you wander around London's residential streets, you will see rows of brick terraced houses, most of which are either Victorian (1837-1901) or Edwardian (1901-1910), and in certain areas of town there are still many buildings that are Georgian (1714-1830). Given their age, these properties would have had gas, electricity, and indoor plumbing added as part of their modernization. This means that sometimes the layout of a house may be less than ideal by modern standards. For example, it may be difficult to find an older house with an en-suite master bedroom, though improvements in plumbing equipment and updated building regulations are making this easier.

While many visitors to this city may be conscious of London's age, they often fail to realize just how much London's roads and homes continue to be shaped by the past. I certainly believe that one of London's most charming aspects is that it does value the past and tries hard to preserve its history... even if I do secretly long for a garage.

on one, and then getting straight onto the paperwork. If it goes well it can all be over in a few days or a week. However, you can also encounter problems at each step along the way—maybe finding it hard to find an affordable place, having trouble with your references, or finding that the landlord has decided to pull out of the agreement or given the property to another potential tenant offering more rent.

It is worth noting that some areas of London are popular with expats because they offer more places to rent that are geared toward overseas tenants, making them an expat ghetto. There are bits of town that are desirable, yet mainly owner-occupied—and it is very hard to find rental property in these areas. Professional landlords invest in property where they know they are likely to attract renters, so some areas have much more rental property available, and sometimes more expats of all nationalities.

The rental (or "letting") process in the United Kingdom is different from that in the United States, and there are certain key factors that you should know as a potential tenant in London. There are no realtors who will compile places for you to view and advocate for you during the process. There are also leases, the calculation of the monthly rent, and security deposits.

### TYPES OF LEASES

There are a few tenancy options available in London. First, there is a short-term let, which is used for temporary housing for anything from a few weeks up to six months. These can be ideal for your fact-finding trip or as a place to land while you find longer-term accommodations. The advantage of these is that they are fully furnished and all the utilities and taxes are included (except for telephone calls). Then there are long-term leases, which are taken out for at least six months, with a year (or more) much more likely, and will usually be an assured shorthold tenancy. This type of lease can cover furnished or unfurnished property. If possible, you should try to get a tenant-only diplomatic (or break) clause in your long-term lease so you have the option to end the tenancy early if necessary. Ideally this will be a six-month break clause, which means that after four months you can give two months' notice of you ending the tenancy. This is especially useful for expats who have been transferred to London, as there is always the chance that your project or role will be terminated and you will be asked to return to the United States. Also make sure you have the option to renew the lease, and agree what the annual increase will be if you do renew (based on increases in the Retail Price Index with upper and lower percentage limits). If you have a relocation agent make sure they check the lease before you sign, and enlist a solicitor to review your lease (there may even be someone at work you can use).



### CALCULATING THE MONTHLY RENT

One of the first things that you need to know about rental property in London is that the prices are usually priced by the week (such as £500pw), even though you will pay by the calendar month. Furthermore, the monthly rental is *not* just the weekly rent multiplied by four. Instead, the monthly rent is worked out by multiplying the weekly rent by 52 and then dividing it by 12 (for example, £500 per week × 52 weeks ÷ 12 months = £2,166.67 per month). Don't make the mistake of just multiplying the rental price per week by four—the actual price over a 12-month period will be more.

### LETTING AGENTS AND FEES

Another thing you should bear in mind concerns the realtors (called "letting agents" or "leasing negotiators"). Estate agents do not work for the potential tenant—they work for the landlord. Good ones will try to please you and the landlord; bad ones will misrepresent the situation and say nearly anything to get you to sign the lease. You should be cautious about anything that they say or agree to, and always get it in writing or include it in the lease. At the moment, letting agents aren't regulated, so they are pretty much a law unto themselves. Don't be surprised if they show you property above your budget and then promise that the landlord will take reduced offers. While there may be some room for negotiation, this will depend on the state of the rental market and cannot be relied upon.

You should expect to pay the letting agent an administration fee for processing your

## Useful Real Estate Terms

Here is a list of important British real estate terms for both buyers and renters:

- **Administration fees:** Fees charged by letting agents for processing references and preparing the lease and inventory.
- **Agent:** A person (or a company) who has been authorized to act on behalf of a landlord, such as a letting, management, or estate agent (realtor).
- **Assured shorthold tenancy:** This type of tenancy gives the landlord the right to repossess their property at the end of the lease.
- **Bedsit:** A single occupancy room with shared bathroom in a private house, usually used by students.
- **Break clause:** This clause can be included in a fixed-term tenancy agreement and enables either the tenant or landlord to terminate the tenancy earlier than the end of the original fixed term. It is also sometimes called a release clause.
- **Completion:** This is the point at which ownership of a property is transferred from the seller to the buyer and the balance of the purchase price (minus the deposit) is handed over.
- **Contractual tenancy agreement:** This type of tenancy agreement may be used when the annual rent is greater than £100,000.
- **Conversion:** An older house that has been remodeled into two or more flats or maisonettes; may also refer to a warehouse or another industrial building that has been turned into residential property.
- **Conveyance:** The legal term for the transferring of property ownership from one person to another.
- **Cottage:** An old, rustic, smaller house that often has a garden, where centuries ago the residents would grow vegetables and flowers.
- **Council tax:** This is an annual tax charged by local authorities in the United Kingdom that is based on the relative value of the property. Both homeowners and tenants must pay this tax, although students living in student accommodations may be exempt.
- **Detached:** Property that stands alone and is not attached to a neighboring house.
- **Direct debit:** An instruction from a bank account holder to authorize regular collection of money from their account; often used to pay bills or mortgage payments.
- **Exchange contracts:** This is the point at which the seller and buyer are legally bound to go through with the property sale and the deposit is paid to the seller. Up until this point either party can pull out of the purchase.
- **Flat:** The British term for an apartment, usually on one floor of a building. Many flats in London are in houses that have been converted to flats.
- **Freehold:** A type of ownership in which the property owner owns the property and the land that it stands on in perpetuity.
- **Gas safety regulations:** Landlords must have annual gas safety checks carried out, and a copy of the report must be given to the tenant.
- **Ground rent:** The money paid to the freeholder for use of the land and property.
- **Holding deposit:** Also known as a pre-tenancy agreement fee or reservation fee, this is a nominal amount (usually one or two weeks' rent) that a potential tenant pays to get a property taken off the market, and it shows their good faith in renting the property. If the letting doesn't proceed because the lessee pulled

out, then the deposit will not be returned. If it goes ahead, then the funds can be applied to the first month's rent or the security deposit.

- **Inventory:** This lists the contents, condition, and state of a property, including the garden and garage if applicable. Ideally, an independent inventory clerk will assess a property before and after a tenancy, with a report going to the landlord and the tenant.
- **Joint tenancy:** Joint ownership of a property by two or more people, whereby a partner's share is "inherited" by the other partners upon his or her death.
- **Land Registry:** A register of property in the United Kingdom, which records freehold and leasehold properties (if the lease is for seven years or more).
- **Leasehold:** This is a type of long-term tenancy for property (often for a flat or apartment) where the land that the property stands on is owned by the freeholder. The leasehold will pay the freeholder ground rent fees. When the lease expires, ownership of the property returns to the freeholder, though a new lease is usually organized.
- **Let:** The British term for renting.
- **Local authority search:** This is carried out on behalf of the buyer and asks the local authority about any outstanding enforcement issues or future developments that could affect the property or nearby areas.
- **Maisonette:** An apartment that is set over two or more floors.
- **Mansion block:** A period building (usually Victorian or Edwardian) specifically designed to contain generously proportioned flats. These tend to be in the more upmarket areas of town.
- **Mews house:** A small terraced house converted from an old stable and carriage building, often on a cobbled street. Usually in the traditionally wealthy areas of town, these houses have lots of character and often come with a garage.
- **Purpose-built block:** A modern apartment building that was built just to contain apartments.
- **Reference check:** A landlord (or his or her agent) checks a potential tenant's suitability to pay the rent, their ID, and their track record on previous rentals. This often involves contacting previous landlords and the potential tenant's employer (or accountant if self-employed).
- **Semi-detached:** Property joined to another house on just one side.
- **Service charge:** An annual fee to help cover the cost of running a building and looking after communal areas.
- **Stamp duty land tax:** A tax levied on legal documents that need a stamp, such as deeds of title; similar to a transfer tax in the United States.
- **Standing order:** A request by an account holder that instructs the bank to send a specified amount of money to a particular account on a regular basis; often used to pay rent (similar to a monthly bank transfer).
- **Tenancy deposit scheme:** All landlords, or their agents, who take deposits for assured shorthold tenancies must register a security deposit with a tenancy deposit scheme to protect the tenant's deposit and provide a mediation service.
- **Terraced houses:** A row of houses linked to each other on both sides; very common in London.
- **Townhouse:** A Georgian or Victorian house set out over several floors, sometimes with as many as five floors.

references and preparing the lease (this can be £180 or more). You may also be asked to pay for an inventory/check-in or checkout fee, which currently runs £150 up to several hundred pounds depending on the size of the property. An inventory check will happen when you check in and check out of the property. This fee covers the cost of an independent inventory clerk who will come in and make a note of the state of the property, along with all the furnishings and fittings, before you move in and again when you leave. You will split the costs with the landlord. The idea is that the state of the property when you move out will be compared to its state when you moved in, allowing for some wear and tear. You will need to get the place professionally cleaned before the checkout, and be sure to fill and paint any holes you put in the walls and replace blown light bulbs. If you've looked after the place and any furnishings you should get your security deposit back. Otherwise, the landlord will keep some (or all) of the deposit to cover the costs to repair the "dilapidations." If you can, you should be at the inventory check-in, so that you can point out any damage or problems with the property before you move in.

Sometimes the letting agents and/or landlords of less expensive properties are not as responsive or well-regulated as those marketing more expensive property. Be wary of these agents, and read your lease with care. Use only agents who are in the **Association of Residential Letting Agencies** (www.arla.co.uk), **The Property Ombudsman** (www.tpos.co.uk), or the **National Approved Letting Scheme** (www.nalscheme.co.uk), and pay close attention to how your security deposit is handled.

### HOLDING DEPOSIT

If you find the home of your dreams and want to secure it, then you can place what is known as a "holding deposit" (or pre-agreement fee). This fee (usually a week or two's rent) confirms your good faith and serious commitment to renting the property, but it is not legally binding. It should get the landlord to take the property off the market while you negotiate terms and sort out the lease. You hand over the holding deposit money straightaway (sometimes you can use a credit card) and sign an agreement that says that you will lose the deposit if you back out for any reason, and the landlord will return the deposit if they pull out. Make sure you list any conditions you want included as part of the agreement, such as the amount of rent, the start date, or having the place thoroughly cleaned. Once the lease is signed, the holding deposit money is usually applied to the security deposit or the first month's rent.

### SECURITY DEPOSIT

This deposit is used as security against damages and unpaid rent; it is usually equal to six weeks' rent in London. For a long time landlords in the United Kingdom used to view the security deposit as their money regardless of the state of the property when the tenant moved out. Needless to say, getting your security deposit back used to be a nightmare. However, the rules governing security deposits have been changed, and landlords (or management agents) are now required to join a government-approved tenancy deposit scheme. These schemes give the tenant some protection from landlords who refuse to return the deposit for no good reason, and they provide a dispute-resolution service to help settle any issues quickly. Within 14 days of moving in, the

© LES SMITHSON

By looking in an estate agent's window, you can get an idea of what is available and how much it costs.



landlord or the management agent should tell you where your deposit is registered and provide information on the scheme they are using. Be sure to follow up if you don't hear from them. Landlords are starting to realize that a security deposit is just that, a deposit, and must be returned if the property and furnishings haven't been damaged and no rent is owed.

### REFERENCES

Before the lease is signed, you will be asked to provide the letting agent (or landlord) with some information and references to prove that you can pay the rent and are suitable as a tenant. These will include an employer's reference, a bank statement, a passport, and a second form of ID (such as a US driver's license). You may also be asked to provide a previous landlord's reference and perhaps a recent bill. For Americans new to London these references can be difficult to pull together, as you may not have a bank account or a pay slip yet. If you own your own home in the United States, you may not be able to provide a previous landlord's reference (in which case ask if a character reference will suffice). Landlords and letting agents that are used to overseas tenants should be a bit more understanding and make a few allowances. It is a good idea to pull together as many references as possible before you start your home search. Increasingly, letting agents are using referencing companies to collect and process this information (sometimes online), and there is yet another charge for this, usually upwards of £35.

## Finding the Right Place

Knowing where to start your search for a home is probably the hardest part of relocating to London. Which areas can you afford? Are they safe? What will the commute be like? What are the local schools like? Your search will be more fruitful if you can list your priorities, including cost, commute, and size. Do you need an outdoor space? What local amenities would you want? Is off-street parking a must? You need to be realistic about what is available in your chosen neighborhood in your price bracket and be willing to compromise if necessary. If schools aren't a worry, then you can select a location based on your budget, your commute, and the neighborhood's ambiance. Ideally, you'll want a simple commute with no more than one interchange, with backup options for when your local Tube has delays or is suspended. So start your search based on this criterion and then visit the areas that fit the bill. Don't be afraid to ask around for suggestions from trusted colleagues who know London—they may know a hidden gem in an up-and-coming (yet still affordable) area of town.



If you have kids, the location of their school will probably dictate where you live, so make this your first priority. You may decide that you want to be able to walk to school, and so you need to be within a mile or so of the school or just a few stops away on the Tube. Or, you may not be worried about using the car for the school run, which will give you more options. In any case, find your school first (make sure that you have a place if it is private) before you decide on a home.

One shock that you may find hard to swallow is the high rental cost of London property—it is one of the most expensive places to live in the world. In the swanky residential areas of Chelsea, South Kensington, or Westminster, average rental prices are astronomical—around £950-1,100 per week (£4,116-4,766 per month) for a two-bedroom apartment. More affordable, yet still desirable, areas aren't that much of a bargain at around £500-700 per week or £2,166-4,333 per month. While these prices may not be a huge surprise to New Yorkers, they still come as a shock.

## Let the Search Begin

Now that you've done a bit of research and selected an area or two where you would consider living, you can start your home search in earnest. Probably the first place to start is online at one of the big property websites covering all of the United Kingdom, such as Rightmove (www.rightmove.co.uk), Zoopla (www.zoopla.co.uk), or Prime Location (www.primelocation.com). Unfortunately, these websites aren't necessarily bang up-to-date, so they may be advertising property that has already been rented, but they will give you an idea of what is on the market and the cost. Determine which letting agents are listing the most appropriate properties and check out their websites. It may also be worthwhile to drop by or give them a call to find out about their latest listings and to arrange some viewings. Many of them offer email or SMS alerts, which will make your life a bit easier. If the market has more demand than supply (as is critically the case in London currently), then it may take you several episodes of house hunting to find anything that you like, or at least can live with. While you are viewing, remember to check the amount of storage (always a problem in London property), the water pressure, the size of the fridge (these may be small in a one-bedroom flat), and the appliances. Also consider the property's location and proximity to shops, the station, school, or gym. Take pictures of each property as an aide-mémoire; after you've seen a few places in close succession they all start to merge into one.

## Student Accommodations

If you plan to be one of a growing number of foreign students who come to study in London each year, then there are several options. Although it may be difficult, for your first year you should try getting accommodations in one of the halls of residence at your university, which will include utilities and broadband connections, offer easy access to campus, and have good security. It is worth noting that there are privately run halls of residence for students as well, some of which specialize in the international student market. You will also find purpose-built self-catering student accommodations in London.

Of course living in "halls" (as it is called here) isn't the only option. You may want to share an apartment or house with other students or even take a room with a family. As the bulk of your student living expenses will be on accommodations, you need to choose wisely. Another point to remember is that if you are a student in halls or sharing with other full-time students, then you shouldn't have to pay council tax. For more information check out the University of London's student accommodation websites (http://housing.london.ac.uk and www.studenthousing.lon.ac.uk). As well as these websites, there are numerous online student accommodation web portals that can help you find a house or flat share in London.

### FLAT OR HOUSE SHARE

Like students in the United States, many British and foreign students, especially those who are in their second or third year of study, opt for shared accommodations in an apartment (flat) or house. At least with a flat or house share, the cost of the utilities can be shared between several people. Just make sure that you all come to an agreement about bills, food, and cleaning before you all move in. Although many student

Signs promote places to buy or rent.

## How to Reduce your Rent

If finding affordable accommodations is your top priority, it helps to understand how properties are valued in London. Factors such as location and popularity are important, but so are the number of bedrooms and the distance from the Tube station. A compromise may be one way to save yourself a bit of money.

1. Live farther from London, in Zone 3 of the public transportation or beyond. If you are looking in southwest London, prices go up the closer you are to Richmond or Wimbledon. Prices become more affordable (and the properties larger) farther away from the center of town, especially if the area isn't on the Underground.
2. If you can't afford your favorite location, look a stop or two farther up the Tube line and away from central London (such as Shepherd's Bush rather than Notting Hill, or Kentish Town instead of Camden Town).
3. Look in neighborhoods far from a Tube station, then take the bus to get to and from a station.
4. Apartments on the upper floors of a high-rise have more light and command higher prices. Look for apartments on the bottom floors, including the lower ground floor (basement).
5. Flats on the top floors in a converted five- or six-floor house or in an apartment building without an elevator can be more affordable; many people do not want to climb that many stairs.
6. Look only at properties that are currently vacant, and offer less than the asking price for a fast move-in (such as in a week's time)—the landlord may accept it.
7. If you can control when you move to London, try looking for a place to rent during the winter months. There will be fewer properties to choose from, but the landlord may be more willing to consider a lower price.
8. Is it time to reconsider your requirements? For example, although you may expect visitors from the US, can you afford to have a spare room that you may only use for a handful of weeks?



houses or flats are much farther out of town (or in a slightly dodgy area), these locations offer a more affordable accommodation solution—even if you do need to shell out more in travel costs.

### BEING A LODGER

One type of student accommodation that is never really used in the States is being a lodger. This is where you live in a spare room in a house or flat with a live-in landlord, and perhaps their family. This tends to be the cheapest form of accommodation on offer (as all the bills are included). If you want to live in a home away from home, with meals and cleaning (except for laundry) included, becoming a lodger in a family house may be a good idea. You may also be able to find lodging with an individual landlord or a couple, who are perhaps looking for someone else to share the bills. Just be sure to get the ground rules established first about visitors (including overnight ones) and access to the rest of the house if you rent a room with a live-in landlord. The lodging market isn't regulated, so be sure to ask if the landlord has permission from the mortgage holder or landlord, and check them out to see if you think you'll get on. It is a good idea to ask for a written agreement, as there are no statutory rules to protect lodgers.

## BUYING

If you can't stomach the idea of renting for months on end or wasting money on rent when that income could be working for you through home ownership, then perhaps buying is the best solution for you. (If you are going to be in London for several years, it makes sense.) One positive aspect of home ownership in London is that property values in the capital are steadily climbing, though the same can't always be said of the rest of the country. This is no doubt due to the general shortage of prime living property in London as wells as overseas investors looking to a safe investment with good return. If you have a lot of capital to invest, are a good bet for a mortgage, and have the patience of a saint, then home ownership is worth considering.

A word of warning: Home buying in the United Kingdom is a lengthy process, and in a seller's market you may encounter disappointment along the way if you are "gazumped." This is when a seller pulls out of a deal and gives the property to another potential buyer offering more money, and sellers can do this several weeks into the home-buying process—right up until the contracts are exchanged. Gazumping is the scourge of buying property in the United Kingdom and the cause of a lot of heartbreak and numerous sleepless nights. Yet when demand constantly outstrips supply, greed can enter the equation and the seller gives the place to the highest bidder. Another point to bear in mind is that house buying tends to fall into a chain of property purchases, with each successive purchase depending on the selling and purchasing going smoothly so that the capital is in place for the next property. Sometimes this chain breaks down, causing delays or cancellation of the whole process. If you are still undeterred about buying property in London, here is a short breakdown of the home-buying process.



### Getting a Mortgage

Your first step will be to work out how much you can afford and to secure a mortgage offer. Unfortunately, the days of 100 percent mortgages are long gone, and banks now insist on a hefty deposit (10-15 percent) before they will give you a mortgage. How much you can borrow for your mortgage will be determined by the size of your deposit and your annual earnings. As a general guide, a lender will usually let you borrow up to four times your annual salary, or 2.5 times your joint income if you are buying as a couple. As buying a home is such a major financial undertaking, you should get some professional advice about which type of mortgage would suit you and how much you can afford. The types and range of mortgages on offer in the United Kingdom can be slightly different from those offered in the United States; for example, interest-only mortgages are available, though they are not as popular as they once were. Equally, a fixed-rate interest mortgage is fairly popular, as are capped and tracker rate mortgages, though you can get an adjustable-rate mortgage. Loans in the United Kingdom are based on your income and credit history and require a deposit of 10-15 percent, though these figures depend on the mortgage lender. A mortgage advisor or lender will be able to take you through all the various options and offer advice on which one could work for you.

### Finding Your Ideal Home and Making an Offer

Once you have some idea of your budget, you can start looking for your dream home. Once again you can start your search online to get an idea of what is available where and the asking price. Property prices vary enormously across London, and many of the areas favored by expats are in the expensive parts of town. A house or large luxurious apartment in London's most desirable neighborhoods can be several million pounds (even tens of millions), though a house or large apartment in a more affordable (but still nice) neighborhood may start around the £1 million mark, perhaps a bit less.

To get an up-to-date idea of property prices where you are thinking of buying, contact estate agents that are listing properties in your chosen area and start viewing. Remember that the estate agent's bread is buttered by the seller, not the buyer, so they will be representing their interests, not yours. Once you have found the right place and made an offer, don't be surprised if you need to negotiate on the price. Whatever you do, don't get trapped in a bidding war that you cannot afford.



There are standard costs associated with a home purchase. These include a fee for the mortgage valuation, which depends on the cost of the property you are buying but can be as much as £1,500. Expect to pay at least £250 for a general "home buyer's" survey, which will reveal any obvious structural problems. A full structural survey, which is much more detailed, can cost as much as £1,000; it provides a thorough examination of the building to make sure it is structurally sound and/or highlight possible problems. (Given the age and cost of some of the property in London, you may want the peace of mind of a full structural survey, especially if you plan to buy an older property and do extensive remodeling after the purchase.) Another cost is the property search by the local authority (around £100 or more), which will bring to light any nearby planning applications that could affect the property. The solicitor's fee can be as much as £1,500. Stamp duty is a tax that applies to all property transactions; if you buy a place worth more than £125,000, you will be liable for stamp duty charges. The amount you will pay depends upon the value of the property; currently, stamp duty is a minimum of £1,250 and can be much, much higher. You also have to pay a fee to the Land Registry office for transferring the registered ownership to yourself. The cost for this varies according to the purchase price of the property, currently ranging £40-910.

One major difference in owning property in the United Kingdom concerns freehold and leasehold property. Freehold property is where you own the land and/or property in perpetuity. A leasehold property is one where you own a lease on a property, giving you a temporary right to the property. With this type of property you will have to pay the freeholder an annual service charge and you will just be leasing the property on which the building is built. Huge swaths of central London's most valuable property are built on land owned by the Duke of Westminster, making him one of Britain's wealthiest people. Be sure to find out if the property you are buying is leasehold or freehold.

## Conveyancing

This is the term used to cover the actual process of transferring the deed of title from the current owner of the property to the buyer. So, once you've agreed on a price, you should finalize your mortgage arrangements and get your deposit together. You also need to get a solicitor or licensed conveyancer to handle all the legal paperwork. If you don't know a good conveyancing solicitor, ask someone for a recommendation (this is where being active in an expat club or school can pay real dividends). Although the seller's solicitor will draw up the final contracts, your solicitor will organize a land search on the property, to ensure that there are no problems with ownership of the property, questions of rights of way, or problematic future developments—you don't want to buy a house in leafy Middlesex only to find out in a year's time that your backyard is meant to be part of Heathrow's third runway.

You need to organize a valuation of the property for your mortgage lender. You should also get a survey done on the property so that you can be sure that the building is safe and sound and complies with building regulations. Sometimes it is cheaper to have the same surveyor do the valuation and the survey.

Once all the checks have been made, you will exchange contracts and hand over your deposit. This is when the purchase of the property is fully binding. Up until this time either party could pull out (although they would lose some money on the various fees). The final step is known as completion, and this is when the final funds are transferred to the seller and you become the new owner. There are several more fees and expenses to pay on completion, such as stamp duty land tax (similar to transfer tax), sales tax, and the Land Registry fee.



### Refurbishing and Restoring Your Home

Seldom are the homes that you buy exactly as you want them to be, and many people take the opportunity to refurbish their home when they finally take ownership. This assumes that you still have a bit of money left to pay for redecoration or building work. Just remember that many homes in London are in a conservation area, which preserves the character of London's older buildings. The upshot is that you will only be able to carry out certain building work. Your conveyancing should have highlighted if your new home is in a conservation area, and your local council will be able to tell you more. You may also need to get planning permission from the local council for some building work, but your architect or contractor (in Britain, use the term "builder") will be able to guide you through this process.

## SEASONAL DEMAND FOR PROPERTY

There is a distinct seasonal demand for property, for both rentals and purchases. Usually the demand and stock levels for rentals decline in the winter months and peak in the summer months, though in central London there is a general turnover of one- and two-bedroom flats throughout the year. Family-size properties and houses are much harder to find in the winter, and tend to come to market in early summer. If you are moving with your family, try to do your house-hunting then. The peak season for rentals is during the summer months, and you may find that you are competing with 20 other house hunters for each property on the market. In high demand areas such as Shoreditch, Angel, Bloomsbury, and Wandsworth, places can be rented within a few hours of coming on the market.

Spring is the traditional time to start looking for a new home to buy, and this is when many homeowners put their houses on the market so that they can upsize (or downsize) depending on their needs. To buy a place, do your house search in the spring and try to organize your mortgage by the beginning of March. This puts you in a good position to secure any home you decide to put an offer on.

## Living in a Historical Home

One of London's greatest assets is its wide range of historical architecture—from beautiful cathedrals to medieval castles and stately homes. Even mundane homes in London can be historically and architecturally significant. With such a wealth of historical buildings on offer it is little surprise that the country carefully guards these ancient structures. And while preserving these beautiful buildings for generations to come is praiseworthy indeed, for those who purchase a historic home the challenges that they face trying to combine a modern family home with historic architecture can be difficult, as was the case with Ann and Peter, who bought a Grade II listed home in Highgate.

The house stands on a main road in Highgate Village on top of Highgate Hill, giving it amazing panoramic views of the City of London's skyline. The five-story house was originally built around 1805 to house British soldiers during the Napoleonic Wars, but successive years had seen it fall into neglect. Even though the property was just a collection of ramshackle pre-war flats when Ann and Peter first saw it, they still felt its charm. Drawn to its sense of history, they were keen to return it to its Regency heritage. This is just as well, really, because the property was a Grade II listed building, which means that any refurbishment must be sympathetic to its original architecture—both inside and out.

Here in London, the preservation of historical buildings falls to the English Heritage organization, and since 1950 it has been working to conserve and preserve old and important buildings by listing them. This ensures that the architectural and historical interest of the building is carefully considered before any alterations, either outside or inside, are given planning permission. All buildings built before 1700 (and in anything like their original condition) and most buildings built between 1700 and 1840 are listed. Exceptional buildings are listed as Grade I, while important or special-interest buildings are Grade II.

What the couple hadn't been completely prepared for was the red tape that they would have to go through to get planning permission to refurbish the building. Everything from wallpaper to light fixtures had to be carefully considered. Yet their time and effort paid off, and once all the work was finished they had a beautiful home. Of course, now that their family has expanded, they would love more space and to be able to add a conservatory or have an office in the backyard, yet neither would be allowed. Although living in a well-preserved historic property is truly special, I'm sure there are times when Ann and Peter wish they hadn't bought that particular home.

# Household Expenses

In addition to your monthly rent or mortgage payment, you will need to budget for utilities and local taxes (council taxes). I suggest that you budget at least £350 per month to cover these expenses—probably more if energy prices start to climb. Another thing to cover is household insurance. Homeowners need both building (required for mortgage) and contents insurance, while renters just need the latter. Building insurance provides cover for the actual fabric of the building, such as rebuilding costs, while contents insurance protects your possessions from theft or fire and flood damage. The cost of your home insurance will depend on several factors, including the home's size, location, and age, as well as the amount of cover required. If you own your property, then its maintenance will be down to you.

If you buy an apartment in a block of flats you may also be asked to pay for a service charge to cover the maintenance of the building and communal areas such as hallways or the garden (often this is covered by the rent). Landlords may also sometimes pass on the service charges to their renters, in addition to the rent, so be sure to ask about this before you sign the lease.

## COUNCIL TAX

Once you've moved in, you must register for council tax at your local borough or county (if you've opted to live in Greater London). This is the case for both home-owners and renters (assuming they are not in student accommodations). Usually this can be done online and will only take a minute or two. The council tax is based on the assumption that two people will be living in a property. However, if you are living alone, you should be able to get a 25 percent rebate off your council tax bill. Council tax rates vary from borough to borough, but the average cost for property (known as Band D) was £1,296 in 2014, and broadly ranged £822-1,985 in London's 32 boroughs.



## TV LICENSE

A cost that you need to pay if you plan to have a TV will be a TV license. Anyone who watches or records television programs as they're being broadcast must, by law, have a TV license, no matter what device they are using to view the program. The annual charge for a TV license is currently £145.50 for a color TV and can be paid online or over the phone. Students need a TV license if they have a TV or are watching live TV programs on their computer or cell phone while the device is plugged into a wall socket.

## UTILITIES

Once you move into your property, transfer the utility (electricity, gas, and water) accounts to your name, as well as the telephone and broadband service. This can be done with a phone call to the relevant company with meter readings when you move in. If you are a really lucky tenant, sometimes your management agent will transfer the utilities for you, and if you're using a relocation company they should be able to help. If you can find out the name of the gas and electricity company before the move you can get the ball rolling on the transferring of utilities before you actually move in. Ask the agent handling your lease or purchase if they can find who the utility providers are and who is going to do what on the day of the move. You don't have to use the property's existing gas and electricity providers, and you can shop around for a better deal if you want, but this may just compound your stress level at a very tense time. If you are renting and do switch providers, be sure to let your landlord know. In 2014, the average gas and electricity bill was around £110 a month (£250 for a family of four). You also have to set up an account for your telephone and broadband provider when you move in.

### Thames Water

The only mains water provider to London is Thames Water, and an average monthly household bill runs around £30. London's water is very hard and you will need to de-scale your coffee maker and electric kettle regularly; however, the mains water tastes pretty good. You may also need to add water-softening tablets to the washing machine to prevent it from getting covered in lime scale and put specialized salt in the dishwasher.

Your water bills will depend on whether your property is metered or unmetered. If it is the former then Thames Water aims to read the meters and send out a bill every six months. If it is unmetered then you will be sent an annual bill (running from April 1 to the following March 31). These bills are based on the value of the property (as used to determine council taxes) and a standing charge.

# LANGUAGE AND EDUCATION

The United Kingdom and the United States are "two countries separated by a common language." The 400 or so years of isolation between us, the influence of immigrants, and the natural evolution of regional dialects have all contributed to the gulf between the two versions of English that we experience today. While we can usually get the gist of what the other is talking about, confusion can creep in when someone uses a term that the other nationality is unfamiliar with. I had one such embarrassing moment not long after I arrived here as a student, when I went to the pub with some fellow students. One of the girls turned to me and said, "I'm thinking of getting fringe—like yours." I frantically did a mental survey of my clothes . . . nope, nothing had fringe on it. I nodded at her and mumbled, "Fringe?" She laughed and picked up some of her hair and swept it across her forehead like bangs. "Yes," she said . . . *"Fringe!"* I nodded in embarrassment. Who would have thought that fringe means bangs? Oddly enough I've been here so long that I too use odd British idioms, which completely throws my expat friends, such as describing the winter's flu as "lurgy" (slang for an infectious disease that makes you feel unwell).

Another area where you would think that the British and the Americans would be

© GARRY KNIGHT

quite similar is in education, but even here there are differences. While the schooling for younger children is broadly similar (in that the children are taught to read and write, understand arithmetic, and so on), once you get to the high school years, there's quite a bit of divergence. Understanding the differences as well as the similarities between the educational systems will help ease your transition as you settle into life in London.

# Understanding British English



For the most part our shared media means that we already tend to understand each other's words and idioms. You probably already know that lift means elevator or that football is soccer. Yet it will probably take you a while to become familiar with all of the variations between our two versions of English, especially if you consider slang, pronunciation, and regional variations. At least our shared language means that we can quickly pick up British terminology and idioms. More importantly, you will have the English to say "I'm confused, what do you mean?" or "Can you say it again, please?" even if it is a bit embarrassing.

One Americanism that the British do *not* like is the use of "what?" when you have not heard or understood someone. In these circumstances "what?" is considered ill-mannered. Instead, try to remember to say "pardon" or "I'm sorry." It might seem a minor offense to say "what" rather than "pardon," but I would say that this is one word commonly used by Americans that really grates on the British. I, on the other hand, shudder when they use "have got," when "have" is all they need—so I guess it is just "horses for courses" (as they say here). We each have our own foibles, which we will just have to accommodate.

## REGIONAL DIALECTS

If you aren't that familiar with Britain, you may believe that everyone here speaks like Roger Moore and Helen Mirren—or even Keira Knightley and Hugh Grant—but you would be sadly mistaken. Britain has an enormous range of regional accents, from Welsh to Brummie (from Birmingham), Geordie (from Newcastle), and Glaswegian, to name but a few. To get a sense of Britain's regional accents, think of Michael Caine with his London Cockney accent, Russell Brand with his Essex twang, or Robbie Coltrane with a Scottish accent. Given that it is geographically small in comparison to the United States, it is odd that there are such pronounced regional dialects in Britain—many more than we have in the States. Until you become used to them, these regional accents can occasionally be incomprehensible—especially on the phone. It is also worth bearing in mind that in England someone's accent can be a sign of their background, with the middle and upper classes tending to have a less regionally pronounced accent. Thankfully, London accents are fairly easy to grasp, although you may struggle with the accents of some of the city's immigrant population. At least you don't have to learn a whole new language to get around in London, even if you do encounter the occasional confusing dialogue. Just be sure to remember that Southwark is pronounced "SUTH-uck"; they won't know what you mean if you pronounce it as it is spelled.

© NEIL LANG/123RF.COM

Although we share a language, there are some spelling differences.



### BRITISH SPELLING

The Americans and the British don't just use different words—they also use different spellings and even syntax. The obvious spelling differences are the adding of "u" to words that end in "or" (colour, favour) and the changing of "er" endings to "re" (theatre, centre). But there are numerous other ones, such as "programme"—in Britain, "program" is only correct when referring to a computer program. The really odd one is "gaol" for jail, although this seems to be a bit archaic these days. The easiest way to deal with British spelling will be to just switch your computer's spell-checker to UK English, which should catch any anomalies.

## Education

Deciding on a school for your children will be one of the most difficult aspects of your move to London, and will make or break your stay here. It is vital that you understand all the educational options available to you so that you can make an informed decision about the best education for your children. You should also consider your children's ages, their adaptability, and where you might be in a couple of years' time, as these could be important factors in your school selection. A couple of years in a British elementary school won't be as disruptive to their education as it would be later on once they're in high school.

To get a place at a school really just depends on whether there is a vacancy. If it's a selective school then your child will need to pass any entrance or assessment tests. If it's a private school, you must be able to afford it or have school fees included in your

## Cockney Rhyming Slang

Cockney rhyming slang is a dialect unique to London—especially the East End of London. A cockney is said to be anyone who was born within earshot of the sound of "Bow Bells"—the bells of Bow Church in the City of London. The construction of Cockney rhyming slang takes two common words, a phrase or famous person that rhymes with the intended word, and instead of saying the intended word uses the rhyming word. The important thing about this slang is that users may only say the first word of the two-word rhyme. A classic and common example of this is "look," which rhymes with butcher's hook, hence the slang word of "butchers," which is said instead of the word "look." Sometimes it helps to understand the rhyme if you say it with a London accent, for instance dropping a leading "h" and adding an "r" at the end of an "a," so that the word "half" becomes "arff."

Like all languages, Cockney rhyming slang is constantly evolving, but here is a list of some of the most common (or funniest) slang words you may encounter. The italicized words are the ones used.

| **Expression** | **Meaning** |
|---|---|
| *Adam and Eve* | Believe |
| *Barnet* (as in Barnet Fair) | Hair |
| *Barney* (for barn owl) | Row (argue/fight) |
| *Boat race* | Face |
| *Boracic* (as in boracic lint) | Skint (broke) |
| *Bread* (for bread and honey) | Money |
| *Brown bread* | Dead |
| *Butchers* (as in butcher's hook) | Look |
| *Chewing the fat* | Chat |
| *My old china* (for china plate) | Mate |
| *Cobbler's* (for cobbler's awls) | Balls (testicles) |
| *I've not heard a dickie* (as in a dickie bird) | Word |
| *Dickie* (dickie dirt) | Shirt |
| *Dickie* (for Uncle Dick) | Sick |
| *Giraffe* | Laugh |
| *Half inch* | Pinch (to steal) |
| *Hampsteads* (for Hampstead Heath) | Teeth |
| *Jam jar* | Car |
| *Loaf* (for loaf of bread) | Head |
| *Mincies* (for mince pies) | Eyes |
| *Mutton* (as in Mutton and Jeff) | Deaf |
| *Plates* (as in plates of meat) | Feet |
| *Rabbit* (for rabbit and pork) | Talk |
| *Rosie* (for Rosie Lee) | Tea |
| *Ruby* (for Ruby Murray) | Curry |
| *Scarper* (as in Scapa Flow) | Go |
| *Sherman* (for Sherman tank) | Yanks |
| *Tea leaf* | Thief |
| *On your/his/my Tod* (for Tod Sloan) | Alone |
| *Tom* (for tomfoolery) | Jewelry |
| *Trouble and strife* | Wife |
| *Whistle* (for whistle and flute) | Suit |

corporate relocation package. Vaccination records are not usually required to get a place at a school, though a recent school report would be helpful.

A good starting point for your school hunt is to speak to friends, family, and colleagues—anyone you trust who has some experience of London's schools. Ideally they will have kids similar in age to your own. You should also consult the Good Schools Guide (www.goodschoolsguide.co.uk) and visit the website of any school that you are interested in. Another online resource is the school guide provided by the London-based children's quarterly publication *Angels and Urchins* (www.angelsandurchins.co.uk/directories/schools), which is good for primary schools both private and state. Two dedicated online school guides are www.schoolsnet.com, which offers a school guide based on parental reviews, and www.schoolswebdirectory.co.uk, which provides information about schools searchable by borough or county. You can also read the results of a government inspection of most schools at www.ofsted.gov.uk; just bear in mind that some private schools are inspected by the Independent Schools Inspectorate (ISI; www.isi.net).



As London is a world-class city attracting numerous nationalities, there are several educational curriculums available here. For example, you can choose a British school, stick with the American curriculum at an American school, or opt for an international school offering the International Baccalaureate (IB) curriculum. For the most part the educational content of these different schools doesn't vary that much for children in elementary school, and all cover subjects such as literacy, numeracy, natural and social sciences, as well as art and physical education. However, the situation changes for teenagers, who are required to study certain topics as per the requirements of the formal qualification of their educational systems, be it a high school diploma, International Baccalaureate diploma, or British General Certificate of Secondary Education (GCSEs) or Advanced Level (A Levels). If you'd prefer that your teenage children continue with their American education, there are American schools—both in town and in Greater London—where they can study for their high school diploma and the Advanced Placement program.

To avoid confusion, you should refer to the free schools provided by the local authority (what we refer to as "public schools") as "state schools." In England, a public school is one of the elite private boarding secondary schools, such as Eton, Rugby, or Westminster. The term "public" was given to these schools because they were open to the wealthy public (of any religion) in contrast to other schools that were open to just certain religions.

Another confusing term for Americans will be the word "college." This can refer to a "sixth-form college" (for years 12 and 13), which is where students aged 16 to 18 can go to get the appropriate national qualification to apply to a British university or vocational qualification. Illogically, a college can also be part of a university. For example, Kings College is part of the University of London, and Trinity College is part of the University of Cambridge. It's a bit of academic snobbery, but if you are studying for a BA or BS, or a higher degree (referred to as "post-graduate"), then you should say that you're studying at university or "uni"—college is for kids.

## Getting a School Place

In the past few years the demand for primary school places has shot up right across London, forcing some state schools to use temporary classrooms and increase class sizes. In some parts of town there is an under-capacity of up to 25 percent. If you are intending to send your children to a state school (be it for financial or ethical reasons), you will need to do a considerable amount of planning before you move. The website of the Advisory Centre for Education (www.ace-ed.org.uk) is a good place to start for information about getting a place at a state school.

Many London boroughs have a deadline in mid-January for admissions the following September, although for some secondary schools, it may be in November of the previous year. If you miss this deadline then you need to do an "in-year" application, during which you select your top six schools within the area. If your favorite school has a great reputation, it will probably be oversubscribed, in which case you will be placed on a waiting list until a place comes up at a school in the right class for your child, and will be given a school place elsewhere. The school will give priority to people who met the application deadline but didn't get a place. As a family that has just moved into the area, you will be way down the waiting list to get a place at any well-regarded school.

There is also a "catch 22" situation with applying to a state school, as you must provide proof of your address (such as a utility bill) so they can see if you live in the borough and are in the school's catchment area. However, as you are relocating you may not have an address yet and possibly hope to base your home selection on its proximity to your children's school. That can make it very hard, if not impossible, to coordinate schooling through the state system and housing at the same time. You could try choosing a borough and contacting the local authority's department of education to see which schools have spaces, and then check these out individually. Of course there is every chance that the borough's educational department won't help you if you are not yet a resident of the borough, leaving you a bit high and dry.

If you are wondering just what in the world a "catchment area" is, don't worry, you're not alone. Many expats I know didn't have a clue what this meant when they started their school search. In essence it is a defined area around a school, and residents within this area are given first priority for that school. However, it is important to realize that living in the catchment area *does not* guarantee a place at that school. The local authority is only obliged to find you a place at a school, not necessarily at the nearest one. Other admissions factors will be given greater priority by the school, such as whether the child has special educational needs or a sibling already at the school.

Going private is one way to avoid the problem of deadlines and catchment areas, though this is no guarantee that you will get a place at your first choice. London's private schools are equally oversubscribed and difficult to get into, especially the nursery and primary schools. Your best bet for either a state or private school will be to look at several schools (just about all private schools have websites, and so do many of the state schools). You can read their government inspection reports at OFSTED (www.ofsted.gov.uk) or the Independent Schools Inspectorate (www.isi.net) and should contact them to see if they have any places in the right year group. Schools that cater to expat families (especially those in the suburbs) tend to have a regular turnover of pupils, and so may be better able to offer a place, though they will probably want you to start at the beginning of a term, if possible.

To help support your child's admission application bring a copy of his or her most recent school report. You can show this to the head or admissions manager when you visit the school so that they have a sense of where your child is academically. If you decide to go for a religious school you will have to have a letter of recommendation from your clergyperson and baptism certificates. Vaccination records are currently not required for a school place.

## ENGLISH EDUCATIONAL STRUCTURE

England's educational structure is very different from that in the United States, as in England there is nationally set course work and standardized testing, which must be passed to achieve your educational qualifications. This is very different from the American system, where the local educational authority and state government determine what should be covered in each grade and how the children's progress will be assessed. Certainly there is no nationally standardized mandatory testing across all 50 states.

In Britain, kids start full-time education at age 4, and there is usually no middle/ junior high school—just primary school for ages 4-11 followed by secondary school for 11- to 16-year-olds, with some continuing until age 18. A few private schools in London do have a lower, middle, and upper school, though those schools offer schooling from the age of 4 all the way up to the age of 18. A few pre-prep private schools cater to the 4- to 7-year-old age group, some state elementary schools have an infant school (ages 4-7), and there is a junior school for children ages 8-11. A few private primary schools continue until age 13 for boys—setting them up for entry to a private school with a 13 and older entrance, such as a boarding school.

Some kids go to "sixth form" (perhaps at a sixth-form college) for the last two years of their schooling before they head to university. It used to be that the last five years of mandatory schooling in England (ages 11 to 15 or 16) were referred to as "forms," starting with first form for 11-year-olds. Those who stayed on in school to get a higher qualification so that they could go to university went into the sixth form (which was broken down into the lower sixth (age 16 or 17) and upper sixth (age 17 or 18). The whole system changed in the early 1990s, doing away with forms and replacing them with year numbers. So, there is a Reception year at the age of 4, followed by Year 1 (age 5), continuing until Year 13 (age 17 or 18). Nevertheless, use of the term "sixth form" has continued, and private schools in particular are quite likely to use this term.

September is the cut-off month for each school year, with pre-September birthdays going in one year and the rest of that calendar year going in the one below. By law, children should have started their schooling no later than the term following their 5th birthday, and they must continue until at least age 16 (though the government is considering changing this to age 18). There are three terms to the British school year, and it stretches from early September to mid-July, with a one- or two-week break in the middle of each term and two or three weeks between terms (taking in the Christmas and Easter holidays). The summer break is around six or seven weeks long (private schools have longer summer breaks). American schools loosely follow the American school calendar, adapted to work with British and American national holidays.

In England, teenage students specialize in certain subjects at the age of 14, which may affect what subjects they can study at a British university. Specializing so early in a child's academic career is the norm in Europe, where many children finish their formal schooling at the age of 16. Only those who are academically inclined continue in full-time education past this age. The rest start work, do vocational training, or both. More and more British students are recognizing the benefits of higher education and staying on at school. In the past two decades the number of British students furthering their studies has dramatically increased, and now around half of all 18-year-olds go to higher education.

Another major difference between the United States and the United Kingdom is that the academic curriculum is not secular, even at state schools. Faith schools are commonplace, and here in London you'll find Church of England, Catholic, Jewish, Hindu, and Islamic faith schools—these can be either state or private. Faith schools require that you are actively practicing your religion. If you decide on a religious school, you may be asked to provide a letter of reference from your pastor, rabbi, or priest (and so on) as part of your application.

Another aspect of British education that may be unexpected is the large number of single-sex schools, especially at secondary school level. For girls in particular a single-sex school is seen as potentially providing a significant academic advantage. It also means that they might go through their formative teenage years without the opposite sex around, which could make attending a coeducational university a more drastic transition. Yet I seem to be in a minority among my British friends, most of whom are in favor of single-sex secondary schooling for their kids.



## Nursery (Preschool)

Children can go to a fee-paying preschool anytime from the age of 2 until the age of 4 or 5, depending on whether the school they are going on to offers a Reception class. Some state primary schools also offer half-day nursery school for 3-year-olds to help with the transition to full-time school the following year, though competition for places at these free nursery schools can be fierce. The emphasis at preschool tends to revolve around learning through play, with the child expected to have some basic numeracy and literacy skills by the age of 4. It is quite common to find Montessori nurseries in London, though there are very few Montessori primary schools. If both you and your partner work full-time, there are day-care nurseries that will look after children that are just a few months old until they are old enough for full-time school. These are expensive, especially in London, but are one way to get full-time child care.

## Primary School (ages 4 to 11)

As you'd expect, the main subjects in primary school are literacy and numeracy, history, geography, sciences, and physical education. State schools in England follow the national curriculum, which requires that certain subjects are taught by a certain age. Private elementary schools following the English curriculum do not necessarily follow the national curriculum. Instead they will probably be "prep schools," which aim to prepare the children for entrance to their selective secondary school. As well as literacy, numeracy, science, and other core subjects, private schools are more likely to teach a foreign language at this age and offer instrumental lessons.

## Secondary School (ages 11 to 16 or 18)

Secondary school combines both middle school and high school. After three years, children in England and Wales select four or so subjects that they want to study in addition to the required subjects of English, math, and sciences (biology, physics, and chemistry). Optional subjects include history, a foreign language, geography, drama, art, and so on. In Year 11 (age 15/16) they take the General Certificate of Secondary Education (GCSE) exams in the subject they've studied. Both state and private schools take GCSE exams, and capable students usually take nine or more GCSEs. Students who do well in these exams may decide to continue in full-time education in Years 12 and 13 (the sixth form) and study for their Advanced Level qualification (A Levels). There are two stages to A Levels: the AS after one year and the A2 in the second year. As with GCSEs, A Levels are achieved by passing the national exams held in May and June. More importantly, A Levels are needed to gain entrance to a British university. Those who don't want to study at university can start work or go to a vocational/technical college. The current government has big plans for education and wants to improve standards, especially at secondary school. You should be able to find out about the latest changes to the English state education system at www.education.gov.uk.

### International Baccalaureate (IB) Diplomas

This is an international qualification used in 146 countries around the world, including the United Kingdom. The IB program is broken up into three age groups: primary for ages 3 to 12, middle years for ages 11 to 16, and diploma for the final two years before university. Most universities on either side of the Atlantic will accept applicants with an IB diploma. One of the advantages of an IB education is that it offers a broad curriculum, where students are required to study languages, social sciences, and formal sciences as well as math and arts subjects. The IB provides a broad-based approach to learning and may be a good educational choice if you or your partner's career requires your family to be based overseas, relocating every few years to a different country. Unfortunately, only private schools offer the IB program in London at the moment.



## STATE OR INDEPENDENT (PRIVATE FEE-PAYING) EDUCATION

When considering schooling for your children, one of the first things to decide is whether you want—or can afford—a fee-paying education. If you want to stay within the American curriculum, you have no choice and have to go for one of the private American schools. Another option would be to send your children to a private British school—be it a day school or a boarding school. More than 7 percent of English children attend a private school, with the numbers for London rising to more than 10 percent. Private schools may require children to pass an entrance test and be interviewed before they are offered a place. This is especially true in secondary school and at selective prep schools.

### State Schools

English state schools follow a national curriculum that concentrates on subjects such as English, math, science, information technology, history, geography, foreign languages (for 11- to 14-year-olds), music, and art, as well as physical education. These children will have to sit national tests at ages 7, 11, and 14 to assess their numeracy and literacy skills learning—the Standard Assessment Tests (SATs, pronounced "sats," as in the plural of "sat"). Doing well in these tests is vital for schools, as they are judged on performance tables (sometimes called league tables) according to their results. Another compulsory subject is religious education. This is very different from the United States, where most religious schools are private. Generally, schools take a balanced approach to religious education, teaching about all of the world's major faiths. Many of the best state schools academically—at primary and secondary levels—are faith schools. It is not unheard of for people desperate to get a place at a good school to find religion or

## Expat Student Profile

**Name**: Rebecca Gold
**Age**: 20
**From**: New York

**What are you studying and how long is your course?** My official course is Study Abroad, which allows me to select my own modules rather than have them preselected for me. I'm a computer science major at home, and I'm taking two classes in that department. Additionally, I am taking an English literature course about 17th-century British theater and a Classics course that takes me on trips to museums throughout London.

**Why did you choose London?** Several factors, really. Firstly, I've always wanted to go to the UK (whether due to imported British media, such as *Doctor Who*, or other drawing factors). I wanted to see London (Big Ben and other touristy stuff). Secondly, I had several friends who have studied abroad here in the past and had an excellent time. Finally, when deciding where I wanted to study abroad (and therefore live for six months), language and cultural familiarity, while still being in a different place, was an important factor.

**Was the application process difficult? Did you apply directly?** I applied for the ability to study abroad through my university. The process was not particularly difficult, but involved several essays. I am told that my being a STEM (Science/Tech/Engineering/Math) student and my preference for semesters made my application easier. It seems that fewer STEM majors study abroad. Once I was on the Study Abroad program, I then applied directly to King's College, London which was a very easy process.

**Was getting a visa difficult? How did you do this?** I did not need to get a visa before arriving in the UK. I went to customs and border control at the airport with a letter from my home institution and a letter from King's College. I was granted a student visitor visa, allowing me to stay for the duration of my six-month course.

**Where are you living, what is it like, and who organized this?** I'm living at Moonraker Point, which is one of the dorms for King's students (primarily first years). I got accommodation through King's.

I found out after moving in that I was in "the posh dorm." It's very expensive (£206.50 per week) and there are a great deal of international/study abroad students here. I have my own bedroom and bathroom in a flat with four other students, and we share a kitchen. Three of us are study abroad students and one is a full-time King's College student from China.

**Has it been easy to settle in and make friends?** I've spent a good deal of time in places far away from my family at home in the US (I go to school a three-hour plane ride from my parents), so homesickness isn't all that much of an issue. I spent a fair amount of time Skyping with friends and family, especially in the first few weeks of being in London.

I made a point to join clubs and societies to meet other students with similar interests. I have found that, compared to some other study abroad students at King's that I have met, I have settled in quite easily. I credit joining in and regular attendance/participation in King's College societies as the main reason why I have so many British friends and an active social life.

**What has surprised you about life in London?** Dealing with the change! I still spend time digging through my coin purse to figure out how to make the right change. I'll be with British friends, asking "Which one is 10 pence?" My wallet has gotten quite heavy because I don't know how to make exact change. I was also very thrown by the different sizes of paper money.

Also, the way places and things are pronounced has thrown me a bit. I'm living in Southwark and it took me more than a week to get the pronunciation down. Other things, like pronouncing "Thames" as "tame-s," rather than "tems," were particularly annoying.

Bus strikes—now those are very weird! They're very politely publicized in advance and perplexingly official.

change faiths suddenly, just so they can secure a place at their first choice school. When trying to assess potential state schools, look at their placement on the local authority's performance tables to get a sense of how well the pupils of that school did on their SATs (or GCSE and A Level exams if you are looking at a secondary school). This information should be on the borough's website or the Department of Education website (www.education.gov.uk), or visit Locrating (www.locrating.com). There are also online league tables showing the performance of private and state secondary schools in the national exams (such as those offered by the United Kingdom's national newspapers)—just bear in mind that some of the schools included will be selective.

The quality of London's state schools can be very hit or miss. As a general rule, religious schools often enjoy a better reputation than the secular ones, but this is by no means a guarantee of good schooling. Certainly any good state school in London (and elsewhere in the United Kingdom, for that matter) will most probably be heavily oversubscribed, making it difficult to secure a place (or several, if you have more than one child). Your challenge may be to find a state school that can take your children, even if it's not exactly where you want to live or your first choice school.

At time of publication, London had a state schooling supply crisis—there are several boroughs with at least a 10 percent shortage of school places. For some boroughs, this figure is expected to rise to 25 percent by 2015, making getting a place at a state school for one or more kids a challenge. Local authorities are under a legal obligation to provide schooling, but the places that they offer may be miles away or at different schools for each child—hardly ideal. There are a few selective state secondary schools in London (known as grammar schools), with more in the counties that surround the capital. These are very difficult to get into, yet can be a great idea for bright children who will thrive in these academic hothouses.



## Private Schools

There are numerous private schools to choose from in the London area, and you may find it much easier to get a place at one of these. However, even many private schools are full. For more information on private schools, you can look online at the Good Schools Guide (www.goodschoolsguide.co.uk) or buy their book by the same name. Another good online resource for private schools is the Independent Schools Council; you can search for schools that are members on their website (www.isc.co.uk). Of course the real question is whether you can afford to go private. Perhaps you will be one of the lucky ones and have this as part of your relocation package.

In case you are wondering about the cost of non-boarding school fees, there can be quite a significant difference in these from one school to the next, usually because of the school's reputation and facilities. Currently, the average annual amount for non-boarder fees in London is £14,800. Generally, fees are less for the elementary years, which range £11,400-22,000 per annum. The cost for secondary schools is greater, anywhere between £15,250 and £25,650 annually. Bear in mind that schools often offer financial aid (called "bursaries") as well as scholarships, so be sure to ask about these.

Often, private secondary schools are selective and may require that your child pass an interview and entrance exams (covering math and English, and possibly verbal and non-verbal reasoning). Other schools, especially non-selective primary schools, are more likely to base an admission decision on their assessment of the child, in which case they may ask the child to join the class for a few hours so that the teacher can assess them, or they may just ask for a school report. Selective primary schools may want the child to sit for exams in English and math to see that they are at an appropriate level in these subjects. You are much more likely to find a place (or three) at a private school, although even some of these may not be able to accommodate all your children. As a general rule, private schools tend to have smaller class sizes than state schools (usually around 20 per class). The government guidelines say that primary class sizes should be no more than 30 per class, but with greater numbers of children looking for places, class sizes seem to be creeping up (a recent study found that around one in eight under-11s in England had class sizes of 30 or more). Whether you decide on a state or private school is a very personal decision and will very much depend on your finances.



## UNIVERSITIES AND COLLEGES

For years and years, only a few of the British academic elite would get an undergraduate degree, usually those from the upper or middle classes. Now, about one-quarter of the population have an undergraduate degree, following a real push by the government to get more teenagers to stay on in school and go to university. In England and Wales, undergraduates study for three years (in Scotland it's four) and usually just study subjects that relate to their major (called a "degree" here). Just as in the rest of the English educational system, there is a heavy emphasis on exams to assess your grasp of a subject at university.

Those of you thinking of studying here will be pleased to learn that London has one of the world's largest concentrations of universities and higher education institutions, many of which have a world-wide reputation, including Imperial College and University College London. Several specialist schools of higher education offer

the University College London

undergraduate or higher degrees. These only offer one or two specialist subjects, but many of them enjoy an international reputation for excellence, such as the London College of Business. With up to 40 different places of higher education learning, it should come as no surprise that the city has a very large student population (including many from overseas). Whether you are looking to do your undergraduate or advanced degree, London can be a great place to study. The bad news is that studying in London isn't cheap. Tuition fees for foreign students at British universities are high and significantly more than the amount charged to British and EU students. For example, in 2014-2015 an American starting a BS in chemistry at Imperial College London was required to pay £26,000 (around US$41,600) for each year of the three-year course, while a British student attending the exact same course will pay £9,000 (around US$14,400) per annum. Tuition fees charged to foreign students at other educational institutions will vary.

There are a few foreign universities based in London, including the American International University in London and New York University's London campus. Several American universities have an exchange program with the various colleges that form the University of London, giving American students yet another way to study here.

# HEALTH

Although we love to moan about the state of health care in the United Kingdom, when compared internationally it becomes clear that the care provided here is pretty good (even if it's not as thorough as that in France). In the United Kingdom, most health care is provided through a public health service—the National Health Service. This provides health care to all permanent residents of the United Kingdom and is *free* at the point of use, with the cost covered by general taxes and National Insurance contributions. However, here in England we do pay something toward the cost of dental and ophthalmic services, long-term care, and prescriptions. One consequence of the devolution of power to the individual countries that make up the United Kingdom is that the charges for health care services vary depending on the country. The United Kingdom also has private medical health care, which is paid for through medical insurance, and about 12 percent of the people have some sort of private medical insurance, often as a job perk. To qualify for free NHS treatment you must be considered to be "ordinarily resident" here. You will not qualify for free primary care or non-emergency hospital treatment if you are not considered to be a resident of the United Kingdom, so you should organize some private insurance to cover you during any visits and until you are settled here and can register with an NHS general practitioner.

© DAVID HOLT

London is blessed with several leading hospitals, including several highly regarded specialist ones. This makes it easier to get specialist medical care here in the capital, and you shouldn't have to travel too far to the hospital. This is not always the case elsewhere in the country, where people may well have to travel some distance (perhaps even to London) to get specialist treatment. Also, in contrast to many other areas of the United Kingdom, in London access to both NHS and private medical care is readily available. Many doctors offer private health services on Harley Street in Westminster (home to the medical profession since Victorian times) and other streets nearby.

## National Health Service



The National Health Service (NHS) is the United Kingdom's free public health system and was formed back in 1948. It was created as part of the sweeping reforms introduced by the Labour government when it came to power after World War II. At the core of the NHS's ideology is the aim to provide a comprehensive and universal health care system that is free at the point of access for British residents. Providing they can prove that they are resident here, immigrants to the United Kingdom can also use NHS services.

There are two main points of access to the NHS. First, there is the primary care provided by a general practitioner (GP) at a local surgery (doctor's office) or walk-in clinic for minor illnesses. Second, there is treatment at a hospital as an emergency patient. US expats who are working or studying in London should be able to register with an NHS general practitioner if they can prove that they are an "ordinary resident" here and that they live locally. However, there are no set guidelines for GPs to follow regarding what is and is not "ordinary resident." To help establish your residency, you may be asked to provide some form of ID: a National Insurance number, a copy of your visa that allows you to live and work in the United Kingdom, or documentation from your employer stating that you will be working in the United Kingdom for a few years. Students need their Tier 4 visa allowing them to live and study here and maybe a letter from their university. In either case, you may need proof of your address (such as a long-term tenancy agreement or utility bill).

On the NHS website (www.nhs.uk/NHSEngland), you can find information about health services near where you live, including general practitioners (GPs). You may also want to ask a local friend which "GP's surgery" (doctor's office) they are registered with and if they would recommend them. To register with a local GP, you should contact the surgery and ask if they are taking on new patients and what is needed to be added to their list of patients. When you register at the GP's, you'll be asked to fill in a GMS1 form. You may also be asked to provide a bit of information about yourself and to make an appointment with the nurse for a health check. You may also need the relevant documentation to prove that you are resident in the United Kingdom. It will be up to the GP to decide whether to accept you. If they don't, the GP does not have to give a reason for their rejection. If you would prefer to be treated privately, you may be able to find a GP to take you on as a private patient; whether this will be covered by insurance will depend on the type of policy you have.

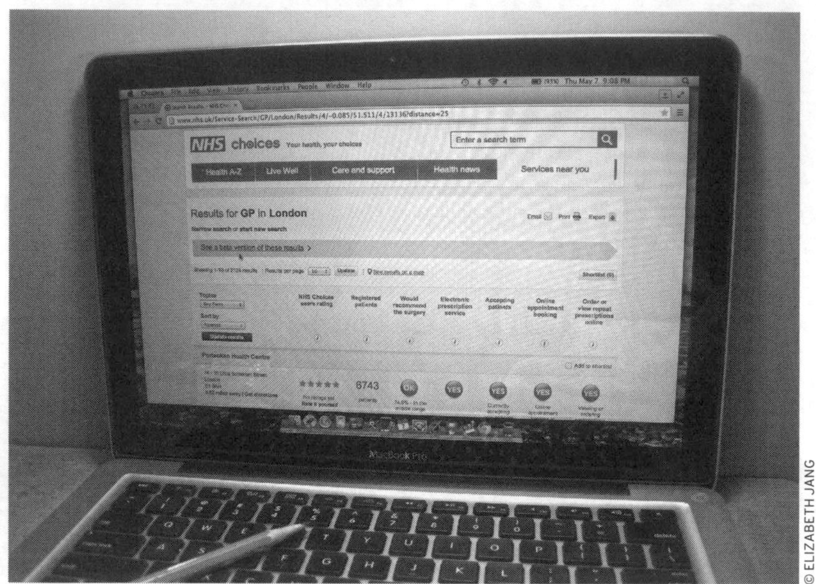




You can search the NHS website for a GP near you.



Emergency medical treatment is provided at NHS hospitals. It is up to the hospital to decide whether it will charge you for the treatment or any follow-up care. If you are registered with a doctor and have an NHS number, then your emergency hospital treatment should be free. If you don't have an NHS number because you haven't registered with a GP yet, but need hospital treatment, you should get this free of charge, providing you can prove that you are legally living and working in the United Kingdom.

If you're planning to study full-time in London for more than six months, then you will be eligible for free medical treatment with the NHS by a GP or in a hospital. However, your partner and any children will not and will require private health coverage. If your course of study is for exactly six months, then you may be treated by the NHS on a temporary resident basis if you have an urgent health problem. Those studying for three months or less will not be eligible for the NHS service. In these circumstances, you should have some sort of private medical coverage. For more information on the National Health Service, visit the website of the Department of Health (www.gov.uk/government/organisations/department-of-health) and the NHS's own website (www.nhs.uk).

# Private Health Care

Of course, the National Health Service isn't the only type of medical care here—there is also a thriving private medical care system with numerous hospitals and clinics. One big advantage of private medical care is that it gives you some say in when and where your treatment will take place, as well as in choosing your medical practitioner. Depending on which type of private medical coverage you have, you may be able to go to a specialist directly, such as a pediatrician. How much you'll be expected to pay for any prescriptions or vaccinations depends on the plan.

Popular British providers of private medical care include BUPA, PPP, and Standard Life. Often private medical insurance is an added perk provided by UK employers. If you've moved to London through an intra-company transfer, you may be able to extend your employer-sponsored American health insurance to cover you in the United Kingdom. Try checking with your human resources department or relocation manager to see if this is possible or to find out if private UK health insurance will be included in the package. Even if your employer doesn't offer private medical coverage or you will be self-employed, you can still take out private medical insurance for you and your family.

Private medical insurance in the United Kingdom isn't cheap, and most British people rely on the NHS service. When looking at private medical insurance in the United Kingdom remember that some policies are designed just to supplement the NHS service, so that people can get hospital treatment a bit faster or have a private hospital room, while using their NHS GP for regular or emergency care. As an expat, you may find that an international health insurance policy suits your needs best, as it may allow you to go directly to a private specialist consultant (such as a pediatrician) without needing a GP's referral. You'll find a list of private doctors and clinics for visiting Americans on the US Embassy's website (http://london.usembassy.gov).

# Types of Medical Care

## NHS DIRECT

The NHS has a telephone advice service (dial 111); you can also find out about local GPs, dentists, and hospital and emergency care services on its website (www.nhs.uk). The telephone service allows you to speak to a nurse to get non-emergency medical advice for particular symptoms or medical treatments. While getting an accurate diagnosis over the phone isn't always straightforward, sometimes all you need is a bit of reassurance that you don't need to worry about your child's high fever or that you really should see a doctor about your recurring heartburn. Ideally you should be registered with an NHS GP to use the NHS phone service (you may be asked for your GP's details so your records are kept up-to-date), though anyone with Internet access should be able to use the website (www.nhsdirect.nhs.uk).

## HOSPITALS AND CLINICS

London has numerous hospitals, some of which enjoy a global reputation, such as the Great Ormond Street Hospital for Sick Children, Moorfield's Eye Hospital, and St. Bartholomew Hospital (the oldest hospital in Britain—founded in 1123!). There are both NHS and private hospitals available, and many NHS hospitals offer private wards, which give the patient a bit more in the way of home comforts. Certainly NHS rooms tend to be basic and may be communal. If you are hospitalized in an NHS hospital, you may find that you are in a ward with several other people. You may have just a curtain around the bed for privacy, and the bathroom may be at the other end of the corridor. By comparison, a private single hospital room will be much more comfortable, offering an en-suite bathroom and personal TV.



If you have an accident and need emergency treatment, go straight to the hospital or dial 999 for an ambulance. Not all hospitals have emergency (A&E, or "accident and emergency") wards, though there might be a minor injuries unit (for sprains, fractures, and minor emergencies) at a small local hospital. These can be a godsend, especially for children, as the treatment tends to be much faster than at large emergency units. Walk-in centers are another option for minor ailments.

If you develop a condition that requires specialist medical treatment, your GP will refer you on to a "consultant" at a local hospital. So, for example, when I became pregnant I was referred to an OB/GYN at my local hospital and I attended the maternity clinic there. You should also know that, in the United Kingdom, general practitioners are referred to as "doctors," while specialist consultants (such as OB/GYNs) are referred to by Mr., Mrs., or Ms. as appropriate. Sometimes there are long waiting lists for

© KAREN WHITE

Sometimes an ambulance bicycle can be the fastest way to respond to an emergency.

certain specialist treatments, which is why occasionally people choose to go the private route. A few years ago my mother-in-law needed to have a cataract operation. She had already had one eye done on the NHS, but for the second one she decided to have it done privately so that she could plan when and where it would be done.

Unlike in the United States, where people may go directly to specialist doctors, here in the United Kingdom most specialist treatment is carried out by consultants at NHS hospitals, so you need a GP's referral first. If you are wondering about pediatric care for your children, this is usually carried out by your local NHS GP, and you are only referred to an NHS pediatrician if your child requires more specialist care. For example, my asthmatic son was referred to a specialist pediatric allergies and asthma clinic at our local NHS hospital. Now that his condition is under control he is monitored by our local GP.



## PHARMACIES AND PRESCRIPTIONS

You'll find pharmacies ("chemists") on most high streets, with the larger ones selling makeup, perfume, etc., and some even offer an optician. You can get over-the-counter medicine for several common complaints, such as minor eye infections and yeast infections. If in doubt, ask to speak to the pharmacist, who should be able to advise if there is a suitable over-the-counter treatment available.

In England adults must pay something toward their NHS prescriptions, although contraception prescriptions are free of charge. Children under 16 and full-time students up to the age of 18 do not have to pay for prescriptions, nor do people over the age of 60 or those with a medical exemption. At the moment the charge for a prescription is £8.05 (around US$12.88) per medication, though this will probably increase in the future.

Your US prescription will not apply in the United Kingdom, so you will need to see a UK doctor for a repeat prescription. It's a good idea to get a copy of your US medical records and bring them with you as part of the move, especially if you have an ongoing medical condition that requires treatment.

## DENTAL CARE

The NHS does provide some dental care, but its aim is to just keep the teeth and gums healthy, so it will not cover the cost of cosmetic dentistry. The service is only free to some residents, such as children under 18, full-time students under the age of 19, and pregnant women. For the rest of the population there is a reduced cost for dental care, with an upper limit on the amount payable for a course of treatment. Here in London the majority of dentists are private, and it can be very hard to find a dentist, especially a good one, who will take you on as an NHS patient. For help with finding a good dentist, you could try asking a colleague to recommend a dentist or ask someone else whose opinion you value. You can also look online at the NHS's website for a local dentist.

Like many Europeans, the British aren't that bothered by their dental care. However, orthodontists and cosmetic dentistry are becoming more and more popular, and it's not uncommon to see teenagers with braces. It shouldn't be too difficult to find a dentist that offers orthodontic treatments, and there are a few orthodontic clinics in town. Occasionally the NHS will cover the cost of braces if the bite is very badly aligned; your dentist should be able to provide more guidance.

## EYE CARE

Eye tests are carried out by either a registered ophthalmic optician (an "optometrist") or an ophthalmic practitioner. Once again the NHS will provide free eye care (including some types of glasses) to people who are registered as blind, children under 16, or full-time students under the age of 19. People over the age of 60, those with diabetes or glaucoma (or over the age of 40 and with a family member with these conditions), and people on social benefits also get free eye care. In England, everyone else must pay a fee for their eye tests and glasses or contact lenses.

Just about every high street and many shopping malls have opticians. After your eye test, the optician will give you a prescription, though you don't have to buy your glasses or contacts from them. Sometimes the optician will throw in the cost of the eye test if you get your glasses or lenses from them. There are also several private laser eye clinics in London, if this strikes your fancy.



# Preventative Medicine

As the saying goes, "prevention is better than a cure," so you may want to be proactive about your (and your family's) health and well-being while you are in London. Although getting an annual check-up with a doctor in the UK isn't as prevalent for the young as it is in the United States, dentists and opticians do offer this service. Nevertheless, you should still be able to get the preventative medical treatment you are after, be it an annual flu jab or contraception and STD advice from your GP or a clinic. Also, alternative medicine is thriving here in London and you should find numerous therapies available.

## VACCINATIONS

You shouldn't need to get any vaccinations to travel to the United Kingdom; just make sure your (and your family's) tetanus and MMR (measles, mumps, and rubella) immunizations are up-to-date. You may also want to get a flu jab if you're arriving during the season (November to April). Although schools in the United Kingdom do not require that children's vaccinations be up-to-date, you may want to bring a copy of their medical and vaccination records with you to show your GP.

Children registered with a GP are vaccinated free of charge for most of the same illnesses in the United Kingdom as in the United States, although the United Kingdom doesn't yet vaccinate against chickenpox. If you are keen to have your children vaccinated for this, you should contact your GP to see if they will do it and how much it will cost. The latest vaccination to be introduced in the United Kingdom is the one to protect against papilloma virus (HPV), and it is being given to 14-year-old girls (usually at school) assuming their parents give permission. If you are worried about keeping up-to-date with your vaccinations, contact your GP and they will organize a booster, if necessary.

London is one of the world's major travel hubs, and it is very easy to get a plane from here to some of the most exotic locations in the world. If your travel plans include a trip to some far-flung corner of the world while you are here, then you may well need travel shots or malaria medicine. Be sure to find out what vaccination you may need well in advance of your trip and then contact your GP to see if they can help and to find out how much it will cost.

## SEXUALLY TRANSMITTED DISEASES

Sexually transmitted diseases (STDs) are a concern anywhere in the world, and London is no exception. The highest rates for reported STDs are among young adults, aged 15 to 24; the most common and fastest-spreading disease is chlamydia. Cases of gonorrhea, genital herpes, warts, and syphilis are also on the rise. Approximately 100,000 people in the United Kingdom live with HIV. Exercise the same care and safety measures in the United Kingdom as you would in the United States. Condoms are available in pharmacies and supermarkets (sometimes even in a pub through a vending machine)—finding one shouldn't be difficult. If you are concerned that you have a sexually transmitted disease, see your GP or visit one of the specialist walk-in STD clinics in London.



## ALTERNATIVE THERAPIES

There seems to be no end to the range of complementary medical treatment you can get in London: everything from Chinese medicine and acupuncture to naturopathy and Ayurvedic medicine, and loads more. Homeopathy also has a strong following in London; the capital is home to Europe's largest and only public sector provider of complementary medicine, the Royal London Hospital for Integrated Medicine. This NHS trust hospital provides a range of complementary medicine, from allergy and nutritional medicine to complementary cancer care and musculoskeletal treatment. Numerous

© KAREN WHITE

an alternative health center in Belsize Park

jogging along the River Thames



private alternative medicine clinics offer everything from osteopathy, chiropractic therapy, and physiotherapy to Pilates and Alexander Technique, to name but a few.

## FITNESS

### Yoga Centers

If you are looking for something that can improve your well-being and fitness, as well as help you to relax, then you may want to give yoga a try. There are yoga centers all around London, and you can choose from numerous types of yoga, from Hatha and Ashtanga to the hot and steamy Bikram. Yoga is very popular with London's fashionable mothers and mothers-to-be (known as "yummy-mummies"). Many yoga centers also offer other exercise classes, such as Pilates—equally popular with trendy Londoners looking to keep fit.

### Sports Clubs

It's fairly easy to find a local gym where you can "keep fit." Some employers will even help cover the cost of a gym membership. There are numerous public and private gyms across town, some with swimming pools or squash courts. Private gym memberships can be expensive, especially for those that function more like a country club, with tennis courts, dining, swim lessons for the kids, and social opportunities. Some of the large gym chains include Esporta, Virgin Active, David Lloyd, and the Harbour Club. Amenities vary; sport clubs with a swimming pool are a bit of a premium. Local councils also offer "leisure centers," and some can be fairly nice, offering indoor swimming, weight rooms, and a range of exercise classes—you may even find an indoor rock-climbing wall.

### Outdoor Activities

If indoor classes and gyms aren't for you, don't despair. One of the best things about London is the abundance of local green spaces and parks where you can run, jog, or take an energetic walk. If you enjoy rowing, tennis, or golf, you'll find a few clubs that you can join. If you love English-style horse riding there are a few stables in Greater London—usually to the north or west of town. Astonishingly, you can also ride in Hyde Park—assuming you can afford it.

Believe it or not, bike riding (or "cycling" as it is called here) is quite popular, even though you take your life in your hands to brave London's busy streets on a bike. Just a few words of warning: The sidewalk is for pedestrians and not bike riders, so stay in the road (young children are an exception), and bike riders must obey the rules of the road, such as stopping at a red light. Many of London's parks are mainly for pedestrians, so stick to the designated "cycle path" in the parks where cycling is allowed, such as Hampstead Heath and the Royal Parks.



## Environmental Factors

With more than 8 million people packed into 600 square miles (1,550 square kilometers), it should be no surprise that London suffers from noise, light, and air pollution. Litter can also be a problem, as there isn't an attitude of "zero tolerance" to littering that you get in France or the United States. We used to live near a small corner shop, and our front garden was always filled with empty candy wrappers and potato chip bags dropped by teenage kids on their way to and from school. The really frustrating thing was that there were garbage cans nearby where they could have easily dumped their garbage, but instead they just dropped it in the street. Perhaps they were just going through a rebellious phase, but the result needlessly left our street covered with bits of rubbish.

### AIR QUALITY

Just speak to any asthma sufferer and you will soon hear all about London's poor air quality. Although the authorities are trying their best to improve the air quality, London is struggling to reduce the amount of tiny particulates (called PM10) in the air to within the limits set by the European Union (EU). These, combined with high levels of nitrogen oxide, have given London the dubious accolade of having the worst air quality in Europe.

Two roads in particular suffer from very poor air quality due to their heavy traffic congestion: the A501 road, which stretches from Marylebone to City Road where it connects with Old Street; and Oxford Street in the West End, with its plethora of diesel buses, taxis, and high levels of nitrogen dioxide.

London has taken steps to improve its air quality, such as introducing a congestion charge for private vehicles in central London. By 2020, the city plans to introduce an ultra-low emission zone in central London. It is also implementing a zero emissions policy for newly licensed taxis, as well as further tightening the low emission restrictions for trucks and buses in Greater London.

## WATER QUALITY

Although it hasn't always been the case, thankfully London's water quality is now very good—if not the best in England. As in much of southern England, the water in London is very "hard," so you will need to de-chalk your kettles, irons, and coffeemakers on a regular basis, but at least the water is fine to drink (especially after it has been filtered). One problem with London's water isn't the quality but the age of the system. Most of London's underground pipework is Victorian cast iron piping, which has degenerated over the years, making it prone to leaks and even major bursts of the water main pipes where whole streets can be flooded. Since 2007, Thames Water (the water provider for the London region) has started to replace the antiquated Victorian pipes with plastic ones. This leads to major road works, and while the inconvenience makes Londoners moan, we all know that our leaking water pipes must be upgraded, and soon!



## SMOKING

The United Kingdom has had strict anti-smoking legislation in enclosed public places since 2007, so don't light up "a fag" in a pub, restaurant, or anywhere else that is inside. The reason behind the ban is to protect the health of others from the effects of secondary smoke and to deter smokers. The government's actions to deter smokers also included restricting advertising and displays of tobacco products in some stores. Despite the appearance of smokers huddled together outside their office entrances for a nicotine fix, there seems to be a gentle decline in the number of smokers. Those who do smoke can find many pubs and restaurants with outdoor tables where smokers can drink or dine while having an occasional cigarette (even if London doesn't always have the weather for it). The use of electronic cigarettes seems to be on the rise, though there can be restrictions on use in public spaces.

The UK has strict public smoking policies.

The minimum age for buying cigarettes and electronic cigarettes is 18 (the same as for drinking alcohol), and the government levies a heavy duty on tobacco. Under current UK legislation the smoking of cannabis is illegal (be it indoors or outside). That said, a mix of hash and tobacco in a "spiff" is fairly common, especially among British teens. Oddly enough, statistics suggest that London's teenagers are less likely to be taking drugs or drinking to excess than their suburban counterparts.

## Cholera and London's Sewers

For centuries London had been plagued by periodic outbreaks of cholera, causing the deaths of thousands of residents. Back in the mid-19th century, it was commonly thought that the cause of cholera was miasma (a vapor). However, an enterprising doctor (Dr. John Snow—one of the forefathers of modern epidemiology) found that, instead of a vapor, cholera was caused by poor sanitation and contaminated drinking water. You see, at the time, the River Thames (the main source of drinking water) was also an open sewer. Once this link was established it was clear that Parliament would have to act, but it dragged its feet due to lack of funding.

During the summer of 1858, Parliament was finally forced to act as the stench of untreated human waste in the Thames made life in London unbearable. After the Great Stink of 1858, the government conceded something needed to be done urgently, and works finally began on a modern sewerage system for London. The project fell to the civil engineer Joseph Bazalgette, who designed an extensive underground sewer system that moved London's waste out to the Thames Estuary, downstream of the population. Once there, it would be pumped up and held in a reservoir until it could be washed out to sea at high tide. Construction lasted for six years and created 450 miles (724 kilometers) of underground sewer mains. For the most part gravity forced the sewage eastward, although some pumping stations were installed. The Thames Embankment, along the north edge of the Thames through central London, was the result of these sewer works. Underground it incorporated the sewers from West London, as well as the part of the Circle line, while aboveground there is a wide road, some gardens, and a paved sidewalk along the river's edge. When you walk along the sidewalk next to the river, you have no idea what is flowing beneath your feet.

During the last century much of London's sewer system has been expanded. Today waste is no longer washed out to sea but goes to one of the Thames Water's 351 treatment works spread out across the region. As part of a system update, the water company is replacing London's Victorian sewers with those fit for the 21st century.

DAILY LIFE

# Access for People with Disabilities

London has made a concerted effort to improve access for those with a disability, through changes to its building regulations for public buildings and public transport. This isn't always easy given the age of many of the buildings and the Underground network. The Equality Act aims to protect people with disabilities and prevent disability discrimination. It provides legal rights for people with disabilities in a number of areas, such as employment, education, access to goods, services, and facilities. However, disabled access building codes only apply to recently built buildings.

The good news is that most buses have been fitted with a ramp to allow wheelchair users to get on and off the bus, and the Docklands Light Railway also provides access for wheelchair users. However, much of the Underground network uses escalators and stairs to get to and from the train platforms, although a few stations offer elevators.

Transport for London plans to improve access for wheelchair users and is introducing more step-free access at stations. For more information, visit Transport for London's website (www.tfl.gov.uk/transport-accessibility).

The United Kingdom runs a national scheme for disabled parking called the Blue Badge Scheme. Registering for this will give you a badge that you can display on the dashboard, which will give you free parking in some places and allow you to park in disabled bays. Parking can be a problem in central London, which is why some boroughs also have their own badges for residents with disabilities. For more information contact your local borough.



# Safety

London is a fairly safe place, providing that you exercise a bit of street knowledge and are careful with your smartphone, purse, and wallet. Pickpockets and muggers are your main concern; try to be aware of your surroundings, especially at ATMs or out at night. Cell phones in particular are at risk; someone on a bike or a scooter could grab it out of your hands while you are using it to text for directions. Pickpockets can be a problem in London, especially in crowded areas such as markets or on the Tube; however, violent crimes are rare and are mainly gang-related. While not unheard of, rape and sexual harassment are unlikely—though Rohypnol dosed into drinks in clubs does happen, so always keep an eye on your drink. When taking a taxi, use only black cabs or a licensed minicab, which must be pre-ordered.

© GEORGE REDGRAVE

London Transport Police

London has pockets of social housing throughout, sometimes even in fairly affluent areas. Theft can be troublesome in both wealthy and low-income areas. Just be sure to exercise common sense, make sure your home is secure, and be aware of your surroundings and possessions when you are on the streets—your best defense is prevention.

If you have been a victim of a crime you should contact the police to report it. You should call 999 if it is an emergency or dial 0300/123 1212 for non-emergencies.

# EMPLOYMENT

You may think that all it takes to start a new life in London is to buy your tickets, pack your bags, and away you go . . . leaving the question of gainful employment until you arrive. Unfortunately, life isn't that simple, and it is actually illegal to travel to London as just a tourist with the express purpose of finding a job. That's not to say that it never happens—it does—it is just that it is technically against the law to job hunt with a tourist visa. However, if you are lucky enough to have British or EU dual nationality, things are different. You can just jump on a plane and start to look for a job in London. Everyone else, however, will need to become eligible for employment in the United Kingdom by getting the right visa first. Now that the United Kingdom has tightened up its visa rules, for most people this means getting a job in London before you move or being transferred to the London office by your American employer. If you are incredibly wealthy and have an entrepreneurial bent, then you may be able to move over here to start or invest in a business.

# Work Opportunities

So where do you start? There are two routes to getting a work visa for the United Kingdom. Which one you'll qualify for depends on your education, skills, and talent. If you are highly skilled, well educated, and a world-renowned expert in your field, you could try for a Tier 1 visa for exceptionally skilled workers, investors, or entrepreneurs. The Tier 1 visa will allow you to start up your own business or become employed while you are in London. Given the United Kingdom's rigorous rules and tight quotas for Tier 1 visas, however, your most likely option for finding a job in London will be through sponsored employment with a Tier 2 visa. Yet even Tier 2 visas are by no means a walkover. You still need to be well educated and skilled, as well as on a good salary. You will need to work in one of the professions on the Tier 2 Shortage Occupation List so that your potential employer has a case for sponsoring you—and even then they may prefer to use someone from the EU. (For details about visa requirements, visit the UK Visas and Immigration website at www.gov.uk/government/organisations/uk-visas-and-immigration.) By far the easiest way to get a job in London is to transfer here with your American employer.



## INTRA-COMPANY TRANSFERS

As one of the world's most important financial centers, London has numerous American multinational companies. If you already work for an investment bank, you could try to put out some tentacles to learn about suitable vacancies in the London offices. Even if you don't work for an investment bank, there may be another US-based multinational that you could work for, perhaps a media organization or IT company—any firm with a London office. However, your employer will need to prove that they need you to fulfill a role that a British national isn't able to do. While the government recognizes that multinationals want to shift employees around the world to meet their business objectives, they do not want to allow this flexibility at the expense of its native workforce.

The first step to moving to London via an intra-company transfer will be to have a job with a multinational company with an office in London and to work for them at a fairly high level for at least one year. In addition to investment banks, there are other American organizations with London offices, such as large accountancy and legal firms, retailers, media, and IT organizations. If you are really determined to work in London this way (and depending on your skills and experience, it may be the only option open to you), then do some leg work—find out what options are open to you and plan ahead. At the same time, you need to be realistic. Work visas are not given to manual or secretarial positions, or employees on a low salary, except perhaps for a graduate trainee's visa (assuming that your American employer offers such a scheme). Another option will be to work as your US employer's sole representative in the UK (though you will need to be at a high level in the organization) or to be an employee of a US news agency.

### Relocation Packages

If your skills are a valuable asset to your employer and they need you (and those skills) in the London office, usually your employer will try to encourage you to move by easing the transition with a relocation package. When the world's economy was booming, American expats could expect to receive generous relocation packages. However, today's relocation packages are much more moderate. Basically there are two elements to a relocation package: to cover the additional expense incurred by the move and to help with the move and settling in. Typically a relocation package will include the cost of airfare, moving company fees, and temporary housing, and it may include getting a relocation company to help with the move. If you are lucky, an annual trip to the United States will be thrown in for good measure. As London is more expensive than the United States, a relocation package for here may include a cost of living adjustment (COLA). If you are being paid in dollars, you may be given some exchange rate protection as well. Some other things you may want to ask for include private health coverage, a housing stipend, and a lump sum payment to help with the cost of electrical goods or furniture. You may even want transportation and school fees covered. Just what you end up with will depend upon negotiations between you and your employer: what they offer versus what you can winkle out of them. Don't forget that you will also need help when you head back to the States, so make sure repatriation is included as part of the package.



## GENERAL EMPLOYMENT WITH SPONSORING EMPLOYER

If you don't want to (or can't) transfer to London through your American employer, you will have to try your luck with a British employer and get a general Tier 2 work visa. To receive one of these visas, you must be sponsored by a British business; you'll have to get the job first, though, by applying to an advertised role. If a British employer offers a job to someone requiring a Tier 2 work visa, they must prove that they were unable to find a qualified EU national or UK resident to fulfill the role. Meeting this criterion often proves too arduous for a busy company—many do not bother with non-EU applicants and wait instead until they can offer a British or EU resident the position.

It is easier for an employer to sponsor your Tier 2 visa if you work in a profession where there is a national shortage, such as those detailed by the Tier 2 Shortage Occupation List (www.gov.uk/government/publications/tier-2-shortage-occupation-list-from-6-april-2013). All of the roles on the list are highly specialized—you must work in a particular field within a specific industry to qualify. Some of the roles currently on the list include production managers and directors in the field of mining and energy production, geotechnical engineers within the field of construction-related ground engineering, and drilling engineers for the oil and gas industry. Electrical engineers specializing in the field of electrical transmission and distribution are also in demand. Medical professionals, including neonatal intensive care units and radiographers, are also listed. Other in-demand professions include high school teachers of math, chemistry, or physics. Within media, technical directors of visual effects and 2D/3D computer animation for film, television, or video games sectors are also on the shortage list. If you are an exceptionally talented and well-paid chef, you may also be able to find employment (and get a UK work visa). You will still need to achieve the correct level of points (based on your education, language skills, salary, and so on) to qualify for a general Tier 2 visa.

It's worth noting that some elite sportspeople and ministers of religion can qualify for a Tier 2 visa. Their work permit will still need to be sponsored by an employer, and their skills and training, education, and knowledge of English must give them enough points to qualify for this sponsored visa.

## NON-SPONSORED EMPLOYMENT

If you are a world-renowned expert in your field, have millions of pounds to invest in a UK business, or have £500,000 to invest in setting up a UK business, then you could try to apply for a Tier 1 visa. The UK government awards only 1,000 Tier 1 visas each year, but if you feel you have what it takes, then by all means apply for a Tier 1 work permit. However, they may be as scarce as hen's teeth.



## STUDENT EMPLOYMENT

If you are a full-time student at a recognized British institution of higher learning and are studying for your bachelor's degree or higher, then you may be able to work during term time on the weekends and full-time during the summer break. If you are unsure whether or not you can work, check your visa. Although a weekend job won't allow you to support yourself completely while studying, it may help to cover some bills or a clothing allowance. Many students work in retail shops in the capital, be it well-known American brands or local stores.

© WILLIAM PERUGINI/123RF.COM

Your new job in London may be in a skyscraper.

# Self-Employment

As a self-employed Yank based in London, I sympathize with anyone who has a similar ambition. I really just fell into the role as something I could do part-time and still be able to care for my family. More importantly, I had already established my residency in London. Unfortunately, those planning to move to London and start their own business will probably need to get the ever-elusive Tier 1 work permit for entrepreneurs. It is likely that getting one of these will be very difficult, but if you think you have the right qualities and have the required funds this is one avenue open to you.

Another group of expats who may be interested in self-employment are the "trailing spouses." If you are moving to London with your spouse because he or she has been relocated by a US employer or has a sponsored British employer, you may want to become self-employed while you are living in the United Kingdom, assuming that your visa allows you to work here as well. This means you can still keep your hand in and further your career, even though you have moved to London. Of course, whether this will work for someone depends upon their profession.

## BUSINESS CONSIDERATIONS

If you plan to start your own business in the United Kingdom you will need to decide how you want to trade (the legal form of your business). Here there are three different legal forms for a self-employed business. They can be:

- A sole trader—the simplest way of starting a business, but you are liable if something goes wrong.
- A partnership—similar to sole traders with the exception that two or more people run the business.
- A limited company—similar to being incorporated in the United States, with the business being completely separate from the people who run it.

You must decide which way of trading is most appropriate for your business. Some companies offering freelance contract work will only do business with a limited company, so you may have to go that route if you plan on being a freelance consultant. To do this you need to register your company with Companies House (which can be done online at www.companieshouse.gov.uk). You will find more information about starting a limited company and becoming self-employed on the UK government's business link website (www.gov.uk/browse/business). It is a good idea to get some advice from a British-trained accountant and solicitor before you embark on your new enterprise, especially if you decide to become a limited company.

### Accounting and Taxes

If you are self-employed you must let the tax department (Her Majesty's Revenue and Customs, or HMRC) know. You may also need to register for value-added tax (VAT).

This is the United Kingdom's sales tax, which is levied on some goods and services and should be paid to HMRC. Whether you as a self-employed person will have to pay VAT depends on the type of business you have and how much it earns. To register for UK taxes for the self-employed and learn more about what you will need to do, go to the HMRC website (www.hmrc.gov.uk/selfemployed). Just as in the States, you will need to be very careful about your bookkeeping and accounting records. This will be important for your personal taxes and National Insurance contributions, as well as those of your business.

### Insurance

Another consideration will be to get certain types of insurance. Which type of insurance you need depends on what type of business you are running and how it is set up. Insurance that you may need to take out includes public liability insurance so that you are covered in case a member of the public is injured or their property is damaged as a result of carelessness by you or an employee. If you plan on employing people you must have employer's liability insurance to provide some protection in case an employee is hurt (or becomes ill) as a result of their job. You may also want to protect your office, equipment, or stock with specialist insurance.



### Starting the Business

As with any business start-up, do your research and develop a clear business plan. Make sure that you have enough funding to get the business rolling and to cover your living expenses. If you've never started a business before, plan to do a lot of research before launching any enterprise in the United Kingdom. For more information about starting a business in the United Kingdom, the government website (www.gov.uk/starting-up-a-business); the Citizens Advice Bureau website (www.adviceguide.org.uk), which covers self-employment; and the Professional Contractors Group (PCG; www.ipse.co.uk) are all good starting points.

One factor to bear in mind is your business's location. Prices for commercial property in Central London are expensive; if you don't need to be centrally located, save your money and look for a property slightly out of town. You could also use your home for your business; if you are renting, check the terms of your lease agreement to ensure that this is allowed.

### Business Practices

For the most part, business practices are much the same in the United Kingdom as they are in the States. You may find the British slightly more formal, especially if they are a bit older. Most people will shake hands upon introduction, though they won't necessarily at subsequent meetings. If someone has a title, be sure to use it—they may be used to a bit of reverence—at least until you are told otherwise. Time-keeping is important to the British, so always be there on time or call if you're going to be a few minutes late. Business cards are often politely exchanged, then quickly put in a pocket with just a cursory glance. Dress as you would in the United States, or slightly more formally, with dark business suits when appropriate.

# The Job Hunt

So, now that you've established how you are going to get your work permit for the United Kingdom, your next step will be to find a job to make your dream come true. You should start by revamping your résumé so that it is following the standard layout of the British curriculum vitae (CV). Start your CV with your contact details and your objective, and then list your key achievements and skills, following with your work experience (or academic achievements if you don't have much work experience). You do not need to include your date of birth on your CV, nor do you need a picture. Try to keep it all on one page if possible. You can find several examples of a British CV online.



The Internet has dramatically changed international job-hunting, and it would be a good place to start your search. Numerous websites list jobs in London and the United Kingdom, such as www.jobserve.co.uk, www.efinancialcareers.co.uk, www.jobsite.co.uk, and www.topjobs.co.uk. Several British newspapers also advertise jobs, such as the *Guardian* (www.guardian.co.uk/jobs) and *Daily Telegraph* (www.jobs.telegraph.co.uk). Particular sectors are catered for on different days, such as medical and health vacancies on Wednesday in the *Guardian,* so scan through these websites on a regular basis. You could, of course, turn to a recruitment consultant to help you land a job in London, and it is well worth registering with a few that specialize in your sector. Networking can also be a great way to get a job, be it through LinkedIn (www.linkedin.com) or your own contacts. You may also want to contact FOCUS Information Services (www.focus-info.org/career), which can provide specialist job-hunting help for positions in London and elsewhere in the United Kingdom.

## INTERVIEWS

There is hardly anything in life as stressful as a job interview. It is always a battle to come across as intelligent and informed, even though your stomach is in knots and your hands may be shaking. The interview process is much the same here as in the United States—giving both you and the prospective employer a chance to size each other up and determine if you are right for the job. You should dress formally, in a dark business suit with a tie or skirt and low heels, as appropriate. Although you will be nervous, you should enunciate your words correctly and avoid Americanisms. Don't try to put on a British accent (unless it is an audition for an acting role); it will be obvious that you are faking it.

In the interview you should explain your experience, skills, and qualifications, highlighting why you are perfect for the job. Don't forget that you may need to put this information into context. Don't assume that the interviewer knows that much about the company, organization, or institution where you gained your skills. Ask how much they know about relevant facts and briefly fill in any pertinent information. Bear in mind that even some well-known brands in the United States are unheard of here in the United Kingdom, so the onus will be on you to give a bit of background highlighting the similarity where possible. I would also warn about coming across as too much of a "know-it-all," as arrogance (especially from foreigners) will not go down well with a British employer. Remember, things will be done differently here, and you want to show that you can adapt to this new environment.

Finally, think carefully about how you answer the ubiquitous question of "Where do you see yourself in five years?" Unless you are going for a casual job or a short-term contract, the employer is going to want some assurances that you plan on remaining in the United Kingdom for some time. Try not to imply that you will only be in the United Kingdom for a limited period. Would you give a job to someone who was only planning on being in town for a few months or was unsure how long they were going to be around? Say that you plan to be here some time or hope to remain indefinitely. I always told employers that my husband is British (he is) and that having lived in both countries we have decided that London is our home, so we have no intention of leaving here—all of which is true. Most employers will be looking for a long-term commitment, so you must be prepared to give them this.



# Labor Laws

The rights of workers here in the United Kingdom are fairly well protected. In fact, I found that one of the most pronounced differences between employment in the United Kingdom and the United States was the difference in guaranteed rights. For example, paid vacation (holiday) entitlement is much more generous here, with other employee rights such as some sick pay or maximum working hours also governed by law.

## EMPLOYMENT BENEFITS

All UK employees should receive from their employer a statement that details information about the role. This includes a brief description about the role, where the employee will work, and the start date of the job. It should also include details about the salary and when the employee will be paid. Here in the United Kingdom, salaries are usually paid by bank transfer on a monthly basis in arrears. So on top of all the expense of setting up home here in London, you may need to work for a month before you get paid. Make sure you have enough saved up to see you through while you settle in to your new home and job. The statement from your employer should also list your holiday entitlement, the hours you need to work, and your sick pay entitlement (and the procedures for your company with regards to this).

### Holiday Entitlement

Without a doubt one of the best perks of a job in the United Kingdom is the statutory annual paid leave. With so much to see and do in Europe, you will probably want to use every last second of your holiday entitlement. Compared to in the States, paid vacation time is quite generous in the United Kingdom—a statutory 28 days per annum for someone working full-time, five days a week. This is just the minimum amount of paid holiday entitlement, and there is every chance that your employer will give you more than this if you are in a fairly senior role. Part-time workers are also entitled to some paid vacation; the amount depends on how many hours you work. The English have eight national holidays, helping to boost your vacation leave even further.

## Maternity and Paternity Rights

Starting or expanding your family while you are overseas can create a whole new set of challenges. As well as getting used to the maternity care provided in the United Kingdom, there is the added problem that some family members might not be nearby, making you feel a bit more isolated. I know my own mother worried because, while she really wanted to be here after the birth of my two children, she also recognized that there wasn't much practical help that she could provide. She couldn't help with errands and shopping, as she didn't know her way around. She also knew that the jet lag would make her a bit less functional for a few days. Moral support and a spare pair of hands were all she could really offer. Thankfully my husband was also around to help with more practical matters.

If you plan to start or extend your family while in London, you may want to know what you can expect in the way of maternity and paternity leave. Fortunately, both of these are statutory rights for UK employees, providing they meet the terms of the qualifying period.

Your employer may have more generous maternity and paternity arrangements in place, so check with your HR department for more details. Also bear in mind that legislation is subject to change. For more information about maternity and paternity rights and adoption leave, visit www.direct.gov.uk.

### MATERNITY LEAVE

As an employee in the United Kingdom, a pregnant woman is entitled to 26 weeks of ordinary maternity leave and a further 26 weeks of maternity leave, giving her one whole year to care for her infant. It doesn't matter how long she has worked for the employer, or whether she is full- or part-time. To get the statutory maternity leave, a pregnant woman must let her employer know at least 15 weeks before the child is due. If she has worked for her employer for 26 weeks by the 15th week before the baby is due, then she should get *paid* leave for 39 weeks. But she will need to let her employer know when she plans to take her maternity leave at least 28 days before the baby is due. She also needs to give them a copy of the maternity certificate provided by her midwife or doctor. It may be best to give them this certificate with her notice for her maternity leave. If a woman doesn't qualify for paid maternity leave, then she may be able to get a maternity allowance. Employees also have the right to have time off for antenatal checkups. Once your maternity leave is finished, your employer must allow you to return to work. You also have the right to the same job (and terms and conditions). However, if your employer can prove that it is not "reasonably practical" for you to return to the same role (for example, if it no longer exists due to restructuring) then you must be offered an alternative position with the same terms and conditions.

As soon as you start your job in London, you will start to build up your holiday entitlement. Just how the entitlement is worked out depends on the system used by your employer, but your holiday entitlement should be made clear in your employment contract. You still need permission from your employer regarding when you can take your vacations and whether any unused entitlement can be carried over into the next leave year. When you leave your job, you should be paid for any unused holidays you have built up.

## Sick Pay

Most minor illnesses or injuries, which only require a day or two off work while you recover, are not a big issue usually—just call in sick or do whatever is required by your contract. However, if you become seriously ill or injured, you should be able to receive

**PATERNITY LEAVE**

Fathers are also entitled to paid leave to help care for their partner and the newborn following the birth or an adoption. This can be a great help to a mother who may be getting by on very little sleep, especially if there are other children to care for in the family. The statutory qualifying period for paternity leave requires the father-to-be to have worked for his employer for more than 26 weeks, by the 15th week before the baby is due. These employees can expect to get a week or two of consecutive paternity leave and may qualify for ordinary paternity leave pay. Your window of opportunity to take your paternity leave is anytime between the child's birth (or adoption date) and 56 days after the birth (or due date if the baby is premature). You don't have to be in a heterosexual partnership to get paternity leave—it also applies to same-sex partnerships as well. If your partner plans to return to work early, you may also be able to share some of their remaining maternity leave to provide child care.

**ADOPTION LEAVE**

If you adopt a UK child while you are employed in the United Kingdom, the statutory adoption leave and pay is similar to maternity leave in that you can get 52 weeks of leave (made up of 26 weeks of ordinary adoption leave followed by 26 weeks of additional adoption leave). You will need to give your employer sufficient proof of your adoption within seven days of being matched with a child, which is usually a matching certificate from your UK adoption agency. If this is not possible you must tell them as soon as you can. If you are adopting from overseas the rules vary slightly, and you will need to get official notification from a central authority confirming your adoption. In England this is done by the Department of Education. If you are adopting a relative from overseas, you may qualify for statutory adoption leave and pay, so long as you have been assessed and deemed to be a suitable adoptive parent. A co-adopter may also be able to get up to 26 weeks' additional paternity leave, in addition to the two week's statutory paternity leave to which they may also be entitled. Unwed heterosexual couples and same-sex couples can adopt children in England, though only one person will qualify for extended adoption leave, while the other will just be able to get 26 days of adoption leave. It should also be pointed out that not all adoptions qualify for statutory adoption leave. You will not qualify for it if you arrange a private adoption, but you will if you have a child through surrogacy. Adopting a stepchild will not qualify you for adoption leave, though your employer may have more generous adoption leave arrangements than the statutory scheme.

some paid sick leave; how much pay you get will depend upon your employment contract. As a minimum, a full-time employee can expect to get statutory sick pay (currently £87.55) for up to 28 weeks. The more senior your role, the better the perks, including paid sick leave (but ask your HR department if you are unsure). Don't be surprised if you must follow particular rules regarding letting your employer know you are ill. This may include immediately providing a medical certificate from your doctor if you are going to be off sick for several days or weeks or calling in by a particular time. You should find more information about paid sick leave in your employment contract.

## Maximum Hours of Work

While not as generous as in France (where the standard number of hours per week is just 35), in the United Kingdom you will usually work at least 38-40 hours per week (usually 9am to 6pm, with an hour for lunch). You also have the right to take a break during the working day and to have some days off during the week. Whether you will get overtime for working more than 40 hours will depend upon your employment contract. There is, however, an upper limit on the maximum number of hours per week you can be required to work, currently 48 hours. Of course you can agree to do more than 48 hours, but this will be an arrangement that you come to with your employer. It also has to be said that in some professions "presenteeism" is the norm, and sometimes employees feel they need to work long hours just to prove their worth or to get through their workload. If you've been drafted into the London office to help with a major business project, you may well have a monstrously heavy workload, but then you probably anticipated this before your arrival. One can only hope that you have the time and energy to enjoy a bit of life in London. At the other end of the scale, if you are on an hourly wage (perhaps as a student with a weekend job), whether you get overtime pay depends upon your employer (and contract). They may set the threshold for overtime pay in excess of what is required by full-time employees (for example, more than 40 hours in a week).



## EMPLOYEES' RIGHTS

The Equality Act of 2010 requires that people are judged by their character, not their race, gender, sexual orientation, religion or belief, age, or disabilities. Rights enshrined by law include not forcing employees to work longer hours than the worker agrees to. Employees must also be given a set amount of notice prior to dismissal (based on length of service) and receive statutory sick pay. Employees have the right to ask for flexible working hours and the right to take unpaid parental leave in case of an emergency. If a company is taken over by another company, the terms of someone's employment cannot be reduced; the worker cannot be dismissed by the new company without a good reason, be it economic or organizational.

If you are laid off (called being "made redundant" here), you can expect to get a compensation payment only if you have been working for the same employer for more than two years. There are fixed rules for the amount you should be given (again based on the length of service), and you can't be made redundant just because you are 65 years old. Employers can dismiss employees for misconduct or their inability to perform their duties as required by their employment contract. In most cases, an employer will give you around one month's notice of your termination, though it may be a bit more at some companies.

The United Kingdom operates a standard minimum wage, based on age, which is the minimum that a worker can be paid. The minimum wage is not that high—just £6.50 per hour if you are more than 20 years old—but it's what you can expect if you work part-time in retail or in a restaurant while you are a student. Some employers will top up your wages with a London Living Allowance to help cover the high cost of living in the capital. Given the high cost of living, the Greater London Authority is encouraging London businesses to pay the London Living Wage (currently £9.15 per hour), though they cannot force employers to pay this rate.

Legislation is subject to change and workers' rights are no exception. When in doubt, contact the Citizens Advice Bureau (www.citizensadvice.org.uk) for more information.

## Trade Unions

The trade union movement is quite strong in the United Kingdom, and as the movement forms part of the basis of the Labour Party, they have real political clout here. Unison, the union representing public servants, is particularly large (with around 1.3 million members) and includes employees from a wide variety of public sector organizations, including the National Health Service, local government, and police and probation services. As you would expect, the union campaigns tirelessly to protect jobs, pay, and pension provisions for all its members, and it defends workers' rights. Other trade unions in Britain are equally committed to protecting their members' interests, although union membership in the private sector has dramatically declined in the past few decades. Generally, unions are not prevalent among management, which is the level at which most Americans will be working in London if they are here with a Tier 2 visa.

# FINANCE

Although the United Kingdom is a fully paid-up member of the European Union, it has not yet relinquished control of its currency and joined the "eurozone." To be honest, it's hard to imagine that happening given the economic troubles within the eurozone. The British are reluctant members of the EU, looking to benefit economically from the union but only on their terms. The financial collapse of some eurozone members, and the subsequent gulf between the prosperous economy of Germany and that of the struggling Greeks, Spanish, Irish, and Portuguese (and the subsequent strain this has put on their shared currency) means that it is unlikely the United Kingdom will join the eurozone anytime soon—if ever.

One fact of life in London is the high cost of living. London is an expensive place to live and work—in fact it is currently *the* most expensive city in the world. One reason that London has knocked Hong Kong off of the list of the world's most expensive cities is the soaring property prices. The high cost of transportation plus the high value of the pound against the dollar has also made London a very expensive place to live. Many everyday expenses, such as rent, food, utilities, gas, transportation, and sales tax (currently 20 percent)—even going to the movies—are generally more expensive in London than they are in most American cities. Be prepared for London to be a much

more expensive place than you are used to. It is a price well worth paying to live in this fabulous city.

## Cost of Living

The cost of living in the United Kingdom is generally quite high, often because of the amount of tax and duty charged on many items. On top of this, prices in London are generally higher than in the rest of the country; the cost of renting in London is more than double that of the rest of the United Kingdom. Certainly if you are coming from a small town in the Midwest, you may be shocked by the high prices in London—but then a spell in New York City would be equally jaw-dropping. Just how much money you will need in London will depend on your tastes and requirements—where you live and how you live, as well as what you are willing to compromise on to make ends meet.

According to the latest findings of an international cost of living comparison for London by Xpatulator, the British capital is now the 12th most expensive place to live as an expat. The data used by Xpatulator to work out the cost of living compares prices in each city for the same quantity and quality of goods and services, which are representative of an expat's lifestyle, using New York as the base. The data collected includes items such as accommodations and utilities, food and fuel, as well as health care and transportation. More importantly, this data may form the basis of any cost of living adjustment provided by your employer in your relocation package. It is important to remember that these comparisons convert prices to dollars, so the level of the exchange rate is important.

So, why is this island so expensive? Taxes and duties tend to be higher here, but there is also another factor at play. Although Britain is a big island, it is nevertheless an island, and it has to import a lot of its food and goods. As you would expect, this tends to push the prices up—just ask any Hawaiian. It seems to me that as it is an island, UK businesses often charge as much as they can get away with. I am forever flabbergasted that I can buy four peaches in France (around 100 miles/160 kilometers away) for less than €3, whereas four peaches here in London will set me back around £5—and I'm talking about the prices in the summer when peaches are in season. The difference is that the peaches here have to be ferried or flown in. So keep this fact in the back of your mind if you are shocked by the prices sometimes charged here.

### BALANCING YOUR BUDGET

Depending on your relocation package or salary, you may find living in London to be a bit of a squeeze at first. To balance the books, you may have to compromise on your lifestyle and accommodations while you are in London. It is likely that accommodations will be your greatest expense. Just how much your accommodations will cost will depend on the usual factors, such as the size of the property, how near it is to town, and the ambience of the neighborhood, as well as the proximity to public transport.

The average monthly rental asking price in the greater London area is more than £1,600 for a two-bedroom flat. This is an average across the city, including areas with social housing as well as more expensive areas, and encompasses properties of different sizes. More importantly, London's rents are currently on the rise and during the past year have increased by around 11 percent on average, and much more in some parts of town. More and more would-be buyers are forced to continue renting, as they are unable to secure a mortgage. The price of an average terraced house in London has increased in value by 20 percent to nearly £789,000. The city is one of the few places in the United Kingdom where property prices are still on the rise.

Another cost that you will need to cover is local property taxes (called council tax). Even if you are renting, you still need to register and pay for this tax, although students in student accommodations are exempt. Unfortunately, this tax isn't just a trifling cost. In 2014-2015, the average council tax in London for an averagely priced property was just under £1,300 for the year. Bear in mind that the council tax in England is based on the value of a property (as valued in 1991). Homes in nicer areas of town (which tend to be where many expats live) may be higher than the average simply because the value of the property when purchased was above average, though population density can also come into play.



Your budget will also need to cover the cost of home insurance. The premiums for this are partially based on postcode, so if you live in (or near) a burglary hot spot, your premiums may be a little more expensive than in some other areas.

You also have to factor the monthly (or quarterly) utility costs into this equation. The current average annual bill in the United Kingdom for gas and electricity for two people is around £1,800, perhaps less if you are living in a modern, energy-efficient apartment building. Don't forget the annual TV license (currently £145.50), so that you can enjoy watching the BBC and endless reruns of American TV on most of the other channels.

Getting around town will currently set you back £1,104 for an annual Travelcard for Transport for London's two most central Underground zones, and fares increase the farther out you go. Though prices have dropped from their £1.40 per liter prices a few years ago, gas costs are still pretty hefty, coming in at around £1.25 per liter in 2014.

Food and fresh produce can be expensive, depending on what and where you are buying. How much you spend on food will hinge on several factors, not least of which is your cooking abilities. As a very general guide, consumer goods and groceries in London tend to be a bit more expensive than in the United States (excluding New York City), though this depends on where you shop. Some supermarkets concentrate on quality (such as Whole Foods, Waitrose, and Marks and Spencer), whereas for others it is all about price (including Asda or Lidl). Street markets (such as the weekday markets on Chapel Street in Islington or Brixton Market in South London, Portobello Road Market in Notting Hill on Friday, or the Saturday Broadway Market close to Bethnal Green Tube) can be a great place to get fresh fruits and vegetables, and they are often cheaper than in the supermarkets. If you prefer organic produce, there are several farmers markets dotted around London, with the Friday and Saturday market in Borough, the Saturday Pimlico Road Market, and the Sunday markets in Islington,

Marylebone, and Queen's Park—all well worth visiting and a great place to get some local organic produce.

Your weekly food bill will quickly shoot up if you plan on eating out or getting a meal to go (called "takeaways") every night. The cost of eating out is more or less the same as in the largest American cities, though fast food strikes me as less expensive in the United States.

# Banking



## CURRENCY

Here in the United Kingdom the currency used is British pounds sterling, shown as £, which stands for the Latin word *librae.* Paper bills come in four denominations—£5 (which is green), £10 (blue), £20 (brown), and £50 (red), although the £50 is not commonly used (probably because ATMs don't tend to issue them). Unlike US currency, these bills (or "banknotes" as they are called here) all get bigger in size as the denomination increases. As for coins, these are in "pence," and the abbreviation is "p" (pronounced "pee"). Denominations include 1p (or a "penny"), 2p (or "tuppence"), 5p, 10p, 20p, and 50p as well as £1 and £2. Compared to American change, UK coins are large and heavy. The 1p and 2p coins are copper colored and the pound coins are golden, with the other four coins all colored silver.

Banknotes come in four denominations: £5, £10, £20, and £50.

In case you are wondering where "shillings" come in, unfortunately these are no longer in use. In 1971 the United Kingdom's currency was decimalized to just pounds and pence, with there being 100 pence to the pound. Prior to decimalization, the pound was divided into 20 shillings and each shilling was worth 12 pence, making the pound worth 240 pence.

## BRITISH BANK ACCOUNTS

Unless you are going to be in London for just a few months, chances are you will need to have a British bank account to pay your bills, so opening a bank account should be one of your first priorities. Here in the United Kingdom there are two main types of banking accounts readily available: a current account (checking) and a deposit account (savings). As in the States, you can open an account in a bank or a building society (like a savings and loan), or both if you really want to. It is worth noting that unless you request it (and pay for the privilege), banks will not return your canceled checks (spelled "cheques"). With the rise in popularity of online banking, as well as direct debit and standing orders, people don't tend to write many checks these days. Most British banks and building societies offer at least one current account that receives interest, and most have an online presence if you prefer to bank this way. Make sure that you get a check guarantee/debit card with your account. There will be a range of accounts available, some free (providing you have enough money in your account), while others charge a monthly fee but come with added extras, such as preferential interest rates. I'm afraid you can't rely on your bank if you want a safe deposit box; they simply don't have room. Instead you need to use a company that specializes in safe deposit boxes.

There are numerous banks and building societies to choose from, including well-known names such as Barclays, Lloyds, HSBC, Citibank, and NatWest. To be perfectly honest I'd say that the service between them all is "much of a muchness." The opening hours tend to be 9am-5pm Monday-Friday, with some open Saturday morning as well. They won't be open on national holidays. I recommend that you choose a bank that is convenient to get to (maybe one near work) or ask colleagues which bank they'd recommend. If you are coming to London through an intra-company transfer, try asking your HR/relocation department for a recommendation or whether the company has a link with a particular bank. Also consider whether you are going to be paid in dollars or in pounds sterling. If your US employer is going to continue to pay you in dollars and just give you a cost of living adjustment, you may want both a dollar account and a sterling account. Luckily, most of the major banks offer offshore accounts that can hold numerous currencies.

### Opening an Account

It often comes as a surprise just how hard it is to open a banking account in the United Kingdom—not forgetting the amount of time it can sometimes take. The anti-money-laundering legislation here is notoriously complicated, with the result that banks are very careful to check the identity of people opening an account and their resident status. The long and short of it is that you will need to provide the banks

## Bringing Cash In and Out of the UK

As it may take a while to establish yourself in the United Kingdom and get a bank account organized, you may want to come to London with a fairly large wedge of cash in your wallet. While it is always nice to have cash on hand, there are limits on how much you can bring in and out of any European Union country without declaring it first. At the present, you only need to declare cash you are bringing in or taking out of the United Kingdom (or elsewhere in the EU) if it is €10,000 or more, or the equivalent in other currencies. And this doesn't just mean banknotes and change—banker's drafts or traveler's checks are also covered under the term "cash."

If you plan to move through the border control with more than this amount, you'll need to declare it as you enter or leave the United Kingdom. You can declare your cash by filling in the Customs and Excise C9011 form and posting it in the drop box at the airport. This form is available at the airport, or you can download it online at www.gov.uk/bringing-cash-into-uk on the Travel Abroad pages. As with most official documents, it is best if you have a copy for your records to provide proof that you have declared your cash, so make a photocopy if you are using the online form. The form in the airport is on a self-copying paper, so remember to take your copy before you put your form in the box.

Be warned that you face a hefty fine if you fail to declare your cash or lie on the form. If you are worried that your cash will be seized if you declare it, rest assured that the authorities are only likely to do this if they suspect that it will be used for something illegal. If you are aboveboard, you should have nothing to worry about.



with several different bits of documentation before they will give you an account. Just what is required to open an account may vary from bank to bank, but you will probably need to provide:

- A couple forms of ID (such as your passport and US driver's license)
- A copy of your visa
- A copy of a recent utility or council tax bill (this can be a tricky one for expats)
- A confirmation sponsorship letter from your UK employer or university

Once you have your documentation together, you must pay a visit to a branch to open an account; pre-book an appointment with one of the bank's representatives (call or drop by beforehand to arrange this and see what they require). Since you don't have a credit history in the United Kingdom yet, the bank has no way of checking up on you and your identity, so they will want to speak with you in person. Once you've handed in your documentation and filled in an application for an account, your bank account should follow within a week or so.

One of the biggest difficulties for expats when it comes to opening a bank account is that to get a flat or house you need to have a bank account so that you can pay the rent by bank transfer, but in order to get a bank account you need proof of an address—a bit of a chicken and egg situation. Some banks are more understanding about this than others, especially those in the City, where there is a large international workforce. A letter from your employer stating your role and salary, their sponsorship, and the confirmation details of your corporate housing address (if any) can be a big help in smoothing the way for a bank account.

## BANKING SERVICES AND CREDIT CARDS

Most rents are paid by a standing order, which is a written instruction by you to pay a fixed amount to a particular party by bank transfer. You can also instruct the bank to make sure that the amount is paid by a particular day each month. To set up a standing order you need to fill in a standing order mandate with all the relevant information. When it comes to paying the bills, some providers will give you a discount if you pay by direct debit. Unlike a standing order where you set the amount to be paid, with a direct debit you tell the bank that you've agreed that another party (such as the electricity company) can collect money from your account. More importantly, the amount withdrawn can vary each month, providing that you are told how much is being debited.



### ATMs

Although you can queue up in a bank to get cash from the teller, the easiest way to get cash is from an ATM (also known as a "cash point," "cash machine," or, my favorite, "hole in the wall"). These are widely available and you'll find them at banks and building societies, as well as in malls and stores. Sometimes you may incur a small charge for using an ATM, though you will be warned about this by the machine. As in the United States, you can use ATMs to request a statement, deposit checks, or see

© KAREN WHITE

The Bank of England is the UK's central bank and was founded in 1694.

your balance. You can use either your debit or credit card to get cash from an ATM, though by withdrawing cash on a credit card you may incur interest on the withdrawal straightaway, making this an expensive option. You should also be able to use debit cards from a dollar account to get cash while you are in London, though once again you may incur a charge.

You should always be careful at ATMs, and be sure to cover the keypad when entering your PIN, as well as being aware of your surroundings and who is nearby. Before you use the ATM, check it out just in case it has been fitted with an illegal card skimmer and hidden camera or card trap. If in doubt, don't use it. Whenever possible, I try to use an ATM inside a bank, as these should be a bit safer.



## Debit and Credit Cards

One of the hardest things for expats to get used to when they move to London is that suddenly they have no credit history. If you are employed, a letter from your employer detailing your salary should help to facilitate matters; most banks have a minimum salary requirement for credit cards. It may take a few months before your bank will trust you with a credit card, especially if you are a student. Until then, make use of your debit card, which should come as part of your bank account (perhaps as a check guarantee card) to pay for purchases and withdraw cash. Debit cards are accepted just as often as a credit card, though you will be debited straightaway for purchases with this card. You can also use debit cards to pay over the phone or online—just be sure to provide all the information they ask for, such as when the card was issued and its expiry date.

When it comes to using cards, either credit or debit, you do not sign to authorize payment here in the United Kingdom. Instead you enter a PIN on a debit/credit card reader, which is similar to those that you use at checkouts in American stores. Most restaurants have a mobile debit/credit reader, which is brought to the table for you to enter your PIN. Using a PIN to authorize payment is seen as a more secure procedure than just asking for a signature. On the odd occasion when the PIN machine isn't working, you may be asked to sign a receipt, though this rarely happens. You can also use your American credit card in London, in which case you will just be asked to sign the receipt to authorize payment.

## Exchange Rates

For many expats, the international transferring of money just becomes a way of life. And there will probably be times when you will want to send dollars by wire transfer to your UK bank account (or vice versa). As you will quickly come to realize, exchange rates can vary enormously, and depending on what is happening in the markets, there can be a dramatic change from day to day or month to month. In just the past year, the rate for the US dollar to the pound has ranged US$1.58-1.71, and in 2007 it broke through the US$2 barrier. So it will pay dividends to keep a watchful eye over the exchange rate. It is fairly easy to set up a wire transfer from your dollar account to your British bank account, although you may have to pay for the service. Transfers usually take at least 48 hours, with five working days more likely. If you prefer, you could use a foreign currency check to transfer money, for example from your US account to your

British one. This will take a bit longer to clear than a wire transfer, and there may be a charge with this service.

### OFFSHORE BANKING

Several of the leading British banks also offer offshore banking options, and depending on your circumstances, these may be worth considering. These tend to be on one of the British Crown Dependency islands where there is a low tax jurisdiction, such as the Isle of Man, Gibraltar, or Guernsey and Jersey in the Channel Islands. These banks often allow you to have an account in several different currencies, such as dollars, pounds, or euros, making them ideal for individuals who earn in one currency and withdraw in another. There may be some tax advantages to having an overseas banks account, depending on your residency status and circumstances. Before you set up an offshore bank account, get some financial advice to see if this could be appropriate for you and your circumstances.



## Taxes

Certainly Benjamin Franklin hit the nail on the head when he said that "in this world nothing can be said to be certain, except death and taxes." As an American working in London, you will get the dubious pleasure of having to file income taxes in two countries noted for their complex tax rules. One of the first taxes you will encounter here in London is sales tax (known as value-added tax or VAT). This is now a massive 20 percent for most items, although many foods are not charged VAT. Sadly, chocolate isn't considered a food and so VAT is charged on this. If you have a family, you'll be pleased to learn that children's clothes and footwear are also "zero rated," while students (and everyone else really) will be glad to know that books and printed matter are also free of sales tax. Some items, such as kids' car seats and domestic electricity, have a reduced rate of VAT, currently 5 percent.

### UK TAXES

Don't be fooled into thinking that as you aren't a British citizen you won't need to pay UK taxes—you will. All resident workers in the United Kingdom are required to file for income tax on their earnings. The amount you will be required to pay depends on how much you earn, how you are paid, and your employment. There are two types of income-related tax in the United Kingdom—income tax and National Insurance (similar to Social Security). The United Kingdom uses a system of progressive rates for income tax and currently has three different tax bands. If you earn £0-31,865, the tax rate is 20 percent, which is called the Basic Rate of tax. The Higher Rate of 40 percent applies for earnings £31,866-150,000. Finally, there is the Additional Rate of tax at 45 percent for earnings over £150,000. Remember, this is a progressive rate of tax, so you only pay the percentage of tax that applies for earnings within a particular tax bracket. At the moment, the tax-free Personal Allowance limit is £10,000 (assuming you are not more than 65 years old), and you will only qualify for this if your income is below £100,000. The other UK income-related tax is National Insurance, and you will also have to pay this unless you can get an Exemption Certificate from your American employer. The United Kingdom has a reciprocal agreement on Social Security with the United States, and your American employer may be able to issue you an Exception Certificate before you move to the United Kingdom to exempt you from National Insurance contributions while you are working here. If you are moving here as part of an intra-company transfer ask your HR or relocation department about this before you make the move.

The situation for American expats with regard to taxes in the United Kingdom is very complex and will depend on their residency status. If you are going to be on a good salary here in London you should get specialist advice for your UK and US taxes. However, if you are a student and just have a Saturday job in a local store, your UK taxes will be quite straightforward and will be automatically deducted from your pay. Her Majesty's Revenue and Customs website (www.hmrc.gov.uk) offers helpful information and guidance, as well as tax forms and filing instructions. I've found the HMRC's online tax form is quite easy to complete, but then my taxes are rather simple.

There are key differences between the American and British tax regimes. The United Kingdom's tax year runs from April 6 to April 5 of the following year (not from January 1 to December 31 as in the United States). Completed paper UK tax returns must be filed by the end of October. Online tax returns and any payments are due by the end of January—giving you nine months past the end of the tax year to submit your return.

If you are employed, income tax and National Insurance (if appropriate) will automatically be deducted from your earnings through what is known as the pay-as-you-earn (PAYE) system. Your pay slip should show you how much tax and NI contributions have been deducted from your monthly pay. The situation is slightly different if you are self-employed. In these cases, you will need to keep records of your income and expenditures, then complete an annual tax return to determine the amount of income tax and National Insurance due—and don't forget to register for VAT. You'll probably need to pay any income tax that you owe in a couple of installments, as well as a final payment to cover any outstanding amounts. Employees with complicated tax arrangements also need to file a self-assessment form. As well as your UK income, you can also be taxed on any income from UK investments, as well as income from outside the United Kingdom, and this is where it can start to get a bit tricky.

The United Kingdom has a dazzling array of categories for residency status, but for American expats, these are important because their UK income tax liability will depend on their residency status. You can be a resident or a non-resident, as well as domicile and non-domicile. If all this sounds complicated, that's because it is, especially the issues of residency, domicile, and tax on foreign income and gains. Her Majesty's Revenue and Customs (HMRC—the UK government's tax authority) has a statutory residence test to help expats determine whether or not they are a UK resident for tax purposes. It is a good idea to get some professional UK tax planning advice before you start work in London. If you are part of an intra-company transfer, you may find that your HR department or expatriate employee department can also help. Sometimes UK tax advice is provided as part of a relocation package. If you aren't so lucky there are a few UK firms specializing in the tax matters of expat Americans in London; these include Buzzacott Chartered Accountants (www.buzzacott.co.uk) and MacIntyre Hudson Chartered Accountants (www.macintyrehudson.co.uk). You should be able to find more online or ask for a recommendation on one of the numerous expat forums. The United Kingdom and the United States have a double taxation agreement, so you should not need to pay taxes in both countries on the same income—at least that's the theory.

## US TAXES



Many Americans are blissfully unaware that they are subject to income taxes on their world-wide income and must file US taxes regardless of where in the world they are living and working. This doesn't mean that they will necessarily have to pay taxes in the United States, but the rules require them to file. If you have no other income and have already paid taxes in a foreign country that has a double taxation agreement with the United States (such as paying your UK taxes through the PAYE scheme), then all you may need to do is complete your US forms. Filing dates for Americans overseas are automatically extended until June 15, though you should make any necessary payments by April 15, if you want to avoid paying added interest and perhaps penalties. And remember, the US Treasury Department now requires that all Americans complete and return a Report of Foreign Bank and Financial Accounts (FBAR) if they have foreign financial accounts (including bank accounts and other investments) and the total amount in these foreign accounts comes to more than US$10,000 at any point during a tax year.

There are two key tax exclusions/deductions that American expats in London may be able to benefit from—the Foreign Earned Income Exclusion and the Housing Cost Amount Exclusion/Deduction. But you will first need to qualify under either the bona fide residence test or the physical presence test. Assuming you do qualify for the Foreign Earned Income Exclusion, you will be allowed to exclude some of your income earned overseas (currently the first US$97,600) from income tax. Working couples can each claim this exclusion. Again, a qualifying US taxpayer whose tax home is in another country may be able to make use of the Foreign Housing Exclusion to exclude from their gross income some employer-provided housing expenses. If you are self-employed and live in another country you may qualify for the Foreign Housing Deduction. In either case, the calculation for the deduction or exclusion is quite complicated and will depend on factors such as income, costs, and location. For more help with your US taxes, you can contact your US accountant or a CPA who has specialized in the expat market (there is a list of specialist accountants on the London embassy's website under citizen services). The US Embassy in London also has an IRS department. Although my US accountant doesn't believe me, I've always found the people at the London IRS office to be very helpful, looking after bewildered Brits and expat Americans in their stride.

# Investing

Another financial matter you may want to consider is investing while you are in the United Kingdom. As the London Stock Exchange is one of the world's largest and oldest, you may well be tempted to invest in some of the equities traded there. The London Stock Exchange (or LSE) was established back in 1698, when shares were first traded in the city's coffee houses. The Financial Times Stock Exchange (FTSE) 100 is the main index for shares listed on the London Stock Exchange and is similar to the New York Stock Exchange's Dow Jones Industrial Average. As its name implies, the FTSE 100 (or "footies" as it is often called) consists of the 100 most highly capitalized UK companies listed on the London stock market. There are also other share indexes, such as the FTSE 250, FTSE 350, or FTSE All-Share index, but the FTSE 100 is by far the most popular, and represents around 80 percent of the market capitalization for the London Stock Exchange. Businesses included on the list are in numerous sectors, ranging from the financial industry to consumer goods, mining to oil and gas, not to forget telecommunications or pharmaceuticals, among others.

Before you start investing in the United Kingdom, you need to determine whether investing in the United Kingdom makes sense with regard to your tax planning and long-term plans, so get some financial planning advice first with someone who understands American and UK taxes. If, indeed, it does make sense for you and you are so inclined, there are numerous investment possibilities and they tend to be similarly

DAILY LIFE

You may want to consider investing in British equities.

structured to those in the United States. As the City of London is one of the world's leading financial centers, you will be well placed to learn about UK investment opportunities. These could be equities, bonds, retirement products, cash savings, hedge funds, and property.

If you don't plan on living in the United Kingdom permanently for the rest of your life, you may feel that you would be better off keeping your investments dollar-based. This could be because investing in the United Kingdom may not be tax efficient for you and/or you may not want to be at the mercy of the currency markets. On the other hand, you may not want to have all your eggs in a dollar basket, and are looking to add another type of investment to your portfolio. Whichever is the case for you, be sure to get some financial and tax planning with someone who understands the issues faced by Americans living in London before you make any major investments. There are numerous companies offering this service, but try to get a recommendation from someone you know and trust who is in a similar situation.



Here is a quick summary of some of the more popular investment options in the United Kingdom.

## SAVINGS

As in the United States, banks and building societies offer a wide range of saving options that will give you some interest on your savings. These include fixed-rate and fixed-term deposits, as well as regular savings accounts. There are also UK tax-free savings accounts known as Individual Savings Accounts (or ISAs), which currently allow you to invest up to £15,000 annually in cash savings, though some banks may require a minimum deposit. But remember, ISAs are unlikely to be tax-free in the United States. In case you are worried about whether your money will be safe, you should know that the UK government has promised to protect the first £85,000 of an individual's cash savings in the event of their bank or building society going under. This limit is applied "per individual, per bank," so joint account customers can get a refund of up to £170,000 if their bank collapses.

## EQUITIES

Direct investment in the stock market isn't as prevalent in the United Kingdom as it is in the United States, perhaps because they are a bit more risk adverse here. Instead they may invest in managed investment funds called a "unit trust," which is similar to a mutual fund. Generally there will be a management fee (usually between 0.75 and 1.5 percent) and perhaps setup and exit fees for these investments. It is possible to invest some money that is free of UK income and capital gains tax with an investment ISA. The current annual limit for this is the same as that for a cash ISA (£15,000) and once again there may be a minimum amount required. You can, of course, buy and sell individual UK stocks if you prefer this to managed funds.

## RETIREMENT

Saving for retirement should be one of our first financial priorities. As in the United States, the legislation that governs UK pensions is very complex. In the United Kingdom most people save for retirement through a company pension plan or a personal pension plan, paying regular contributions and using the accrued benefits to buy an annuity upon retirement. At the moment, the United Kingdom does not offer anything akin to a 401K, so you do not have access to your retirement savings prior to retirement. The nearest thing to an Individual Retirement Account (IRA) would be a Self-Invested Personal Pension (or SIPP). A SIPP allows the holder to save for their retirement in a UK tax-efficient way, and provides greater control over the investment options, including a greater say about when to take the pension benefits. However, these are usually favored just by wealthy individuals who are investment savvy, and the administration costs are a bit high. Even with a SIPP, you will at some point be required to use your pension pot, which will probably be paid in sterling and will expose you to currency fluctuation. Although your UK pension savings may be tax efficient here, you may still have to pay US tax on these investments. Whether saving for retirement in the United Kingdom is a good idea for you as an American will depend on your circumstances and long-term plans. As with most financial matters for US expats living in London, retirement planning requires specialist advice.



## PROPERTY

You may think that investing in property in the United Kingdom would be a wise move, given the assumption that home ownership is better than renting. However, this may not be the case for some expats in London, especially when you throw in the high cost of buying and selling property in the United Kingdom and the risks of currency fluctuations. You may also lose out on some US tax benefits if your employer is helping you with your rent and other living expenses while you are in the United Kingdom. Nevertheless, the continued high demand for property in London, a strong increase in property values in London (up by 20 percent in 2014), and the weariness of renting year after year may combine to tempt you into buying property.

# COMMUNICATIONS

Without a doubt, one of the factors that makes London easier to move to than many other places is that you don't have a major communication barrier to overcome. The United Kingdom speaks English (well, a version of it at least), and it has a good telecommunications infrastructure in place. Here you simply don't have to face that overwhelming isolation that comes from living in a country where you don't speak the native language. The TV, newspapers, and Internet will all be in English (with American versions readily available), so you shouldn't feel isolated linguistically. Sure, you are bound to encounter the odd occasion where you don't quite understand what is being said or why, but they will be the laughable exceptions, rather than the rule. Being able to just pick up a local newspaper and read it with ease or flick through the TV channels without struggling to understand what is being said should make it easier for you to settle into your new life in London. As for communicating with family and friends back home, the Internet should make this quite easy and affordable, especially if you use email, a social network messaging system, or voice-over-the-Internet application.

© KAREN WHITE

# Telephone and Internet Services

## TELEPHONE SERVICE

The country code for the United Kingdom is 44, and there are three main area code prefixes for London: 020 7, 020 8, and 020 3. Area codes are called "STD codes" (in case you're wondering, STD stands for "subscriber trunk dialing" and means that you don't need an operator to place the call). Originally, 020 7 was meant to cover central London with the 020 8 number for outer London. Of course, as it is a massive metropolis, London soon needed more phone numbers, so the 020 3 prefix was introduced.

If you are calling London from the United States, then you do not need to dial the leading 0 in the area code—just dial 011 44 20 and then the rest of the number. If you are in London and call a number with a different area code on a landline, then you can drop the 020 and just start dialing with 7, 8, or 3, as required. With a cell phone, however, you must include the 020 part of the prefix.

Outside of London, the area code prefixes follow the National Telephone Numbering Plan, and area codes can be anything from three to six digits long. The numbering system is not geographic, so don't expect all Scottish numbers to begin with a certain number, for example. Unlike in the United States, where all phone numbers are usually seven digits long and the area codes are three digits, the number of digits in a British telephone number and a regional STD dialing code can vary. You can even get STD dialing codes that are longer than the actual phone number.

All British cell phone numbers start with 07 and are 11 digits long. The prefixes for "freephone" numbers (toll-free numbers) in the United Kingdom are 0800 and 0808. British mobile operators usually charge for calls to freephone numbers, so it is best to use a landline or the number given for use with cell phones. A premium rate is charged for numbers that start with 09, and calls cost much more than the standard rate. The United Kingdom also has what is known as a business rate number (0843, 0844, 0845, 0870, and 0871); these are normally used for customer service or support lines. Calling these numbers costs more per minute than a normal landline call (1-12p more per minute) and even more from a cell phone (as much as 40p per minute).

Attitudes toward receiving phone calls at night are generally a bit more conservative here than they are in the States. As a guide I do not tend to phone past 9pm unless I know the person really, really well or it's an emergency—I'll send a text message or email instead. Perhaps this is a hangover from when I had younger kids that could be easily awakened by the sound of a phone ringing, but still I try to be considerate about when I use the phone here.

### Public Phone Boxes

Even though most Londoners have cell phones, you'll still find brightly painted red call boxes dotted around town. The ones that say "telephone" are coin operated and the ones that say "phone card" only take cards. These days the minimum cost for a call from a public phone call box is 60p (20p for the call and 40p for the connection), which gives you up to 30 minutes for either a local or national call, though some phone numbers are excluded from this tariff. With the old-style British public phones, you should dial first and only insert your change when you hear the beeping sound (your cue to put the coins in), which means that the call has been answered. With the more modern phone boxes, you put the money in first before you dial, as you do in the States. Other ways to pay for your call from a public phone box include getting a phone card from British Telecom (www.bt.com) or using your credit/debit card and PIN. If you are going to make several international calls, you may want to get an international phone card from your local post office. Some of the call boxes in London (as elsewhere in the United Kingdom) are very sophisticated these days and will let you send a text message, email, or fax. And if you see a green phone box, this is the result of an initiative to turn some disused red phone boxes into solar charging stations for cell phones.



## Landlines

Once you have found your flat or house, in addition to getting the utilities set up you may want to get a fixed-line phone account—and more importantly an ADSL Internet connection. When house-hunting, ask if the property has a telephone line already installed, as this will make getting a fixed-line phone and broadband connection (which usually comes through the phone line) a bit easier. The main telephone provider in the United Kingdom is British Telecom, though there are numerous other providers as well, with even the Post Office and Cable & Wireless Communications getting in on the act. Generally, these companies offer bundled packages of a telephone line, Internet, and cable or satellite TV (sometimes with great deals), but you can have just a landline and Internet if you prefer. If you know that you will want to see regular NFL games or get CNN (both available on pay-to-view TV), then you may as well go for one of the bundled packages. Cell phone providers have also entered the fixed-line market, and you may be able to get a contract covering your landline, pay-to-view TV, and broadband connection along with your cell phone.

You will still find red phone boxes in London that use phone cards.

### DOMESTIC AND INTERNATIONAL CALLS

Unlike in the States, you do *not* automatically get unlimited local daytime calls with your fixed-line phone in the United Kingdom. The rates for a landline vary and are based on the price of the line rental, the number of calls, when they are made, and the package you have decided to get. The standard telephone packages offer unlimited UK landline calls on the weekend, or in the evening and on the weekend, or anytime. Just how much you will pay if you call outside these times (or

## Going Mobile

Do a straw poll of a few people asking what 10 items they could not do without and a cell phone would probably be fairly near the top of the list. When a friend of mine decided that it was time to switch from her American smartphone to a British cell phone (they call it a "mobile phone" here), her challenge of getting a "real" cell phone began.

As a recently arrived American in London, my friend Amy encountered a classic example of the problems that can arise when you suddenly do not have a credit history. To make matters worse, as a full-time mother of young children, she was really just adjunct to her employed American husband, so it wasn't as if she could ask her employer to help her establish credit. Her husband, of course, was fine because he had a corporate cell phone; however, she was not so lucky.

She decided to take out a very basic (or "bog standard," as they say here) pay-as-you-go cell phone for six months while the phone company determined if they could trust her with a monthly phone subscription. If you've had a cell phone account for years in the States, it comes as quite a shock to only be able to have a pay-as-you-go account, with all the hassle of regularly topping it up. Amy tried her best to get a phone on account, contacting many different providers, but they all said the same thing—get a pay-as-you-go for six months and then come back to us. So, for six months she had a pay-as-you-go phone and got regular top ups every few weeks. As soon as she could, she switched to a phone with an account and got a smartphone just like the one she had back home. By contrast, when I made the switch from pay-as-you-go to a contract, I think it took all of about 10 minutes, and most of that was finding the right smartphone. Of course, I already had several years of credit history (and a few UK credit cards), so they could easily check if I was a credit risk.

It just goes to show that even simple things like getting a cell phone on a monthly account can be tough when you don't have the right credit history.



for calls lasting more than an hour) will depend on the package, but expect to pay around 9p per minute for a call to a UK landline, with calls to UK cell phones usually around 12p per minute. It's quite common for people here to just opt for unlimited evening and/or weekend calls, and pay the extra for any daytime calls—especially as so many people have a cell phone subscription that includes a certain amount of call time each month as part of their plan. As you'd expect, the price of international phone calls is more expensive during the day. If you are calling the United States, it's at least five hours behind London, so unless it's an emergency you'll probably want to wait until the evening. For example, a daytime phone call will be around 21p per minute, which drops to 14p at night. If you know you'll want to make lots of international phone calls, look for a plan that offers this, but don't forget that you could save a bit of money and use a voice-over-the-Internet application.

For many people, their main motivation for getting a fixed land line is to get broadband access, which is why they tend to bundle the phone, broadband, and pay-to-view television together in one package. The ranges and prices of these bundled packages tend to change quite frequently, so be sure to shop around to see what is on offer. Expect to pay at least £10-35 per month, or less if you are fine with the free-to-view TV channels.

### Cellular Phones

Cell phones, or "mobile phones" as they are referred to here, are just as ubiquitous

© KAREN WHITE

The use of mobile phones is ubiquitous in London.

in London as they are in the United States, perhaps more so. You will need to switch your American cell phone to a British one fairly soon after you arrive if you want to avoid expensive long-distance phone calls and hefty data roaming charges while in the United Kingdom. There are five main network operators in the United Kingdom: O2, Orange/EE, T-Mobile, Three, and Vodafone. Several other companies sell mobile phone packages that use the network of one of these operators, making the range of choice a bit overwhelming. Bear in mind that the network coverage isn't comprehensive for all the networks, so you may have difficulty getting a signal in some areas. No doubt this is a problem the world over as far as cell phone usage goes.

There are two main ways to pay for a cell phone: through a monthly subscription or pre-paid vouchers known as pay-as-you-go. You can buy phone vouchers all over the place, from newsagents to the post office, cell phone shops, banks and supermarkets, and of course online and by phone. The monthly phone plans offer a mix of call minutes, SMS (short message service), and data. The price you pay will depend on the package and handset that you choose (assuming you are also buying a phone). It is also possible to buy your phone outright (or maybe use your American phone if the SIM is unlocked) and have a SIM-only contract or pay-as-you-go phone. The cost of a UK cell phone can range dramatically depending on the phone, though incoming calls are free in the United Kingdom. A basic smartphone on a two-year contract with 500 minutes and 250 megabytes of data, with no upfront costs for the phone, can start at £14 per month. For the latest iPhone, expect to pay around £45 or more for 24 months with unlimited minutes and text and 250 megabytes of data. With a pay-as-you-go phone, the cost of the phone will start at around £5, though a basic smartphone would be closer to £50. If you want to use your cell phone to make international calls (which at around £1 per minute will be very expensive), then you will need to add this to your package, and may want to pay a bit more each month for cheaper international phone calls. Most people in Britain have a phone subscription, but you may have to use a pay-as-you-go phone for six months to build up a credit history with the phone company before you can sign up for a monthly plan. If you are working in the UK, ask a few network providers if they will give you a contract if you provide your own phone and pay a hefty deposit. If you are relocating to London as a sponsored employee, hopefully your employer will provide a mobile phone as part of your employment package.



## INTERNET AND BROADBAND

If you are anything like me, one of your first priorities will be to sort out your broadband or Wi-Fi connection. I know I would really struggle if I didn't have access to the Internet for days on end, unless I'm on vacation, in which case it would be a welcome change. One way to set up an Internet account is to bundle it with your telephone (and possibly pay-to-view television) provider. Just how much this will cost depends on the package and current offers, though you should expect to pay around £10-20 per month for a landline phone and broadband, and a bit more for super-fast broadband. If you just want broadband there are plenty of providers, but expect to pay £7.50-20 per month, depending on the speed.

If you prefer to have wireless Internet access at your house, broadband providers can usually organize this, or you can get your own wireless network device. Sometimes setting up an Internet connection and pay-to-view TV can be a bit trying as you may have to make an appointment for the provider to come fit all the lines and cables, and of course, you may have to pay for the privilege of getting it set up. Thankfully, most properties are already set up for the Internet, though this isn't necessarily the case with satellite or cable TV. You can always go to one of the numerous coffee shops or fast food joints offering a free wireless connection to the Internet. Or you could get a pay-as-you-go mobile Wi-Fi or dongle to connect your devices to the Internet without a modem. These are available from cell phone stores for as little as £10 per month, which gives you 3G access to 1 gigabyte of data, while pay-as-you-go options are available for around £30 for 2G of data and last for a month. Instead, you may want to join BT Openzone, a Wi-Fi network with hot spots throughout the capital; this costs around £30 per month or you can order a prepaid voucher. For more information about BT Openzone, including how to subscribe, visit its website (www.btwifi.co.uk).

Of course there are also Internet cafés, which charge around £2 per hour, as well as computers at public libraries, which you can often use for free for at least an hour, assuming that you have joined the library and pre-book your slot.

# Postal and Courier Services

## POSTAL SERVICE

There are post offices on most high streets where you can buy stamps or send parcels, though really big parcels may need to be sent via a special courier, such as UPS or Parcelforce. You can also pay for your car's road tax or apply for a driving license. British post offices offer a range of financial and banking services, everything from paying bills to offering savings accounts and home insurance.



The normal hours for the post office are 9am-5:30pm weekdays and 9am-12:30pm on Saturday, though there may be some variations at your nearest branch. If something is being delivered to you and you're out, you will need to take the missed delivery card and some ID (and lots of patience) to your delivery office (also called a "sorting office") to collect it. Please note that the sorting offices are not at your local post office. The address and hours for your local delivery office should be on your missed delivery card, or you can ask for its address at your local post office. Sometimes the lines at these offices are horrendous and the staff can be a bit surly. If you prefer, you can organize redelivery through the Royal Mail's website (www.royalmail.com).

If you want a letter to get there within a few days then you should send it first class (currently 62p). Use second class (currently 53p) if it is less urgent. The weight limit for these is 100 grams, which is around 20 pages of standard photocopying paper, although you'll also need to allow for the weight of the envelope. Your letter must also be in a standard envelope (240 mm by 165 mm); anything larger will need to

Drop your letters in the red postbox.

## British Postal History and Stamps

The British are justifiably proud of their postal history—not only was England the first country to introduce postage stamps, but it was also the first country to establish a quality service that covered all of the British Isles, as well as the British Empire.

The British postal service can be traced back to Tudor times, when Henry VIII started the Royal Mail. Before then it fell to the sender to establish how their letter was going to be delivered to the recipient. In 1635, the Royal Mail service was extended to the public, and a whole network of regular coaches, postal roads, and houses was established. At this time, it was the common practice for a letter to be paid for by the recipient, and it could take ages. Around the middle of the 17th century, the Post Master General introduced a postmark with the date and location on it, in response to complaints about the length of time it took for letters to be delivered. The British postal system struggled on for around 170 years, though it was plagued by inefficiency and a complex charging structure based on weight and distance covered.

In 1840 the government finally took steps to improve the postal system (and the finances of the Royal Mail) and finally implemented many of the suggestions of Sir Rowland Hill, a champion of postal reform and author of *Post Office Reform: Its Importance and Practicability*. A key element of Sir Rowland's reform was to encourage people to prepay their postage on letters and parcels. This move would save the postal service money, as it would improve the efficiency of postal workers out delivering letters, who would no longer need to calculate the postage or handle money if the recipient was to pay the postage. To this end the postal service introduced a flat rate for letters and parcels that covered all of Britain and Ireland—the first of its kind in the world. The new service charged one penny in old money for up to one ounce in weight, regardless of the distance covered. This is the modern-day equivalent of around £1.20 for each letter. Although a bit expensive, the new flat rate charge proved to be popular, and postal usage dramatically increased.

Sir Rowland Hill had also realized that to facilitate prepayment it made sense to use an adhesive label of some kind to show that the letter had been paid for. This laid the foundation for the world's first postage stamp—the Penny Black—which was also introduced in 1840 as part of the postal reforms. These stamps were not perforated, but had to be cut with scissors. Unfortunately, the use of the Penny Black didn't last for long, as it was hard to see the red cancellation franking over the black ink. Soon a red stamp (the Red Penny) was introduced and the cancellation ink changed to black.

Since then hundreds of stamps have been introduced in the United Kingdom, and thankfully postage rates are a bit more affordable than they were in 1840, with a first-class stamp now costing just 62 pence for a 100-gram letter.



go as a large letter, which costs a bit more (currently 93p for first class). You can, of course, send letters by special delivery or express mail for a guaranteed faster delivery. If you want to make sure that it is received, you can send it "recorded," which requires the receiver to sign for it. Stamps are widely available from newsagents and supermarkets as well as post offices and online (www.royalmail.com/personal/uk-delivery/online-postage).

Postal rates for international letters are based on the weight; a 60-gram letter to the United States via standard international post costs about £2.15. When I mail these I simply go to my local post office and have them weigh it so I have the right postage. Remember, you are not supposed to use first- or second-class stamps for international mail. Instead you should use stamps that have their value printed on them, so that the postal workers can see the amount of postage paid.

### COURIERS AND INTERNATIONAL SHIPPING

Sending things back to the States (or anywhere else in the world for that matter), such as birthday and holiday gifts, can usually be done at the post office (and sent via Royal Mail's courier division—Parcelforce). However, the item must weigh less than 30 kilograms, and there are size limits depending on the destination. Parcels can be sent via airmail or surface mail, and the post office counter service should be able to give you an idea how long each will take. Sometimes there isn't much of a difference in price between these, so ask at the post office counter how much for each. A packet weighing less than 2 kilograms can be sent airmail as a "small packet." A 2-kilogram package sent to the United States as an airmail "small packet" would currently cost around £23, whereas a parcel that is just a bit heavier, say 2.2 kilograms, would set you back by around £32 for economy airmail. Be sure to bear this in mind when you're birthday and holiday shopping for family and friends back home—go for small, lightweight, non-breakable items. The last posting date for holiday airmail shipments to the United States tends to be in early December and in mid-October for surface mail. You can get more precise dates from your local post office. If you miss the last postal date with the UK postal service you could always try one of the American-owned courier services operating in the United Kingdom, such as UPS, FedEx, or DHL.



## Media

The British media has been well regarded for centuries, be it the United Kingdom's newspapers, the Reuters news agency, or the BBC. There are more than a dozen different daily newspapers in Britain and numerous magazines covering everything from special interests to celebrity gossip. The BBC is probably the dominant player in the media field at the moment, certainly as far as the web and broadcast media are concerned. There are two 24-hour news stations generally available in the United Kingdom, with the American versions available with some pay-to-view television packages. The BBC alone offers seven different nationwide radio stations, along with its regional stations, and there are music stations catering to all musical preferences.

### TELEVISION

The excellent quality of British TV means that it is generally held in high regard around the world. Certainly my American family (who don't tend to watch much TV in the States) really enjoys the eclectic mix of programs that you get here, ranging from informative wildlife documentaries on BBC2 to satirical humor and gripping drama on BBC1. They were a bit taken aback, however, by the suddenness of the 9pm "watershed" (as it is called here), when swearing and some nudity are allowed—this is something to keep an eye on if you have children who may stay up a bit later on the weekend. If you are a big fan of certain American shows, you may be a bit disappointed after your move here. Assuming that your favorite program has been bought by a British channel and is on air here, the programs shown will probably be a bit behind the US plot, so you may have to watch reruns for a while.

There are five main terrestrial channels in England: BBC1, BBC2, ITV, Channel Four, and Channel Five. Most of these stations offer regional variations, and both the BBC and ITV have local London news. Only the BBC channels are commercial free. Both BBC1 and ITV offer a wide range of programs, including dramas, news, sports, and light entertainment. BBC2 is more likely to show documentaries, as well as programs relating to the arts. Channel Four also shows documentaries, dramas, and comedy. On the other hand, Channel Five mainly seems to show American or Aussie programs along with light entertainment shows. There are also numerous digital channels, some of which are free to view, such as the digital BBC channels, including the News Channel, BBC4, and CBeebies and CBBC for kids. There are also free-to-view commercial channels, which often show repeats. Other digital channels include commercial pay-to-view programs, such as Sky TV or ESPN.

Using satellite or cable TV isn't as pervasive in the United Kingdom as it is in the United States, but the services are available. If there is an antenna (called "aerial" here), you should be able to get Freeview TV, which includes the five main channels (BBC1, BBC2, ITV, Channel Four, and Channel Five) and a whole host of other digital channels, some of which are only on in the evening. Even though both the BBC and ITV show some sports programming, if you are a big sports fan (especially of American sports) you will probably want a satellite or cable subscription so that you can get ESPN or the Sky sports channels. Just how much you'll pay each month for cable or satellite TV will depend on the package; these currently start at £24.50 per month in addition to your standard package and any installation costs. If you have property in a conservation area, you may not be able to install a satellite receiver, in which case you'll have to see if you can get cable TV. If you are renting it is unlikely that you would be able to install a satellite dish. At www.cable.co.uk you can type in your postcode to see if there is a cable provider in the area.

Don't forget that you will need to also get a TV license if you plan on watching any TV at home in the United Kingdom, and you will need it whether you plan on watching TV via Freeview, a pay-to-view contract, or even the Internet. This applies to students. You can get a TV license online or by check or bank transfer, and the current cost for a color TV is £145.50 per annum. Another way to pay is through a PayPoint. These are usually in newsagents, convenience stores, supermarkets, and gas stations, and you can use this service to pay all your household bills. To find your local PayPoint go to www.paypoint.co.uk.

## RADIO

One of the things that I appreciate most about living in the United Kingdom is that the art of radio broadcasting hasn't succumbed to just playing the top 10 in the music charts or the songs that the record companies want to promote. Here you can hear plays, long-standing soap operas, informative programs, light-hearted discussions, and a wide variety of music—all on the radio. The BBC in particular tries hard to keep the art of radio broadcasting alive and original. It offers 10 national radio stations, as well as regional stations in England, Scotland, Wales, and Northern Ireland. These stations provide a wide range of programs. You'll find pop music and the top 10 on Radio 1 and Radio 1X, chat and music on Radio 2, classical music on Radio 3, news, drama, and chat on Radio 4 and Radio 4 Extra, sports on Radio 5 and Radio 5 Live, with Radio 6 playing a variety of musical genres. The final radio station is the Asian Network. Of course the BBC isn't the only one providing radio stations. Other commercial stations in London offer everything from easy listening to classical and rap—there's even a Polish rock station.

## NEWSPAPERS AND MAGAZINES



British newspapers have a long and well-established history, with publications such as *The Times,* which has been around since 1788. Today there are several daily newspapers in the United Kingdom, as well as the daily evening London paper the *Evening Standard.* You can also easily find the *Herald Tribune* if you want to keep up to date with events on the other side of the Atlantic. The editorial stance of each of the main national papers often depends on the political leanings of the publication: *The Times, The Financial Times, The Daily Telegraph,* the *Daily Express,* and the *Daily Mail* all lean toward the right; the *Guardian, Mirror,* and *The Sun* all lean toward the left; and *The Independent* takes the middle left ground.

To get a daily paper you can drop by your local newsagent or a kiosk—there is usually one near each Tube or train station. Having a paper delivered may be a bit trickier. If you really want to do this, you should drop by your local newsagent and see if they offer this service, and if they don't ask if there is a newsagent in the area that does. It's also worth remembering that most newspapers are also online if that is easier, though you may have to pay a subscription.

### Broadsheets and Tabloids

British newspapers have two classes: the broadsheets and the tabloids. You can easily separate the two types of journalism into the "quality" press providing in-depth journalism (the broadsheets) and the "popular" press, which tends toward simplistic news coverage and sometimes has a jingoistic editorial slant (the tabloids). While the former concentrate on groundbreaking national, international, and political news, the latter take a more sensationalistic approach, concentrating on celebrity gossip and human-interest stories, with some featuring the added enticement of buxom topless female models.

In days gone by, the bigger quality newspapers would be on larger sheets of paper, hence the name "broadsheet," while the popular press would be in the smaller tabloid form. This marked difference between quality and popular newspapers has been around since the early 20th century, though it wasn't until the 1970s that *The Sun* introduced scantily clad girls to its pages, a trend that some other tabloids quickly adopted. (The use of Page Three girls, as they are known, hasn't been without controversy, and there have been several campaigns to put an end to this policy, but as of yet no laws have been passed that would stop the practice.) Nowadays, due to rising production and paper costs, even some of the quality papers have reduced their size to a more compact format, although the content and editorial stance remain the same. And of course, a smaller paper has the added benefit of being easier to read while on a crowded Tube train during the morning commute.

You can pick up a copy of a newspaper at a news kiosk by the station.

In Britain you'll also find a wide range of magazines to cover most topics, from the weekly celebrity gossip magazines to industry-specific publications and leisure interests. If you want a particular magazine, you can ask your local newsagent if they can order in or hold a copy for you. Most of the larger supermarkets also offer a range of popular magazines, with bookstores more likely to carry technical or industry-specific publications.

# TRAVEL AND TRANSPORTATION

For a city of its size and age, London is blessed with good public transportation, which includes the Underground (the "Tube"), its iconic red buses, trains, Docklands Light Railway, and river boats. On top of that, bicycling, driving, and taxis are all very common ways to get around town, even if the streets are sometimes very crowded. London is also a major transportation hub for rail and air travel, with 10 major railway termini, including St. Pancras International—home to the Eurostar to Belgium and France. London's Heathrow Airport is one of the busiest in the world, so getting around town, Britain, and the rest of the world is fairly easy if you are based in London.

When it comes to finding a home, one of your first considerations should be your daily commute to work or university, so you should try to get your head around London's transportation network sooner rather than later. You will probably want a straightforward journey, perhaps with just one Underground line change for your commute. Ideally, you will have another Underground line, train station, or bus stop nearby so that you have a backup option if your regular line is down for some reason. It is all too common for one of the Underground lines to be out of action for a while, be it due to a broken-down train, a signal failure, or an incident with a passenger under

the rails. If you decide to live out of town and commute by rail into town, then bear in mind the travel time on both the train and the Underground. Commuting by car will very much depend on where you are working. In the City or the West End, parking a car will be expensive and problematic, and you will also have to pay a further charge for the privilege of taking a car into and around the center of London.

# Public Transportation

Ask any visitor to London what 10 things they find memorable about the city and their reply will probably include a mention of the Underground. This is hardly surprising, as London's Underground was introduced back in 1863, making it the oldest underground railway in the world. By contrast, North America's first subway, in Boston, opened in 1897, and the Paris Metro didn't open until 1900. One downside to having the oldest underground system in the world is that it always seems to need refurbishment, which can be very frustrating for its passengers. At the moment it seems that one or two lines are closed every weekend for engineering work, which can make getting around on Saturday and Sunday a bit of a challenge. The temperature on the Underground's trains can sometimes get unbearable during summertime heat waves, and has been recorded at more than 117°F (47°C). New air-conditioned trains introduced on the shallower Underground lines, such as the Circle, District, Hammersmith & City, and Metropolitan lines, should help ease these heat waves. Transport for London is also working to help cool the deeper lines by improving ventilation and introducing lighter trains, though this is likely to take some time; be sure to carry a bottle of water with you during hot summer days. However, the Underground isn't the only way to get around town. London also has an extensive network of buses and overground train services, and these can be ideal for getting around town without having to go in and out of central London to change Underground lines.

## TRANSPORT FOR LONDON

London's transportation network is overseen by Transport for London (TfL), part of the Greater London Authority. Although London's mayor is responsible for London's strategy for public transport and sets the prices for fares on the TfL network, the day-to-day running of the system falls to the commissioner of Transport for London. The overall network is a mixture of the Underground, some London Overground trains, the Docklands Light Railway (DLR), buses, trams, and the occasional river boat.

### Zones, Fares, and Oyster Cards

Fares for the Underground, DLR, and Overground trains within the TfL network are based on travel between its nine zones, with Zone 1 being the most central, Zone 6 extending out to Heathrow airport, and Zones 7-9 stretching out to Amersham or Chesham in the suburban county of Buckinghamshire. Fares are based on the zones traveled through, with there being a higher rate for peak-hour travel. You can pay for your travel with a single ticket (currently £4 to travel in Zones 1-2) bought in the station. You could also use a daily, weekly, monthly, or annual pre-pay travel pass known

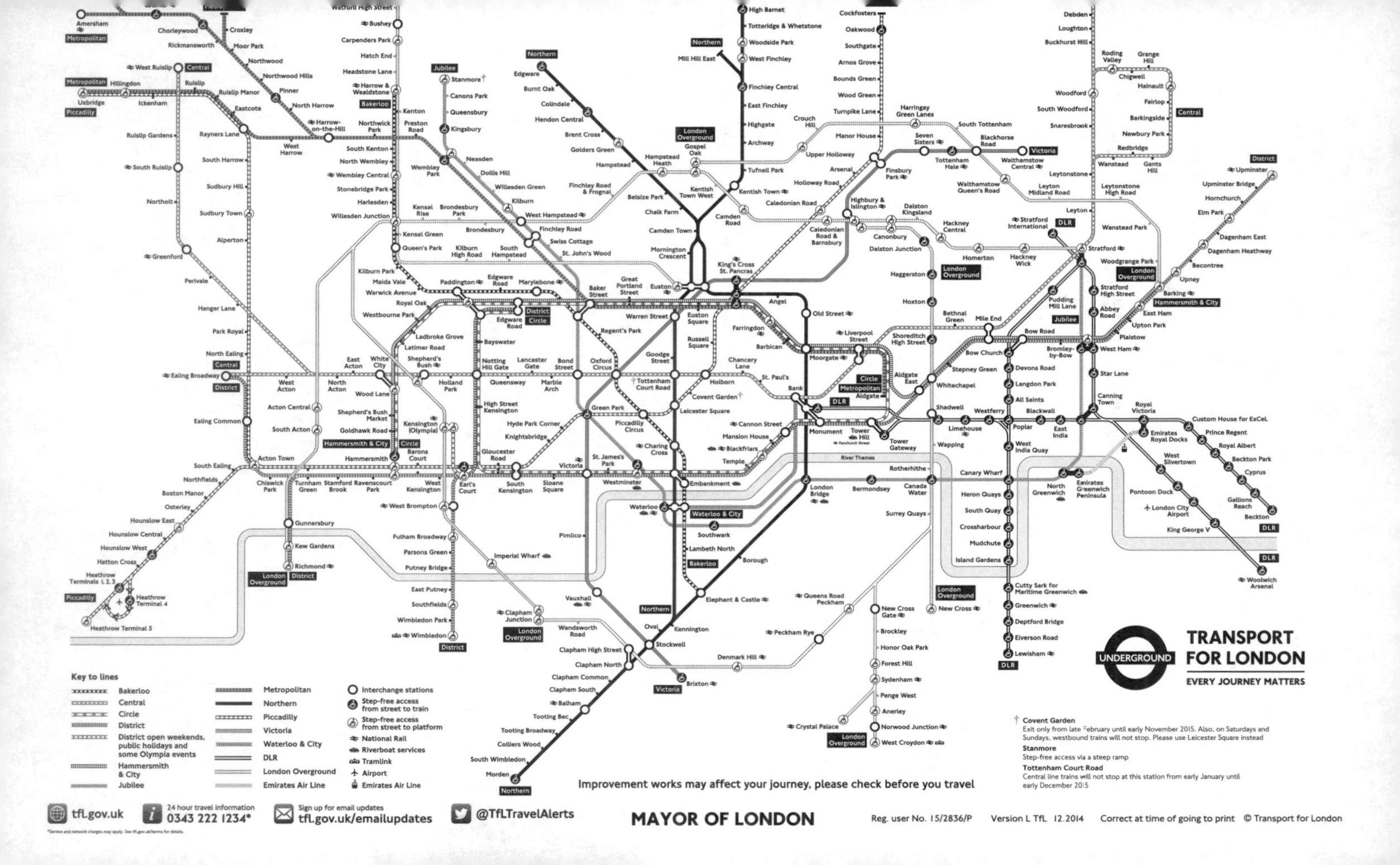

Amersham
Chorleywood
Rickmansworth
Croxley
Moor Park
Northwood
Northwood Hills
Pinner
North Harrow
Harrow-on-the-Hill
West Harrow
Metropolitan
Hillingdon
Uxbridge
Ickenham
Ruislip
Ruislip Manor
Eastcote
Rayners Lane
Ruislip Gardens
West Ruislip
South Ruislip
South Harrow
Sudbury Hill
Sudbury Town
Northolt
Alperton
Greenford
Perivale
Hanger Lane
Park Royal
North Ealing
Ealing Broadway
Ealing Common
West Acton
North Acton
East Acton
White City
Acton Central
South Acton
Acton Town
South Ealing
Northfields
Boston Manor
Osterley
Hounslow East
Hounslow Central
Hounslow West
Hatton Cross
Heathrow Terminals 1, 2, 3
Heathrow Terminal 4
Heathrow Terminal 5
Piccadilly
Central
Chiswick Park
Turnham Green
Stamford Brook
Ravenscourt Park
Hammersmith
Gunnersbury
Kew Gardens
Richmond
London Overground
District
Watford High Street
Bushey
Carpenders Park
Hatch End
Headstone Lane
Harrow & Wealdstone
Bakerloo
Kenton
Northwick Park
Preston Road
South Kenton
North Wembley
Wembley Central
Stonebridge Park
Harlesden
Willesden Junction
Kensal Rise
Brondesbury Park
Brondesbury
Kensal Green
Queen's Park
Kilburn Park
Maida Vale
Warwick Avenue
Royal Oak
Westbourne Park
Ladbroke Grove
Latimer Road
Shepherd's Bush
Shepherd's Bush Market
Wood Lane
Goldhawk Road
Kensington (Olympia)
Hammersmith & City
Circle
Barons Court
West Kensington
West Brompton
Fulham Broadway
Parsons Green
Putney Bridge
East Putney
Southfields
Wimbledon Park
Wimbledon
Imperial Wharf
Jubilee
Stanmore
Canons Park
Queensbury
Kingsbury
Wembley Park
Neasden
Dollis Hill
Willesden Green
Kilburn
West Hampstead
Finchley Road
Swiss Cottage
St. John's Wood
Kilburn High Road
South Hampstead
Finchley Road & Frognal
Paddington
Edgware Road
Marylebone
Baker Street
Holland Park
Notting Hill Gate
Bayswater
Queensway
Lancaster Gate
Marble Arch
Bond Street
High Street Kensington
Gloucester Road
Earl's Court
South Kensington
Sloane Square
Knightsbridge
Hyde Park Corner
Victoria
Pimlico
Northern
Edgware
Burnt Oak
Colindale
Hendon Central
Brent Cross
Golders Green
Hampstead
Belsize Park
Chalk Farm
Camden Town
Mornington Crescent
Hampstead Heath
Gospel Oak
Kentish Town West
Camden Road
Mill Hill East
High Barnet
Totteridge & Whetstone
Woodside Park
West Finchley
Finchley Central
East Finchley
Highgate
Archway
Tufnell Park
Kentish Town
Crouch Hill
Upper Holloway
Euston
King's Cross St. Pancras
Great Portland Street
Warren Street
Euston Square
Regent's Park
Oxford Circus
Goodge Street
Russell Square
Tottenham Court Road
Holborn
Covent Garden
Leicester Square
Green Park
Piccadilly Circus
Charing Cross
St. James's Park
Westminster
Embankment
Waterloo
Waterloo & City
Southwark
Lambeth North
Elephant & Castle
Borough
Vauxhall
Oval
Kennington
Stockwell
Clapham Junction
Wandsworth Road
Clapham High Street
Clapham North
Clapham Common
Clapham South
Balham
Tooting Bec
Tooting Broadway
Colliers Wood
South Wimbledon
Morden
Brixton
Denmark Hill
Peckham Rye
Queens Road Peckham
Farringdon
Barbican
Chancery Lane
St. Paul's
Bank
Cannon Street
Mansion House
Blackfriars
Temple
Angel
Old Street
Moorgate
Liverpool Street
Aldgate
Aldgate East
Monument
Tower Hill
Fenchurch Street
Tower Gateway
DLR
River Thames
London Bridge
Bermondsey
Rotherhithe
Canada Water
Surrey Quays
Wapping
Shadwell
Whitechapel
Shoreditch High Street
Hoxton
Haggerston
Dalston Junction
Dalston Kingsland
Canonbury
Highbury & Islington
Caledonian Road & Barnsbury
Caledonian Road
Holloway Road
Arsenal
Finsbury Park
Manor House
Turnpike Lane
Wood Green
Bounds Green
Arnos Grove
Southgate
Oakwood
Cockfosters
Harringay Green Lanes
Seven Sisters
Tottenham Hale
Blackhorse Road
Walthamstow Central
South Tottenham
Walthamstow Queen's Road
Leyton Midland Road
Hackney Central
Homerton
Hackney Wick
Bethnal Green
Mile End
Stepney Green
Bow Church
Bow Road
Limehouse
Westferry
Poplar
Devons Road
Langdon Park
All Saints
Blackwall
East India
West India Quay
Canary Wharf
Heron Quays
South Quay
Crossharbour
Mudchute
Island Gardens
Cutty Sark for Maritime Greenwich
Greenwich
Deptford Bridge
Elverson Road
Lewisham
New Cross Gate
New Cross
Brockley
Honor Oak Park
Forest Hill
Sydenham
Penge West
Anerley
Crystal Palace
Norwood Junction
West Croydon
Stratford International
Stratford
Pudding Mill Lane
Bromley-by-Bow
West Ham
Star Lane
Canning Town
Royal Victoria
Custom House for ExCeL
Prince Regent
Royal Albert
Beckton Park
Cyprus
Gallions Reach
Beckton
Emirates Royal Docks
Emirates Greenwich Peninsula
North Greenwich
West Silvertown
Pontoon Dock
London City Airport
King George V
Woolwich Arsenal
Abbey Road
Stratford High Street
Plaistow
Upton Park
East Ham
Barking
Upney
Becontree
Dagenham Heathway
Dagenham East
Elm Park
Hornchurch
Upminster Bridge
Upminster
Woodgrange Park
Wanstead Park
Leyton
Leytonstone
Leytonstone High Road
Wanstead
Redbridge
Gants Hill
Newbury Park
Barkingside
Fairlop
Hainault
Grange Hill
Chigwell
Roding Valley
Woodford
South Woodford
Snaresbrook
Buckhurst Hill
Loughton
Debden
Key to lines
Bakerloo
Central
Circle
District
District open weekends, public holidays and some Olympia events
Hammersmith & City
Jubilee
Metropolitan
Northern
Piccadilly
Victoria
Waterloo & City
DLR
London Overground
Emirates Air Line
Interchange stations
Step-free access from street to train
Step-free access from street to platform
National Rail
Riverboat services
Tramlink
Airport
Emirates Air Line
Improvement works may affect your journey, please check before you travel
UNDERGROUND
TRANSPORT FOR LONDON
EVERY JOURNEY MATTERS
† Covent Garden
Exit only from late February until early November 2015. Also, on Saturdays and Sundays, westbound trains will not stop. Please use Leicester Square instead
Stanmore
Step-free access via a steep ramp
Tottenham Court Road
Central line trains will not stop at this station from early January until early December 2015
tfl.gov.uk
24 hour travel information 0343 222 1234*
Sign up for email updates tfl.gov.uk/emailupdates
@TfLTravelAlerts
*Service and network charges may apply. See tfl.gov.uk/terms for details.
MAYOR OF LONDON
Reg. user No. 15/2836/P
Version L TfL 12.2014
Correct at time of going to print
© Transport for London

© LES SMITHSON

Londoners head to the Liverpool Street tube station.



as a "Travelcard." These allow you to make unlimited journeys within the zone(s) covered, and are good on the Tube, buses, Overground trains, and Docklands Light Railway. A one-day Travelcard for Zone 1 costs £12, while a one-day Travelcard for Zones 1-6 costs nearly £17, though this drops to just £12 if you travel off-peak. These are just one-day Travelcards, and you'll save money if you get a weekly, monthly, or annual pass. You can buy tickets and Travelcards in the Underground or train station at the ticket machines or at the staffed ticket offices or online at www.tfl.gov.uk. Remember that paying for each individual journey is *the* most expensive way to travel, and you are much better off getting a travel pass of some sort.

Another way to pay for the Tube is with a pay-as-you-go Oyster card. Transport for London introduced its smartcard with an embedded radio-frequency identification (RFID) chip—the Oyster card—back in 2003. Travelers simply swipe in and out of the ticket gates by touching their Oyster card to the yellow contact pad. They can top up their cards as and when they need them in the station or online, or they can register a credit card with TfL to have their Oyster card's credit automatically topped up when it falls below a certain level. An Oyster card can be used under the pay-as-you-go system or be loaded with a Travelcard. Best of all, you can use your Oyster card several times in a day and the amount you pay will be capped. The current daily cap for Zone 1-2 usage is £6.40. Just like a paper Travelcard from a ticket machine, Oyster cards can be used on the Underground, Overground trains, buses, National Rail services within London, and the Docklands Light Railway. You can also get an Oyster card online if you are in the United Kingdom or at most Underground stations. I suggest that you get an Oyster card fairly quickly, because TfL encourages people to use it rather than tickets or Travelcards and has adjusted its fares to reflect this. Single journeys using an Oyster card cost significantly less than single cash tickets.

The most recent addition to Transport for London's fare payment scheme is the acceptance of contactless payment via Visa, MasterCard, Maestro, or American Express. You will know if your card offers contactless payments if it displays the contactless symbol. The system also includes some contactless mobile payment applications, such as mobile phones (assuming they are set up for contactless payments). Fares using this payment method are the same as those for a pay-as-you-go Oyster card.

One bit of good news is that students and children pay a bit less to use public transportation in London. Those aged 10 or under can travel for free on the Underground, buses, DLR, and Overground, providing they are with an adult using an Oyster card. To do this go to the staffed ticket gate and the guard will let you both through; just make sure that the adult swipes in and out as usual. Kids between 10 and 15 get a reduced rate for their travel on the Tube and other trains in town, providing they have a photo Oyster card. Those between 11 and 15 can ride on the buses for free, but again they need a photo Oyster card. Full-time students aged 16 to 18 can use the public transportation network for half price and may be able to qualify for free bus travel with a photo Oyster card. Full-time students over age 18 qualify for a 30 percent discount off a weekly (or longer) Travelcard, though they also need a photo Oyster card.



## THE UNDERGROUND (TUBE)

Each year more than one billion passengers are carried by the Underground, and in peak times of the year, such as the busy pre-Christmas period, passenger numbers swell to more than four million a day. By anyone's standard, that is a lot of people using the Underground system and its 11 different train lines, and it is small wonder that at peak times traveling on a train can seem more like being a sardine packed in a can, rather than a commuter on a train. Unsurprisingly, when so many people are packed into such a cramped space, there is a whole new level of etiquette for Tube travel. On escalators, you stand on the right and walk up the steps on the left. Certainly, don't stop moving at the top or bottom of the escalator—this blocks the way for the rest of the passengers coming off the escalator. Be sure to let passengers off the train first before you dive in after a seat. Women passengers who are expecting can now get a "baby on board" badge, so please give up your seat if you see one and can't justify having a seat yourself. Likewise, offer your seat to parents with young children who may be unable to maintain their balance as the train bumps along. It goes without saying that the elderly, injured, or disabled should be offered a seat as there are no specially designated seats for them on the Tube. Otherwise, keep your head down and generally keep yourself to yourself, just like everyone else.

Unlike its name suggests, the Underground isn't completely underground. At least four of its lines (the Circle, District, Hammersmith & City, and Metropolitan lines) can be classed as subsurface routes, while the rest (the Bakerloo, Central, Jubilee, Northern, Piccadilly, Victoria, and Waterloo & City lines) are the deeper Tube routes, at least while they are in central London. Nearly all of the Underground lines go aboveground for some of their journeys, which is why there can be major delays when it snows.

Traveling on the Tube during the rush hour (usually 7:30am-9:30am and 5pm-7pm) can be a nightmare, with people being packed into very crowded trains. If you aren't commuting, try to avoid traveling during the rush hour if you can. One last bit of advice: If you are traveling with children, always hold their hands and keep them near on the platform and train. I have a friend whose eldest daughter (just 7 at the time) got on a train only to turn around and see her mother and sister still on the platform just as the train pulled out. Luckily, all was well and the child got off at the next stop, with the mother and sibling following behind on the next train. Everyone was reunited within 10 minutes or so, but it was an anxious time for all.

## LONDON BUSES

One of the most iconic sights you'll see in London is the bright red double-decker buses. Unfortunately, the old-style open-backed Routemasters with a conductor selling tickets are seldom used these days. Instead, we get a newly designed and much more environmentally friendly Routemaster bus. Like the old Routemaster, these buses have a conductor (at least in busy central London), who does not take fares but supervises the rear platform to make sure people get on and off safely.

London's buses are now cash-free so you will need an Oyster card, Travelcard, one-day bus pass, or contactless payment method to pay the £1.50 fare. London's newer buses are appropriate for wheelchair users and parents with a child in a stroller; they have a ramp that can be lowered so that travelers can get on the bus more easily. Nothing beats seeing London from the front row on the top deck of a bus. When my children were young, we used to take a bus down Oxford and Regents Street every December, sitting in the front row on the top deck to see the Christmas lights. It was a fantastic way to experience the holiday without fighting your way through the hordes of shoppers on the street below.

To catch a ride on a bus you need to be at a bus stop—look for a red bus sign on top of a pole. There may well be a line ("queue") of people already waiting for the bus, so don't barge on in front of those who are already there. One vital piece of information is that there are two types of bus stops: a normal stop where the driver pulls in to let on passengers and a request stop where a bus will only stop if hailed. Always check to see if you are at a request bus stop by looking at the sign on the bus stop—it will say Request Stop on it. If in doubt, just put out your arm so that the driver knows you want to get on. You should find details of the bus routes on the bus stop pole and read the banner above the bus's windshield (referred to as a "windscreen" here) to see its route number and destination.

## DOCKLANDS LIGHT RAILWAY

This electronic tram system services Docklands and City Airport, as well as going over the River Thames to Greenwich and beyond. This area was once home to London's docks, which used to be the largest in the world. Now, following redevelopment in the late 1980s and '90s, the docks have been turned into modern offices and residential buildings, and are home to numerous commercial and investment banks. Because it is above ground and snakes through the ultramodern Docklands complex, this train can be a fun way to explore this area of London. Fares for the DLR are the same as those charged for the Tube; a single journey in Zone 1 costs £4.80 (or £2.30 with Oyster at off-peak times), and trains tend to come every 10 minutes or so.

## LONDON OVERGROUND

Complementing the Underground system is London's network of overground trains, connecting greater West and East London without having to go through the middle of town. The London Overground now runs on both sides of the Thames, creating a Zone 2 ring around London (though you need to switch trains at Clapham Junction and Highbury & Islington stations). The train network also travels through Zone 3 in northeast London, as well as linking suburban Watford, Hertfordshire, to Euston station in central London. Prior to 2007, when TfL took over the network, these train lines used to be run by the private railway companies and were more expensive than the Underground. However, now that these trains are part of TfL, a journey on the Overground costs the same as the Tube or DLR. Remember that this is a rail service and that trains can be 20 minutes apart, though more popular lines run every 10 minutes or so, with a reduced service on the weekends.

Other train networks ferry commuters from the suburbs (and farther afield) into the capital, but they are not part of the TfL network. Instead they are owned and run by individual railroad companies. These include South West Trains from southwest of London, Thameslink from the north, Chiltern Railways from the west, and Southeastern Railway from southeast of town. There is also a tram line in South London linking Wimbledon with Beckenham Junction (in southeast London) via Croydon.



## RIVER BOAT

You may not think of traveling by river boat as a credible option for getting around London, but you would be mistaken. If you are working near the river, then using one of Thames Clippers' river boats is an enjoyable, if more expensive, way to travel to and from work, and you can use an Oyster card to pay for your journey. There are

a train taking passengers across the river in Barnes

Seeing London from the river gives you a whole new perspective on the city.

also several other river boat cruises, which will take you either east toward Docklands or west downriver to Hampton Court in Surrey. Traveling on the river is a great way to see London, especially Tower Bridge. The river boats tend to come every 20 minutes or so, with the frequency increasing to every 10 minutes during rush hour. With tickets for a single journey for an adult currently running £8.78-16.20 (depending on distance traveled), a ride on a river boat isn't as affordable as the Underground or bus, but it certainly is a fun way to travel. If you have an Oyster card or Travelcard you should be able to get a reduced rate on your river boat fares.

# Taxis

One of London's most iconic images is that of a black taxicab and its odd carriage-like interior with pull-down backward-facing seats. However, it's worth noting that the black cab is not the only cab available in London. You can also use "minicabs," which are private cars for hire. Both of these types of cabs should be licensed by the London authorities—the wonderfully named Public Carriage Office.

## BLACK CABS

Black cabs are the only taxis that can be hailed in the street or used from a designated taxi rank. These tend to be located near to where people are likely to need a taxi, such as outside train stations, grand hotels, tourist attractions, or large shopping areas.

You can tell if a taxi is available by looking at the yellow light on the front of the black cab's roof. If it is lit up, then the cab is available. Black cabs can also be

© KAREN WHITE

Find a black cab at a taxi rank.

pre-booked over the phone, but there is a fee (at least £2) for this service. To qualify as a black-cab driver, you must pass a challenging test covering some 25,000 central London streets and memorize the quickest routes between certain destinations. This is known as getting "the Knowledge," and it usually takes two years to qualify as a black-cab driver.

All of the fares in a black cab are metered and depend on the distance and journey time, the number of passengers, and the time of day. For example, a two-mile journey for one person taking around 10 minutes during a weekday should be around £8.60-13.80. Fares for journeys comprise a single minimum tariff (currently £2.40 during the daytime in town) and a charge of 20 pence for each additional 126.2 meters or 27.1 seconds (whichever is reached first). As you'd expect, longer journeys are more expensive, and luggage or bulky shopping will also push the fare up. Black cabs can take up to six people, with luggage going in the front next to the driver. The usual tip for a taxi driver is to round up the fare to the nearest pound.

## MINICABS

The other type of cab available in London is a minicab. All minicabs must be pre-booked by phone or email and are generally less expensive than a black cab. Unlike a black cab, a minicab is a privately owned car, and the driver has not undergone the same level of training as a black-cab driver. Minicabs are not metered, so you should ask how much the fare will be when you make the booking.

It is important to only use a reputable minicab firm that is licensed by the London authorities—they will have a Transport for London license disc on both their front and back windshields. Your hotel should be able to organize a minicab for you from a reputable firm. You can also search for details on nearby licensed minicab firms on the Transport for London website (www.tfl.gov.uk) under the section on taxis and minicabs.

You should never use an unlicensed minicab. If you are approached in the streets by a person offering their services as a driver, don't be tempted to get in the car. The chances are they are illegal, unlicensed, and uninsured—and could potentially be very dangerous. Remember, minicabs must always be pre-booked. Only a black cab can pick up paying passengers in the street.

# Driving



For many expats, the prospect of driving in London fills them with dread. Not only will they be driving on the wrong side of the road, but the congestion on the streets, the occasional narrow road, and the steady stream of bicycle riders, pedestrians, motorbikes, and scooters all mean that you need to have your wits about you. Depending on where you live and your lifestyle, you can get by in London without a car fairly easily, though you will probably rely on black cabs and become pretty familiar with your local minicab firm. However, if you live more than five miles (eight kilometers) from the middle of town or in the rural counties surrounding town, then you will probably need to get a car to get around. The same is perhaps true if you live south of the river.

To be honest with you, driving in London isn't that difficult generally. All it takes is a bit of practice and a good idea of where you are going or a GPS to guide you. I tend to avoid driving in central London, as the congestion makes it faster to take the Tube or walk. There are, of course, differences between driving in the United States and the United Kingdom besides the obvious driving on the left side of the road. Although it's been a while since I lived in the States, I'd say that the attitude to driving after drinking is very different between the two countries. The laws are quite strict in England about how much alcohol can be in your system when you drive: the legal limit is just 80 milligrams of alcohol for every 100 milliliters of blood in your body. Driving under the influence is generally frowned upon, so people obey the laws and don't drink and drive—period.

## CONGESTION CHARGE AND PARKING PERMITS

If you decide to buy a car and drive in London, be aware that there is a special charge for taking a car into the center of town—the "congestion charge." It runs Monday-Friday 7am-6pm, except for public holidays. The charge is currently £11.50, though there are substantial discounts for residents who live within the congestion charge zone. There is no charge for cars registered to a disabled individual. The London authorities introduced the congestion charge back in 2003 and extended it west through Kensington and Chelsea in 2007. This move was deeply unpopular with residents and local businesses, so the western extension was abandoned in 2011.

The congestion charge was introduced to reduce pollution and congestion in the middle of town, and it has had some success at helping to ease both. The system works by a series of CCTV cameras that photograph license plates as they enter the charging zone. People have until midnight to pay the fee, though I tend to pay

## The Lowdown on Parking

There are days when I seem to spend all my time looking for a parking place. These tend to be the very busy days, when I'm down on the Kings Road in Chelsea doing some shopping before heading up to Hampstead to collect my son from school. We then go to Westminster to see a concert or play at my daughter's school. I dread to think how much time and money I really spend circling around and around trying to find a pay-and-display parking space in these areas. Yes, I know I really should use public transportation, but this involves going in and out of Zone 1 to change lines and takes just as long, if not longer, as it takes me to drive it. Plus there is the hefty walk at the other end, as the Tube isn't always near to where you are going, which isn't great in the evening with two kids in tow. So, if you are thinking about owning or occasionally renting a car you need to know a little bit about parking in London.

First of all, nearly all the London boroughs have some sort of controlled residential parking, which requires residents to get a permit to park on the street. Driveways and garages are rare, so parking on the street may be your only option. The price and requirements for the residence permits vary from borough to borough and depend on the engine size of your car, but you should expect anything from £120 up to £400 annually, with hefty charges for owning a second car. In most boroughs the permit allows permit holders to park in just certain areas around their home, although the permit for Kensington and Chelsea allows holders to use it anywhere in the borough. The times of the controlled parking vary with the location, with some just being Monday-Friday 7am-6:30pm, while others are seven days a week. So, if you live near a popular shopping area you may find that spaces are used by visitors to the area once the controlled hours have stopped. Nonresidents parking in a controlled area should always check the time of the controlled parking exactly where they are parked. There should be signs with the times and days listed on them. I learned this the hard way and once made the mistake of assuming that as the controlled parking didn't apply on one street that it wouldn't apply just around the corner. Of course I was wrong and my car was towed—a very expensive mistake on my part.

In addition to the restrictions posted on signs there are markings for stopping (and parking) restrictions that are painted on the road, just next to the curb. A double yellow line means that you can't park there, and a single yellow means that parking is restricted to certain hours, which should be posted on a sign nearby. A double red line is a "red route" and stopping is not allowed—these are just on main roads usually. Loading areas are usually marked out on the road with the word "loading."

There is also the usual "pay-and-display" option, where you get a ticket from a nearby machine and display it on your dashboard. The machines take coins or debit/credit cards with a personal identification number (some now only accept debit/credit cards). Across more of London the local authorities are encouraging car users to pay for parking by registering a credit/debit card with them and then using their cell phone to call or text in their location and the number of minutes they want.

Parking lots are another option, and in some parts of town (such as Covent Garden) they will be your best option. The largest chain of parking lots (or "car parks," as they are called here) is NCP (National Car Parks), and it has numerous parking lots all around central London. These aren't cheap, but if you have no idea how long you are going to stay then they give you some flexibility. And you won't have to circle the street looking for an empty space. Some stores also have parking lots that let you park for an hour or two for free if you do some shopping.

However, if I'm in central London and planning to be there for some time, it is always cheaper to take the Underground or bus, rather than taking the car and parking—especially during weekdays.

© KAREN WHITE

To drive into the heart of London with an ordinary car, you will need to pay the congestion charge.

before I enter the zone on the odd occasion when I take my car into the center of town. I usually just call the automated congestion charge phone line (tel. 0343/222 2222), though I could just as easily pay online through the Transport for London website (www.tfl.gov.uk/modes/driving/congestion-charge). If you forget, you can pay a slightly increased fee the following day—otherwise you'll receive a hefty fine (currently £130). TfL has also introduced an automated payment system, Congestion Charge Auto Pay, which people can sign up for through their website, which is great for absent-minded drivers. As part of its green policy, the London authorities have exempted ultra-low-emission vehicles (vehicles with carbon dioxide emissions below 75 grams per kilometer) from the congestion charge, though you'll need to register the car with TfL.

Another cost to motorists is a resident parking permit. Most of the boroughs require car users to have a resident parking permit to park on their streets—at least during weekdays.

## DRIVER'S LICENSE

You can drive in the United Kingdom with your American license for a year after you've moved here, and you don't need an international license. If you plan on driving with your US license, I suggest that you get a copy of the *Highway Code* first. This book details all the rules of the road, and you will need to study it to get your British driving license. You can only use your US license for a year; after that you will need to get a British license (spelled "licence" here). Learning how to drive to pass the British test will take practice; not only are the laws different, but the way you should use the car is different. For example, you should look in all the mirrors, signal that you are going to move, and then make your maneuver. If you don't do it in this order, you will fail the test. It's not so much a question of learning to drive (as it was when you were 16), it's more a question of learning how to drive here, and more importantly learning how to pass the written and practical driving tests. If you decide to get your British driving license, don't leave it too late before your 12 months are up, and I strongly suggest that you get a few lessons under your belt. Your first step to getting a British license will be to get a "provisional driving license" (similar to a learner's permit) so that you can drive when a fully qualified and experienced driver is in the car. You can do this at your local post office or online at www.gov.uk/browse/driving/driving-licences. A few driving schools offer lessons for people who just need to get their British license, and you may want to use one of these. Don't get disheartened if you don't pass your

## Roundabouts: The British Answer to Four-Way Stops

In Europe they don't use four-way stops at junctions. Instead they use a "roundabout." These are referred to as traffic circles in the United States, and a few states have adopted them. As the name implies, this is a circular junction, with different roads feeding into it. Here in the United Kingdom, cars travel *only* in a clockwise direction around the roundabout. You should yield to the car to your right at a roundabout, so stop and let them go first. If there is a car to your left, they should yield to you. If you can make the maneuver before they arrive, then you should go. And if there is no one to your right, you should proceed around the circle without stopping (just be sure to slow down, look, use your mirrors, and signal before you go).

For most American drivers, it takes a while to become comfortable with roundabouts. The temptation is to stop at the junction and look right, left, and right again as you would at a four-way stop. But roundabouts are designed to keep the traffic flowing, so you should only stop if you need to give way. The real trouble begins when you have more than one lane as you approach a roundabout. Then you will need to be in the correct lane for your maneuver: left lane to turn left (signaling as you approach), left lane to go straight ahead (only signal left as you exit), right lane to turn right (signaling right turn and then switching to left turn as you approach your exit). If you miss your exit, continue around the roundabout—I've been known to do this several times while I look for the right exit. Needless to say, going around busy roundabouts can require lots of concentration.

Adding to this complexity are London's busy streets and the need to be fairly aggressive in your driving to get anywhere, all of which makes maneuvering a busy roundabout a real challenge. Sometimes they can seem like a free-for-all, as assertive drivers rush into the roundabout in a bid to get through first, or impatient drivers behind you honk their horn because you aren't taking your right-of-way and other drivers are taking advantage of you. However, with a bit of practice and nerves of steel, you will soon become accustomed to driving around roundabouts—and once you're an expert, you can try Hyde Park Corner (a nightmare if ever there was one).



test on the first attempt. Many experienced drivers fail, often because they fall back into their usual "bad" driving habits and fail to follow the rules precisely.

## BUYING AND RENTING A CAR

There's no two ways about it—owning a car is expensive in London, and that's not just because the price of gas (called "petrol" here) is among the highest in the world. The price of a liter of gas has been on a roller coaster ride for the past few years. In 2012, it rose drastically to more than £1.40 following hefty rises in the price of a barrel of crude oil. In 2014, the price dropped as demand for oil slowed down around the world. We may yet see it fall below £1 per liter for the first time in several years. Cars are also expensive, and you'll pay a premium for a new car. There is a good market for second-hand cars; the average asking price is around £5,500. Several weekly publications, such as *Loot* and *Auto Trader,* specialize in listing second-hand cars. One thing to watch for with some older cars is theft. Most newer cars in London have either an alarm or are fitted with an immobilizer, or both, but car theft and theft from cars can be a problem, so don't leave anything of value in them.

Car insurance is a must for all drivers, and the cost depends on several variables, including the type and age of the car, where you live, and your experience as a driver. In the summer of 2014, the average annual cost of comprehensive car insurance was nearly £900. To help reduce your premiums, you could try asking your US insurer for a reference letter, assuming you haven't made any claims lately. In addition to insurance, you'll need to pay an annual road tax for each car you own; this can be done in a post office, by phone, or online (www.taxdisc.direct.gov.uk). You no longer receive a round disc (a "tax disc") to put in the windshield of your car. Today all information is held digitally, and the police and traffic wardens can use a handheld device to check if the car is taxed. The amount of road tax you'll pay depends on the age of your car. Cars registered before 2001 are based on the engine size, and those with an engine under 1,549 cubic centimeters pay around £145 per annum. More modern cars pay according to the car's measured CO2 emissions, with the annual taxes ranging from £20 at the bottom end of the scale up to £500 for heavy polluters. All cars that are more than three years old must undergo an annual road safety and emissions test by the Ministry of Transport, known as getting a "MOT certificate." There is, of course, a fee for this test (£55 in 2014), and you also need to cover the cost of any work the garage needs to carry out to make the car road worthy. You must have your car's MOT certificate and proof of insurance in order to pay your road tax.

If you don't want to own a car but want regular access to one, look into leasing a car. This is fairly common in London, and you'll find several leasing companies online. However, this will be difficult to achieve until you establish a credit history in the United Kingdom. You may find that you have to take out a short-term lease (which is more expensive) until you get your UK credit history established. Another useful alternative to car ownership is to join a car club, such as Zipcar. With Zipcar, users pay an annual fee and you only pay for the time that you actually use the car. This can be by the hour, day, or for as long as you want to use the car; all you need to do is reserve the car, which can be done online, by phone, or through a cell phone application. If you just need a car for the occasional trip to that well-known Swedish furniture store or for a weekend out of town, you can rent a car in the usual way from a car rental company. You'll find many of the major American rental companies are in the United Kingdom, such as Hertz, Avis, Budget, and Thrifty.

## RULES OF THE ROAD

Before you start to drive with any regularity here, you should become at least a bit familiar with the general laws of driving. The most major difference that US drivers need to adjust to is driving on the left. This means that you pass (or "overtake") someone on their right. You also need to realize that although you should be on the left, often London's roads are so narrow that everyone uses the middle of the road, as there is only room for one car between all the parked cars. Just remember that if you encounter an oncoming car you should move over to the left. One aspect of driving here that is the same as in the United States is that you give way to the right at roundabouts. You don't get four-way stops here—they use lights or roundabouts instead. For other intersections, you'll see two parallel dashed painted white lines going across the left side of the road as you approach the intersection. These lines mean that you must give way to traffic at this intersection.

You should also be aware of "zebra crossings," which are recognizable as crosswalks with black and white stripes across them. These give right-of-way to pedestrians, and you must stop and let them cross the road, just as with crosswalks in the United States.

The standard speed limit in towns is 30 miles an hour (48 kilometers per hour). In a fair amount of London this has been reduced to just 20 mph (32 kph), with bumps in the road to enforce your speed.

It is illegal to use a cell phone to talk, text, or send emails while driving. You must use a hands-free system (for example, Bluetooth) for phone calls.

Everyone in the car must wear a seatbelt—both in the front and the back. Children 3-12 and under the height of 135 centimeters (4 feet, 5 inches) must use a booster seat. Once a child has reached the height of 135 centimeters, they do not have to use a booster seat. Children 12 and over (regardless of their height) do not need to use a booster seat. Children under 3 must be in a car seat, and babies cannot be in a rear-facing car seat in the front if there is an active airbag.

To drive you must be at least 17 years old, and at least 16 to ride a moped or motorbike.



## BICYCLING

Those who prefer to travel under their own steam will be pleased to learn that an increasing number of Londoners use two wheels to get around. Although London still has a ways to go, the authorities are trying to make it a friendlier place for "cyclists" by introducing cycle lanes on many roads throughout London. I know plenty of people who regularly commute on bike each day, bravely facing the congested streets and vying with buses and taxis for road space, not to mention breathing in the noxious fumes.

More and more people are traveling around London on bikes.

## On Your Bike

Maybe it's the high cost of public transportation, or perhaps Mayor Boris Johnson has set a bike-friendly example, but more Londoners are taking to a bicycle for their weekday commute. The 2011 census found that the number of Londoners cycling to work has more than doubled in the past 10 years (it's very popular with men in their 30s). Biking to work often provides the fastest and most direct journey into central London, and could be the quickest commute option.

While cycling can be a great way to get to work and to keep fit, it is not without risk. London's busy roads can make riding a bike a bit daunting, and unfortunately fatal accidents do occur. To improve safety for bicyclists, Transport for London has introduced a couple of Cycling Super Highways routes to better separate road traffic from bikes on key routes across London. These routes cover South London to central London and East London to the City of London. Further developments may include the riverside embankment through central London.

Transport for London is also introducing new road safety measures, such as redesigning major junctions and streets, increasing the number of CCTV traffic enforcement cameras, and equipping heavy-goods vehicles with safety equipment. They also offer bicycle training to London school pupils, which my son found to be very educational (he now criticizes every cyclist he sees for not positioning themselves properly in the road or using hand signals).

With major improvements to London's cycling network on the drawing board and better education on bike safety, riding a bike in London may become even more popular.



I admire them, for I'm not sure I would be fearless enough to use a bike downtown. However, getting around by bike can be very enjoyable when you are away from the congestion. In a bid to help promote cycling, London has introduced a "jump on, jump off" self-service, bike-sharing scheme. People can rent bikes for a short journey or to just ride around town. It costs £2 to rent the bike (using a debit or credit card) for a 24-hour period, and the first half hour of each journey is free. Any bike rides for more than 30 minutes will cost an extra £2 per 30 minutes.

## MOTORBIKES OR SCOOTERS

If using a bike sounds like too much hard work, then you could always try a motorbike or scooter. These have the advantage of being able to weave in and around traffic, avoiding the worst of the congestion, getting you to your destination that much quicker. Of course they are not the safest way to travel, as it is all too easy for drivers to not see you, but wearing fluorescent outer clothing and having your lights on should help. Traveling by scooter or motorbike gives you the freedom of a car but at a fraction of the cost. They also don't have to pay the congestion charge (at least not yet) but do have to pay for parking sometimes.

# Outside London

## AIRPORTS

London has five airports, with Heathrow and Gatwick the two best known. The other three are Luton and Stansted, both north of the city, and City Airport in East London. Flights from the United States usually land at either Heathrow or Gatwick, though you can fly to and from the Continent at the other three airports. You can take an express train or Tube to Heathrow and the DLR to City Airport; otherwise you'll need to get a taxi, train, or bus out to one of the other airports.

With security what it is today, the check-in times for the airports can be very long—up to three hours. Be sure to leave enough time for you to get checked in and through security and passport control.



## TRAINS

Back in the mid-1990s, Britain's nationalized railways service (British Rail) was privatized to create several railroad companies, with the infrastructure and rail tracks owned and maintained by a newly formed company called Railtrack. The passenger and freight railroad companies leased the different lines from Railtrack. This was true for both intercity mainline services and smaller commuter railroads. Unfortunately, Railtrack was unable to survive financially and was replaced in 2002 with the state-owned Network Rail. There are currently 24 different railroad companies in the United Kingdom, excluding those run by Transport for London. In order to establish a sense of cohesion for Britain's railroads, the National Rail brand has been created, which

Stansted Airport

A Eurostar train waits at the platform at St. Pancras Station.



promotes Britain's railroads and provides a central point for passengers to find out about services and buy tickets. In recent years, there have been major improvements to the railroads on several lines, which should improve safety, comfort, and reliability.

There are some major new railway lines under development, including Crossrail, which will link Reading (some 40 miles west of London) with Shenfield northeast of Greater London and Abbey Wood in southeast Greater London. Crossrail also has five central London stops and will link with the Underground and some London railway stations. Other projects in the pipeline include HS2—a high-speed train line running from London and Birmingham (stage one) and then linking with Manchester and on to Leeds (stage two).

London is home to several major train stations providing links across the United Kingdom and offering a service to France and Belgium via Eurostar. If you want or need to travel around Britain, you can take a train from London to just about anywhere on the island, though you may have to make a few connections along the way. London is serviced by a variety of intercity lines, such as London Midland, which provides services between Liverpool and London. East Coast Train runs between Scotland and the capital. Visitors to the United Kingdom may also be familiar with rail services such as the Heathrow and Gatwick Express or First Capital Connect's Eurostar services to the Continent. Well-known London commuter lines include Chiltern Railways (from Birmingham, Oxfordshire, and Berkshire), First Capital Connect's Thameslink (from north of London), and Southeastern Railway (offering services across southeast England). Traveling by train can be a good way to get around, even if it isn't the cheapest option. You can reduce the cost of your rail travel by getting a round-trip ticket ("cheap day return") when you buy your ticket. These can be bought online through National Rail (www.nationalrail.co.uk) or in the staffed ticket office of a train station.

If you are traveling with a family (with at least one child between 5 and 15), get an annual family railcard, which currently costs £30. The family railcard gives you one-third off most adult fares and 60 percent off children's fares throughout Great Britain, and can be used by up to four adults and four kids. You can find out about these and other railcards online (www.railcard.co.uk), by calling National Rail Enquiries (tel. 08457/484950), or by asking at a staffed railroad station's ticket office.

## COACHES

Often the most affordable way to travel between towns and cities is on a bus, or "coach," as they say here. Some coach companies just service within a 40-mile (65-kilometer) radius of London, while others cover the whole of the United Kingdom and Ireland. There are coach services between towns and cities, or even to the Continent. You can also go on coach trips to visit particular sights in Britain, such as a day trip to Bath, Stonehenge, and Salisbury; or to Leeds Castle and Canterbury in Kent. The two best known coach companies are Green Line Coaches and National Express, while Premium Tours, among others, offers tours around London as well as farther afield.

# PRIME LIVING LOCATIONS

# OVERVIEW

When people are faced with the prospect of moving to London, often their first concern is to decide where they are going to live, and rightly so. Yet to do this successfully, they must first make some decisions about their priorities. Working out where to live in London will depend on several factors, such as budget, personal and school requirements, and the daily commute. These will be different for everyone and every family. Some people will want to be as close to work or their studies as possible, while others may want a quieter, more suburban atmosphere. Making your relocation to London a success requires you to do a bit of soul-searching and research. Some places are better for couples or single people, while others are more suitable for families. As you will probably start off renting, you will find your house-hunting easier if you stick to areas where there is a large rental market, which tend to be more centrally located. However, there is no obvious answer to the question of where to live in London that works for everyone—it is very much a personal decision.

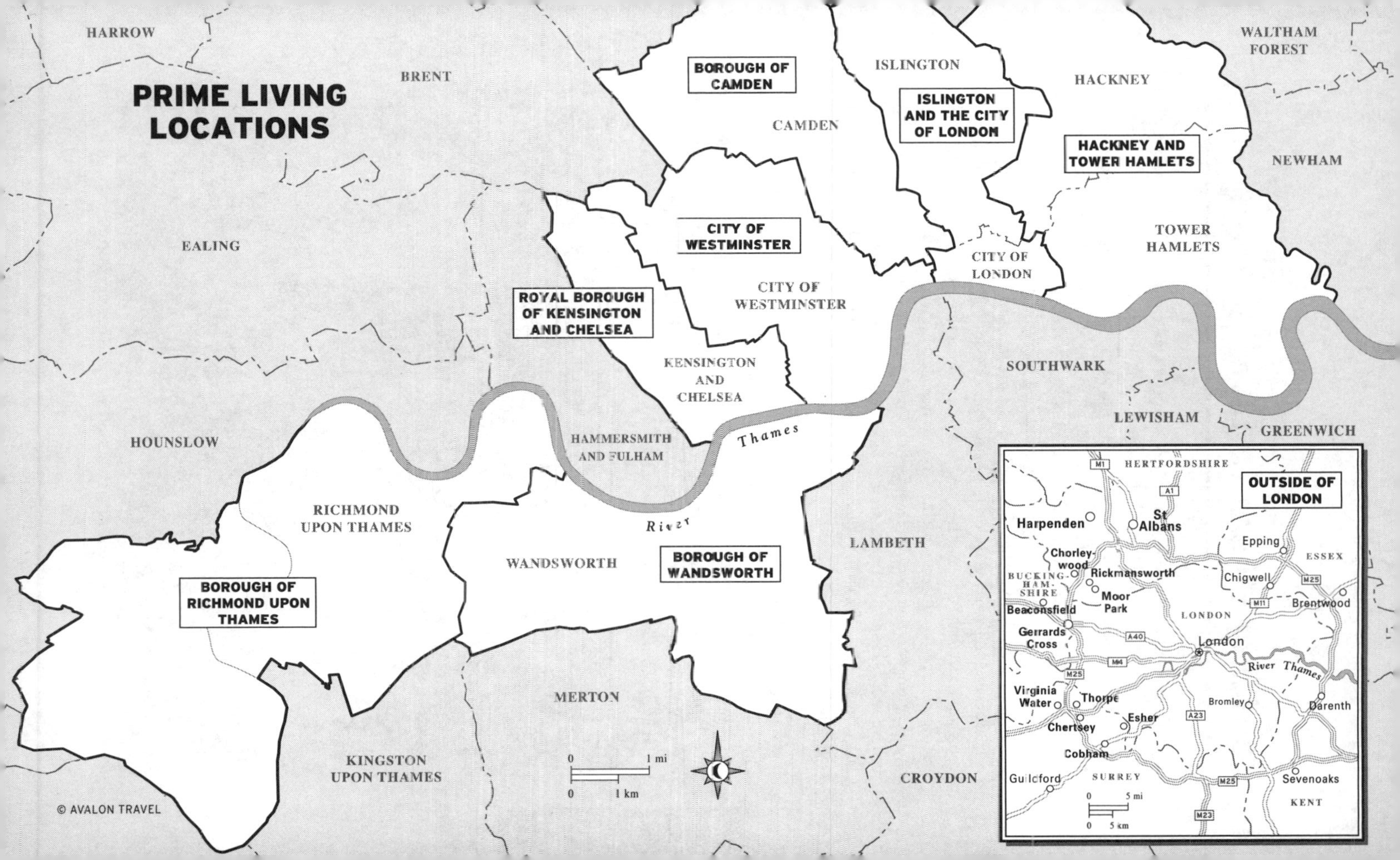
PRIME LIVING LOCATIONS
HARROW
BRENT
EALING
HOUNSLOW
BOROUGH OF CAMDEN
CAMDEN
ISLINGTON
ISLINGTON AND THE CITY OF LONDON
HACKNEY
WALTHAM FOREST
NEWHAM
HACKNEY AND TOWER HAMLETS
TOWER HAMLETS
CITY OF WESTMINSTER
CITY OF LONDON
ROYAL BOROUGH OF KENSINGTON AND CHELSEA
KENSINGTON AND CHELSEA
SOUTHWARK
LEWISHAM
GREENWICH
HAMMERSMITH AND FULHAM
Thames
River
RICHMOND UPON THAMES
WANDSWORTH
BOROUGH OF WANDSWORTH
LAMBETH
BOROUGH OF RICHMOND UPON THAMES
MERTON
KINGSTON UPON THAMES
CROYDON
0 1 mi
0 1 km
OUTSIDE OF LONDON
HERTFORDSHIRE
M1
A1
Harpenden
St Albans
Epping
ESSEX
Chorleywood
Rickmansworth
Chigwell
M25
BUCKINGHAMSHIRE
Moor Park
M11
Brentwood
Beaconsfield
LONDON
Gerrards Cross
A40
London
M4
River Thames
Virginia Water
Thorpe
Bromley
Darenth
Chertsey
Esher
A23
Cobham
Guildford
SURREY
Sevenoaks
0 5 mi
0 5 km
M23
KENT

# Deciding Where to Live

If you are new to London, then one of your biggest challenges will be to find the right neighborhood to live in. This isn't just about being able to get to work easily (though that is a prime consideration); it's also about finding an area that you like and can afford. Factors such as the commute, rental prices, and schools may be part of the equation. You may not be planning to get a car, so easy-to-access shopping (both practical and otherwise) is an important consideration. The best transportation links tend to be in the center of town, so living centrally should make for an easier commute, though this of course depends on where you work—not everyone's work will be in the middle of town. You should also consider your budget, and don't forget that exchange rates fluctuate.

Your own personal requirements—be it a nearby park where you can walk the dog, shopping on your doorstep, or a swimming pool at a local gym—will shape what you believe will be your ideal place to live in London. It will make your location search easier if you take a bit of time to consider these factors and decide on the "must haves" and "nice to haves."

## THE COMMUTE



One of your main considerations when selecting an area of town to live in is the commute. Believe me; standing for hours in a crowded train, packed in like sardines, can quickly make your life a misery. That said, sometimes where we work is really not where we want to live—it may be too congested, urban, isolated, noisy, quiet, expensive, etc. As far as the commute goes, remember that changing between Tube and train lines will

You may want to find a place to live that is a short walk to a grocery store.

complicate your journey and possibly create delays. Try to look in areas that will keep these changes to a minimum. Additionally, all too often there are delays or closures with your main Underground or train line, so also think about backup routes, such as a walk to another station (on another line) or the bus. Also bear in mind that suburban trains often suffer terribly from overcrowding and are expensive—Britain's train fares are considered to be the most expensive in Europe (based on distance traveled).

Now, you may be thinking, "no worries, I'll drive a car," but this will be even more expensive (especially given the price of gas), and parking will be a big problem. The only people I know who regularly use their cars to commute do a reverse commute—living in the city and working in the suburbs or even farther, and they only use their cars because they don't have a way to get from the nearest train station to work.

### SCHOOLS

I strongly suggest that if you have school-aged children you make it a priority to get their schooling sorted out first and then base your decision about where to live on where the kids will be at school. If you are going down the state education route, then you may have no other option but to get your accommodations sorted first. Just remember that living next to the state school of your choice does not mean you will get a place there. Good schools are oversubscribed—especially in London, where there is a worrying shortage of state school places—and you may find your children have been offered a place at a less than ideal school. Most Americans I've spoken to found the process of getting the children's schooling sorted out the hardest part of their relocation to London. Believe me—it is hard for the British who live here, too, and is the cause of many a sleepless night for parents, whatever their nationality. So do your homework, check out the schools, find out about availability in the relevant class year, and get your application in by the deadline.



## Property Prices

London's rental and property prices are among the highest in the world. For those looking for a place to live—whether expats or British national—they seem staggeringly high. On average costs are double those of the rest of the United Kingdom. The problem is that London is suffering from a shortage of housing stock, which is pushing prices up at a dramatic rate. The high price of rentals in central London has pushed hard-pressed Londoners to look elsewhere; as a result, parts of leafy, suburban outer London have seen annual rental values increase up to 20 percent. Many suburban Londoners endure a horrendously long commute to work in the capital, but this may be the only way to afford renting or buying a home.

Prices constantly change, so your best bet is to visit one of the online property portals to get an idea of how much landlords in a particular area are asking for their properties. As a general rule, the closer you are to central London the higher the property prices. The popularity of a neighborhood, the size and general finish of a property, the number of bedrooms, and proximity to a Tube or train station can also affect price.

## You Can't Always Get What You Want

High demand and low supply push up prices for commodity items or consumer goods, and the same market mechanism works in the rental property market. Since the economic downturn a few years ago, when the credit crunch put a stop to easily accessible mortgages, it has been increasingly difficult for Londoners to get on the property ladder, which means that they are renewing their leases and continuing to rent. At the same time, London has seen an increase in its population. Most importantly, the city has failed to anticipate increased housing requirements and hasn't generated enough new homes to meet growing demand. This increased demand and undersupply of homes has led to soaring purchase and rental prices—during 2014 the Camden borough saw an increase of rental values of up to 11 percent. For expats looking to rent in London it means that landlords can be a bit greedy and ask for extremely high rents, as more and more renters chase fewer and fewer properties. This can lead to bidding wars between potential renters or even gazumping—when the landlord gives the property to another tenant who has offered to pay more rent, leaving the original would-be tenant high and dry even though they paid a holding deposit and agreed on terms. The lower end of the market has the most acute shortage, with affordable property the hardest to come by.

Unfortunately, the shortage of housing isn't just limited to London. Across the southeast of England there is a shortage of homes, and property prices are high to both rent and buy. I guess that is what happens on an island with limited room for expansion. Until there is a let-up in demand for property it seems likely that prices will increase right across the capital, with increased competition for good properties.

Given the current state of the property market in London, with demand far outstripping supply, you may have to pay more than you would really want to for your home in London. Or, you may have to settle for what you can get in your price bracket that is closest to your requirements and forgo your preferred living location.



## MORE AFFORDABLE OPTIONS

London is considered the world's most expensive city in which to live and work. This is no doubt due in part to the high cost of property. The shortage of homes in London sent prices skyrocketing, fueled by high demand outstripping supply. Be prepared to settle for what you can get that is closest to your requirements and budget. Sometimes the areas a few stations beyond your first-choice location are a bit more affordable, placing you within easy access of the right area, yet without breaking the bank.

Anything that is fairly central to London (i.e., within Zone 1 or 2 of public transportation) will be on the expensive side; don't expect the rent in areas just beyond Marylebone to drop down to outer London prices. If money is extremely tight, you will have to live farther out, in an area with fewer amenities and leisure activities. Another option is to look for a much smaller place. If prices are still beyond your budget, you may have to do both.

If you are moving to London with your employers on a relocation package, they will be aware of the high cost of living in London, and this should be taken into account in your housing allowance. Before you decide to skimp on housing costs and pocket some of your allowance, do a bit of online research via London property portals to get an idea of rental prices.

# London Boroughs

London is generally referred to by its boroughs and then broken down to smaller neighborhoods (or villages), often based around a particular main street or Underground station. These areas have their own personalities and ambience, with good points and bad ones. Certainly the neighborhoods in Islington will be very different from those in Kensington and Chelsea, although with adjoining areas the distinctions can be more blurred, with perhaps only the nearest Tube station being the real difference between them. Your challenge will be to find the neighborhood that best suits you and your needs. Boroughs such as Westminster, Camden, Islington, and Kensington and Chelsea are popular with the expats. You may also want to consider some relative newcomers, such as Wandsworth, or the neighborhoods around the City of London. For suburban living you could try southwest London in the borough of Richmond—which is adored by the locals. Not everyone is cut out for life in the city, so we have also included a few rural and suburban areas outside of London. You should think of the locations covered as a starting point for possible places to live in London based on the availability of property (mainly for the rental market) and transportation links, as well as well-established and popular neighborhoods. Some places may not have the fastest transportation links but are still worth considering as long as you are realistic about the commute. Yes, most of the places recommended are in the better areas of town, but usually Americans who move to London for work receive a fairly good salary and suitable relocation allowance.



## ROYAL BOROUGH OF KENSINGTON AND CHELSEA

Just slightly west of the center of London, the Kensington and Chelsea borough is one of the most affluent areas in the capital—if not the United Kingdom. Popular neighborhoods include Chelsea, South Kensington, and trendy Notting Hill. The affluence of Kensington and Chelsea's residents can be seen in the abundance of fashionable boutiques and upmarket shops in this borough, with Chelsea, South Kensington, and Holland Park the most exclusive. The chic, trendy area of Notting Hill is very popular and still has a slightly bohemian feel. The area known as Kensington (near to Kensington High Street) has some wonderful accommodations and brilliant

© KAREN WHITE

a row of houses in Holland Park in Kensington

local shopping, while Holland Park is a quieter area and is dominated by the park for which it is named. Unlike in other central London boroughs (such as Camden, Islington, and Westminster), the overriding atmosphere of most of Kensington and Chelsea is one of refined residential neighborhoods with the occasional busy shopping street. With the exception of west Chelsea (which is a 10- to 15-minute walk from a Tube station), transportation links across the borough are fairly good, with many neighborhoods having access to more than one Tube line. If the property price tag for Kensington and Chelsea is too high, you could head west a bit into Hammersmith and Fulham, which is near to the delights of Kensington and Chelsea, yet is a bit easier on the pocket.

## CITY OF WESTMINSTER

When people think of London, chances are they are really thinking of Westminster, with its "Theaterland" and West End shopping, not forgetting its Royal Parks and Buckingham Palace. Although much of the borough is in busy central London, it does have some quiet residential areas, such as St. John's Wood and Maida Vale, which are only a few miles from the heart of the capital. The exclusive neighborhoods of Mayfair, Knightsbridge, and Belgravia offer luxurious apartment living right in the middle of town, while the area around Marylebone successfully mixes offices and retailing units, with prime residential living (Regent's Park is just a few minutes away). Cosmopolitan Bayswater is close to Notting Hill (and can be a bit more affordable), making it well worth considering if you want to be near to this part of London. Within the borough you'll find London's best stores and excellent public transportation throughout, which perhaps explains why this part of London is so popular with Americans.

© KAREN WHITE

shops on St. John's Wood Terrace in Westminster

## BOROUGH OF CAMDEN

A long, thin borough geographically, Camden stretches right down to Covent Garden and the City of London at its southern tip and up to the quiet residential neighborhoods around Hampstead and Highgate in the north of the borough. As with Westminster, there is a noticeable distinction between the north and south of the borough, with the former consisting of quiet leafy residential areas (such as Hampstead, Belsize Park, Highgate, and Primrose Hill) and the latter part of busy, congested central London (in Bloomsbury, Covent Garden, and Holborn). Camden Town is a halfway house between the north and south and is rougher than the other areas recommended, though its trendy edginess is what attracts many residents to this part of London. Generally, the expat community is drawn to the areas near Hampstead, where the atmosphere often centers on local village life. Because the village sits atop Hampstead Hill and has the green open spaces of "the Heath" to one side, this area is slightly isolated, which helps it to maintain a strong village feel, with an active local community. The numerous schools in the Hampstead area are another draw for families to this part of Camden. On the top of the same hill, but on the eastern side of Hampstead Heath, is Highgate, yet another village neighborhood in Camden. West Hampstead is more affordable than the village proper and has a livelier nightlife with some good bars and pubs. The main Underground lines servicing the northern borough are the Jubilee, Metropolitan, and Northern lines, while the southern part is crisscrossed by seven different Underground lines, with three mainline train stations.

## BOROUGH OF ISLINGTON AND THE CITY OF LONDON

Islington lies north of the City of London and is London's second smallest borough. It has a few very desirable residential neighborhoods, such as those running near Upper Street, with more urban living down in Clerkenwell next to the City. Not so long ago, much of Islington was considered quite rough; today, it has some of London's most attractive neighborhoods. At the bottom end of Upper Street is the more urbanized Angel neighborhood, while farther up Upper Street, in Highbury and Islington, Victorian and Georgian terraces dominate. Islington is more socially mixed than many areas to the west of London, with some very smart streets located next to some very deprived ones. Clerkenwell/Finsbury, in the south of the borough (near to the City of London), is a mixed commercial and residential area; it's popular with creative-sector businesses. The recommended parts of Islington are well served by the London Underground (with five different Tube lines), giving residents easy access to the rest of the capital. In addition, Angel and Clerkenwell have the added bonus that City of London workers can walk or take a short bus ride to commute to work.

One of the world's main financial districts, the City of London has the smallest residential population of any of London's boroughs—just 7,000 people. City workers who want to live as near to work as possible often favor property in the City or in one of the neighborhoods just beyond the "Square Mile," such as Clerkenwell, Shoreditch, Spitalfields, or south of the river's edge in Shad Thames by London Bridge station. The City is predominantly a business area and a hive of activity during the weekdays, but is much quieter on the weekends. The City has 10 Tube stations on six different lines and three train stations.

© KAREN WHITE

Shoreditch High Street Overground station in Hackney



## BOROUGHS OF HACKNEY AND TOWER HAMLETS

If you want urban hipster cool and loft-style living, then look no further than the threesome of Shoreditch, Hoxton (in Hackney), and Spitalfields (in nearby Tower Hamlets), all with an edgy feel, lively nightlife, and creative buzz. These are socially mixed boroughs, and their edginess can be attractive if you are someone who would prefer to see London (warts and all) rather than live in the manifestly exclusive areas of West London. Underground stations are thin on the ground in Hackney, though the areas near to Islington and the City of London have easy access to Tube and train stations; the rest of the boroughs rely on buses, the Overground, or trains to get into central London.

Tower Hamlets has witnessed the emergence of London's second financial center in Canary Wharf, an area also known as Docklands. Canary Wharf development was built with upmarket urban living in mind, so apartment complexes (along with stores, dining, and leisure activities) sit next to towering office blocks. Docklands is serviced by the Jubilee line, the Overground (in Canada Water), and Docklands Light Railway (DLR). Between Canary Wharf and the City of London is the area of Victoria Park/Bow, with its mix of modern apartments and Victorian terraces. The area is an oasis of leafy green in the East End and is serviced by the Central, Hammersmith & City, and District lines.

## BOROUGH OF WANDSWORTH

For years South London was a no-go area for expats, but gentrification has floated across the river from Chelsea and Fulham, and now parts of South London are among London's most desirable locations. Neighborhoods such as Battersea and Wandsworth, and even Putney, have undergone a massive gentrification and now attract families looking for good-sized family accommodations. In particular, the area between Clapham and Wandsworth Common teems with young professional families. Given the numerous green spaces nearby (including Clapham Common, Wandsworth Common, and Battersea Park); the restaurants, bars, and boutiques along Northcote Road; and some great local schools, it is no wonder that this part of Wandsworth has its devoted fans. Putney, too, offers some large family homes and good schools, and is popular with families. Both Battersea and Clapham (some of which is in the Lambeth borough) are more popular with young unencumbered professionals looking for fun-filled nightlife. To the south, you'll find the neighborhood of Wimbledon (in both Wandsworth and Merton boroughs), known for both its lawn tennis tournament and its fabulous family homes. Though the current lack of Underground stations near Battersea and Wandsworth does mean that public transportation options are dominated by Clapham Junction (the UK's busiest train station), parts of Clapham, Putney, and Wimbledon are serviced by the Northern and District lines.

## BOROUGH OF RICHMOND UPON THAMES

In the southwestern tip of outer London, the Richmond borough has distinct leanings toward suburbia, with a charming blend of old and new. The neighborhoods of Barnes, Kew, and Richmond are a halfway house between the suburbs and central London, giving you the best of both worlds. With the River Thames to one side and the massive Richmond Park on the other, these slightly suburban areas of London draw young professionals and families. Both Kew and Barnes are small villages with tight communities, helping to reinforce their suburban feel. They are also somewhat isolated by the river, so they don't have the same level of public transportation options as somewhere nearer town, but this is often the price you pay for a more suburban lifestyle. Richmond, on the other hand, is much larger and has better transportation links. A bit farther south is the area known as Kingston upon Thames, and property here is usually a little less expensive than in nearby Richmond. Also in southwest London, but less isolated and suburban, is Chiswick, which is on the north side of the Thames. Chiswick encompasses a relatively large area (with two District line stations) yet still has a thriving community and family-friendly atmosphere.



## OUTSIDE OF LONDON

Not everyone welcomes the prospects of living in the heart of a big city. For them, one of the counties that surround the capital may be a better option. One of the most popular counties for Americans is Surrey, which is southwest of London and is home to several international and American schools. Although Cobham and Esher are small towns and Virginia Water, Chertsey, and Thorpe are villages, these areas of Surrey attract expats keen to maintain their children's American schooling. Less than an hour's train ride from London, these towns and villages have a straightforward commute into town. You'll find a thriving social network of expats in this bit of Surrey—one that will easily match those in London.

West of London is the county of Buckinghamshire, where once again you can find countryside living with a straightforward commute. In this county you may want to consider the very affluent Gerrards Cross and Beaconsfield (with an American School a bus ride away). These towns are nestled in the beautiful Chiltern Hills, yet

© PETER ELVIDGE/123RF.COM

Buckinghamshire is only 30 minutes away from London.



are around 30 minutes from London by train. North of London there is the county of Hertfordshire, where you'll find spacious family homes with large suburban gardens. Popular suburban commuter-belt areas in southern Hertfordshire include Rickmansworth as well as nearby Chorleywood and Moor Park—all of which are on the Metropolitan Tube line. Farther away from London are the suburban towns of St. Albans and Harpenden, which offer fast trains into the capital and small-town suburban living. Of course, other counties surround London, including Essex to the northeast and Kent to the southeast. Although neither has a noticeable American expat community, one may be just what you are looking for.

When considering whether to live outside of London you should bear in mind that the rental market beyond the capital is not as developed as it is in the capital, and that rental options will be more limited. Most Americans who live in Surrey or Buckinghamshire are there for the schools and lifestyle. The best time to house hunt will be during the early summer, when most rental houses are marketed.

# ROYAL BOROUGH OF KENSINGTON AND CHELSEA

For many expats, living in the Royal Borough of Kensington and Chelsea (RBKC) is ideal. It has excellent transportation options with easy links to the City and West End, an upmarket ambience in lovely surroundings. The only downside is the high price tag of property here. From the genteel streets of Chelsea (with its well-heeled inhabitants) to the trendy and picturesque Notting Hill, this borough has a lot to offer, so it's no wonder that it is popular with the international community in London.

In case you are wondering why it's a "royal" borough, this honor was conferred upon the borough of Kensington in 1901 in memory of Queen Victoria, who was born at Kensington Palace. Back in 1965, when the two separate boroughs of Kensington and Chelsea were combined into a new larger borough, the royal patronage was also transferred.

The Royal Borough of Kensington and Chelsea is one of the wealthiest boroughs in London, if not the United Kingdom. It has a high concentration of big earners, many

© KAREN WHITE

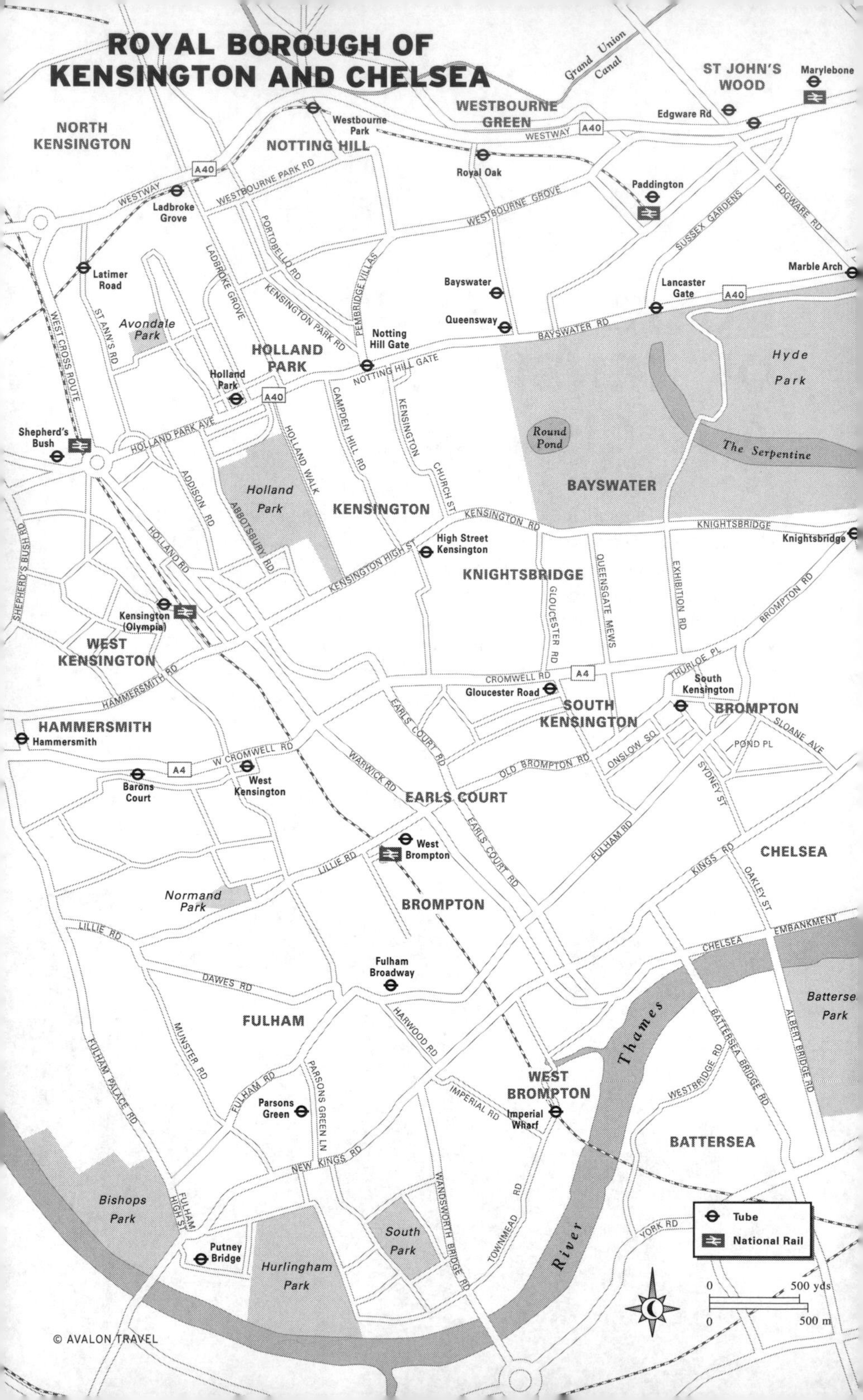
ROYAL BOROUGH OF KENSINGTON AND CHELSEA
Grand Union Canal
ST JOHN'S WOOD
Marylebone
WESTBOURNE GREEN
Edgware Rd
NORTH KENSINGTON
Westbourne Park
NOTTING HILL
WESTWAY
A40
Royal Oak
Paddington
WESTBOURNE PARK RD
WESTBOURNE GROVE
Ladbroke Grove
SUSSEX GARDENS
EDGWARE RD
PORTOBELLO RD
LADBROKE GROVE
Latimer Road
Bayswater
Marble Arch
Lancaster Gate
KENSINGTON PARK RD
PEMBRIDGE VILLAS
Queensway
BAYSWATER RD
ST ANN'S RD
Avondale Park
HOLLAND PARK
Notting Hill Gate
WEST CROSS ROUTE
Hyde Park
Holland Park
NOTTING HILL GATE
CAMPDEN HILL RD
KENSINGTON CHURCH ST
Round Pond
Shepherd's Bush
HOLLAND PARK AVE
HOLLAND WALK
The Serpentine
ADDISON RD
Holland Park
BAYSWATER
ABBOTSBURY RD
KENSINGTON
KENSINGTON RD
HOLLAND RD
SHEPHERD'S BUSH RD
High Street Kensington
KNIGHTSBRIDGE
Knightsbridge
KENSINGTON HIGH ST
KNIGHTSBRIDGE
QUEENSGATE MEWS
EXHIBITION RD
GLOUCESTER RD
BROMPTON RD
Kensington (Olympia)
WEST KENSINGTON
HAMMERSMITH RD
CROMWELL RD
A4
THURLOE PL
South Kensington
Gloucester Road
SOUTH KENSINGTON
BROMPTON
HAMMERSMITH
Hammersmith
EARLS COURT RD
SLOANE AVE
W CROMWELL RD
ONSLOW SQ
POND PL
Barons Court
West Kensington
WARWICK RD
OLD BROMPTON RD
SYDNEY ST
EARLS COURT
FULHAM RD
West Brompton
CHELSEA
LILLIE RD
KINGS RD
Normand Park
BROMPTON
OAKLEY ST
LILLIE RD
CHELSEA EMBANKMENT
Fulham Broadway
DAWES RD
Thames
HARWOOD RD
FULHAM
Batterse Park
BATTERSEA BRIDGE RD
ALBERT BRIDGE RD
MUNSTER RD
WEST BROMPTON
WESTBRIDGE RD
FULHAM PALACE RD
FULHAM RD
IMPERIAL RD
PARSONS GREEN LN
Parsons Green
Imperial Wharf
BATTERSEA
NEW KINGS RD
WANDSWORTH BRIDGE RD
TOWNMEAD RD
Bishops Park
FULHAM HIGH ST
South Park
Tube
National Rail
YORK RD
Putney Bridge
River
Hurlingham Park
0
500 yds
0
500 m

of whom work in the financial markets. Ethnic minorities make up just under one-quarter of the population. After World War II, many immigrants from the Caribbean settled in the Notting Hill area, which is why the Notting Hill Carnival (inspired by similar celebrations in the West Indies) is held here. There is also a sizable Spanish and Portuguese community, with the Spanish School based in Notting Hill. The French community is quite strong in South Kensington, where the Lycée Français and the French Embassy are based. There are some great areas for shopping and dining in Kensington and Chelsea, such as Kings Road in Chelsea, South Kensington on Fulham Road, High Street Kensington, and trendy Notting Hill.

# Where to Live

Just about anywhere in this borough is worth considering as a place to live. North Kensington and the far west of the borough by Earls Court have a slightly rougher reputation, but regeneration and gentrification have improved even these areas. The most popular areas are Notting Hill, Chelsea, South Kensington, and Kensington (by High Street Kensington). Holland Park, which is slightly west of Notting Hill, is another great (if expensive) area. As a rule, rental prices are higher than average for London, and in today's tight rental market they can be astronomical. The weekly rent on a two-bedroom apartment in Chelsea is nearly double that of a similarly sized property in Fulham (west of Chelsea). Likewise, rental prices in Hammersmith/Shepherd's Bush, west of Kensington and Notting Hill, are at least one-third less expensive.



## THE LAY OF THE LAND

The Royal Borough of Kensington and Chelsea is a long thin borough, lying west of the City of Westminster. It runs down to the River Thames's edge in the south of the borough (by Chelsea Embankment and Cheyne Walk) and north to its borders with Westminster and Brent along the Harrow Road. Part of Kensington Gardens lies within its borders, and then there is the delightful Holland Park, with its wandering peacocks and wonderful playground for kids. The early-18th-century fashion for shared gardens behind houses (as in Notting Hill) or houses built around a communal square (as in Kensington) is commonplace throughout much of the borough, giving residents access to a bit of green space. Even though it is considered to be an affluent area (the

© KAREN WHITE

Chelsea Old Town Hall

wealthiest in the United Kingdom), there are pockets of deprivation and a few large areas of social housing where crime can be a problem.

## HOUSING

Much of the RBKC is in a conservation area, helping to preserve its character and looks, and in my opinion adding to its charm. The accommodations tend to be flats or maisonettes (apartments over two floors) converted from the terraced houses. There are also a few mansion blocks, along with some smaller townhouses and mews houses. Generally, there are very few modern apartment blocks or detached house properties in the borough (most of these seem to be in Holland Park). As you may expect, property prices in this borough are among the highest in London, especially in Kensington (W8). Expect to pay £330-1,600 per week for a one-bedroom apartment (the average price is £600). For a two-bedroom apartment, the range is £400-2,500 per week (£900 is the average). Larger three-bedroom homes are at least £600 per week (average £1,950), with very desirable places much more. The most affordable areas in the borough are in North Kensington (W10) or near Earls Court (SW5), or consider farther west in the borough of Hammersmith and Fulham. As for property prices, one-bedroom apartments start at around £575,000, but can go up to more than £1 million for very desirable places. Two-bedroom apartments go for around £1 million, but can easily rise to double that amount or more. Larger homes (three bedrooms or more) are usually around £2 million and more. The population density in RBKC is the second-highest in London, as many of its houses have been turned into separate flats. This helps to keep the local property tax (council tax) fairly low. Council tax ranged £711-2,134 in 2014-2015—the third-lowest in London.



## Chelsea (SW1/SW3/SW10)

Chelsea is a wonderful mix of stunning terraced houses, great (albeit expensive) shopping, and wonderful places to dine. Of course, all this ambience comes at a price, and property prices (to buy or rent) are at the top end here. Knightsbridge in SW1 (the western cousin of exclusive Belgravia in Westminster) can generally be classed as part of Chelsea. This neighborhood boasts period mansion blocks and mews houses, and some Georgian terraced homes, but these aren't as large as those in nearby Belgravia. If you can afford it, Chelsea can be a good place for families as there are some good (mainly private) primary schools in the area. However, it's not particularly close to a park where kids can run around and let off steam. Certainly the wealth of local excellent shopping (everything from groceries to clothing and a great department store) means that you should be able to get by without a car in this area.

### GETTING AROUND

Chelsea's one downfall (and it can be a major headache) is that it is not great for public transportation. The only Tube station for the area is Sloane Square on the Circle and District lines. Your only other options are a hefty walk up to South Kensington or Gloucester Road (both on the Circle, District, and Piccadilly lines). Thankfully, several buses run up and down Kings Road (such as the number 11 to the City or the 22 to Piccadilly Circus). Just a word of warning: Parking can be a nightmare in Chelsea, even with a resident's permit.

## The Pros and Cons of Residents-Only Parking

Parking in London can be a nightmare—and expensive! However, if you are lucky enough to live in the borough of Kensington and Chelsea, you have a distinct advantage when it comes to parking. You see, unlike in other boroughs in London, in Kensington and Chelsea the resident parking permit is borough-wide. There is just one zone for the whole borough, and parking is usually controlled weekdays 8:30am-6:30pm and Saturday 8:30am-1:30pm. These times, however, are extended in certain locations, such as around High Street Kensington or Chelsea, with some limits on Sunday as well. Permit holders can also park for free in the pay-and-display spaces between 8.30am and 9.30am and between 5:30pm and 6:30pm Monday to Saturday.

What this means is that, although you may live in Notting Hill, you can park in resident bays (spaces) right next to Kings Road in Chelsea—some five miles (eight kilometers) away from your home. This is both good and bad news for residents of the borough, depending on where they live. For someone who lives in a residential area, perhaps in Holland Park or North Kensington, it's great news as they can drive and park by the main shopping areas, be it Kings Road (in Chelsea), High Street Kensington, or Notting Hill. However, if you live near these prime shopping areas, you may find that you often cannot find a place to park near to where you live, as residents from elsewhere in the borough are parking on your street.

Thanks to a high density of residents and limited access to off-street parking, the demand for on-street parking space is very high in Kensington and Chelsea. While the borough is taking steps to reduce fraudulent requests for residence parking permits, there are still more permit holders than places in the borough. Given this it is no wonder that you hear stories of people occasionally having to park blocks away from their home if they arrive home late at night. I certainly notice that on the weekends when many people are out shopping, sometimes the resident parking bays near to the shops on High Street Kensington are jammed—even though it's an area where the hours have been extended to just resident permit holders. Yet, if you go there midweek there are plenty of resident-only bays available.

It's also interesting to note that the borough of Islington has a similar scheme (the Residents' Roamer Scheme), which allows residents with a parking permit to park in controlled resident bays or resident shared-use spaces outside their specific parking zone 11am-3pm, with further restrictions around some areas. At all other times, permit holders can only park within their local controlled parking zone (CPZ). The borough decided to introduce the scheme as a short-term measure to help support local shops and allow residents to visit friends and family without having to pay for parking. Its success has prompted the borough to continue with the scheme: I guess the needs of the local economy are more important than environmental concerns.



### Holland Park (W11/W14)

The very grand area known as Holland Park is close to both Notting Hill and Kensington High Street. It boasts a mix of staggeringly expensive large detached homes (just west of Holland Park) and more modest white Victorian terraced houses (some separated into flats), along with apartments in grand mansion blocks and some pretty mews. As with much of the RBKC, rental and purchase prices for property are expensive in the area. Through still fairly central, Holland Park comes across as a leafy village, with beautiful residences and a small parade of shops, with the fashionable boutiques of Notting Hill just a few blocks away—though the very busy Holland Park Road cuts the area in half. For a supermarket, you'll have to head to either High Street

© SAMPETE | DREAMSTIME.COM

a row of townhouses in Kensington



Kensington or the nearby mall in Westfield, though the area has a small grocery store, butcher, and greengrocer.

### GETTING AROUND

Holland Park Tube station is on the Central line, giving you easy access to Oxford Street and the City. Five buses travel on Holland Park Road going in an east-west direction along the top of Hyde Park into the West End (such as the number 94).

## Kensington (W8)

Just south of Notting Hill (on the other side of Notting Hill Gate) is W8—London's most expensive neighborhood. The area stretches between Notting Hill Gate down to the other side of High Street Kensington, though the streets near Kensington Place carry the colossal price tag. The centrality of W8, in addition to good shopping (both practical and otherwise), helps maintain the high demand for property. W8 boasts a good mix of property, from red-brick mansion blocks offering spacious flats to three-story white Victorian terraced houses, many of which have been converted into flats. This neighborhood suits families well with a few good schools, and it is close to both Holland Park and Kensington Gardens. For nightlife, you'll find several great restaurants and pubs, as well as the Gate Cinema by Notting Hill Gate Tube station.

### GETTING AROUND

On the north side of the W8 postcode the Central line at Notting Hill Gate station provides a straight shot into the "Square Mile"—great for those working in the City. The other station in the area is High Street Kensington on the Circle and District

© LAURA SMITHSON

people enjoying a drink outside a pub in Notting Hill



lines on the southern side of this postcode. Bear in mind that traffic on High Street Kensington makes this street unbearably congested at times, but then it is a major thoroughfare for major roads west of London into town, such as the A4. High Street Kensington is serviced on 10 different bus routes, including the number 9 to the West End and the number 10 to King's Cross station.

### Notting Hill (W11)

Most people associate Notting Hill with the movie that shares its name. Believe it or not, two centuries ago trendy affluent Notting Hill was a slum and was called "Potteries and Piggeries" due to the number of potteries and pig farms in the area. Through most of the last century Notting Hill was a run-down neighborhood, and it had race riots in the late 1950s. However, by the 1980s its fortunes had changed; it developed a slightly bohemian reputation and began to be a desirable place to live. These days its streets are home to some of the most expensive property in the country. Just as in the movie, the area around Portobello Market has some wonderful fashion boutiques, quirky specialist shops, a few pleasant places to eat and drink, as well as the odd antiques shop. You can get some groceries on Portobello Road and Notting Hill Gate, and there are larger grocery shops on High Street Kensington, Bayswater (in Westminster) to the east, or in North Kensington. Notting Hill also has some beautiful picture-postcard Victorian residential streets where you can escape the hustle and bustle of London. One of the reasons that Notting Hill is so popular with expats is that it tends to tick many of the boxes for prime living—its nightlife is good for singles and couples, while the nearby parks of Kensington Gardens and Holland Park (both with excellent playgrounds) make it a hit with families. One word of warning, though;

## The Notting Hill Carnival

© I4LCOCL2 | DREAMSTIME.COM

At the end of the summer just before schoolkids start a new year, West London plays host to the largest street festival in Europe—the Notting Hill Carnival. Every year on the August bank holiday (a national holiday usually held on the last weekend in August), the streets of Notting Hill and surrounding areas come together to celebrate London's Afro-Caribbean culture. There is a grand "mas" (masquerade) parade where astonishing floats (sometimes with a steel band) followed by dancers in amazing costumes parade through the streets. Once the float and the dancers have passed, locals and residents are encouraged to follow behind and join in the dancing. The competition between the various groups to have the best costumes and best performance can be intense. The sounds and sights of the Notting Hill Carnival, as well as the camaraderie of Londoners, make this an unforgettable event.

### HISTORY OF THE CARNIVAL

It may be hard to believe, given that Notting Hill is now one of the most expensive and exclusive neighborhoods in London, but back in the post-World War II era Notting Hill was filled with cheap, run-down properties. Many of the Commonwealth citizens who moved to London in the post-war era settled there—especially those from the West Indies. The first carnival was held back in 1964 and consisted mainly of local steel bands getting together for a concert. The music reminded local residents and participants of their Caribbean homeland and the carnival celebrations that are a traditional part of life there. Gradually the event became more formalized and organized, turning into the massive street party that it is today. The London carnival takes its inspiration from similar events in the West Indies, especially in Trinidad and Tobago. Originally, the Trinidadian carnival tradition started in the 19th century as a celebration of the abolition of slavery and the ending of the slave trade. Once the former slaves were emancipated, they could hold festivals filled with dancing, music, and fancy costumes—all of which had been previously forbidden.

### TODAY'S CARNIVAL

London's Notting Hill Carnival is held over the final two days of the August bank holiday and attracts more than a million people annually. The Sunday of the carnival is Children's Day and is a bit less crowded and noisy, tending to quiet down a bit earlier. The Monday is the real carnival celebration, with revelers continuing to drink, dance, and party late into the night. The carnival now covers a massive 20-square-mile (52-square-kilometer) area, taking in not just the Notting Hill area but many of the surrounding neighborhoods as well. Throughout the carnival you'll find stages and sound systems where reggae musicians and steel bands are performing. The streets are dotted with hundreds of food stalls, many selling Jamaican and Trinidadian specialties such as jerk chicken and fried plantains.

In years gone by, the carnival attracted criminal elements who used the crowded streets to help them pickpocket or mug people. With so many drunken people wandering around, fights could break out. In recent years, however, the carnival committee and the police have been able to control most of the criminal activity, though pickpocketing is still an issue.

## Jimi Hendrix in London

On September 18, 1970, one of the world's best ever guitarists died of an alcohol and sleeping pill overdose in a dinky run-down flat in the Samarkand Hotel in Notting Hill. This was a sad end to a very promising career, and it's all that most people know about Jimi Hendrix's life in London. Thought to be perhaps the best rock guitarist ever, Jimi Hendrix's skills and music made him one of the most influential musicians of his era. Well-known British guitarists such as Eric Clapton, Jeff Beck, and Pete Townsend had all been friendly with Hendrix, and he had been known to jam and perform with a few of them.

Born in Seattle, Washington, Hendrix was a master with the guitar, with most of his skills self-taught. Hendrix spent much of his early career in either the South or New York City, where in 1966 he met Chas Chandler, a member of the British band The Animals. Impressed with Hendrix's talent and keen to branch out into management, Chandler brought him to London, to see if he could help him kick-start his musical career here. On his first night in London, Hendrix met Kathy Etchingham, who was his girlfriend for the next two years. Much of what is known about Hendrix comes from her autobiography covering his life and the London music scene in the late 1960s.

During this time in London, Hendrix was to record some of his most popular songs, with his band The Jimi Hendrix Experience, including *Hey Joe* (recorded in 1966), *Purple Haze* (1967), and *The Wind Cries Mary* (1967). All three songs were a big success, making it into the top 10 in the UK charts. His first album, *Are You Experienced,* came out later that year. International success soon followed. Ever the showman, his stage performances would include everything from playing the guitar with just his teeth (a traditional R&B trick) or behind his back to smashing up or setting fire to his guitar.

Hendrix returned to the United States in 1968 to try to get a better foothold in the music scene there. In 1969, he was one of the headline artists to play at Woodstock, where his classic rendition of the *Star-Spangled Banner* became a symbol for the 1960s in the United States. Unfortunately, fame and life in the fast lane began to take their toll on Hendrix, who fell out with members of his backing band. Feeling increasingly alone in his homeland, Hendrix would frequently return to London, where he was appreciated for his musical talent and not just his tricks. He died in the Notting Hill flat of his then-girlfriend, Monika Dannemann, in slightly mysterious circumstances. Yes, his death was due to a bad combination of too many drugs; however, rumors persisted for a while that his passing was intentional, either on his own part or someone else's. Perhaps these grieving fans just couldn't believe that after just four short years of fame Jimi Hendrix was gone.



during the Notting Hill Carnival this area can be mayhem thanks to the crowds and noise. You'll either have to embrace the carnival by getting out and partying or escape for the weekend.

### GETTING AROUND

There are two Underground stations in the Notting Hill area: Notting Hill Gate (Central, Circle, and District lines) and Ladbroke Grove station (Circle and Hammersmith & City lines) to the northwest of the area. Buses tend to run north-south on Ladbroke Grove (such as the number 52 to Victoria or 28 to Fulham and on to Wandsworth) or east-west along Notting Hill Gate (including the number 148 to Victoria).

## Portobello Market

© KAREN WHITE
antiques for sale at the Saturday Portobello Market

Portobello Market is one of London's top tourist attractions, with visitors filling the street on most Saturdays. Although you can get fruit and vegetables as well as clothes, and even second-hand stuff up toward the Goldbourne Road end, my favorite pastime is to browse for antiques in the market. Saturday is the main trading day for antiques, though some of the shops are open during the week and a few stalls set up on Friday and Sunday (especially in peak tourist months). If you're into antiques I suggest that you come on Saturday—bright and early. Ideally you should get there by 9am, giving you time to look around and visit the shops and stalls before the big crowds arrive.

The antiques stalls are at the top end of the market (from Chepstow Villas down Portobello Road). They continue down the hill until Portobello Road crosses Elgin Crescent (by the pub Portobello Gold). This isn't far to walk—just a few blocks—but it's well worth exploring all the shops along the way. The section between Westbourne Grove and Elgin Crescent holds the best antiques shops (these will be on your right as you walk down the hill). There are more than 40 antiques stalls on Portobello Road; some of the shops contain a small maze of antiques stalls, giving you even more collectibles to hanker after. I'd also suggest that you take some time to explore the small parade of antiques shops along Westbourne Grove (between Portobello Road and Kensington Park Road), as there are eight antiques shops on Westbourne.

While you are in the area, you may want to explore along Kensington Church Road. This is back past Notting Hill Gate Tube station heading the other direction toward High Street Kensington—if in doubt jump on a number 52 bus. Along this road you will see some jaw-dropping antiques and works of art. While I can't afford the antiques offered in these shops I do enjoy window-shopping here.

### DIRECTIONS TO PORTOBELLO MARKET

To get to the market is very simple. You should first travel to Notting Hill Gate station (on the Central, Circle, or District line). Make sure to exit on the Pembridge Road exit. Then just turn right and follow Pembridge Road down about a block. Portobello Road will be on your left. You should be able to just follow the crowds for this, but sometimes it helps to know exactly where you are going. The market now stretches out before you and goes on for around half a mile.

## South Kensington (SW7)

On the south side of Hyde Park and Kensington Gardens, stretching down to Chelsea, is the area known as South Kensington. Although the area boasts its own excellent shopping, upmarket Knightsbridge (with its well-known department stores) and equally fashionable Chelsea are just a few minutes away. For that matter, High Street Kensington (one of London's biggest streets for shopping) is just a short bus ride away. This is museum-land, home to the Natural History, Science, and Victoria and Albert Museums. The beautiful Royal Albert Hall for concerts is also nearby, as is Imperial College. Given its proximity to town, nearby facilities, and easy transportation links, South Kensington is understandably one of the most sought-after areas to live in London. Unfortunately, the price tag for property here reflects the desirableness of the area, and the local population is fairly affluent. South Kensington is popular with expats of all nationalities, though I associate it mostly with the French (who tend to live around here so they are near the Lycée Français). True, homes here are expensive, but nearby parks and open spaces, as well as a few good private schools, make it good for families. Property tends toward large Victorian townhouses over several floors; there are a few mansion apartment blocks, though there are also converted mews and smaller homes.

### GETTING AROUND

One of the advantages to living in South Kensington is its good transport links. There are three Underground lines to the area (the Circle, District, and Piccadilly) at both South Kensington and Gloucester Road stations. There are around 10 different bus routes through the area; for example, the number 14 bus travels east to the West End, while the number 49 goes north-south between High Street Kensington through Chelsea and over the River Thames to Battersea. As it is fairly centrally located you shouldn't need to have a car here, which is just as well because parking in South Kensington isn't always easy.



## Fulham (SW6)

If you have your heart set on Kensington or Chelsea but can't afford it, you could try a bit farther west in Fulham (in the borough of Hammersmith and Fulham). This is another great area of town, and much of the fashionableness of Kensington and Chelsea has spread over the borough's borders and into Fulham. While you can't expect miracles as far as property prices go, you can get a similar environment, if a bit less "she-she-la-la." Fulham Broadway and Fulham Road have good local shopping, dining (including an American diner), and movie theaters. Soccer fans will already know the Stamford Bridge (Chelsea Football Club's ground) is around here. Fulham is very popular with families because you can find a range of good quality houses and several good schools (both state and private). Property ranges from luxurious modern apartments on the river's edge to late Victorian and Edwardian terraced houses. Farther west into SW6, you'll get a more residential, slightly suburban feel, with tree-lined streets and family-oriented neighborhoods. There are several parks in the Fulham/Parsons Green area, providing green spaces for kids to play.

In 2014-2015, the council tax for the borough of Hammersmith and Fulham ranged £689-2,068. To give you an idea of property prices in Fulham, a one-bedroom apartment should rent for at least £375 per week, with a two-bedroom place going for

£500-900 or more per week; a riverside apartment runs more than £1,000 a week. Rents for a house in Fulham range anywhere between £650 per week to more than £2,000 per week for larger properties. Those looking to buy should expect to pay at least £450,000 for a one-bedroom flat. The price range for two-bedroom flats is anywhere from £500,000 to more than £1.8 million for a modern flat with river frontage. Houses run £1 million and up for a small three-bedroom to more than £2 million for a large family home in a desirable location.

#### GETTING AROUND

The area has three Underground stations all on the District line (Parsons Green, Putney Bridge, and Fulham Broadway); just remember that the District line isn't London Underground's most reliable of Tube lines. On the plus side, the area is serviced by eight different bus routes, which you may come to rely on if the District line is having a bad day.

### Hammersmith and Shepherd's Bush

If you prefer to live near Kensington or Notting Hill/Holland Park but can't afford the rent, consider living slightly farther west in Hammersmith or Shepherd's Bush. Though these areas are less than two miles away, rental prices can be 20-60 percent less, with luxury flats offering the greatest savings. Of course, the closer you are to the royal borough the more prices increase, but Hammersmith and Shepherd's Bush are well worth considering, providing you are fairly near the Tube stations. The area known as Brook Green, just off of Hammersmith Road, is particularly nice with some great schools, quiet residential Victorian terraced streets, and a leafy enclave and playground. Along Shepherds Bush Road there are converted flats and apartment buildings that lead to Shepherd's Bush Common and the massive Westfield Mall. Redevelopment of the nearby White City area may make this part of town a good option in the future. Rental prices tend to be lower toward Shepherd's Bush; one bedroom flats in this part of town average around £350 per week, with two bedrooms around £200 or more per week,

Brook Green in Hammersmith provides a bit of greenery to the neighborhood.

and add up to another £200 for a three-bedroom place. Housing prices in the area run £375,000-500,000 for a one-bedroom flat, with two bedrooms at least £500,000; riverside property in Hammersmith will run in the millions. For larger properties, you may find something for less than £1 million, but expect to pay £1.5 million or more.

### GETTING AROUND

Four Underground lines (Circle, Hammersmith & City, Piccadilly, and District) service Hammersmith Station. There is a bus station in the Hammersmith roundabout with approximately 17 bus lines, including the number 27 to Notting Hill and number 9 to Aldwych near Covent Garden (via Kensington). Farther north, Shepherd's Bush is on the Overground between Stratford and Clapham Junction and on the Underground's Central line, and there are mainline railroad services between Hertfordshire and Croydon in South London. More than 10 buses run through this area, including the number 31 bus toward Notting Hill and into Camden Town and the number 49 bus to South Kensington.

## Daily Life



The Royal Borough of Kensington and Chelsea is one of the most popular areas of London to live in. True, most people live in an apartment, but its central location and proximity to the West End, with an easy commute to the City or Docklands, make it popular with expat communities and the British. Certainly it is very popular with Americans, and there are two women's clubs in the borough, The Kensington and Chelsea Women's Club and American Women's Club of London. FOCUS Information Services is also based here and is a brilliant resource for expats trying to settle into their new life in London.

### SCHOOLS

The RBKC has four state nursery schools, 27 state primary schools, and six state secondary schools. State schools in Kensington and Chelsea are on the upswing, and some have an outstanding reputation. There are more than 20 private primary or prep schools in Kensington and Chelsea, some of which continue on until age 14 or 18. There are also seven private secondary schools, although most of these are colleges and only take students aged 14 or older. Kensington is home to the excellent (and oversubscribed) French Lycée Français Charles de Gaulle and the Spanish Instituto Español Cañada Blanch. There is also an international school in Notting Hill for ages 3-11, with older children attending the secondary schools in Westminster.

### SHOPPING

Between South Kensington, Kings Road, High Street Kensington, and Notting Hill, this borough offers some of the best shopping in London. A mall has opened just to the west of the borough, in Shepherd's Bush, giving residents even more shopping opportunities. As for groceries, there are several large supermarkets and a few smaller (yet perfectly adequate) grocery stores, including the large Whole Foods Market on High Street Kensington.

## LEISURE

If you want to be near a gym, there are three offered by the borough of Kensington and Chelsea, with several private gyms dotted around. Though there are several movie theaters, there is really only one stage theater—the Royal Court Theater in Sloane Square. Yet what the borough lacks by way of the theater, it certainly makes up for with its museums. The Science Museum, Natural History Museum, and Victoria and Albert Museum—great for children and adults alike—are in South Kensington. Those who enjoy fine dining will be spoiled for choice by the number and quality of the cafés and restaurants in Chelsea and Kensington.

## GETTING AROUND

The borough is well serviced by the Underground and has 13 Tube stations serviced by five of the Underground lines: Central, Circle, District, Hammersmith & City, and Piccadilly. Some parts of RBKC are better serviced by the Underground than others. One problem area is Chelsea, much of which is a fair step away from the Sloane Square or South Kensington Underground station—a bit odd really, given the high price tag to live here. There are no major train stations within the borough, although both Paddington and Victoria are close to its borders. However, the Stratford to Clapham Junction Overground line goes through the borough and has stations at Kensington (Olympia) and West Brompton. Residents in North Kensington could walk the mile or so to Kensal Green station to get the Bakerloo line or trains to Euston station. Those who prefer the bus will find the services in RBKC good, hardly surprising given that it is an inner London borough.

At times the traffic congestion and parking can be a problem in RBKC, though this varies from neighborhood to neighborhood and depends on the location. Having a Kensington and Chelsea resident parking permit is a real advantage to the borough's residents who drive, though the shortage of parking can be an issue. But given that it is so centrally located, you may find that you really don't need a car.

Buses head down Kensington High Street.

# CITY OF WESTMINSTER

The area now regarded as the ancient heart of Westminster was established nearly a thousand years ago, when a royal palace and a church (Westminster Abbey) were first built there by Edward the Confessor. During Norman times these buildings were re-built, creating the current Westminster Abbey and the earlier Palace of Westminster. William the Conqueror used the Palace of Westminster as his royal courts, which led to the area being established as the political center of England (and later the United Kingdom), while the City of London was confirmed as the focal point for commerce in the capital, and beyond. To this day, most of the UK government and the various ministerial bodies have their headquarters in Westminster around the area known as Whitehall, including the prime minister's house—10 Downing Street. Over the centuries the areas surrounding this ancient part of Westminster were developed as the population grew, creating new communities. It is called the City of Westminster because it was awarded this special status when numerous parishes were combined to create one local council as part of the formation of London's boroughs back in 1899. Being a "city" does not give an area any special rights; it's just an honor given to some communities by the monarch.

Forming part of the heart of central London, the City of Westminster is an unusual mix of desirable housing and commerce. The borough includes some of London's

© KAREN WHITE

most popular tourist attractions, such as Oxford Street and Regent Street, Piccadilly Circus, Trafalgar Square, and Buckingham Palace, not to forget Westminster Abbey and the Palace of Westminster (home to Parliament)—a UNESCO World Heritage Site. Although much of it is in the center of town, Westminster also has a substantial residential population. The borough offers a mix of busy urban living (in Mayfair, Belgravia, and Marylebone) and quiet residential areas (in St. John's Wood and Maida Vale). These are some of the nicest areas to live in London, with hefty price tags to match. However, it is also worth bearing in mind that Westminster does have its deprived areas, and is one of London's most socially diverse local authorities, with extremes of wealth and poverty. Though the local government is trying to regenerate some of its more deprived areas, there are still pockets where drugs and gang crime can be a problem. During the past couple of decades many of Westminster's houses in the more central locations have been converted into flats, pushing the borough's population density up.

## Where to Live

The areas in Westminster that tend to be popular with Americans can be split between those right in the heart of London (such as Marylebone) and those slightly north of central London (such as St. John's Wood and Maida Vale), which have a less urban feel. Both have advantages and disadvantages, so whether they will suit you depends on your requirements and budget. While very affluent and central, Belgravia does not seem to be as popular with Americans as it once was. Perhaps this is due to the high cost of property, as well as the high number of wealthy foreign second-home owners, who may only stay in town for a few weeks a year.

### THE LAY OF THE LAND

The centrally located City of Westminster occupies much of what is generally considered central London and constitutes most of the "West End." It lies on the north side of the River Thames, running along the river's edge from Pimlico in the west to Temple in the east (where it borders the City of London). Nearly the entire borough is within Transport for London's Zone 1, making it very easy to get around by public transportation in Westminster. The borough is also blessed with numerous green spaces and parks, including five of the capital's Royal Parks—Green Park, Hyde Park, Kensington Gardens, Regent's Park, and St. James's Park.

### HOUSING

Rental prices can be high in Westminster, but there are a few more affordable areas in the borough that are desirable. Within central London, a one-bedroom apartment will rent for £600-1,200 per week; prices for a two-bedroom flat range £850-2,000, and larger properties range £1,400-4,900 per week. Similarly sized rental properties a bit farther out average £440-480 per week for a one-bedroom apartment and £715-860 for a two-bedroom flat; larger properties range £915-1,400 per week. Housing prices for a one-bedroom flat in the central part of Westminster range from £835,000 up to more

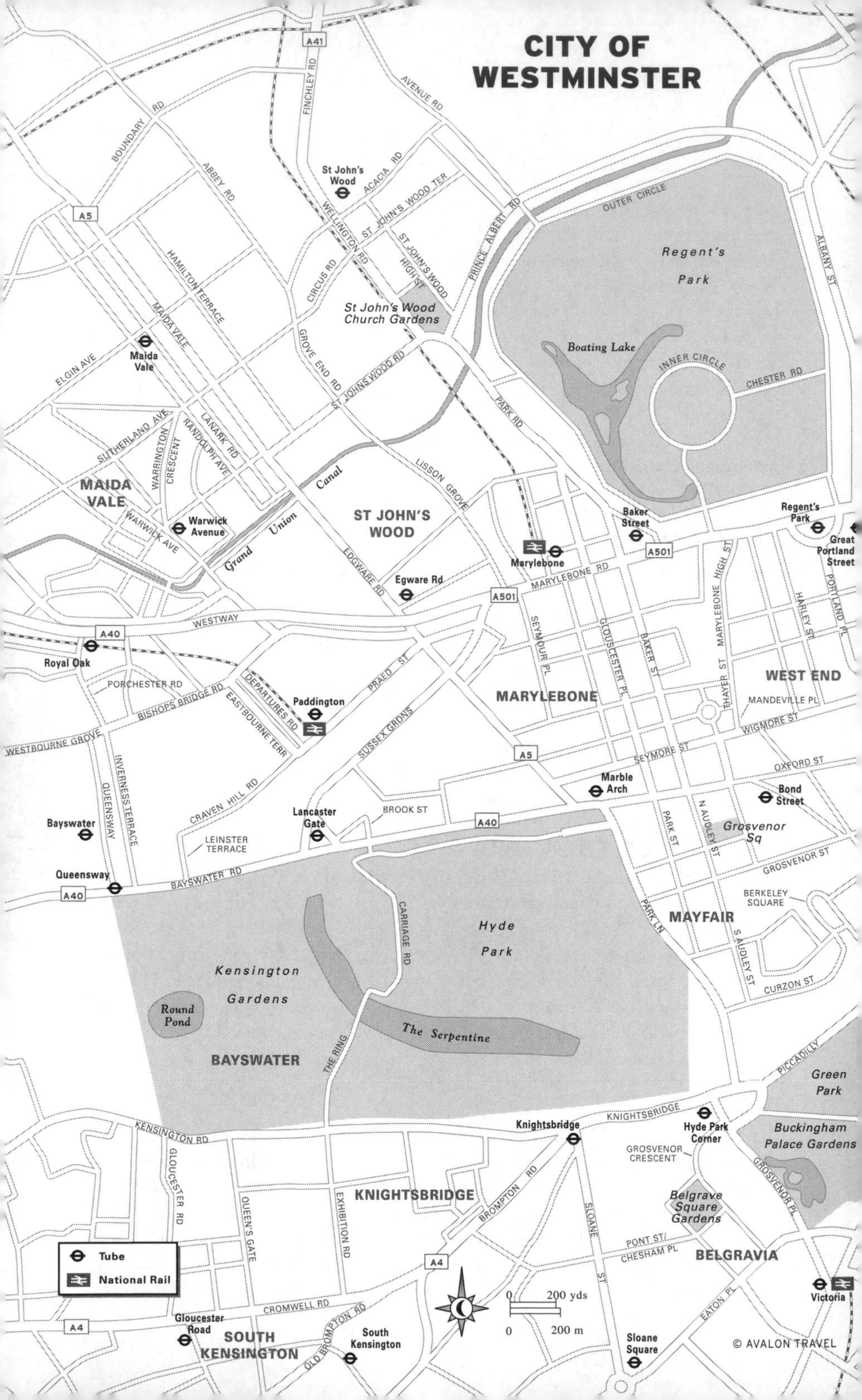
CITY OF WESTMINSTER
A41
FINCHLEY RD
AVENUE RD
BOUNDARY RD
ABBEY RD
St John's Wood
ACACIA RD
A5
WELLINGTON RD
ST JOHN'S WOOD TER
PRINCE ALBERT RD
OUTER CIRCLE
Regent's Park
ALBANY ST
HAMILTON TERRACE
CIRCUS RD
ST JOHN'S WOOD HIGH ST
St John's Wood Church Gardens
MAIDA VALE
Maida Vale
GROVE END RD
Boating Lake
INNER CIRCLE
CHESTER RD
ELGIN AVE
ST JOHNS WOOD RD
PARK RD
SUTHERLAND AVE
WARRINGTON CRESCENT
RANDOLPH AVE
LANARK RD
LISSON GROVE
Canal
MAIDA VALE
Grand Union
ST JOHN'S WOOD
Baker Street
Regent's Park
Great Portland Street
Warwick Avenue
WARWICK AVE
Marylebone
A501
EDGWARE RD
Egware Rd
MARYLEBONE RD
A501
MARYLEBONE HIGH ST
WESTWAY
A40
Royal Oak
SEYMOUR PL
GLOUCESTER PL
BAKER ST
HARLEY ST
PORTLAND PL
PORCHESTER RD
DEPARTURES RD
PRAED ST
WEST END
BISHOPS BRIDGE RD
EASTBOURNE TERR
Paddington
MARYLEBONE
THAYER ST
MANDEVILLE PL
WIGMORE ST
WESTBOURNE GROVE
SUSSEX GRDNS
A5
SEYMORE ST
OXFORD ST
INVERNESS TERRACE
QUEENSWAY
CRAVEN HILL RD
Marble Arch
Bond Street
Lancaster Gate
BROOK ST
Bayswater
LEINSTER TERRACE
A40
PARK ST
N AUDLEY ST
Grosvenor Sq
Queensway
BAYSWATER RD
GROSVENOR ST
A40
CARRIAGE RD
BERKELEY SQUARE
PARK LN
MAYFAIR
Hyde Park
Kensington Gardens
S AUDLEY ST
CURZON ST
Round Pond
The Serpentine
BAYSWATER
THE RING
PICCADILLY
Green Park
KNIGHTSBRIDGE
Hyde Park Corner
Buckingham Palace Gardens
KENSINGTON RD
Knightsbridge
GROSVENOR CRESCENT
GLOUCESTER RD
BROMPTON RD
GROSVENOR PL
QUEEN'S GATE
EXHIBITION RD
KNIGHTSBRIDGE
Belgrave Square Gardens
SLOANE ST
PONT ST/ CHESHAM PL
BELGRAVIA
Tube
National Rail
A4
CROMWELL RD
EATON PL
Victoria
0
200 yds
0
200 m
A4
Gloucester Road
SOUTH KENSINGTON
OLD BROMPTON RD
South Kensington
Sloane Square
© AVALON TRAVEL

## Westminster's Royal Parks

One of the most noticeable (and pleasant) features of central London is the numerous parks and green spaces. In Westminster alone there are five massive Royal Parks, all of which were gardens or hunting grounds for the royalty centuries ago. In 1851, these parks were opened up to the general public by Queen Victoria to give Londoners some access to open spaces. However, the land is still owned by the Crown, which also manages the parks.

### REGENT'S PARK

In the north of the borough is the 195-acre Regent's Park, which was used as a hunting ground in the 17th century and was known as Marylebone Park. Today it is home to London Zoo and lined with gorgeous Regency stucco terrace houses by the noted 18th century architect John Nash (who also remodeled Buckingham Palace). Along the top of the park is the Grand Union canal linking Birmingham with the River Thames. The nearby Primrose Hill Park (in the borough of Camden) is yet another Royal Park, where you can get dramatic views of the city skyline.

### KENSINGTON GARDENS AND HYDE PARK

Covering much of west-central London are Kensington Gardens and Hyde Park, which combine to create an open green space of 592 acres—so it's not quite as big as New York City's Central Park (843 acres), but it is still a good size. On the west side of Kensington Gardens is Kensington Palace (which is a relatively small royal palace, but well worth a visit) as well as the Prince Albert and Diana, Princess of Wales Memorials. The Serpentine Lake straddles both Royal Parks. If you are up to it you can swim in the Serpentine (including during a special Christmas Day race for the very hardy), or you can simply rent a boat and row around the lake for a while. Hyde Park, too, used to be a hunting ground and became part of the royal landholding when Henry VIII bought it for use as a private, enclosed deer-hunting ground. Today the park is used by Londoners for cycling, roller-blading, walking, horse riding, and bike riding, not to forget Speaker's Corner (in the northeast corner by Marble Arch), where people can spout off about whatever is on their mind.

### ST. JAMES'S PARK

Next to Buckingham Palace is St. James's Park, another well-known Royal Park in the City of Westminster. This park once formed the basis for the gardens of St. James's Palace, one of London's oldest royal palaces. This 59-acre park is the farthest east of Westminster's Royal Parks and is the oldest Royal Park. Oddly enough it is home to a flock of pelicans thought to be a gift from a Russian ambassador in the 17th century. If you're into royal pageantry, try to watch Trooping the Colour, which is a ceremony held in St. James's Park on Horse Guards Parade each June to mark the queen's birthday (this should be on TV if you can't get tickets).

### GREEN PARK

Sandwiched between Hyde Park and St. James's Park is the 47-acre Green Park. Here you'll find the gardens of Buckingham Palace, while the palace itself lies juxtaposed to St. James's Park. Unlike the neighboring parks, Green Park doesn't have a lake or pond and has very few memorials. In fact most of it is just lawn with some flower borders and trees.

What is special about all these parks is that they cut a huge swath through central London, ensuring that there is green open space even in the middle of town. Taken as a whole, these five Royal Parks span from Notting Hill in Kensington in the west, down to Victoria station and eastward all the way over to Whitehall, and nearly down to the River Thames—creating a fabulous green oasis through a congested and hectic Westminster.

You'll find quite a few apartment buildings in St. John's Wood.

© KAREN WHITE



than £1.6 million on average, with two-bedroom units ranging £1.5 million to several million pounds. To purchase a larger property, expect to spend at least £2 million and as much as five times that (or more). In the less centrally located areas of Westminster, average purchase prices for a one-bedroom flat range £585,000-754,000, while two-bedroom flats are £862,000-1.1 million, with larger homes £1.2-2 million or more.

One bit of good news for Westminster is that it has the lowest council tax (local property tax) in the country. In 2014-2015, these taxes ranged £451-1,353. Around 40 percent of people living in Westminster are in owner-occupied properties, making it a popular area for renters. Property types range dramatically: everything from grand Georgian houses in Belgravia to beautiful 18th-century stucco houses around Regent's Park, to modern high-rise apartment blocks in Paddington Basin, to family houses up in St. John's Wood.

## Bayswater (W2)

Those looking for a slightly more affordable option to the very expensive Notting Hill in Kensington may want to consider Bayswater, just east of this trendy area and north of Hyde Park. Still fairly centrally located, Bayswater gives you easy access to the shops and restaurants of Notting Hill, as well as some of its own great amenities. It has a few of London's characteristic squares surrounded by white-washed four-floor terraced Victorian townhouses, some of which have been converted into hotels. The nearby Paddington Basin is a modern development and offers high-rise living, while much of the rest of the area is made up of flats converted from the terraced houses. The shopping in this area is quite good—even for groceries. Plus you are near to the great boutiques and shops of Westbourne Grove and Notting Hill, with Portobello Market an easy walk away. Bayswater is very cosmopolitan and the population is quite mixed—traditionally there are large Greek and Brazilian populations, with a sizable Arab community living along Edgware Road to the east.

#### GETTING AROUND

While Bayswater station is on the Circle and District lines, there are numerous other lines near this area, such as the Metropolitan line (at Royal Oak or Westbourne Park station), the Central line at Queensway, or Bakerloo line from Paddington station. Certainly, going west to Heathrow via the Heathrow Express or east to the City on the Central or Circle line is easy from Bayswater. As for buses, on Bayswater Road there is the popular cross-town number 23 to the City, with the number 94 taking you to Piccadilly Circus and the number 27 from Westbourne Grove heading toward Kensington and west to Chiswick.

### Belgravia (SW1X)

Sandwiched between Buckingham Palace, Hyde Park, and Knightsbridge, the area known as Belgravia has always been an affluent area consisting of beautiful regency squares and Georgian terraces, most of which have been converted into luxurious apartments. Much of the property has been bought by wealthy foreigners, either as an investment or as a second home. Individuals and companies from Russian and China, as well as the Arab Gulf States, have all invested in this area, reducing some of its British charm. The area is home to some good schools, which may be one reason to consider living here (though I think I'd be tempted to live in Kensington and Chelsea and have a slightly longer walk to school). Nearby Pimlico, southwest of Belgravia, is a more affordable option with the bonus that Pimlico station is on the Victoria line.

#### GETTING AROUND

The main Underground line serving Belgravia is the Piccadilly line, with stations at Hyde Park Corner and Knightsbridge; Sloane Square on the Central and District lines is nearby. Useful buses include the number 22, which goes between Piccadilly Circus and Chelsea; the number 52, going to High Street Kensington or south to Victoria train station; and numerous other buses that will take you all around London.

### Maida Vale (W9)

To the west of St. John's Wood (just the other side of the main Maida Vale Road) is the area known as Maida Vale. This area gives you easy access to town and St. John's Wood, and is another option for families. Maida Vale is a tranquil residential area, noted for its fine homes, pretty streets, and Little Venice (home to some of London's canal-based residents, with some nice waterside cafés and pubs). The streets near the Tube stations create a nice, well-off residential neighborhood; the property consists of Victorian and Edwardian mansion blocks (some of which have a communal garden) in addition to some terraced houses, with the odd high-rise apartment building for good measure. Many of the houses in Maida Vale have been converted into flats, though you can sometimes find a house. Maida Vale has a few cafés and shops, a pharmacy, and a small grocery store (as well as a post office), but it doesn't have the range of shops of nearby St. John's Wood.

© KAREN WHITE

an Edwardian mansion block in Maida Vale



### GETTING AROUND

Both Maida Vale and Warwick Avenue stations are on the Bakerloo line. From Warwick Avenue it is about a 10- to 15-minute walk to St. John's Wood Tube station on the Jubilee line. The area is serviced by the number 6 and 98 buses, both of which take you into the West End. The number 414 will take you to South Kensington and near the river by Putney, while the number 46 is useful for those who want to get to Hampstead.

## Marylebone (W1M)

To the southwest of Regent's Park is Marylebone village, which has a wonderful mix of commerce and residential living. This area has numerous terraced Georgian and Victorian houses (some of which have been converted into offices), as well as pretty mews and the odd Edwardian mansion block. Due to its desirable central location, rental prices can be steep here, but not always (and they're generally more affordable than either Mayfair or Belgravia). With Oxford Street nearby, this area is ideal for shoppers. Unlike in many centrally located areas, groceries are fairly easy to get in Marylebone, and the area has a farmers market on Sunday. As well as several boutiques, there are some great restaurants, cafés, and pubs on Marylebone High Street. The area also has a few primary and secondary schools (both state and private). For such a centrally located area, Marylebone has a real village feel, with annual summer and winter fairs, so it caters to families relatively well. For those looking to recharge their batteries with a bit of fresh air and greenery, Regent's Park is just a few blocks away and is popular with runners and walkers.

#### GETTING AROUND

Marylebone is surrounded by three Tube stations: Baker Street (on the Jubilee, Bakerloo, Circle, and Metropolitan lines), Bond Street (on the Central and Jubilee lines), and Regent's Park (on the Bakerloo line). Oxford Street station (on the Bakerloo, Victoria, and Central lines) is nearby. So you can easily get just about anywhere on the Underground network. Buses tend to run along Marylebone Road (such as the numbers 18, 30, and 205 leading toward Euston and King's Cross to the east) or on Oxford Street (such as the numbers 23 and 25 heading east toward the City), with the number 10 going west on Oxford Street toward Knightsbridge and Kensington.

### Mayfair (W1S)

If you are after something a bit more exclusive than Marylebone, try nearby Mayfair. Tucked between Piccadilly to the south, Regent Street to the east, Oxford Street to the north, and Hyde Park to the west, Mayfair is just about as centrally located as you can get in Westminster. Since it's known for its exclusive hotels, expensive jewelers, and designer boutiques, it may seem incongruous that Mayfair should increasingly be home to many of London's private equity firms, small investment banks, and hedge funds. The area has some very expensive residential property, which may be of interest if you are working in the area and have a generous housing allowance.

#### GETTING AROUND

Given its proximity to Piccadilly Circus (Piccadilly and Bakerloo lines) and Green Park (Jubilee, Piccadilly, and Victoria lines) stations, getting around by the Underground is easy from Mayfair. From Piccadilly Circus buses will take you all over town, such as numbers 15 and 23 to the City; numbers 9 and 14, which head west to Kensington; and number 13, which goes north to St. John's Wood.

### St. John's Wood (NW8)

In the leafy streets north of Regent's Park you'll find the neighborhood known as St. John's Wood. This area is very popular with Americans because it's home to the American School in London (ASL)—the only American school in the heart of London. Even if you don't have children or they don't go to ASL, Americans tend to flock to St. John's Wood, perhaps because there are so many other Americans here. This can be an expensive area of town, but it's a quiet, safe, family-friendly area, with nice cafés and a great high street, plus it is under four miles from Charing Cross (the traditional center of London). Certainly it ticks many boxes for American expats moving to London.

#### GETTING AROUND

The St. John's Wood station is on the Jubilee line, which is very useful for those who commute to the West End and Docklands. Residents to the east of the area can easily walk to the Bakerloo line in Maida Vale or Warwick Avenue, while those who live near Primrose Hill Park can walk through the park to get to the Northern line

### Benjamin Franklin in London

Although he was one of the founding fathers of the United States, and was born and raised in Boston, Massachusetts, Benjamin Franklin lived in London for many years. Franklin first came to London in 1725 in a bid to increase his understanding of the printing process and improve his typesetting skills. He returned to Philadelphia a year later and by 1729 had started working on *The Pennsylvania Gazette*. He first published *Poor Richard's Almanac* in 1733.

During the coming years he established himself as a statesman and was elected to the Pennsylvania General Assembly in 1751. Six years later he returned once again to London, this time as a diplomat for the Pennsylvania Assembly. For this trip, he had to leave his wife, Debra, in Pennsylvania, as she was too afraid of the sea to make the long voyage. However, he did bring along his son William as a companion. Once in London he took up lodging at 36 Craven Street. He was to become a lifelong friend of his landlord, Margaret Stevenson, and her daughter, Polly. Franklin's task while in London was to get the Penns (the founding family of Pennsylvania) to provide more funds to support the colony and its fights with the French and Native Americans. The Penn family agreed to Franklin's request in 1762, and he soon set sail for home.

Unfortunately, Franklin was to return to London within just two years, this time to try to get the king to grant Pennsylvania the status of a royal colony. Once again he took up lodging at 36 Craven Street. This trip to London was to last more than 10 years, during which time he became a leading negotiator between the Crown, the French, and the American colonies. In 1765 the British Parliament passed the Stamp Act, which imposed a stamp duty on legal documents, newspapers, and several other items. The money raised was to be used to defend the colonies. The tax did not go down well with Franklin or the colonies back home, and tension between the two factions was heightened. During this time Franklin worked tirelessly to reconcile the two sides, but relations took a turn for the worse after levies were imposed by Parliament on items such as glass, paper, and tea.

In 1775, when it became clear that a war of independence was unavoidable, Franklin returned home to Pennsylvania. Once again he journeyed across the Atlantic in 1778–though this time it was to France to drum up support for the American War of Independence against Britain. He remained in France as an ambassador until 1785, when he was relieved of his duties by Thomas Jefferson. Franklin finished his days in Pennsylvania, passing away five years later.



in Chalk Farm, if this line works better for them. The area is serviced by buses up to Hampstead (number 46) and east to Camden Town and Islington (number 274), while the number 139 takes travelers to the heart of the West End. Several buses (including numbers 13, 113, and 187) travel northward up the main thoroughfare of Wellington Road/Finchley Road.

## Daily Life

Westminster is one of the most popular areas for Americans to live, and St. John's Wood is especially popular with families. Given the large American community here, meeting up with other expats through schools, women's clubs, and organizations (such as the St. John's Wood Women's Club) will be easy. Yet you shouldn't feel that you must live near an expat community to meet other Americans, as it is easy enough to get involved with these clubs and organizations without living nearby. For somewhere more lively, head to Bayswater, with its proximity to the pubs, bars, and restaurants of Notting Hill.

## SCHOOLS

The state schools in Westminster are rising in reputation; the borough has many state schools that are considered good, with some that are outstanding, including a few religious schools. Within the borough there are 42 state primary schools, many of which are Church of England schools, and 11 secondary schools. There are also around 15 private primary schools with 12 secondary schools. This includes the American School in London (ASL), which follows the American curriculum. As you'd expect, ASL is popular with American families that have relocated to London because it provides continuity of education for the children. However, it is a *very popular* school, and the waiting lists can be lengthy.

## SHOPPING

For shopaholics Westminster is paradise. It is home to one of Europe's largest shopping precincts: the area around Oxford Street, Regent Street, and upmarket Bond Street. And along its western border with the Royal Borough of Kensington and Chelsea is the prestigious shopping area of Belgravia and Knightsbridge and the well-known department stores of that area (Harvey Nichols and Harrods). Quaint Marylebone High Street offers a rest from crowded West End shopping in a village atmosphere, and it has a great farmers market on Sunday and the fun Cabbages and Frocks Market on Saturday. Those looking for a taste of home will want to know that Panzer's Deli (13-19 Circus Rd. NW8 6BP) in St. John's Wood stocks many American goodies. There are also several small- and medium-sized grocery stores scattered throughout the borough, so restocking the fridge shouldn't be a problem.

## LEISURE

The West End (in Westminster and part of Camden) is home to 40 theaters, as well as the Royal Opera House, Royal Albert Hall, and Wigmore Hall. Leicester Square, in the heart of the West End, boasts several movie theaters (referred to as "cinemas" here), and this is where many movie premieres are held. Top museums include the National Gallery and National Portrait Gallery near Trafalgar Square, as well as the Tate Gallery in the southwest of the borough. Popular with kids and adults alike is the London Zoo in Regent's Park—another feature of the borough. There are numerous leisure centers run by the local council, some of which have pools. On top of this there are a few private gyms where you can work out and socialize. Cricket fans (or those curious to learn more about it) will be pleased to learn that the home of cricket in England and Wales, The Lord's Cricket Ground, is in St. John's Wood. Some of London's best restaurants, nightclubs, and pubs are in Westminster.

## GETTING AROUND

As so much of Westminster is within the center of town, getting around by the Underground is straightforward in this borough. Ten of the 11 Underground lines

© KAREN WHITE

St. Johns Wood High Street has a lovely selection of shops.



go through Westminster, with only the Waterloo & City not traversing the borough. There are 30 Underground stations in Westminster—more than in any other borough in London. It is also well serviced by buses, which crisscross the city in all directions. Although the Overground does not service the area, Westminster does have four major train stations, including Victoria (connecting with Gatwick airport), Charing Cross (for trains to and from Kent), Paddington (for Heathrow and even Wales), and Marylebone (servicing commuters from Buckinghamshire and farther afield). Westminster also borders the river with piers by Westminster Bridge and Charing Cross, where you can take a Thames Clippers ferry upriver to Tower Bridge or to Greenwich. If you are thinking of getting a car, bear in mind that a car right in the heart of town will be expensive and parking will be a problem. As you creep northward through the borough parking gets a bit easier, although I always find it hard to get pay-and-display parking in St. John's Wood.

# BOROUGH OF CAMDEN

Known for its village atmosphere, the northern half of the borough of Camden provides a slightly suburban rural feel, although it is just four miles (six kilometers) from Charing Cross station (the traditional middle of London). The borough was created from the metropolitan boroughs of Hampstead, Holborn, and St. Pancras in the mid-1960s when the government reformed London's local authorities. The borough took its name from Camden Town (one of its neighborhoods), which was named after Charles Pratt, the first Earl Camden, who first developed this area in 1791.

Popular neighborhoods in the north of the borough include Hampstead, Belsize Park, and Primrose Hill (near Regent's Park). Closer to central London, there is Camden Town: an odd mix of well-heeled Londoners living in grand Georgian houses and the trendy (and touristy) weekend Camden Market. The southern half of the borough is home to Bloomsbury and much of the University of London, making it popular with students, though the newly built apartment complexes by King's Cross are popular with wealthy professionals. Camden has the highest proportion of university students in London, around a tenth of its residents. It is also an old borough with many properties dating back to Georgian times. Around half of the borough is in a conservation area, helping to preserve the character and look of its different neighborhoods. Be aware that crime can be a problem here, especially in Camden Town.

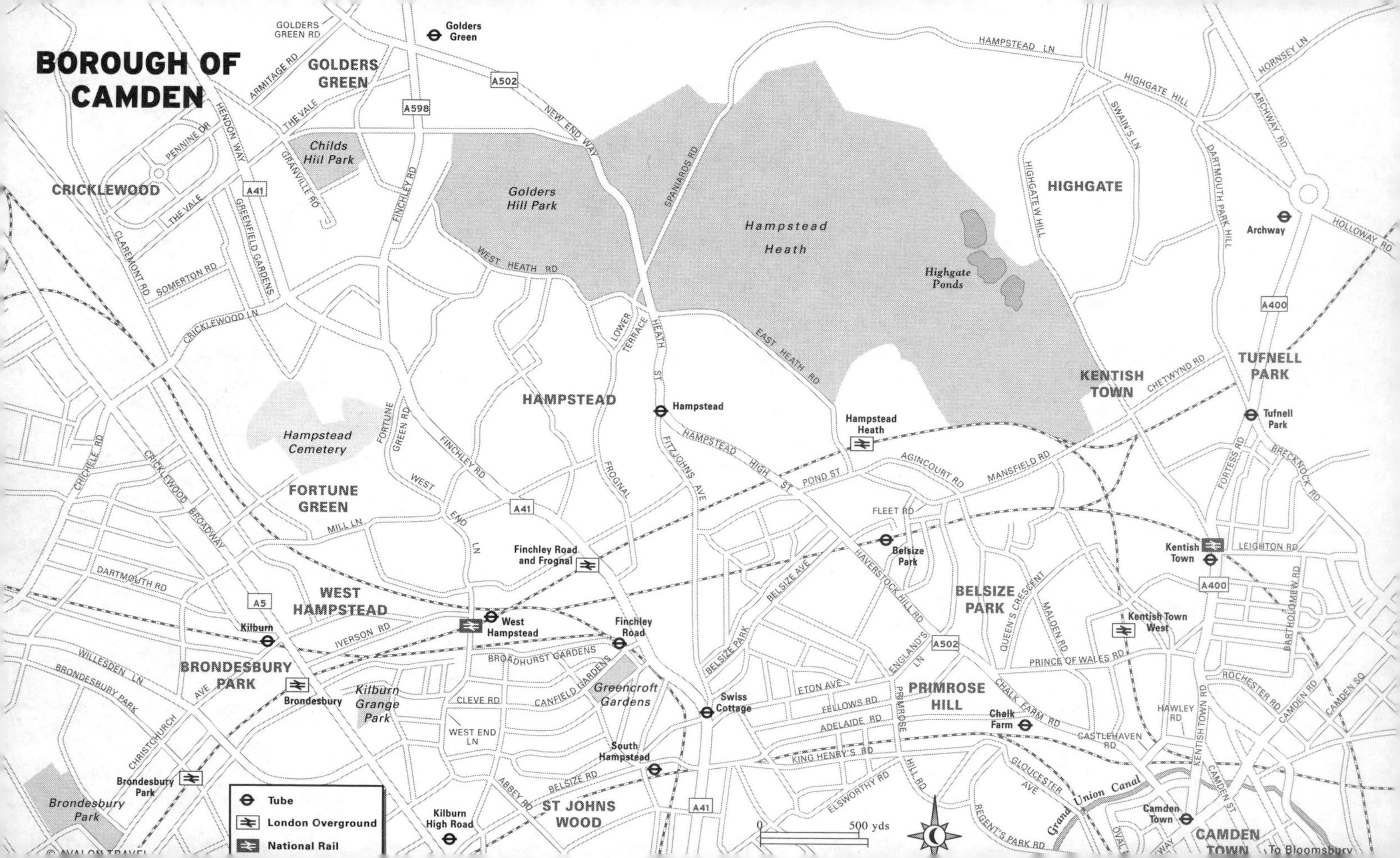
BOROUGH OF CAMDEN
Tube
London Overground
National Rail
0
500 yds
To Bloomsbury
GOLDERS GREEN
CRICKLEWOOD
HAMPSTEAD
HIGHGATE
KENTISH TOWN
TUFNELL PARK
FORTUNE GREEN
WEST HAMPSTEAD
BRONDESBURY PARK
BELSIZE PARK
PRIMROSE HILL
ST JOHNS WOOD
CAMDEN TOWN
Hampstead Heath
Highgate Ponds
Golders Hill Park
Childs Hill Park
Hampstead Cemetery
Kilburn Grange Park
Greencroft Gardens
Brondesbury Park
Grand Union Canal
Golders Green
Archway
Tufnell Park
Hampstead
Hampstead Heath
Belsize Park
Kentish Town
Kentish Town West
Chalk Farm
Camden Town
Swiss Cottage
Finchley Road
Finchley Road and Frognal
West Hampstead
South Hampstead
Kilburn
Brondesbury
Brondesbury Park
Kilburn High Road
GOLDERS GREEN RD
ARMITAGE RD
THE VALE
HENDON WAY
PENNINE DR
GRANVILLE RD
GREENFIELD GARDENS
CLAREMONT RD
SOMERTON RD
CRICKLEWOOD LN
CRICKLEWOOD BROADWAY
CHICHELE RD
DARTMOUTH RD
WILLESDEN LN
BRONDESBURY PARK
CHRISTCHURCH AVE
FINCHLEY RD
NEW END WAY
WEST HEATH RD
SPANIARDS RD
LOWER TERRACE
HEATH ST
EAST HEATH RD
HAMPSTEAD LN
HIGHGATE HILL
HIGHGATE W HILL
SWAIN'S LN
ARCHWAY RD
DARTMOUTH PARK HILL
HOLLOWAY RD
HORNSEY LN
CHETWYND RD
FORTESS RD
BRECKNOCK RD
LEIGHTON RD
BARTHOLOMEW RD
ROCHESTER RD
CAMDEN RD
CAMDEN SQ
KENTISH TOWN RD
CAMDEN ST
HAWLEY RD
CASTLEHAVEN RD
PRINCE OF WALES RD
MALDEN RD
QUEEN'S CRESCENT
CHALK FARM RD
GLOUCESTER AVE
REGENT'S PARK RD
OVAL
MANSFIELD RD
AGINCOURT RD
FLEET RD
POND ST
HAMPSTEAD HIGH ST
FITZJOHNS AVE
HAVERSTOCK HILL RD
BELSIZE AVE
BELSIZE PARK
ENGLAND'S LN
ETON AVE
FELLOWS RD
ADELAIDE RD
KING HENRY'S RD
PRIMROSE HILL RD
ELSWORTHY RD
FROGNAL
FORTUNE GREEN RD
WEST END LN
MILL LN
IVERSON RD
BROADHURST GARDENS
CANFIELD GARDENS
CLEVE RD
BELSIZE RD
ABBEY RD
A41
A502
A598
A400
A5
© AVALON TRAVEL

# Where to Live

The most popular part of Camden to live in for Americans tends to be up in Hampstead, with its quaint village atmosphere and nearby heathland. The nearby neighborhoods of Highgate (on the east side of Hampstead Heath), Belsize Park, and Primrose Hill are also popular with the expat community. All of these areas have a quiet residential feel about them, although they are just a few miles from the heart of London. Those who want to live somewhere with an edgier feel may want to consider Camden, with its lively nightlife and fringe theaters. Right in the middle of town is Bloomsbury, where students mix with tourists and office workers. There has been a lot of redevelopment near King's Cross station, including a few modern apartment blocks.

## THE LAY OF THE LAND

Camden lies north of the River Thames and stretches from Hampstead in the north right into the heart of the West End, with Covent Garden and Holborn. The borough is one of London's smallest—just 8.5 square miles (22 square kilometers) in size. It borders the boroughs of the City of Westminster and the City of London in the south, Brent to the west, Barnet and Haringey on its northern edge, and Islington to the southeast. There is a strong contrast between the north and south of the borough, with lots of residential neighborhoods and green open spaces in the north and the busy, congested south of the borough in central London. The north of the borough by Hampstead is an affluent area, home to some of London's wealthiest individuals, and is dominated by a 790-acre park, Hampstead Heath. The borough has quite a liberal feel to it and the local council is left-of-center—unusual for such a wealthy area. There is severe deprivation in some parts of the borough, notably around Somers Town (by Euston station) and parts of Camden Town and Kentish Town.

© KAREN WHITE

a row of terraced houses in Camden Town

## HOUSING

The housing in Camden is the standard London mix of terraced houses, mansion blocks, and converted flats. There are a few mews houses in Belsize Park, and you'll find charming old cottages in Hampstead. A considerable amount of the property in Hampstead village is Georgian or Victorian and fairly well preserved. Most of the University of London's student accommodation buildings are in the borough, either near the university in Bloomsbury or elsewhere in

## The Wild Heart of London

Dominating much of northwest London is the ancient wooded parkland known as **Hampstead Heath.** The 790-acre park is owned and managed by the Corporation of London, and it stretches between Hampstead to the west and Highgate to the east. It's about a 20- to 30-minute walk across the Heath between the two villages. For nearly 200 years the Heath has been a popular place for Londoners to walk and take in the clean fresh air. The wild rambling heath climbs up one of London's highest hills to give spectacular views of the city below. A wonderful mixture of open grassy fields and wooded areas, the Heath has several ponds (originally reservoirs for drinking water from the River Fleet) that step down the hill toward Parliament Hill Fields at the bottom of the park. Some of the ponds are open to swimmers (usually in the summer months) and have been since Victorian times, though the female-only pond wasn't open until 1925.

The area that incorporates Hampstead Heath has a long history, and was mentioned in the *Domesday Book* of 1086 when the land was recorded as belonging to one of the monasteries at Westminster Abbey. In the early 18th century the village of Hampstead became a spa, though by the early 19th century it had turned into a desirable residence for Londoners wanting to escape the crowded conditions of London. This led to greater demand of land to develop, and some of the Heath land was sold off to meet this requirement. However, the popularity of the Heath as an open space and common land stilted the development of the village. In 1888 the Heath was finally established as parkland. Since then Hampstead Heath has expanded to include Parliament Hill Fields in the south, the manor of Kenwood, and the Heath extension that heads downhill toward the areas known as Golders Green and Hampstead Garden Suburb.

Today, the lower southeastern corner of the Heath contains Parliament Hill Fields, an open grassy area with a playground, tennis courts, running track, and open-air swimming pool (called a "lido" here in the United Kingdom). Atop Hampstead Hill is the picturesque regency house of Kenwood Park. Now one of the stately homes managed and maintained by English Heritage, Kenwood Park was one of the locations used in the film *Notting Hill.* On a completely different note, the heavily wooded West Heath is a notorious location for nighttime cruising in London.

The Heath allows Londoners to get occasional glimpses of British wildlife. Muntjac deer are known to roam there, as do ubiquitous red foxes, gray squirrels, and rabbits. It's a wonderful place for bird-watching, as it's home to several varieties of water fowl, kingfishers, and ring-necked parakeets (escapees that have gone native and now can be found across much of western London). While walking on the Heath I have heard owls and seen numerous rabbits running in and out of the rhododendron bushes by Kenwood House. A healthy walk around Hampstead Heath is a great way to recharge your batteries without having to leave the city.

the borough. The average price of a one-bedroom apartment in Camden is around £430 per week, and can range £350-700 per week. For a two-bedroom place, prices range £400-1,300, with the average weekly rent around £620 per week. The average price for a family home runs between £1,000 for a three-bedroom place to £1,555 for a four-bedroom property, but expect to pay at least £1,000 up to several thousand per week.

Housing prices for a one-bedroom flat in the Camden borough start at £560,000; a two-bedroom flat lists at around £882,000, though in expensive areas such as Bloomsbury and Hampstead expect to pay more than £1 million. Houses usually start at £1.5 million and can run several million. Students may be less choosy about their accommodations and able to rent a studio in Bloomsbury for around £230 per week; a single university dorm room comes in at around £200 per week. Camden's council tax is about average for a central London borough; in 2014-2015, the charges ranged £880-2,641 per annum.

## Belsize Park (NW3)

Just down the hill from Hampstead village is its neighbor, Belsize Park. This is a fashionable, affluent area of town, which is reflected in the property prices. Belsize Park tends to have larger white stucco Victorian townhouses, many of which have been converted into flats, and there are a few grand red-brick mansions with large apartments, along with a number of pretty mews. One of the best things about Belsize Park is that it's just a 15-minute walk away from two large parks—Hampstead Heath to the northeast and Primrose Hill to the south. As this is predominantly a residential area, the shopping in Belsize Park tends to be just smaller convenience stores, with a handful of cafés and restaurants (and a good delicatessen). But the area is just a 15-minute walk (uphill) or a short bus or Tube ride away from Hampstead village, where there is better shopping. The area has maintained its residential feel, even though it is just three miles (five kilometers) from the city center.

### GETTING AROUND

Belsize Park has two Tube stations: Belsize Park station (Northern line) and nearby Swiss Cottage station (Jubilee line). The number 268 bus goes through Belsize Park and takes you from Finchley Road up to Hampstead village, while the C11 will take you east along the bottom of the Heath and over to Swiss Cottage.

## Bloomsbury

If you want a more urban environment one option would be Bloomsbury, where you should have just a short walk to work in the City or West End, with local shops and dining on your doorstep. Bloomsbury has some beautiful Georgian and early Victorian terraced houses, often set around garden squares. There are also some modern apartment buildings, some of which are for students. Up by King's Cross station there are ultra-modern apartment complexes, some of which have views over the canal. The University College London and other University of London colleges and buildings are located in Bloomsbury, as is the British Museum. There are numerous hotels near the British Museum, so tourists are a common sight in this part of town. For shopping, the nearby Brunswick Centre has a grocery store as well as several clothes shops,

## The Bohemian Bloomsbury Group

At the southern end of the borough of Camden (in the part of it that is part of central London) is the residential and academic neighborhood known as Bloomsbury. This area is headquarters for the University of London, so there are plenty of academic buildings spread throughout Bloomsbury, including the University of London's student union and Senate House—the university's main library. The area also is home to the British Museum and its amazing collection of ancient artifacts, including exhibits such as ancient carved Greek marbles, the Rosetta Stone, and the 6th-century Anglo-Saxon treasures uncovered in Sutton Hoo in Suffolk on England's east coast.

Along with the British Museum and the university, Bloomsbury is also associated with an influential intellectual, artistic, and literary group that lived in the area during the first half of the 20th century. The Bloomsbury Group was a collection of writers, intellectuals, academics, philosophers, and artists who held informal discussion groups in Bloomsbury in the period from around 1905-1930. The group comprised an extraordinary collection of brilliant, forward-thinking individuals who went on to influence early-20th-century British literature, aesthetics, and art, as well as economics. Given the social mores of Victorian/Edwardian Britain, the Bloomsbury Group took an astonishingly liberal view of issues such as feminism, sexuality, and pacifism.

One of the group's main founders was Virginia Woolf, who moved to Bloomsbury after the death of her father. During this time she met intellectual friends of her brother from Cambridge, who would gather at her house in Gordon Square, Bloomsbury, to share ideas and thoughts on art, literature, philosophy, and economics, creating what became known as the Bloomsbury Group. The economist John Maynard Keynes, the novelist E. M. Forster, and the biographer Lytton Strachey were active members of the group, as was Virginia Woolf's sister, Vanessa Bell, and her husband, Clive, both of whom were artists. Part of the group's motivation was to rebel against the traditional conservative attitudes to art, society, and sexuality that dominated British society's attitudes in the early 20th century. The members of the group pursued intellectual free-thinking and had radical lifestyles forming liaisons with other members, be they of the opposite sex or same sex, or both.

Though deeply controversial at the time, the Bloomsbury Group did pave the way for new thinking on a range of intellectual and artistic subjects. Today you'll see blue plaques all around Gordon Square commemorating their time in Bloomsbury.



a pharmacy, and a few cafés. Tottenham Court Road also has several shops and is great for technical gadgets and furniture. Of course, Oxford Street (Europe's busiest shopping street) is less than two miles away. Bloomsbury has quite a mixed feel; it is bang in the middle of town (with all the offices, noise, and congestion), yet the streets are filled with students heading off to lectures and tourists looking for the British Museum (or their hotel). For a bit of nightlife you can head to Charlotte Street, with its busy pubs and restaurants.

### GETTING AROUND

There are five Tube stations around the Bloomsbury area: Russell Square (Piccadilly line); Euston Square (Circle, Hammersmith & City, and Metropolitan lines); Warren Street (Victoria and Northern lines); Tottenham Court Road (Central and Northern lines), and Goodge Street (Northern line). Euston train station is just a short walk away, as are St. Pancras and King's Cross stations. Eight bus routes head south down

The Camden Market is one of London's most popular shopping destinations.



Gower Street and north up Tottenham Court Road, including the number 24 bus running between Hampstead and Victoria station and the number 390 to Oxford Street and Notting Hill Gate.

## Camden Town (NW1)

Close to town is trendy, yet slightly edgy, Camden Town. Popular with students, young professionals, and creative media types, Camden Town is dominated by its famous busy weekend market. This is a very mixed community with some wealthy families and couples along with some pockets of poverty. Beyond the busy market precinct and Camden High Road (where there is a good range of shopping, including a supermarket) there are some pretty, leafy streets near the Regent's Park end with some very desirable large Georgian terraced homes and attractive Victorian houses. On the down side, there are some very rough parts of Camden Town, where crime and drugs can be a real problem, so it's probably not for you if you're after quiet, hassle-free streets.

### GETTING AROUND

Camden Town station is on the Northern line, with both branches (Edgware and High Barnet) of this line going through it. The station can get very crowded on the weekend because of the market. There is an Overground station on Camden Road, and several buses go in and out of central London via Camden High Street, such as the number 29 to Trafalgar Square or the 214 to the City.

## Hampstead (NW3)

This is a lovely old area a few miles north of central London—perfect for dog owners, nature lovers, and families because of its proximity to Hampstead Heath (a 790-acre natural park run by the Corporation of London). Hampstead still has a strong village feel and strong sense of community, with good high street shopping and several patisseries, cafés, gastropubs, and restaurants. It is also home to several schools and has the highest concentration of private schools in London. With a lovely village atmosphere, numerous schools, and the Heath, Hampstead is popular with wealthy families, including expats. This neighborhood is well known for its artistic, intellectual, literary, and musical connections, and has been home to many leading figures in these fields—from the poet John Keats to Sigmund Freud and the sculptor Henry Moore. Hampstead is one of London's most exclusive neighborhoods, and property demands a high price. Here you can find Georgian cottages with their large front gardens, as well as stucco Regency houses, though most of the streets are Georgian and Victorian terraces. Away from the village you may see some very modern (and exclusive) houses.

### GETTING AROUND

Hampstead Underground station is on the Northern line (Edgware branch). Finchley Road station (Metropolitan and Jubilee lines) is around a 15-minute walk down the hill from Hampstead village. Hampstead lies at the top of London's tallest hill, and much of it was developed in the early 1700s. To this day many of its narrow winding streets have been preserved. While this is charming for visitors and residents, it also means that many roads are unsuitable for buses. There are just four bus routes through Hampstead village: numbers 603 and 210 to Highgate and to the east or northeast, number 46 from Paddington to King's Cross, and number 268 down the hill to Finchley Road. There is also an Overground station at Hampstead Heath station.



## Highgate (N6)

On the other side of Hampstead is another charming old village in London—Highgate. These two villages are often treated as if they were twins, straddling either side of Hampstead Heath. Highgate village is at the top of a 375-foot (114-meter) hill, giving it panoramic views of the city skyline. This is a charming, well-preserved village, making it popular with wealthy commuters. The village has several shops in Georgian premises, as well as a couple of great pubs, some restaurants, and lovely residential streets. Highgate is also known for its cemetery, where Karl Marx is buried. Housing comprises a mix of architectural styles, from well-preserved Georgian townhouses to red-brick Victorian terraces, as well as modern houses and apartment buildings. Property prices in Highgate are among the highest in London, though they tend to be a bit lower than in its twin, Hampstead. Oddly enough, the neighborhood of Highgate is in three different boroughs—Haringey, Islington, and Camden, with most of the actual village area in Camden. Highgate has two private schools and a couple of Haringey state primary schools. If you end up in the Haringey part of Highgate the council tax is a bit higher than in Camden and ranged £989-2,967 in 2014-2015.

### GETTING AROUND

Highgate station is on the Northern line, a 10-minute walk from the village. The area is serviced by five bus routes, some going east-west (such as the number 603) while the numbers 214 and 271 go in a north-south direction down to the City of London.

## Primrose Hill (NW3/NW1)

Tucked between Belsize Park and Camden Town is a small but highly desirable area of London known as Primrose Hill. The neighborhood is popular with well-to-do professionals from the City of London and their families. Situated close to Regent's Park (and bordering the Royal Park that gives it its name), Primrose Hill is one of London's most popular areas, and a great example of a successful urban London village. Although not as high up as the hill in Hampstead Heath, the Primrose Hill Park (just 256 feet/78 meters) still offers wonderful panoramic views of the surrounding neighborhoods. Here you'll find rows of well-preserved, pretty pastel Victorian terraced houses. Primrose Hill has long been one of London's more desirable addresses, due to its proximity to the center of town and its more suburban neighbors a mile or so to the north. The neighborhood has a long parade of shops and restaurants, though you'd be better off heading to nearby Camden Town for your groceries.

### GETTING AROUND

Public transportation isn't easy in Primrose Hill, which helps to explain why the area has kept its charm and is less densely populated than nearby neighborhoods. The nearest Tube station for Primrose Hill is either Chalk Farm or Camden Town (both on the Northern line). The number 31 bus goes along the top of Primrose Hill, and there are a few buses by Chalk Farm station that will take you in or out of town.



## West Hampstead (NW6)

If you want to be near Hampstead but would prefer slightly lower property prices, then consider West Hampstead, which is about 15-20 minutes away on foot and uphill! This area has lots of shops, cafés, and restaurants along West End Lane, with a good gym, a cinema, and a large supermarket not far from Finchley Road station (Metropolitan and Jubilee lines). West Hampstead is a popular destination for a night out owing to the number of local pubs, bars, and restaurants—helping to make the area popular with young professional Londoners as well. You'll find both flats and houses in West Hampstead—anything from Victorian terraced houses to Edwardian mansion blocks and large Victorian townhouses. Parts of West Hampstead are known for having a high number of converted flats, which means that parking, even for residents, can be a problem.

### GETTING AROUND

The West Hampstead Tube station is on the Jubilee line, and the area has three train stations: two for the Overground (West Hampstead and Finchley Road & Frognal station) and the other a Thameslink station (the railway line between the City of London and Hertfordshire, a county north of London). There are several bus routes up the main thoroughfare of Finchley Road, and both the 328 and 139 travel along West End Lane by West Hampstead station.

# Daily Life

There are high numbers of good schools and parks in Camden, so it should come as no surprise that this borough is very popular with American expats, especially around Hampstead. However, it's not just families that are drawn to this area—many couples enjoy Hampstead's friendly village life and parkland. The Hampstead Women's Club is very popular with many expats in the borough and would be a good way to meet other Americans in Camden.

## SCHOOLS

Camden has a profusion of private schools—nearly 30 in all, with six of them continuing from the age of 4 until 18. There are 42 state primary schools, 10 state secondary schools, and one sixth-form college for 16- to 18-year-olds. Some of Camden's state schools have a very good reputation, which means they can have long waiting lists and be difficult to get into. Most of the private schools are in Hampstead or Belsize Park, making these areas particularly popular with families.

## SHOPPING



While Camden doesn't have the notable shopping precincts of Westminster's Oxford Street or Kensington and Chelsea's Kings Road, Hampstead High Road is still a destination for shoppers and sightseers. Along this road you'll find clothes stores and designer boutiques, a pharmacy, cafés and restaurants, and several banks, with even more shops around the corner on Heath Street. Another shopping destination in the

© KAREN WHITE

You'll find a wide variety of shops in Camden including green grocers.

© KAREN WHITE

There are some great pubs in Camden.

borough is Camden Lock and the surrounding market—a favorite with tourists and younger Londoners. Although there are numerous shops selling tourist souvenirs, there are still parts of the market that sell great secondhand clothing and older furniture. Near the station you'll find several national chains as well as a small Whole Foods Market. The borough has some large supermarkets dotted around, where you can get groceries, and most of its villages have a smaller grocery store where you can get some provisions. Those looking for electronics of any sort may want to go to Tottenham Court Road, where there is a profusion of these shops. And the area around Covent Garden (some of which is in Camden) is another popular shopping destination.

## LEISURE

As well as Camden's open green spaces, which are ideal for walkers and joggers, Hampstead Heath also has a few ponds where you can swim in the summer. Without a doubt Camden's most important museum is the British Museum in Bloomsbury, which attracts both tourists and Londoners in equal measure. In Hampstead Heath there is the stately home of Kenwood, while in Hampstead village you'll find the Fenton House (a 17th-century merchant's house with a walled garden) and the Keats House museum. The borough has a strong alternative music and theater scene—especially in Camden Town itself. The Camden Town area has a lively nightlife, with several popular pubs and bars.

## GETTING AROUND

The southern part of Camden (which is in central London) has 10 Tube stations, while the northern half has a bit fewer, just seven Underground stations. Most of the areas popular with Americans are in the northern half of the borough, and so will mainly depend upon the Northern line. Although there is a bus service up to Hampstead (and its nearby neighborhoods), the service is limited by the narrow roads in this part of town. However, the main thoroughfare of Finchley Road has several bus routes taking you in and out of the West End. The bus service in Camden's centrally located half is very comprehensive. On the other side of the Heath, the village of Highgate has a good bus service, either into the City or east to nearby Muswell Hill. As in other areas in London where there is a high concentration of converted flats, parking can be tough, but it's easier for local residents with a permit.

# ISLINGTON AND THE CITY OF LONDON

With its Roman walls and medieval churches, as well as eye-catching skyscrapers and striking modern architecture, the City of London is an incongruous mix of old and new. Although hundreds of thousands of people work in the City of London, only 7,000 people reside here. As housing is so limited, many city workers have elected to live in nearby neighborhoods, such as Clerkenwell, Shoreditch, Spitalfields, or south of the river, as well as in other parts of London. Unencumbered singles or couples who work in the City and want an extra-easy commute—as well as Americans who work in the City of London's financial sector and are relocating to London with work—should consider living here, even if it can be a bit quiet on the weekends.

If being near the City of London is a top priority, but you want somewhere with a bit of life on the weekends, then you may want to consider somewhere in the Islington borough.

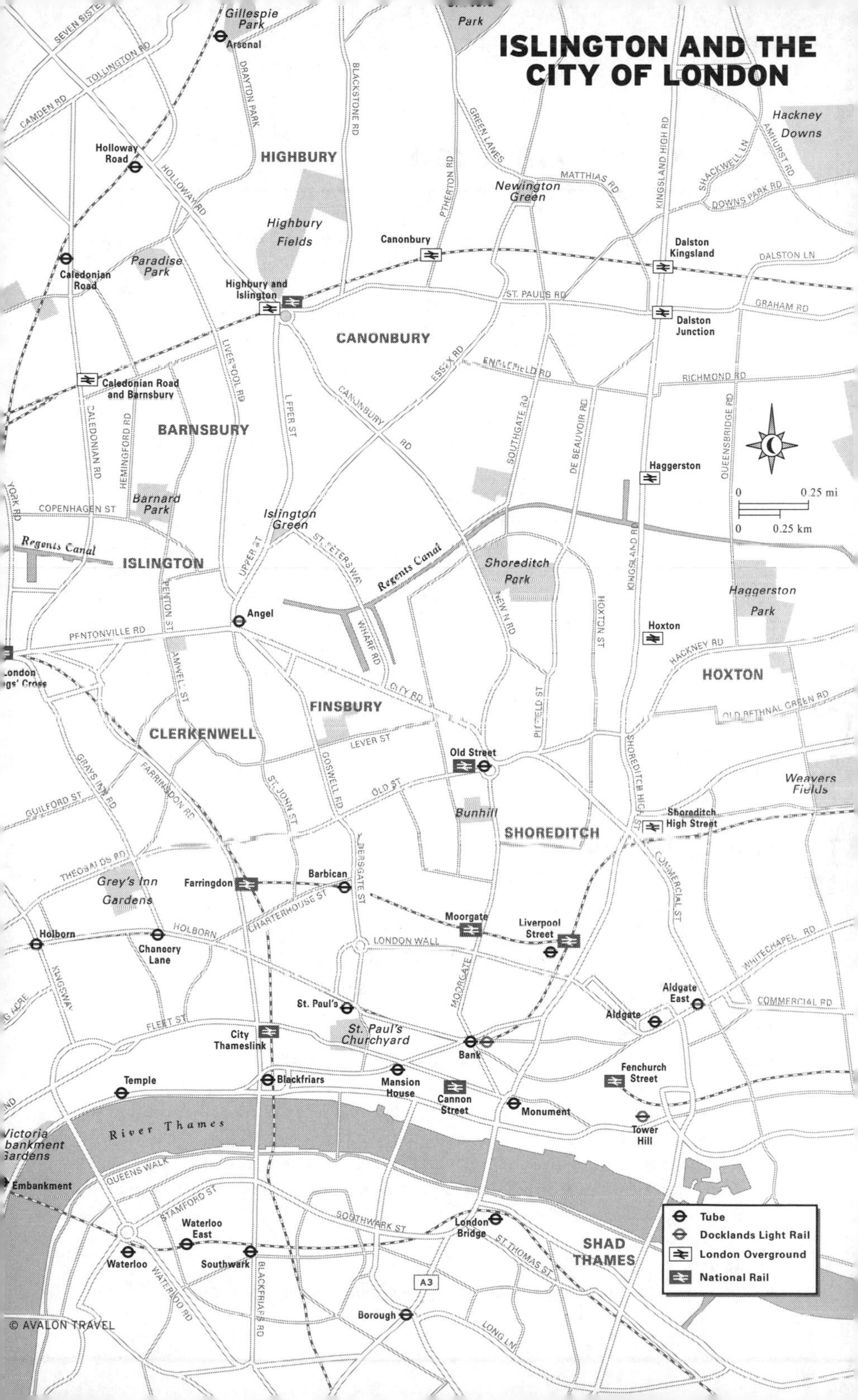
ISLINGTON AND THE CITY OF LONDON
HIGHBURY
CANONBURY
BARNSBURY
ISLINGTON
FINSBURY
CLERKENWELL
SHOREDITCH
HOXTON
SHAD THAMES
Gillespie Park
Arsenal
Holloway Road
Highbury Fields
Paradise Park
Caledonian Road
Highbury and Islington
Canonbury
Newington Green
Dalston Kingsland
Dalston Junction
Hackney Downs
Caledonian Road and Barnsbury
Haggerston
Barnard Park
Islington Green
Regents Canal
Shoreditch Park
Haggerston Park
Angel
Hoxton
Old Street
Bunhill
Weavers Fields
Shoreditch High Street
Grey's Inn Gardens
Farringdon
Barbican
Moorgate
Liverpool Street
Holborn
Chancery Lane
St. Paul's
St. Paul's Churchyard
City Thameslink
Aldgate East
Aldgate
Bank
Temple
Blackfriars
Mansion House
Cannon Street
Monument
Fenchurch Street
Tower Hill
River Thames
Victoria Embankment Gardens
Embankment
Waterloo East
Waterloo
Southwark
London Bridge
Borough
A3
Tube
Docklands Light Rail
London Overground
National Rail
0 0.25 mi
0 0.25 km
© AVALON TRAVEL

# Borough of Islington

Some of this small, densely populated borough borders the City of London, in the neighborhood known as Clerkenwell/Finsbury. Back in the 17th century, Clerkenwell was a very fashionable place to live; these days it is more popular with young city workers and creative types that work nearby. The area around Angel station has terraced homes set around Georgian squares. Its well-proportioned homes and central location, as well as a vibrant nightlife, make this area popular with city types, both singles and families. The area offers very easy access to the City of London and the West End, with a great selection of shops (both frivolous and practical). Farther up Upper Street is Highbury & Islington station, where the area is less urbanized than around Angel station, and prices are moderately lower.

Up until just a few decades ago, most of Islington was a bit rough, with high levels of poverty. However, parts of the borough have seen a tremendous resurgence of fortune, and today certain neighborhoods are very desirable. The area around Upper Street and Angel station has become gentrified, with people attracted to the well-built Georgian townhouses and modern apartment blocks. The area boasts some of the most sought-after property in London, with the added bonus that you can walk to work if you are based in the City. Right in the heart of central London, the areas of Finsbury and Clerkenwell have also undergone a transformation as property developers, followed by wealthy city professionals, have moved into the area. Of course, this affluence hasn't been spread across all of Islington, and parts remain deprived and run down, with crime levels among the worst in London. Taken as a whole, the borough offers a mixed bag of wealth and deprivation. Yet for many who live in the area, this slightly edgy fusion is exactly what they love.



## WHERE TO LIVE

The most popular areas of Islington with American expats tend to be the neighborhoods around Upper Street (by Angel station and up the road by Highbury & Islington station) and the Clerkenwell/Finsbury area. For more affordable properties that are still within easy reach of Upper Street, check out the area toward Caledonian Road or farther east toward Canonbury or De Beauvoir Town (in Hackney).

### The Lay of the Land

Islington is an inner-city London borough, spanning from the City of London in the south up to Archway in the north of the borough. At around six square miles (15 square kilometers), it is London's third-smallest borough, yet it is the capital's second most densely populated borough behind Kensington and Chelsea. Islington is very diverse socially, with a sizable population from ethnic minority backgrounds. Although pockets of Islington are quite deprived, it does contain areas of affluence, which tend to be the areas nearest central London.

### Housing

Islington is an old area of town, and many of the homes here are either Georgian or

## London's Secluded Waterways

Have you ever stopped to think how large heavy objects were transported before the advent of trucks or even the railways? Well of course the answer was to move them around on the water, either by sea, rivers, or canals. The Chinese were the first to adapt rivers for use as canals, though there is some debate about when and who invented the mechanism of a canal lock.

The great age of canal building in the United Kingdom started in the mid-1700s, with the Bridgewater Canal outside Manchester the first. Its success acted as a catalyst for more canals, especially in the Midlands and northern England to serve the heavy industry there. At the time, London's industry was serviced by its massive port, and as it didn't have coal mines there wasn't much need for a system of canals. However, by the end of the 18th century it was clear that a canal was needed to link the River Thames with the canals in the north through the creation of the Grand Junction Canal and the Regent's Canal. Although horses continued to draw boats along London's canals until the mid-20th century, these days the canals are usually just used for leisure purposes and boating. You can even take a boat trip between Little Venice by Warwick Avenue and Camden Lock in Camden Town.

Nowadays these canals are easily visible as they traverse parts of the capital. The Grand Junction Canal runs from Brentford in the west to Little Venice in Westminster, where it links with the Regent's Canal, which sweeps across Camden, Islington, and Hackney before heading south through Tower Hamlets and the River Thames at Limehouse Basin. In particular, the Regent's Canal has become a very picturesque sight in London, starting with the houseboats moored in Little Venice. Nearly nine miles long, the canal also serves as the northern border of nearby Regent's Park, passing in front of the animals at the zoo before heading on to Camden Lock. Next the canal passes through Islington, which is a wonderfully peaceful place to walk before the canal enters a tunnel that takes it under Islington High Street. Afterwards it emerges into the City Road Basin and Wenlock Basin, where old warehouses have been transformed into some stunning modern apartments with canal-side views.

The Regent's Canal is certainly one of London's greatest hidden treasures. It can be a great place to walk or have a bike ride. You may also want to explore where it joins the river at Limehouse Basin, where sea-going motor cruisers and commercial barges mix with traditional Thames sailing crafts and narrowboats, all battling the tides on the Thames.



Victorian. As in many London boroughs, the neighborhoods can be quite mixed, with rows of valuable homes set next to council housing (local authority housing for those on a limited income). More modern apartment blocks and lofts can be found in the converted warehouses that overlook the Regent's and Grand Union Canals east of Angel station (toward Hoxton), and in Clerkenwell, as well as a few off of Upper Street. Property prices increase the closer you are to central London, but your transportation costs will be minimal—especially if you can walk to work. To rent a one-bedroom converted flat in Islington, expect to pay at least £400 per week, but prices can be as much as £900 for somewhere very special. Prices range £550-700 per week for a two-bedroom place, but expect to pay toward the high end of this range. Larger properties will be more than £1,400 (although you may be able to find student-type accommodations for less). If you want to buy, a one-bedroom flat will set you back at least £440,000, though a penthouse will be more than a million (with £550,000 being the average). A two-bedroom can go for anything between £500,000 and £1.6 million.

Larger properties in the Angel/Upper Street area range £1-3 million (and more), though they are a bit less up by Highbury and Islington. A large, refurbished period house in Clerkenwell can run as much as £6 million or more. In 2014-2015, the council tax in Islington was £841-2,522, a bit lower than in neighboring Camden.

### ANGEL/UPPER STREET (N1)

The name "Islington" is often used as a generic term to cover the areas around Angel Tube station and near to Upper Street/Essex Street. The region spans from Islington High Street (by Angel station) to Highbury Fields (behind Highbury & Islington station), encircling the areas around the ever popular Upper Street. The streets in this neighborhood were mainly developed in the Georgian and early Victorian eras, and have flat-fronted traditional terraced houses; some were built around a garden square (such as those by Cloudesley Square with its 19th-century church). In this part of Islington you'll find several one- and two-bedroom flats or maisonettes, mainly from converted houses, and a few three- or four-bedroom houses. There are also a few modern houses and apartment buildings, which may be tucked down alleyways or in a mews. Camden Passage is well known for its antiques shops and is worth a visit if only to look at the antique clocks, furniture, and other curios on sale. All along Upper Street (around a mile in length) there are numerous shops and restaurants to tempt you. The area has a vibrant nightlife, with restaurants, bars, and pubs galore. There is also a small market on Chapel Street where you can get fruit and vegetables, fish, and a few clothing bargains. On Sunday the Islington Farmers' Market is in Chapel Street. This part of Islington has become very popular with wealthy young professionals, as well as a few families, and greater demand has pushed property prices up.

This area has numerous transportation links. Angel station is on the Northern line (via Mill Hill) and is just a mile away from the City. The escalators here are the longest in Western Europe, making for an amazing YouTube video of someone skiing down them. Angel station is also well served by several bus routes, including the number 30 to the West End. Four bus routes travel up and down Upper Street, including the number 43, which goes to London Bridge. Toward the east slightly is Essex Road overground station, which goes to Moorgate station and is yet another way for people to get to the City from the area. Five buses travel Essex Road, with the number 73 taking you to Tottenham Court Road.



### CLERKENWELL/FINSBURY (EC1/WC1)

The Clerkenwell/Finsbury area is a firm favorite with City of London professionals who want to have a short commute. Much of this area's popularity is no doubt due to its proximity to central London, bordering Bloomsbury, Holborn, Farringdon, and the City of London. Originally a fashionable area back in the 17th century, Clerkenwell went into decline in the mid-20th century. A general revival and gentrification of the area began in the 1990s when developers and city professionals poured into the area, which is now known for its nightclubs, pubs, restaurants, and art galleries. The neighborhood is not exclusively residential, as some businesses from the City of London have expanded into the area, as have many of London's design and architectural businesses. Houses are a mix of converted Victorian or Georgian terraces, though the area's housing is dominated by purpose-built apartment blocks, with a few converted warehouses

## A Spot of Lunch at The Eagle

The Eagle on Farringdon was one of the first gastropubs in London.

In the past 20 years or so there has been a distinct change in the attitude of London's pubs toward the food that they offer. Sure, there are those that continue with the standard fare of Sunday roasts and a ploughman's lunch. However, more and more pubs are taking a different approach to the food that they serve, offering exceptional food in the all-important midrange price bracket. Given that most foreigners believe that British food is awful, I thought I'd give you a glimpse into a popular dining trend—the gastropub.

One of the best-known pubs in Clerkenwell for a pint and a meal is **The Eagle** (159 Farringdon Rd., EC1R 3AL, tel. 020/7837 1353, www.theeaglefarringdon.co.uk, nearest Tube: Farringdon). This was one of the first pubs to make the leap from traditional "pub grub" to creative full-flavored food in the unpretentious surroundings and "order at the bar" approach of a pub. The cuisine at The Eagle is an eclectic mix from around the world: black bean soup and chili, linguine and mussels, tapas. The menu is chalked up daily on the blackboard, just as they've always done it—reflecting what is in season and at its best. The last time I was here I had a wonderful steak sandwich for lunch, while my husband had the pork belly with salsa verde, with coffees to follow—just what was needed to warm us up on a cold winter's day.

Usually, the wine you get in a normal pub is pretty dire—after all, you're there to drink beer. However, the gastropub trend has turned this on its head, and a good dining pub will also have a good wine list, because many people see having a glass of wine as an essential part of the whole meal. What is nice about a gastropub is that many of the wines are available by the glass, just in case you don't want to stagger home that night after imbibing a pint or two of beer before you eat and then a whole bottle with your meal.

If you are new to London, I strongly suggest that you try eating in one of London's gastropubs. They offer the right combination of good food and drink in a relaxed environment, and best of all the prices shouldn't break the bank.

offering loft spaces. Given the central location, property prices are on the high side. Clerkenwell Road and St. John's Street are two of the area's main thoroughfares, with St. John Square home to some wonderful places to eat and drink. The area around Amwell Street, with its lovely parade of specialty shops, cafés, and fancy barbers and hairdressers, has a particularly strong village atmosphere and is a very desirable location. The nearby Exmouth Food Market (weekdays 9am-6pm) is a great place to pick up lunch, and it has some unusual regional foods on offer.

This part of London is very well serviced for public transportation, with six Underground stations surrounding its borders: King's Cross (with its five Underground lines), Angel station (to the north), Old Street (to the northeast), Farringdon station to the west and Barbican to the east (both stations are on the Circle, Metropolitan, and Hammersmith & City lines), and Chancery Lane (on the Central line) to the southwest. Farringdon and Old Street are also train stations for the regional train services into London; King's Cross is a National Rail terminus station. The area is crisscrossed by nine bus routes, making it easy to get to the West End or the City.

### HIGHBURY AND ISLINGTON (N1/N5)

At the top end of Upper Street you come to the well-connected Highbury & Islington Underground and Overground station. This area is a bit of a spillover from the slightly wealthier southern half of Upper Street nearest Angel station, yet it still attracts a large contingent of young professionals, drawn to the area because of its transport links and friendly and relaxed atmosphere. Families are also attracted to the area by its large houses, especially those by Highbury Fields. The residents are a mix of City of London professionals, students (there are a couple of universities within a few miles), and residents of social housing—giving you a much greater mix of social classes than in some of London's boroughs out west. Unlike its southern neighbor, Highbury offers a mixture of Georgian and Victorian terraced houses, and property prices tend to be slightly less than those by Angel station. Highbury Fields (a 29-acre park) is nearby and is the largest open space in the borough. The Georgian and Victorian townhouses that surround the park are some of the most desirable residences in the area.



The Highbury & Islington station, which is on the Victoria line, services this area. Three Overground lines travel through Highbury & Islington station, traveling between Richmond or Clapham Junction in southwest London and Stratford in East London, heading south through East London (where you can connect to the Jubilee line to Docklands at Canada Waters station and on to Clapham Junction), and traveling elsewhere in South London. The area by the station has nine bus routes, with both the numbers 4 and 153 going into the City of London, while the number 30 goes to the West End and the number 19 goes to Chelsea via Clerkenwell.

## DAILY LIFE

Families are attracted to Islington by the larger houses in the streets off of Upper Street, with couples and singles attracted to both this area and Clerkenwell, and the expat community is no exception, be they Americans or other European nationalities. However, both good schools and open green spaces are lacking around here, though Angel and Clerkenwell do have the advantage of being within walking or biking distance of the City. Parts of the borough (such as Angel/Upper Street and Clerkenwell) are very popular with young professionals from the City of London. Although there is not a strong American community in the borough, you will still find Islington welcoming.

## Schools

Islington borough has 46 state primary schools; several have a good or very good reputation (but in all probability will be oversubscribed). Islington's eight secondary schools haven't been quite as successful, though a few are well regarded, as is their sixth-form college. There is one private primary school in the Finsbury/Clerkenwell area and a Montessori primary school by Angel in N1. London's Steiner school (for 3- to 18-year-olds) is in nearby Canonbury, which is northeast of Angel station. There is a well-regarded private secondary school of the performing arts in Clerkenwell and a private secondary school for children aged 13 and older in Canonbury. On the plus side, the area is well served for public transportation, so you could easily do the school run by the Tube or Overground.

## Shopping

One of the main advantages of this part of London is the wide range of shops on Upper Street, including supermarkets for groceries and several smaller boutiques offering fashionable clothes and unusual items for the home. As it's so popular, several national (and international) brands have also moved into the area, though they haven't yet crowded out the independents. Some of London's best antiques shopping can be found in Camden Passage by Angel station. Clerkenwell also has some great independent shops, as well as Exmouth Market. About the only type of shopping Islington doesn't have is a major department store, but then getting to Oxford Street is just a few stops on the Underground.

## Leisure

Islington is a vibrant borough with an active fringe theater scene with several smaller theaters (including a few pub theaters) in the N1 area. Around Angel and Upper Street there is a plethora of fantastic restaurants and a vibrant nightlife, as well as two movie theaters. London's main contemporary dance theater—Saddler's Wells—is in Clerkenwell on Rosebery Avenue. The borough also has some great antiques in the Camden Passage Antiques Gallery. There are a few private gyms dotted around Angel and Clerkenwell, if a workout is your idea of a good time. Islington is an inner-city borough and is very built up, so large open green spaces are scarce; about the only one is Highbury Fields park, though there are a few smaller parks and garden squares. However, soccer fans will be pleased to know that Arsenal's Emirates Stadium (between Holloway Road and Arsenal stations on the Piccadilly line) is in the borough.

## Getting Around

As an inner-London borough, Islington is well serviced by public transportation with links to the City, the West End, and other areas of London. There are 10 Underground stations (on six different lines) and 10 train or Overground stations, including the termini at Farringdon and Old Street stations. Buses in the borough can take you west to the West End or south into the City, as well as north to Highgate in Camden (and Haringey) or south of the river to Waterloo station. The borough of Islington has the second-lowest percentage of car ownership in England and Wales. If you are down in Clerkenwell it is unlikely that you will want a car, but if you're up toward Angel or Highbury a car (or car club membership) may be an idea. The borough of Islington has the Residents' Roamer Scheme, which allows residents with a parking permit to park in controlled resident bays or resident shared-use spaces outside their specific parking zone 11am-3pm, with further restrictions around some areas. At all other times, permit holders can only park within their local controlled parking zone (CPZ).

# The City of London

The City of London is unique in Britain; it isn't a borough or public administrative body in the conventional sense. Instead it is a corporation, run by elected residents *and businesses,* that takes on the responsibilities of a local authority, providing services such as road maintenance, street lighting, refuse collection, and so on. The City of London even has its own police force, which is separate from the London Metropolitan police. Residential housing is very limited in the City: Office blocks and retail units tend to dominate the buildings here. Given that the City of London is one of the world's main financial centers, it isn't surprising that those who live here tend to be well-educated and very well-paid professionals (in fact, this is the best-educated "borough" in London, followed by Wandsworth). The majority of residents live alone in one- or two-bedroom apartments, and it's not unheard of for some wealthier individuals to take an apartment in the City and have a large house out in the country. One thing to be aware of with the City is that it can be quiet on the weekends. Yet this tranquility makes it a great place to explore on a Sunday afternoon.



## WHERE TO LIVE

### The Lay of the Land

The City of London (also known as the "Square Mile") is tiny—just slightly larger than a square mile (1.12 square miles/2.9 square kilometers). It is the historical nucleus of modern-day London based on the old Roman walls that were erected to protect the settlement and port there more than 1,500 years ago. Even today the City of London's boundaries remain similar to what they were when the City was granted some autonomy by William the Conqueror in 1075. The Thames River forms its southern border, with Hackney and Tower Hamlets to the east, Islington to the north, and Camden and the City of Westminster to the west.

© KAREN WHITE

a twisting alleyway in the City of London

## The Great Fire of London

On the night of Sunday, September 2, 1666, a fire was accidentally started in a bakery on Pudding Lane in the City of London. The fire spread rapidly across the wooden and thatch-roofed buildings along the narrow medieval streets of the City. It raged for four days and destroyed more than 13,000 homes and 87 churches, including the original St. Paul's Cathedral. It also demolished most of the buildings that belonged to the City of London authorities. The loss of life attributed to the fire was considered to be low (fewer than 10 people), though historians now doubt this figure because record-keeping for the lower and middle classes was poor, and the extreme heat of the fire may have made it difficult to identify any cremated bodies.

The fire was so destructive partly because of indecision by the mayor of London about whether the City should set firebreaks to halt the progress of the fire. This delay meant that by the time firebreaks were finally put in place they proved ineffective against the fierce firestorm that had formed. The fear caused by the fire led some people to become suspicious of French and Dutch immigrants (at the time the English were at war with the Dutch, and to a lesser degree the French, in the Second Anglo-Dutch War), and when order on the streets broke down, some poor innocents of these nationalities were lynched or beaten. By the third day the ineffectual mayor of London was replaced by King Charles II, who put his brother, the Duke of York, in charge.

After four days, the fire had spread across most of the ancient City of London and threatened King Charles II's Whitehall Palace (the main residence for British monarchs in London from 1530 until the end of the 17th century). Although the palace was saved (only to be lost to another fire 30 years later), it wasn't until the strong east winds subsided and gunpowder was used to create a more effective firebreak that the Great Fire of London was finally conquered.

The social and economic consequences of the Great Fire were huge, with many people destitute and homeless. Although Charles II hoped to rebuild London as a city full of piazzas and wide avenues, confusion over the ownership of property meant these ambitions couldn't be realized. In the end, the City of London was rebuilt along the same lines as before the fire, although some beautiful buildings were created in its aftermath, such as the current St. Paul's Cathedral. A 62-meter-tall monument, designed by Sir Christopher Wren, was erected on Pudding Lane to mark the point where the fire started. A much smaller monument (The Golden Boy of Pye Corner) marks the spot where the fire stopped.



### Housing (EC1 to EC4)

There isn't a lot of residential property in the City of London, and what there is tends to be modern purpose-built apartment buildings (built in the latter half of the 20th century or earlier in the 21st century) comprising one-bedroom and two-bedroom apartments. One of the largest residential complexes in the City is the Barbican complex. This comprises Europe's largest multi-arts and conference venue (the Barbican Centre) and the Barbican Estate, a large collection of residential blocks and high-rise buildings. There are, of course, other residential buildings in the City (including the odd riverside apartment), and more are being developed, but property developers have tended to favor offices over apartment buildings. To rent a flat in the City of London, expect to pay at least £550 per week for a one-bedroom apartment and around £750 for a two-bedroom flat; larger properties will be around £1,200 per week. Buying a one-bedroom flat will cost at least £700,000-800,000, with two- or three-bedroom

## Historical Financial Institutions in the City of London

Even though it is just over a square mile (2.9 square kilometers), the City of London (also known as the "Square Mile" or just as the "City") is a leading global business and financial center, equal in stature to New York City. As one of the world's largest trading capitals, the City hosts more than 500 financial institutions, with more Japanese banks than Tokyo and more American banks than New York City. However, it is worth pointing out that this is not a recent development for the Square Mile. It has played a crucial role in Britain's (and the world's) trade and commerce for centuries. As far back as Roman times it was a major trading port with the rest of the Roman Empire. Yet it was the start of the British Empire in Elizabeth I's reign that really helped to establish the City of London as a leading center of trade and commerce.

the Royal Exchange Building

© KAREN WHITE

### THE ROYAL EXCHANGE

By Queen Elizabeth I's reign the City of London had become a major center for banking and international trade. In 1565 the Royal Exchange was created to act as a center of commerce for London's merchants. The aim of the Royal Exchange was to emulate the Bourse in Antwerp as a trading exchange, giving London's merchants and tradesmen a place to meet so they could conduct business. It continued in this capacity for more than 400 years, finally finishing as center for commerce in 1939. Although the Royal Exchange is no longer used for its original purpose (the building is now filled with luxury shops and restaurants), its location on the corner of Cornhill and Threadneedle



flats £1.3-2.5 million and upwards. In 2014-2015, the charge for council tax in the City of London ranged £627-1,884.

## Other Popular Areas Nearby

If you aren't tempted by nearby Clerkenwell in Islington, Hoxton or Shoreditch in Hackney, or even Spitalfields in Tower Hamlets, yet want to live near to the City of London, you may want to head south across the Thames and check out the converted warehouse properties and modern apartments in Shad Thames.

### SHAD THAMES (SE1)

Many City of London workers head south of the river into the Southwark borough. One of the best developments is Shad Thames, near London Bridge. Southwark is just a short walk across the river on one of the bridges into the City, and it offers great views of the City and Tower Bridge. In Shad Thames, large warehouses on the river's

Street is still at the heart of the banking and financial services industries in the Square Mile, with the Bank of England just over the road.

**LONDON STOCK EXCHANGE**

Another historical financial institution in London is the London Stock Exchange, which is one of the world's oldest, dating back more than 300 years. The London Stock Exchange started life in 1698 in the City's coffee houses, when John Castaing had the brainchild of trading marketable securities from a list of stock and commodity prices. The list was entitled *The Course of the Exchange and Other Things*, and in time it led to the creation of the London Stock Exchange. Originally, London's stockbrokers were not allowed to trade in the Royal Exchange because of their rowdy behavior, so they had to continue to trade in coffee shops in the vicinity, such as Jonathan's (their original home) and Garraway's. Eventually the London Stock Exchange built its own premises, though it was still part exchange, part coffee shop. It continued in this vein for the next hundred years or so, until in 1801 when the Stock Exchange moved into dedicated premises in Capel Court and began to be more regulated—marking the start of a modern stock exchange. Today the London Stock Market (now in its premises in Paternoster Square close to St. Paul's Cathedral) lies at the heart of the world's financial community and is one of the largest stock exchanges in the world.

**LLOYD'S OF LONDON**

Yet another financial institution that emerged from London's 17th-century coffee houses was Lloyd's of London—one of the world's leading insurance markets. Back in 1688 Edward Lloyd ran a coffee house on Tower Street that was popular with sailors, ship owners, and merchants, and Lloyd became known as a trustworthy source of information on shipping news. Soon the coffee house established a reputation as a place where wealthy businessmen could buy and invest in marine insurance—a vital element of London's trade with the expanding British Empire. By the 1770s the underwriters at Lloyd's had a more formal structure and had moved to the Royal Exchange. Through the years Lloyd's went from strength to strength, meeting its obligations in the wake of natural disasters, shipwrecks, and conflicts. Today, the Lloyd's marketplace insures most of business listed on both the London Stock Exchange and New York Dow Jones.



edge have been converted into apartment buildings, along with some newer modern apartments, making this area suitable for wealthy, professional, and single city workers, as well as couples.

Property prices for this riverside neighborhood are high, especially flats with a view of the river. The best-known converted warehouse complex is the massive Butler's Wharf. To rent one of the luxury riverside flats in Shad Thames, expect to pay around £550 per week for a one-bedroom and at least £700 per week for a two-bedroom. If you want to buy, expect to pay around £800,000 for a one-bedroom and around £1.5 million for a two-bedroom flat, although they can be much more. Council tax in Southwark in 2014-2015 ranged £807-2,422. Helping to confirm London Bridge and Shad Thames's regeneration is the Shard, London Bridge—Europe's tallest building. Notable attractions in the area include London's largest food market, Borough Market (held on Friday and Saturday); the Design Museum; Shakespeare's Globe Theatre;

and the Tate Modern. Groceries can be ordered online or picked up from a store by London Bridge station.

Those who would prefer to take a bus rather than walk across the bridge can take one of the numerous buses from London Bridge station across the river into the City (such as the number 17 or number 43) or the number 344 on Southwark Bridge Road. The area also connects well to London's second big business district, Canary Wharf, via the Jubilee line at London Bridge station.

## DAILY LIFE

### Schools

Now that the City is so dominated by commerce and business, most of the state schools have left the City of London. Today there are just two state primary schools within the City's boundaries, though there are four private schools (some of which take children from the age of 4, though others don't take children until they are age 7 or older). There are no state secondary schools, although the Corporation of London does sponsor three secondary schools in neighboring boroughs, and there are three private secondary schools.

### Shopping

Shops in the City, including upmarket national chains, target workers. Several smaller grocery stores dot the City as well. Leadenhall Market (on Grace Church Street), with its cobbled roads and glass roof, is a lovely old-fashioned shopping district, and is a great place to shop or stop for lunch or coffee or a drink—depending on what takes your fancy. There are practical (and frivolous) shops near St. Paul's where you can shop for clothes or a gift, or buy food for the weekend. A mall nearby St. Paul's has places to eat and shop—the rooftop restaurant has some lovely views of the City and is a great place for a post-work drink on a warm summer's evening.



### Leisure

The cultural heart of the City of London is the Barbican Centre, which holds music and dance concerts as well as plays—it even has a movie theater. Near the Barbican is the Museum of London, which has exhibits that demonstrate the history of this fascinating and historic part of London. There are some great pubs and restaurants in the City, but if you are looking for exciting nightlife and clubs, head to Shoreditch and Hoxton—you won't find it here. The City does have plenty of private health clubs and gyms, which workers escape to during lunch or after work for a workout. Most of the open spaces are ancient churchyards, with a few landscaped gardens where city workers go for an alfresco lunch.

## Getting Around

With more than 300,000 people commuting in each weekday, the City of London is well serviced by public transportation. Within the Square Mile there are 10 Underground stations on the Central, Circle, District, Northern, Metropolitan, and Hammersmith & City lines. There are also two Docklands Light Railway stations (at Bank and Tower Gateway in nearby Tower Hamlets). There are four National Rail terminus stations: Liverpool Street, Fenchurch Street, Moorgate, and Cannon Street. Just over the river there is London Bridge station. Thameslink railway also has two stations at City Thameslink and Blackfriars. Numerous buses travel through the City of London, though it is often faster to walk around it. There is no need for a car in this area; parking would be difficult and expensive.

# HACKNEY AND TOWER HAMLETS

There was a time not so long ago when many young professionals wouldn't be caught dead in the East End, let alone live there. But times have certainly changed. The City of London's march moved eastward with the development of Docklands and London's second financial center in Canary Wharf (with its luxury riverside apartments). The redevelopment of Stratford as part of London's Olympic 2012 legacy also helped turn around the fortunes of the East End. Today, East London is home to some of London's most desirable neighborhoods. Most affected by the City of London's expansion are the border areas of Hoxton, Shoreditch, and Spitalfields. These neighborhoods attract both city workers and young creative types who want to live in a vibrant, hip area. Prices have increased considerably and are still on the rise, as the demand for residential property increases.

© KAREN WHITE

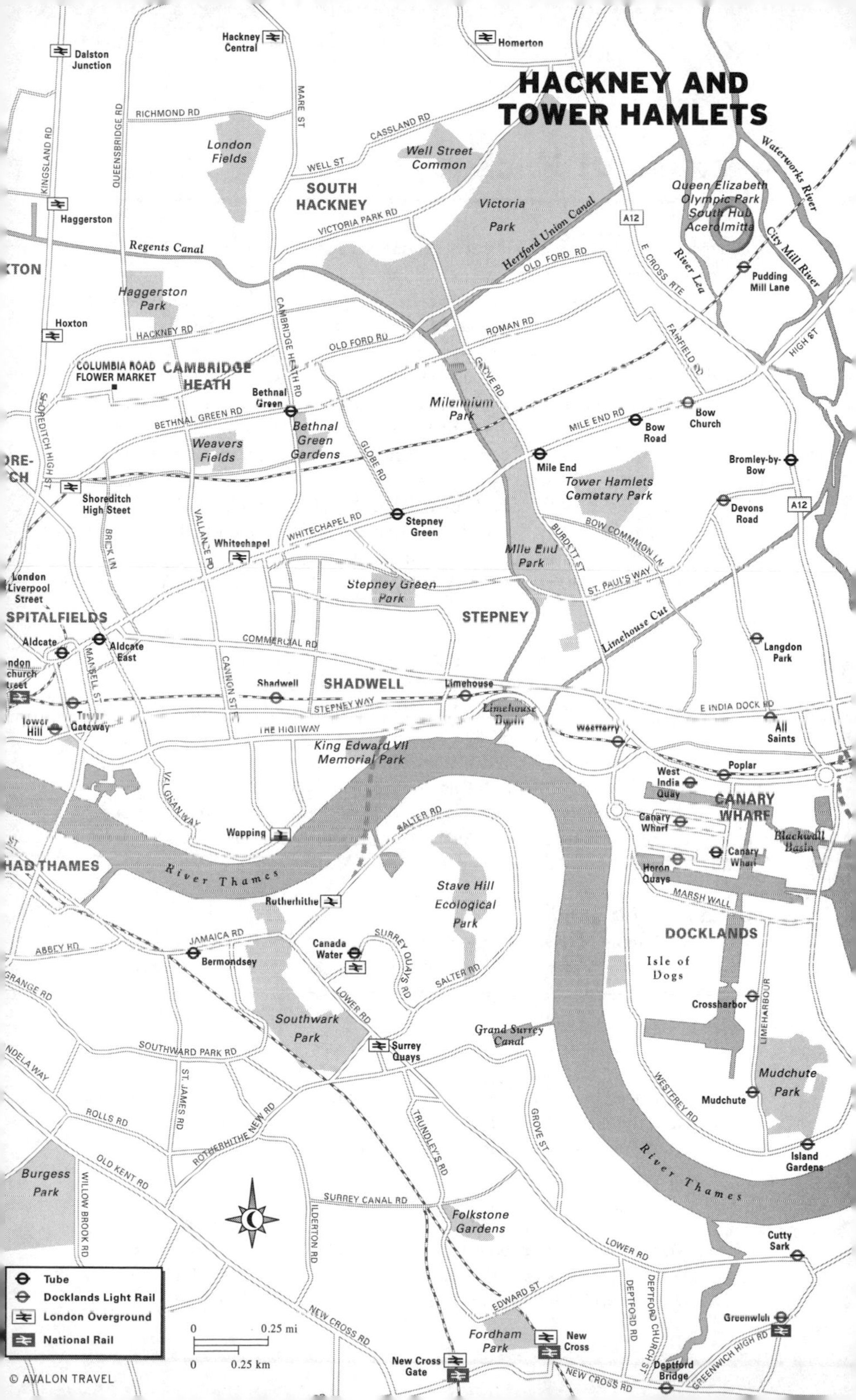
HACKNEY AND TOWER HAMLETS
Dalston Junction
Hackney Central
Homerton
Haggerston
Hoxton
London Fields
Well Street Common
SOUTH HACKNEY
Victoria Park
Queen Elizabeth Olympic Park South Hub
Regents Canal
Hertford Union Canal
Waterworks River
City Mill River
River Lea
Pudding Mill Lane
Haggerston Park
COLUMBIA ROAD FLOWER MARKET
CAMBRIDGE HEATH
Bethnal Green
Bethnal Green Gardens
Weavers Fields
Millennium Park
Mile End
Bow Road
Bow Church
Bromley-by-Bow
Devons Road
Tower Hamlets Cemetary Park
Shoreditch High Street
Stepney Green
Whitechapel
Mile End Park
Stepney Green Park
London Liverpool Street
SPITALFIELDS
STEPNEY
Limehouse Cut
Aldgate
Aldgate East
Langdon Park
Shadwell
SHADWELL
Limehouse
Limehouse Basin
Tower Hill
Tower Gateway
All Saints
King Edward VII Memorial Park
Poplar
West India Quay
CANARY WHARF
Canary Wharf
Blackwall Basin
Heron Quays
Wapping
SHAD THAMES
River Thames
Rotherhithe
Stave Hill Ecological Park
DOCKLANDS
Canada Water
Bermondsey
Isle of Dogs
Crossharbor
Southwark Park
Grand Surrey Canal
Surrey Quays
Mudchute Park
Mudchute
Island Gardens
Burgess Park
Folkstone Gardens
Cutty Sark
Greenwich
Fordham Park
New Cross
New Cross Gate
Deptford Bridge
A12
RICHMOND RD
KINGSLAND RD
QUEENSBRIDGE RD
MARE ST
CASSLAND RD
WELL ST
VICTORIA PARK RD
OLD FORD RD
E. CROSS RTE
HACKNEY RD
CAMBRIDGE HEATH RD
ROMAN RD
FAIRFIELD RD
HIGH ST
GROVE RD
BETHNAL GREEN RD
MILE END RD
GLOBE RD
SHOREDITCH HIGH ST
WHITECHAPEL RD
BRICK LN
VALLANCE RD
BOW COMMMON LN
BURDETT ST
ST. PAUL'S WAY
COMMERCIAL RD
MANSELL ST
CANNON ST
STEPNEY WAY
E INDIA DOCK RD
THE HIGHWAY
SALTER RD
MARSH WALL
JAMAICA RD
SURREY QUAYS RD
ABBEY RD
GRANGE RD
LOWER RD
LIMEHARBOUR
SOUTHWARD PARK RD
WESTFREY RD
ST. JAMES RD
ROLLS RD
ROTHERHITHE NEW RD
TRUNDLEY'S RD
GROVE ST
OLD KENT RD
WILLOW BROOK RD
SURREY CANAL RD
ILDERTON RD
EDWARD ST
DEPTFORD RD
DEPTFORD CHURCH ST
NEW CROSS RD
GREENWICH HIGH RD
Tube
Docklands Light Rail
London Overground
National Rail
0 0.25 mi
0 0.25 km
© AVALON TRAVEL

# Borough of Hackney

Hackney has a long, established history that dates back to Roman times, when much of the borough was used as farmland to feed Roman London. The River Lea has traditionally marked the boundary between the counties of Middlesex (London) and Essex. In the northeast corner of Hackney is the area known as Stamford Hill, home to a large Jewish population (particularly Hasidic Jews) who have populated this neighborhood since Victorian times. Although Hackney has a well-deserved reputation for being a bit dodgy (there is a high crime rate in parts of the borough), the west side of the borough has undergone a dramatic renaissance in recent years. This once rundown area now offers wonderful commercial and residential properties, trendy shops, and a great nightlife.

Hoxton, Shoreditch, and Spitalfields are London's hippest areas. The trio is also home to London's tech center, referred to as "Silicon Roundabout" due to the high number of technology companies and startups based near the Old Street roundabout. Despite the gentrification of parts of its western border, Hackney still has some crime-ridden areas.

## WHERE TO LIVE



The most popular neighborhoods for expats in Hackney, especially younger professionals looking for a trendy location, are Shoreditch and nearby Hoxton. These lively areas are popular with young city workers, artistic and creative types, and Internet technology professionals. Given Hackney's proximity to the City of London, a considerable amount of the borough maintains its inner-city character, with modern apartment complexes and busy offices. (If finances are tight, consider looking in Finsbury Park or Stoke Newington in the northern part of the borough.) On its eastern edge, Hackney has benefited from the regeneration of Stratford and the Queen Elizabeth Olympic Park area, providing yet another option.

### The Lay of the Land

The London Borough of Hackney covers just 7.4 square miles (19 square kilometers). Hackney borders five other boroughs, including Islington to the west, Haringey to the north, and Waltham Forest to the northeast. At its southern borders is Tower Hamlets to the southeast and the City of London to the southwest. The River Lea (London's second-biggest river) marks Hackney's eastern edge, running north-south through East London and feeding into the Thames. In the eastern part of the borough is Hackney Marshes, one of the largest areas of common land in London. It was once a true wetland, though extensive drainage dating from medieval times has turned it into a grassland. Today it is home to 88 full-size soccer pitches.

### Housing

In Hoxton and Shoreditch you'll find a range of housing options, from covered warehouses converted into apartments to skyscrapers and Georgian houses. (Hackney is home to one of London's oldest residential homes, Sutton House, which was built in 1535.) Most expats will live in one of the modern one- and two-bedroom apartment blocks in Hoxton or Shoreditch. The average rent of a one-bedroom apartment is around £450 per week, with prices starting at £320 and topping off at £800 for a luxury flat in Shoreditch. For a two-bedroom flat, the average weekly rent is £635; expect to pay at least £400 for a very basic place and up to more than £1,000 for a penthouse. The average weekly rent for a three-bedroom place is around £750, with prices £550-1,500. Buying a one-bedroom flat in one of these areas will run from £500,000 to more than £1 million for a luxury apartment; the current average asking price is around £685,000. For a two-bedroom flat, that increases to £835,000 but can be much more. Houses or flats with at least three bedrooms may start at around £525,000 and easily increase to several million. Hackney's council tax is on par with the rest of the capital; in 2014-2015, the charges ranged £865-2,595 per annum.

### HOXTON (N1)

North of the City of London, and encompassing some of Islington and Shoreditch/Spitalfields, is the area known as Hoxton. Hoxton sits sandwiched between Angel (in Islington) and Shoreditch, providing easy access to the shops, restaurants, and nightlife of both its neighbors, with some wonderful nightlife of its own in Hoxton Square. Once a very run-down part of central London, this neighborhood is now on the up-and-up (though there is still quite a bit of council housing in the area). Hoxton is also the center of London's technology and creative media, radiating from the "Silicon Roundabout" (Old Street roundabout). Some properties offer an eclectic mix of period terraced houses, though most housing is either in a converted warehouse or modern apartment building.

The nearest Underground station is Old Street on the Northern line, which is also a terminus for British Rail commuter trains. Hoxton station is on the Overground

© KAREN WHITE

Old Street roundabout is also referred to as "Silicon Roundabout."

running between Highbury & Islington station and South London. There are eight bus routes through the Hoxton area; the number 55 bus travels to the West End and Oxford Street, while numbers 48 and 149 head into the City of London.

#### SHOREDITCH (EC1, EC2)

Back in the Elizabethan era, Shoreditch was home to some of London's most famous theatrical playhouses, including the Curtain Theatre, where Shakespeare's company performed until 1599 when the Globe was built in Southwark. Today Shoreditch once again hums with creative energy and is home to one of London's coolest neighborhoods. With its young, vibrant atmosphere, Shoreditch is a popular place to both live and work. Those keen on biking will feel very at home here because bike shops abound, often as an adjunct to a coffee shop or café. Gentrification has transformed this once run-down and crime-ridden area. Shoreditch's aging industrial buildings have been renovated into cool loft apartments, friendly open-plan offices, and lively nightclubs. With neighboring Hoxton and Spitalfields, the neighborhood has become the heart of artsy and urban London. Shoreditch (which straddles both Hackney and Tower Hamlets) is by no means a low-rent living option, but its location means that transportation costs will be lower for those working in central London.

The nearest Underground station is Old Street, which is also a terminus for trains from Hertfordshire (north of the capital). Shoreditch High Street station is on the same Overground line as Hoxton station, with trains running between Highbury & Islington station and South London. Several buses (including night buses) service Shoreditch. The numbers 8, 26, and 35 run through High Street down to the City of London, with number 35 heading over the river and on to London Bridge. Traveling east-west, the number 205 can be used to reach Angel and Upper Street in Islington and on to Paddington Station in West London.



## DAILY LIFE

With their proximity to central London, the City, and Clerkenwell, Hoxton and Shoreditch are popular with young professionals and students. It is expensive to live in the area, but many Londoners just head to Shoreditch to socialize with friends and colleagues.

### Schools

The borough of Hackney has 55 state primary schools and 16 state secondary schools, as well as three sixth-form colleges. There are a few private primary and secondary schools, and many of these have a religious ethos, be it Christian, Jewish, or Muslim. In the Shoreditch and Hoxton areas, there is just one private (nondenominational) primary school and half a dozen state primary schools, with five state secondary schools.

### Shopping

While practical shopping for groceries may be a bit difficult in Shoreditch and Hoxton (there are a couple of grocery stores nearby), quirky independent boutiques, as well as a few well-known brands, make shopping in Shoreditch a real joy. The Boxpark on Bethnal Green Road is a shopping center with a difference—it is made from reclaimed shipping containers and offers food, fashion, and retro shops. Both Shoreditch High Street and nearby Redchurch Street have some wonderful eclectic clothing and

## Columbia Road Flower Market

© KAREN WHITE

a shop in the fabulous Columbia Road Flower Market in Hackney

Tucked up a small road in East London (north of Shoreditch) is one of London's most enchanting markets—the Columbia Road Flower Market. Lined with tiny, terraced cottages and jam-packed full of flowers and plants, Columbia Road is a riot of color in an otherwise bland urban landscape. London's principle market is devoted to selling plants, cut flowers, and gardening paraphernalia; neighboring shops include perfumeries, cafés, and art galleries.

Centuries ago, the market area was a clay pit for the local industry of brick making. Once the clay was exhausted, the area became a notorious slum until the 1840s, when philanthropist Angela Burdett-Coutts bought the land and created the Columbia Road Flower Market. The flower market was originally held on a Saturday, then switched to Sunday in order to accommodate local Jewish traders and clientele. The move to Sunday also gave traders from the Spitalfields and Covent Garden markets a chance to sell their remaining stock.

Today, the Columbia Road Flower Market is one of London's most stunning markets. Towering tree ferns rub shoulders with trimly clipped balls of boxwood, and cut herbaceous flowers in a multitude of colors sit next to delicate grasses gently rustling in the wind. Whether you are after some cheery cut flowers or plants to spruce up your window box, you are sure to find something gorgeous.

The flower market is open 8am-2pm on Sunday. Bargain hunters will find the best deals just before the market closes, though for the best stock you should get there bright and early. The flower market is a 12-minute walk from Old Street station, or take the number 55 bus up Hackney Road.

housewares boutiques. For mainstream mall shopping, jump on the Underground and head into the West End or to the massive mall farther east in Stratford.

### Leisure

If you are after great bars, live music, and clubs, there is no shortage of lively nightlife in Shoreditch and Hoxton. The neighborhoods have some of the best cocktail bars in town, as well as a few great pubs. Shoreditch is home to a great local arts center, which offers a range of creative activities, such as film, dance, theater, and comedy. For a bit of fresh air and green open spaces, head to Hackney Marshes or Victoria Park.

### Getting Around

Manor Park is the only Tube station in the borough, though Islington's Old Street station touches its southwestern edge, with Liverpool Street station in the City of London just a few blocks away. Residents should rely on the Overground network to connect with the Underground, then take a bus or get on a bike. Given the lack of Underground stations, Hackney's most popular neighborhoods are those near the City of London (which has a plethora of Underground stations). The A10 (a former Roman road) is the main road cutting through the borough from north to south; several bus routes follow the road in and out of the City of London. City Road and Great Eastern Street run along the southern edge, with buses in and out of the City.



# Tower Hamlets

You will be hard-pressed to find a more diverse borough than Tower Hamlets; ethnic minorities comprise approximately half of the population. At the heart of London's East End, this borough is one of London's most densely populated, with high levels of social inequality. It is home to some of the capital's most valuable residential and commercial property in Canary Wharf—London's second financial district—and this area attracts the very wealthy with its luxury riverside skyscrapers. The medieval Tower of London and the iconic Tower Bridge form its borders. The borough is home to the famous curry houses of Brick Lane as well as Spitalfields, a hotbed of creative activity—this area embraces everything from fashion to street art.

## WHERE TO LIVE

Expats will be drawn to either the western edge of Tower Hamlets where it borders the City of London, such as Spitalfields, the Docklands and Canary Wharf on the eastern edge of the borough, or the Bow and Victoria Park area in between. The Docklands area sits on a big loop in the River Thames and is filled with old canals that formerly housed London's dockyards. Strategically placed between Canary Wharf and the City of London, Bow offers easy access to either financial center, with Victoria Park providing a leafy green alternative in the urban East End. The area is popular with young professionals and families, as well as the odd student.

## The Lay of the Land

Tower Hamlets is a fairly small borough, just 7.63 square miles (19.77 square kilometers), yet it is very densely populated and includes the largest population of Bangladeshis outside of Bangladesh. The Docklands area is on the borough's southeastern edge; to the west, Spitalfields borders the City of London; and to the north is Hackney. The borough of Newham is east of Tower Hamlets, with the River Lea marking the border between them.

## Housing

Most expats will look to live in Spitalfields (near the City of London), in the Docklands and Canary Wharf, or near Bow and Victoria Park. Spitalfields has undergone a regeneration that includes the development of some modern office blocks and residential properties in apartment buildings and converted warehouses. The Docklands is home to modern apartment buildings, a few townhomes, and some luxury high-rise apartments. Some of Bow's Victorian terraced houses have been converted into flats, and there are some modern apartment buildings here as well.

Rental prices in Spitalfields or Canary Wharf range £350-650 a week for a one-bedroom apartment and £350-1,000 a week for a two-bedroom (Spitalfields is more expensive); the average cost of rent is £630 per week. Rents for a three-bedroom start at £580 per week but can nearly triple for a luxury riverside apartment. Housing prices for a one-bedroom apartment are around £510,000; the average asking price for a two-bedroom flat is around £750,000 in Canary Wharf and a bit more in Spitalfields. Houses or flats with at least three bedrooms may start at around £890,000 and can easily increase to several million.

In Bow and Victoria Park, prices are more affordable. For a one-bedroom flat, expect to pay at least £275 per week and up to £550. For a two-bedroom flat, the weekly rental price ranges between £365 and £500. Larger places rent for £550 per week on average but can be as much as £700. Housing prices for a one-bedroom flat are around £315,000; two-bedroom flats are just under $400,000, while a period house could sell for well over £1 million. Council tax in Tower Hamlets in 2014-2015 ranged £789-2,369.



### DOCKLANDS AND CANARY WHARF (E14)

Although the area is primarily known as a business district, the regeneration of the Docklands and the creation of Canary Wharf have resulted in some urgently needed housing for the capital, in addition to establishing a second massive financial center in London. This area appeals to professional singles and couples, as properties tend to consist of one- and two-bedroom flats. Apartments overlooking the river can command a hefty price. The area sits in a loop of the Thames River, a bit of an oasis in what is otherwise a bleak part of the Tower Hamlets. It can be a hassle getting in and out of the Docklands, but thankfully a mall, cinema, supermarket, and several good cafés and restaurants are nearby. If your job in London will be based in Docklands, consider living in the area—just make sure that you can easily get to Canary Wharf so that you can access the rest of London via the Underground.

Canary Wharf is serviced by the Jubilee line, the Docklands Light Railway, and five bus routes; the number 135 travels west to the City of London and Liverpool Street station. Crossrail will also stop in Canary Wharf and should reduce travel times between there and Liverpool Street station to just six minutes.

### SPITALFIELDS (E1)

Spitalfields was home to French Huguenot lace makers in the 18th century and Eastern European Jews in the 19th century. It was also the site of a few of Jack the Ripper's victims, so it has a checkered past. Along with neighboring Hoxton and Shoreditch, Spitalfields has undergone a great deal of urban regeneration, including towering office blocks, such as those in the Bishopsgate and Aldgate area. Spitalfields Market (one of London's best markets) and Petticoat Lane Market are here, as is Brick Lane. The neighborhood sports an edgy vibe, with great music venues and clubs and notable art galleries, making it one of the capital's most diverse areas.

There are no Tube stations in Spitalfields, though it isn't far from Liverpool Street station (on the Central, Circle, and Metropolitan lines). Aldgate East station (on the District and Hammersmith & City lines) is also near the area. Several buses travel up and down Bishopsgate (such as the number 35), and the number 67 travels along Commercial Road.

### BOW AND VICTORIA PARK (E3/E9)

Conveniently located between both Canary Wharf and the City of London is the neighborhood of Bow and Victoria Park. Victoria Park was established in the 1840s as the first park built for the public. During the summer months, it is home to open-air pop and rock concerts. The north side of the park borders Hackney, and there are some lovely Victorian terraced family homes (and the odd modern apartment building) with independent shops and places to eat and drink along Lauriston Road and

Canary Wharf

© LES SMITHSON
Brick Lane gives way to a bustling market on Sundays.



Victoria Park Road. On the southern side of Victoria Park is Bow in Tower Hamlets. Here there is a mix of period terraced homes and modern apartment buildings, some of which overlook the Regent's Canal. You'll find more conventional shops, trendy coffee shops and cafés, and the Saturday market on Roman Road. Both sides of the park have decent gastropubs for dining and/or drinking.

The southern side of Victoria Park is near Mile End on the Central, District, and Hammersmith & City lines; Bow Road on the District and Hammersmith & City lines; and the DLR station at Bow Church. North of the park, the nearest Overground station is Homerton; trains at London Fields can take you into Liverpool Street. The number 425 bus runs along Grove Road (which cuts through the park) to Mile End.

## DAILY LIFE

### Schools

There are 70 state primary schools in Tower Hamlets, with 17 secondary schools and one sixth-form college. There are eight private primary schools, though many have a religious orientation, with three independent secondary schools—a Christian school and two Muslim schools.

### Shopping

In addition to the markets and boutiques in Spitalfields, the Canary Wharf complex includes a fairly large shopping center with 200 shops and boutiques, as well as a few grocery stores. For practical items such as groceries, there are small local grocery stores and a few supermarkets in Docklands. Stratford, just a few stops up the Central line, is home to a large mall. The western side of the borough provides easy access to Islington and Upper Street or the West End for shopping.

© KAREN WHITE

shops along Lauriston Road in Victoria Park



## Leisure

Spitalfields has a lively nightlife, with some great pubs, clubs, and places to eat. Docklands offers chic and trendy riverside restaurants, and there is a movie theater in Canary Wharf. Both Spitalfields and Canary Wharf have a few gyms where you can work off the calories you gained by eating out. Victoria Park is your best bet for green open spaces, with its ponds, pavilion, tennis courts, and sports ground.

## Getting Around

Tower Hamlets is well served by public transportation with five Underground lines—the Central, Circle, District, Hammersmith & City, and the Jubilee in Canary Wharf—at nine different stations. The DLR services much of the borough, linking Docklands with the City of London and Stratford in the east, and the Overground runs through some of its western edge. Crossrail (with stops in Whitechapel and Canary Wharf) will improve the borough's connectivity with the rest of London and southeast England.

# BOROUGH OF WANDSWORTH

For a long while, expats wouldn't even contemplate living south of the river, unless it was in the more suburban area of Richmond. However, things have changed dramatically in parts of South London, especially in the borough of Wandsworth, which is now home to some very desirable places to live in London. Of course, residents have to contend with getting around London with fewer Underground stations, but the advantages in terms of amenities and property/rental prices help to make up for any inconvenience.

Wandsworth is known for two things: It has one of the lowest council tax charges in the country and is a big favorite with London families. Parts of the borough are known as "Nappy Valley" because of the larger number of middle-class, affluent families that live there ("nappy" is the British word for diaper). The local population has seen tremendous growth in the past 20 years, fueled by the recent influx of young professional workers and families.

Confusingly, there are several names used to describe this part of town—Battersea, Wandsworth, and even Clapham. Around 20 years ago when people started to spill out of Chelsea and over the river they would call it Clapham, after the local train station Clapham Junction. As the area became gentrified and affluent, the large detached

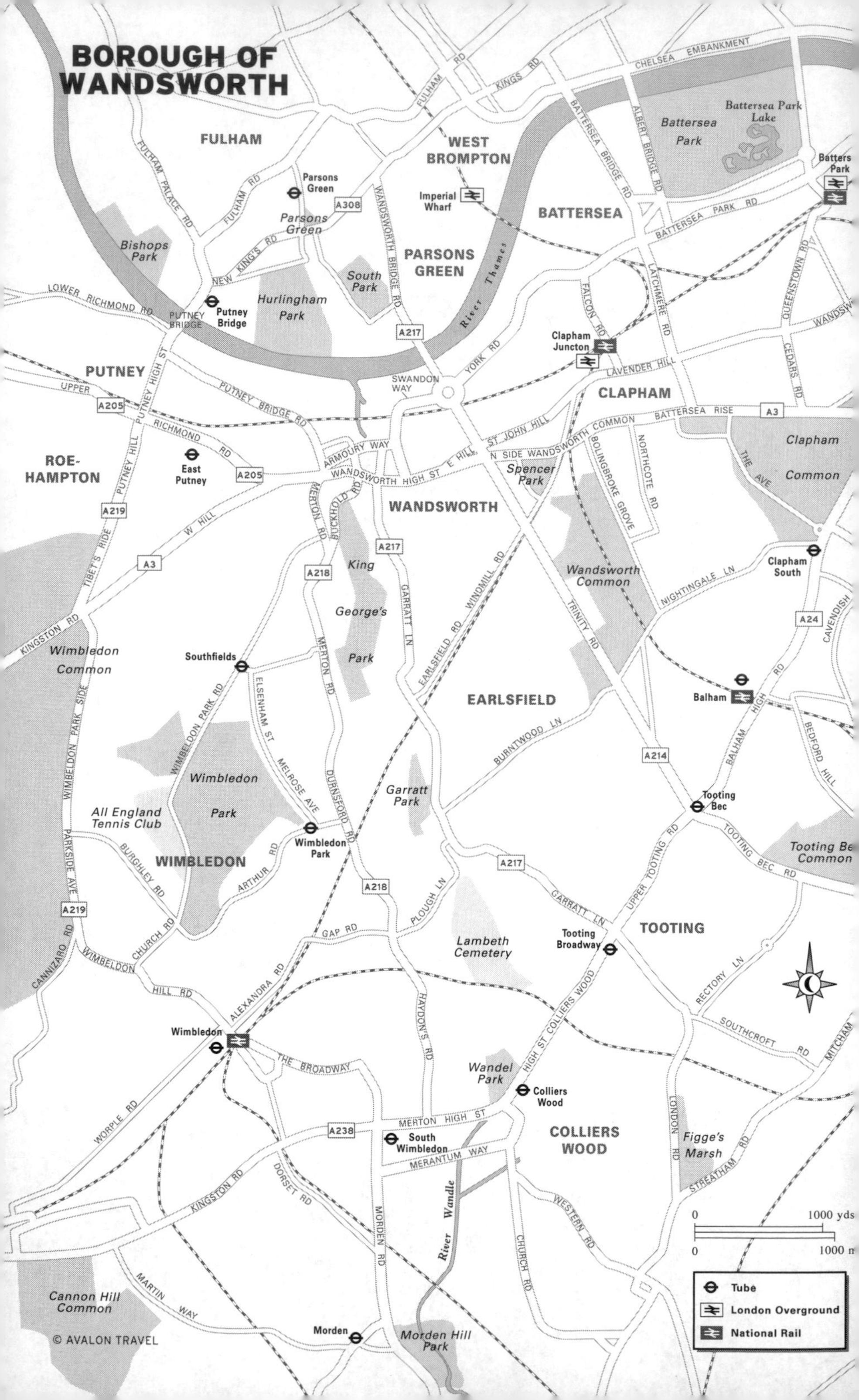

BOROUGH OF WANDSWORTH
FULHAM
WEST BROMPTON
BATTERSEA
PARSONS GREEN
PUTNEY
CLAPHAM
ROE-HAMPTON
WANDSWORTH
EARLSFIELD
WIMBLEDON
TOOTING
COLLIERS WOOD
Parsons Green
Imperial Wharf
Putney Bridge
Clapham Junction
East Putney
Clapham South
Southfields
Balham
Tooting Bec
Wimbledon Park
Tooting Broadway
Wimbledon
Colliers Wood
South Wimbledon
Morden
Bishops Park
Hurlingham Park
South Park
Battersea Park
Battersea Park Lake
Clapham Common
Spencer Park
King George's Park
Wandsworth Common
Wimbledon Common
Wimbledon Park
All England Tennis Club
Garratt Park
Lambeth Cemetery
Wandel Park
Figge's Marsh
Cannon Hill Common
Morden Hall Park
River Thames
River Wandle
CHELSEA EMBANKMENT
KINGS RD
FULHAM RD
FULHAM PALACE RD
NEW KING'S RD
WANDSWORTH BRIDGE RD
BATTERSEA BRIDGE RD
ALBERT BRIDGE RD
BATTERSEA PARK RD
LOWER RICHMOND RD
PUTNEY BRIDGE RD
UPPER RICHMOND RD
PUTNEY HIGH ST
YORK RD
FALCON RD
LATCHMERE RD
QUEENSTOWN RD
CEDARS RD
LAVENDER HILL
BATTERSEA RISE
SWANDON WAY
ARMOURY WAY
WANDSWORTH HIGH ST
E HILL
ST JOHN HILL
N SIDE WANDSWORTH COMMON
NORTHCOTE RD
BOLINGBROKE GROVE
THE AVE
PUTNEY HILL
W HILL
TIBBET'S RIDE
KINGSTON RD
MERTON RD
BUCKHOLD RD
GARRATT LN
WINDMILL RD
EARLSFIELD RD
TRINITY RD
NIGHTINGALE LN
CAVENDISH
BALHAM HIGH RD
BEDFORD HILL
BURNTWOOD LN
WIMBLEDON PARK RD
ELSENHAM ST
MELROSE AVE
DURNSFORD RD
WIMBLEDON PARK SIDE
PARKSIDE AVE
BURGHLEY RD
ARTHUR RD
UPPER TOOTING RD
TOOTING BEC RD
PLOUGH LN
GAP RD
CHURCH RD
WIMBLEDON HILL RD
CANNIZARO RD
ALEXANDRA RD
HAYDON'S RD
HIGH ST COLLIERS WOOD
RECTORY LN
SOUTHCROFT RD
MITCHAM
THE BROADWAY
WORPLE RD
MERTON HIGH ST
MERANTUM WAY
KINGSTON RD
DORSET RD
MORDEN RD
CHURCH RD
WESTERN RD
LONDON RD
STREATHAM RD
MARTIN WAY
A308
A217
A205
A3
A219
A218
A214
A24
A238
0
1000 yds
1000 m
Tube
London Overground
National Rail
© AVALON TRAVEL

Victorian houses by Wandsworth Common shot up in value (and are now worth several million pounds), making Wandsworth and parts of Battersea very desirable places to live. Of course, now everyone who lives in the borough now says that they live in Wandsworth, so they can associate themselves with this prime bit of real estate. Local realtors may also list property as being in Wandsworth (as in the borough) but which are not near Wandsworth Common (and the more desirable neighborhoods)—so look for places "between the commons" (that is to say, between Clapham Common and Wandsworth Common) if this is your chosen location.

As a London borough, Wandsworth is generally prosperous and has one of the highest average incomes in London. Unusual for an inner London borough, Wandsworth doesn't have areas of extreme deprivation, though there are some pockets of poverty in the borough. The American Embassy will be moving to Wandsworth in Nines Elms neighborhood once the new building is completed in 2017. To improve public transportation in this part of London, Transport for London is extending the Northern line down into Battersea from Kennington station, and the line should be operational by 2020. No doubt this part of Wandsworth will quickly become highly desirable commercial and residential real estate. Yet even without an extension of the Northern line Wandsworth still has a lot to offer. The borough has an abundance of family homes on quiet residential streets. Plus, there has already been quite a significant amount of urban regeneration in the past few years, such as turning defunct factories and wharfs into modern riverside developments.



# Where to Live

Wandsworth is a bit of an odd borough, as there are some very nice neighborhoods as well as many areas that could do with some redevelopment. The best neighborhoods are near Clapham Junction train station (Battersea) and near Wandsworth Common (Wandsworth). Farther west, the area known as Putney has some great homes, good amenities and schools, as well as a Tube station, making it another area well worth considering.

## THE LAY OF THE LAND

Wandsworth is around six miles (10 kilometers) southwest of the West End, just across Wandsworth Bridge from Fulham. The borough of Wandsworth takes its name from the River Wandle, which enters the Thames in the village of Wandsworth. It is the largest of the inner London boroughs, covering an area of 13.2 square miles (34 square kilometers), and borders four boroughs south of the river (Lambeth, Merton, Kingston upon Thames, and Richmond upon Thames), with Hammersmith and Fulham, Kensington and Chelsea, and the City of Westminster on the other side of the river. In addition to Battersea Park (200 acres), there are three large parks (or "commons" as they are called in Wandsworth): Wandsworth Common (172 acres), Clapham Common (220 acres and shared with Lambeth), and the massive Wimbledon Common (1,140 acres shared with Merton). A common used to be a bit of waste land that some villagers (commoners) could use to graze their livestock. Over time, these commons developed into public parks and are usually managed by the local council.

## London's North/South Divide

It wasn't too many years ago that London's communities were more socially split by the River Thames, with the water being viewed by some as a border between two countries: North London and South London. (For years, if I ever had an occasion to venture over the river, my husband or friends would remind me to "take my passport.") No doubt some of the north/south divide in London stems from some people's desire to accept only what they know and feel at ease with. This can be more pronounced in a massive city like London, where its residents cling tenaciously to certain areas that are familiar, rarely straying beyond the known borders. I, too, have been guilty of this; Richmond was the only part of South London that I felt comfortable in, as it is a breeze to get there via the Overground trains.

However, things have changed for South London, and it's now treated with much more respect as increasing numbers of North Londoners head over the river into boroughs such as Wandsworth, attracted by the large (and often more affordable) properties there. A regeneration of neighborhoods south of the river, including new property developments, and improving transportation infrastructure have tempted confirmed North Londoners across the river. Sky-high property prices in and around central London have forced many North Londoners to look beyond their borders to new pastures. The result has been that neighborhoods, such as those in Lambeth, have been gentrified by the popularity of Clapham (and Brixton) with young professionals. The construction of Europe's tallest building, the Shard Tower by London Bridge in Southwark, has furthered the City of London's expansion south of the river and supplemented the regeneration of this part of inner London. Even sleepy Putney and Battersea have seen an influx of wealthy professionals in the few past decades, who headed over the bridges in search of more affordable housing and good schools.

Many North London families are tempted south of the river, where they believe they can get more for their money, as the area offers larger houses with ample gardens. There is also a belief that they have a better quality of life, as the commons and parks provide open green spaces away from London's busy streets. Plus they can easily jump on a bus and be north of the river if they need a dose of central London (interestingly, my friends in Fulham tend to head south to Putney for shopping and cinemas rather than head east to Fulham Broadway).

The only trouble with South London is the public transportation, which is limited to fewer than a handful of tube stations, making residents reliant on the railroads and buses—not the fastest ways to get around town. Yet, once the Northern line is extended into Battersea in Wandsworth, this part of London will at last be connected with the Tube network and will be an even more desirable place to live. The improvements with the Overground network have also helped to connect parts of South London with the Tube network and London north of the river. It looks like the once sharp divide between North and South London is diminishing.

## HOUSING

There are three main types of property available in Wandsworth: apartments in mansion buildings (especially in Putney), large Victorian or Edwardian terraced and semi-detached or detached houses, and modern luxury riverside flats. One standout feature of Wandsworth's housing stock is that many of the older properties have *not* been converted into flats, which means that this could be a good place to buy a house, even though prices are on the high side. If you are thinking of renting in this part of town, expect weekly rents of at least £350 for a standard one-bedroom, around £650 for a two-bedroom (up to £1,000 or more if it is on the river), and £850-1,200 for a nice family home. To buy, expect to pay around £440,000 for a one bedroom and around £685,000 for a two-bedroom flat, though those with river frontage can be more than £1 million. Houses depend very much upon the location, with larger detached homes near Wandsworth Common going for several million, while smaller terraced houses are usually at least £1 million. The borough also has several conservation areas that help to preserve the look and character of many of its neighborhoods. Its council tax is the second lowest in the United Kingdom, ranging £473-1,418 in 2014-2015.

### Battersea (SW11)

Battersea is an unusual area; its landscape near the river is dominated by a massive coal-fired power station, though thankfully this is somewhat hidden by Battersea Park. The Battersea power station has been decommissioned for years, and there is a building preservation order on it, but all this is changing. In 2012, property developers bought the power station and will turn it into luxury river apartments, as well as shops, restaurants, and a hotel. The project is due to be completed in 2016-2017. Elsewhere in Battersea, redevelopment and gentrification have been achieved without

luxury riverside apartment buildings in Battersea

difficulty, and in a few decades this area has changed beyond all recognition. It's no longer a working-class neighborhood, and has now become home to many of London's well-paid professionals, who have bought property in this area in droves. Battersea's traditional terrace houses have been renovated and extended, making the neighborhood a firm favorite with families (its nickname is "Nappy Valley"). The area is particularly popular with Europeans, especially the French, as there is a French primary school near Clapham Common. The 200-acre Battersea Park runs along the edge of the River Thames and offers spectacular views of the river along with its tennis courts and duck pond. Nearby Clapham and Wandsworth Commons are popular places for runners and dog walkers. This is an affluent and up-and-coming neighborhood, so Battersea is no longer the bargain that it once was, although it is still more affordable than its neighbor across the river, Chelsea.

## GETTING AROUND

The only station in the Battersea area is Clapham Junction—a railway station. The station has the Overground service to Stratford running through it, and it is the start of Overground services through South London to Docklands and through East London to Highbury & Islington station. Many trains heading to London's Waterloo and Victoria stations also stop in Clapham Junction, making it one of the busiest junctions in the United Kingdom. It is so hectic at the station that overcrowding can be a problem at rush hour. Other public transportation options include one of the other train stations, be it Battersea Park into Victoria station or Queenstown Road to Waterloo. You could also take a number 37 bus to the Northern line at Clapham Common station. Clapham Junction has around 20 different bus routes, from the number 319 to Chelsea, to the number 87 into the West End, to the number 49 through Kensington.

There are some lovely pubs in Battersea.

## Putney (SW15)

Running along the river's south bank opposite Fulham is the delightful neighborhood of Putney. Along the river by Putney Bridge you'll find Putney Wharf with its piazza of shops, restaurants, and bars, set next to modern townhouses and loft-style apartments. Just here next to the bridge is the starting point for the annual Oxford and Cambridge boat race. Putney is known for its striking Victorian and Edwardian architecture along leafy green streets—it's a good option for those who want to mix a city lifestyle with some suburban tranquility. As far as housing goes, you'll find a mix of converted one- and two-bedroom apartments here, as well as a few larger places. There's also an excellent high street with lots of well known stores and some good places to go to in the evening for a drink or meal.

### GETTING AROUND

Putney's one downfall is that it's on the District line, which isn't the most dependable of Tube lines, but at least it's on an Underground line, which is more than you can say for much of the borough. If the Tube line is down, you could take a bus to another Tube line, such as the number 22 to Piccadilly, number 37 to Clapham Junction (and get the train), or the number 220 to Hammersmith.

## Wandsworth (SW18)

A bit farther away from the river is the area known as Wandsworth (like the borough). The area is west of Wandsworth Common and south of East Hill Road. This very desirable neighborhood has some of the most expensive townhouses in London in an area known locally as "The Toast Rack." Although this is a relatively small neighborhood, Wandsworth's pretty residential streets and large Victorian houses are a winning combination, making it a highly sought-after London location. The neighborhood gained notoriety as the location for the film *Love Actually,* which showed Wandsworth's lovely properties to good effect. Unfortunately, Wandsworth High Street is a bit uninspiring and can be congested with cars from the A3 (a main route in and out of London heading southwest into Surrey and on to Portsmouth on the south coast). Shopping in the area is dominated by the newly rebuilt Southside Shopping Mall, complete with a supermarket and a movie theater. On Bellevue Road you'll find some fashion boutiques, some good pubs, and places to eat.

### GETTING AROUND

The bad news is that Wandsworth doesn't have a Tube station, just two rail stations (Wandsworth Town and Wandsworth Common), both of which have trains to Victoria station that can be crowded. Residents who live toward Putney may be able to use East Putney Underground station (District line, Wimbledon branch). Twelve different bus routes run along Wandsworth High Road, including the number 87 to the West End and the number 28 to Kensington.

## Clapham (SW4)

Moving slightly to the east there is the South London neighborhood of Clapham in the adjacent borough of Lambeth. This area has a lot to offer young professionals—or the young at heart. It's a vibrant, diverse area bordering Clapham Common, with its High

## Looking After Man's Best Friend

The British have a notorious love of animals, and some of the world's oldest animal shelters are in England. The most famous of these is the Battersea Dogs & Cats Home, which was founded more than 150 years ago. Both then and now, its aim remains the same—to never turn away a dog or cat in need of help.

Battersea Dogs & Cats Home started life as the Temporary Home for Lost and Starving Dogs and was set up in Archway, North London, by the kind-hearted Mary Tealby, who was concerned about the high number of stray dogs roaming the streets of Victorian London. At first the home was ridiculed for helping animals when humans were living in deprivation. However, an article by Charles Dickens helped garner support for the animal shelter when it compared the two extremes of the grand Crufts Dog Show with its pampered pooches and the conditions of the animals that were rescued by Mary Tealby. In 1871 the home moved south of the river to its current home in Battersea, opening up its doors to cats in 1883. Importantly, the home began to achieve social acceptance, and in 1885 it finally gained the royal seal of approval when it was granted a royal patronage by Queen Victoria.

The Battersea Dogs & Cats Home





Street running between two of its three Underground stations (Clapham North and Clapham Common on the Northern line). The third station (Clapham South) is south of Clapham Common. The stores are a collection of standard grocery and drugstores, along with other conveniences such as fast-food chains and coffee shops. The area has several good clubs, bars, and pubs, all of which are popular with twenty-something Britons and Antipodeans. The open-air concerts held in Clapham Common during the summer months are also popular with trendy young Londoners.

The neighborhood attracts a variety of young professionals, as well as some families (who tend to move to the suburbs once their children are of secondary school age). Generally, the properties consist of terraced Victorian houses, many of which have been converted into flats. To buy a one-bedroom converted flat, expect to pay around £455,000, and around £615,000 for a two-bedroom apartment, with Victorian terraced houses usually going for £1-2.5 million in the more desirable areas. Expect to pay at least £350 per week to rent a one-bedroom flat (maybe as much as £450), with prices for a nice two-bedroom place ranging £400-550 or more. Family houses range £600-1,000 and up, depending on the size and location (Abbeville Village is very popular with families). The council tax in Clapham (in the borough of Lambeth) is higher than in nearby Wandsworth, and in 2014-2015 ranged £816-2,449.

The Battersea Dogs & Cats Home ideology is simple: to care for animals in need and to reunite lost animals with their owners or care for them until they can be rehoused. Animals from the home have also come to the aid of their country by working in both world wars. This includes the famous Airedale Jack, a Battersea dog who served in World War I. Although he was fatally wounded on the front line in France, Jack still managed to deliver his vital message to commanding officers (a plea for reinforcements), which saved his battalion. He was posthumously awarded the Victoria Cross medal, Britain's highest military honor.

The Battersea Dogs & Cats Home offers essential services for Londoners, both human and furry, such as behavior retraining for dogs and cats as well as reuniting animals and owners through its Lost Dogs and Cats Line. The home also provides advice and education to the public about pet ownership and the responsibility of caring for animals. Every year around 10,000 dogs and cats are cared for by Battersea Dogs & Cats Home.

An animal from the Battersea Dogs & Cats Home has been asked to serve the nation once again. In early 2011 a rat was seen on national TV news scurrying along outside the front door of 10 Downing Street (the official home of the prime minister). Within days a call had been made to the Battersea Home for a cat to be adopted by Downing Street to help ward off rodents. The only requirements were that it should be a good hunter and good with a variety of people. Answering the call was Larry, a three- or four-year-old short-haired tabby, who had been rescued from the London streets just a few weeks earlier. So far Larry has been doing a sterling job as the official cat in residence at 10 Downing Street and has taken to his new post with relish.

### GETTING AROUND

The area is fairly well connected for public transportation, even though you are south of the river. It has three Tube stations (Clapham North, Clapham Common, and Clapham South) on the Northern line, which can get crowded, but the line is pretty reliable. For Overground connections, trains from Clapham High Street station travel west to Clapham Junction and Highbury & Islington (via Canada Water). Six buses run along Clapham High Street, with the number 88 heading through the West End and on into Camden Town and the number 345 heading toward Battersea (and Clapham Junction rail station) and on into South Kensington.

## Wimbledon (SW19)

Known the world over as host of the annual two-week lawn tennis championships each summer, Wimbledon is one of London's finest neighborhoods—with house prices to match. Most of the Wimbledon area is in the borough of Merton (Wandsworth's neighbor to the south), although some of it just creeps into Wandsworth. The area known as Wimbledon comprises a large swath of southwest London and can be separated into three different sections: Wimbledon Village on top of the hill (this is the most expensive area and is nearer the common) and Wimbledon Town at the bottom of the hill (more affordable), with Wimbledon Park/Southfield (SW19/SW18) slightly to the northeast. Wimbledon is favored by families due to its good local schools, both private and state. The village has a relaxed and friendly atmosphere with good amenities and upmarket boutiques, pubs, cafés, and restaurants. Houses in the area are a mix of Victorian and Edwardian terraces, with a few modern townhouses as well as the odd apartment building. In 2015, the price for a family house in Wimbledon Village near the common was around £1.85 million on average, while a family house in Wimbledon Park was around £1.15 million; prices down by the town center were occasionally still under £1 million. A two-bedroom flat in the village goes for at least £500,000 (the average is £700,000), and a one-bedroom place averaged £370,000; a luxury one- or two-bedroom apartment near the common could sell for up to £1 million or more. Prices in Wimbledon Park and Wimbledon town are slightly more affordable depending on the size and distance from the station. Rental prices in the village average around £385 per week for a one-bedroom place and £520 per week for a two-bedroom apartment, while a family house averaged around £1,300 per week (but could be double for a really special house). Prices in both Wimbledon Park and Wimbledon Town are more reasonable, sometimes by as much as 20 percent. In 2014-2015, the borough of Merton's council tax ranged £952-2,857.

#### GETTING AROUND

Wimbledon, Wimbledon Park, and Southfield stations are on the District line; South Wimbledon is on the Northern line. Overground trains out of Wimbledon station go to Waterloo Station. There is a Thameslink service to the City of London, including Blackfriars station. Nine bus routes service Wimbledon station, with the number 219 going north to Clapham Junction and the numbers 131 and 57 heading southeast toward Kingston upon Thames.



## Daily Life

The borough of Wandsworth is very popular with families and has a strong residential feel to it. Although it is an inner London borough, it certainly doesn't feel like one. The area is popular with European expats, some Aussies, and, increasingly, Americans. If you have a young family, the "trailing spouse" will be able to meet other parents in the area through schools and kids' activities. Singles and couples may prefer to live over the river, where they will be near London nightlife, or over in Clapham in nearby Lambeth.

### SCHOOLS

There are several top-performing primary schools in Wandsworth, most of which are Church of England schools, and it has a few noteworthy secondary schools as well. The borough has 60 state primary schools and 11 secondary schools. These schools are very popular, and you will need to live right on the school's doorstep to get into one of the better ones. There are also numerous private primary schools (around 20) with six independent secondary schools in Wandsworth, and it wouldn't be too hard to go

There are some wonderful shops on Northcote Road.



across the river for a school north of the river. One of the ACS International Schools (ACS Cobham) operates a bus service from some areas in Putney and Wimbledon.

## SHOPPING

In Battersea (near Clapham Junction) there are a few department stores and supermarkets, and along Northcote Road (situated between Wandsworth and Clapham Commons) you'll find a wide variety of stores, although independents are being replaced by upmarket national chains. As you'd expect in an area famed for attracting families, there are several shops geared toward children in Wandsworth. There's also an antiques market on Northcote Road, as well as a daily food market. Elsewhere in the borough, Putney High Street has all the usual amenities, from grocery stores to national chains, as well as movie theaters and places to eat and drink. Wandsworth town has a small mall and supermarkets.

## LEISURE

There are loads of restaurants and cafés on Northcote Road/Battersea Rise and in Putney on the High Street. Both Wandsworth town and Putney have movie theaters. If you're after fun-filled nightlife, head to Clapham or Battersea, where there are some great pubs, bars, and clubs. After a long night out, you can clear your head with a run (or walk) in one of the nearby commons, or you could head to the swimming pool at Latchmere Leisure Centre and its wave machine. For more cultural pursuits there is the Battersea Arts Centre (with its experimental theater) and Theatre 503 above The Latchmere pub.

## GETTING AROUND

Although it is an inner London borough, Wandsworth is serviced by just two Underground lines—the Northern and District—at just six stations. However, there are eight railway stations in the borough, including Clapham Junction, one of the busiest stations in the United Kingdom. In theory, you can get a train to either Victoria or Waterloo from these stations. However, overcrowding is an issue, though the railway authorities are trying to rectify the situation. If you decide to live in Wandsworth, you could try it without a car, but I would imagine that your life will be easier with one. Thankfully, residential parking is fairly easy to find in Wandsworth, and the borough has introduced a pay-by-phone scheme for pay-and-display parking.

# BOROUGH OF RICHMOND UPON THAMES

If you are looking for a location that is a good blend of rural suburbia, in an old charming village, yet still within Greater London, then look no further than the borough of Richmond upon Thames—another favorite location for international expats. As it is just 8.2 miles (13 kilometers) southwest of central London, Richmond provides an excellent compromise between the hustle and bustle of city life and the tranquility of the countryside. The borough is a very popular location for families and city workers who don't want to live in central London yet need straightforward access to it.

Richmond has the unique distinction of being the only one of London's boroughs to be on either side of the Thames. It's also home to one of London's World Heritage Sites, the Royal Botanic Gardens, Kew. Compared to most London boroughs, Richmond is less urban and less densely populated, giving it a distinct suburban feel. It's not all good news, however—one of Richmond's major downfalls is that airplanes go in and out of Heathrow Airport along the river, giving residents here a steady stream of roaring airplanes overhead. Many residents didn't realize just how much noise they were living with until the Eyjafjallajökull volcano in Iceland erupted in 2010, grounding airplanes across Europe.

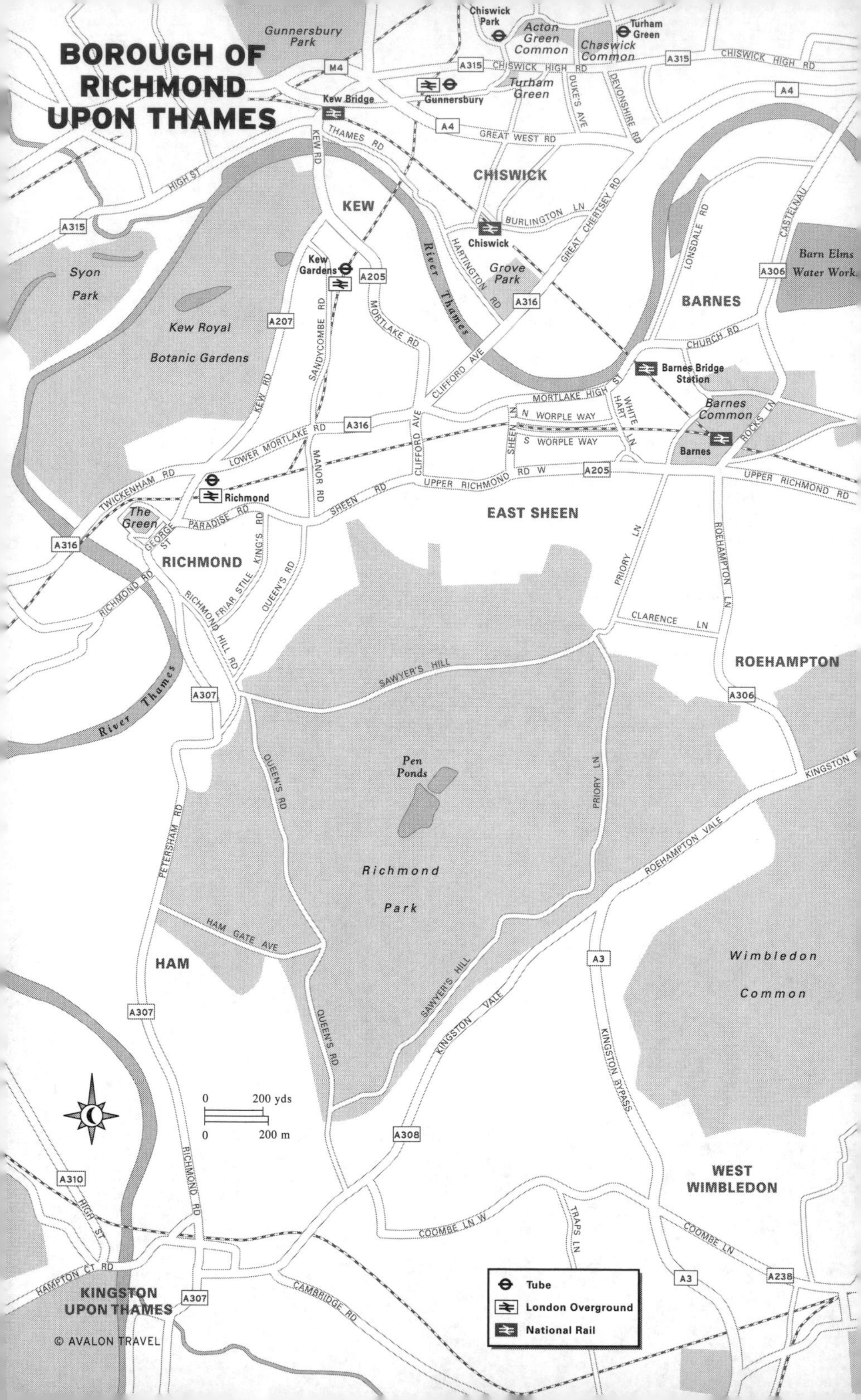
BOROUGH OF RICHMOND UPON THAMES
Gunnersbury Park
Chiswick Park
Acton Green Common
Turham Green
Chaswick Common
M4
A315
CHISWICK HIGH RD
Kew Bridge
Gunnersbury
Turham Green
DUKE'S AVE
DEVONSHIRE RD
A4
GREAT WEST RD
THAMES RD
KEW RD
HIGH ST
CHISWICK
KEW
BURLINGTON LN
GREAT CHERTSEY RD
Chiswick
HARTINGTON RD
Grove Park
A316
River Thames
Syon Park
Kew Gardens
A205
A207
SANDYCOMBE RD
MORTLAKE RD
Kew Royal Botanic Gardens
CLIFFORD AVE
LONSDALE RD
CASTELNAU
Barn Elms Water Work.
A306
BARNES
CHURCH RD
Barnes Bridge Station
MORTLAKE HIGH ST
WHITE HART LN
N WORPLE WAY
S WORPLE WAY
SHEEN LN
Barnes Common
Barnes
ROCKS LN
LOWER MORTLAKE RD
MANOR RD
TWICKENHAM RD
Richmond
UPPER RICHMOND RD W
UPPER RICHMOND RD
SHEEN RD
The Green
PARADISE RD
GEORGE ST
KING'S RD
EAST SHEEN
RICHMOND
FRIAR STILE
QUEEN'S RD
RICHMOND RD
RICHMOND HILL RD
PRIORY LN
CLARENCE LN
ROEHAMPTON LN
ROEHAMPTON
SAWYER'S HILL
A307
Pen Ponds
Richmond Park
PETERSHAM RD
KINGSTON RD
ROEHAMPTON VALE
HAM GATE AVE
HAM
A3
Wimbledon Common
KINGSTON VALE
KINGSTON BYPASS
0 200 yds
0 200 m
A308
A310
HIGH ST
WEST WIMBLEDON
COOMBE LN W
TRAPS LN
COOMBE LN
A238
HAMPTON CT RD
KINGSTON UPON THAMES
CAMBRIDGE RD
Tube
London Overground
National Rail
© AVALON TRAVEL

# Where to Live

The most popular area of Richmond upon Thames is the village of Richmond itself, where there are fairly good transportation options, or in the two peninsulas created by meanders in the River Thames, the neighborhoods of Barnes and Kew. For the most part, the neighborhoods and villages of Richmond have been well preserved, helping to maintain its more rural suburban atmosphere, even if it is less than 10 miles (16 kilometers) to the center of London.

## THE LAY OF THE LAND

The London Borough of Richmond (or the London Borough of Richmond upon Thames as it is formally known) is sandwiched between the twin delights of Richmond Park and the River Thames, and is just 22 square miles (57 square kilometers) in size. The borough is dominated by features that help to limit development in the borough and preserve its character. Richmond Park is London's largest Royal Park, with nearly 2,500 acres of hills, woodlands, and grasslands, and on a clear day you can see as far as St. Paul's Cathedral in the City of London. The borough used to be part of the county of Surrey, which is beyond London's borders. Even today, it's not uncommon for an address to be "Richmond, Surrey" even though this area is now part of London—old habits seem to die hard when it comes to addresses.

## HOUSING

The borough of Richmond has a good selection of large family homes, most of which are Victorian, though there are both older (Georgian) and younger (Edwardian) properties available. Although a few houses have been turned into flats, many of these large houses are intact and still used as single family dwellings. So far, local residents have been successful in deterring attempts by developers to build massive high-rise riverside complexes in the borough.

Although prices are likely to increase in the future, here is a general guide to property prices in Richmond at the moment. In 2015, rent for one-bedroom apartments in the borough averaged around £330 per week but could be as much as £1,000 for a desirable flat on the river's edge. Rent for two-bedroom apartments ranged £500-700 per week (more for ones on the river). The average price for a three-bedroom home runs £750 per week and rises to around £1,000 or more for a four-bedroom house. The average asking price for a one-bedroom apartment is around £334,000; the price for a two-bedroom apartment is around £534,000, though these tend to be quite a bit more in Barnes. A large family house with four or five bedrooms will average around £1.1 million (£1.7 in Barnes), with nice period detached or semi-detached houses often going for more than £2 million. Prices in Hampton and Twickenham, to the west of the borough, tend to be more affordable, but they don't have access to the Tube network; instead people rely on trains and buses. The borough's council tax ranged £1,057-3,173 in 2014-2015, depending on the value of the property.

## Barnes (SW13)

Isolated by a large meander in the River Thames, the neighborhood of Barnes oddly has a countryside feel to it, even though it is less than six miles (10 kilometers) southwest of central London. Barnes lies opposite Hammersmith, just on the other side of the picturesque Hammersmith Bridge. The neighborhood boasts several grand 18th- and 19th-century buildings near the historic village and a pond, which is now part of the Barnes Village Conservation Area. A rural feel (due in part to its wild 120-acre common and wetland habitat) and the large Victorian and Edwardian terraced homes (as well as some decent mid-20th-century houses) make it attractive to wealthy professionals and their families. Barnes is also home to London's Swedish community—the Swedish School is based here. Local shopping can be done on either Barnes High Street (which has a small grocery store) or White Hart Lane, with large supermarkets farther afield in Richmond or Sheen. There are a few good state primary schools and one secondary school. However, it is the few, well-regarded private schools (both in Barnes and over the river in Hammersmith) that attract the many families to this part of Richmond.

### GETTING AROUND

There is no Underground service to Barnes; the nearest Tube station is over the river in Hammersmith, and several buses regularly make the 10-minute journey along Castelnau Road, over the river and into Hammersmith. Barnes has two train stations—Barnes Bridge and Barnes station—from which trains travel to Clapham Junction and on to Waterloo station. Six bus routes have stops at Barnes station, including the number 337 between Clapham Junction and Richmond and numbers 33 and 72 heading over the river into Hammersmith.

Barnes sits in the river's edge.

## The Magic Gardens of Kew

© KAREL MIRAGAYA/123RF.COM

The Royal Botanic Gardens, Kew have been a national treasure trove for botany since Victorian times. This 300-acre garden has the world's largest collection of living plants more than 30,000 so far—while its collection of preserved plant specimens numbers more than seven million. In 2000 Kew launched the Millennium Seed Bank Project to collect seed samples of every plant on the earth, thereby acting as insurance against a species becoming extinct. It's small wonder that the Royal Botanic Gardens, Kew have been made a UNESCO World Heritage Site (one of only four in London).

Kew Gardens were originally created in 1759, and were designed by leading landscape architects of the day, including Capability Brown. The purpose was to study botany and so further our understanding of the subjects. More recently this goal has expanded to include ecology. The standout feature of Kew has to be its five greenhouses (called "glasshouses" in Britain): the Palm, Temperate, Alpine, and Waterlily Houses, as well as the Princess of Wales Conservatory. These take you through tropical rainforests to unusual plants from warmer climates in the temperate house and on to alpine meadows in the latest addition to its glasshouses. Another feature is the treetop walk, which is 59 feet (18 meters) high and 656 feet (200 meters) long, giving visitors a glimpse of what it is like in the tree canopy of Kew's deciduous woodland glade.

While you are wandering around you may want to stop by and see Kew Palace, one of the oldest buildings in Kew Gardens. This incarnation of Kew Palace was first built in 1663 and was known as the Dutch House. It used to be the favorite family home of George III, Queen Charlotte, and their 15 children, and was where the king would retreat to when he suffered from his mental illness. The other royal house in Kew Gardens is Queen Charlotte's Cottage, which has a charming thatched roof and used to be used for royal picnics in the gardens.

The cost to get into Kew Gardens is about £15, but for garden and plant lovers it is worth every penny. Even my son enjoys a day trip there, so long as he can climb up the stairs to the treetop walk and see out across London.

## Kew (TW9)

Certainly the Royal Botanic Gardens are what most people think of when they hear the word Kew. However, it also has some very desirable homes and a small parade of shops in the main village by the station. There are also a few typical high street stores at the Kew Retail Park and a supermarket between Kew and Richmond village. Kew is a residential neighborhood, made popular by its proximity to Kew Gardens. It is a lovely place to live, even with the roar of the airplanes overhead and traffic from the A205. The neighborhood is characterized by its large detached and semi-detached properties. Kew Green conservation area has both Victorian and Georgian houses, though there are also younger properties in the area, including some from the 1930s. A fair few of these properties have been converted into flats, though there are some intact houses. Kew has a couple of fairly good state primary schools and five very popular private ones.

### GETTING AROUND

There is only one Underground station in Kew proper—Kew Gardens (on the District Line), which also services a London Overground line. Kew Gardens station is also serviced by three bus routes; the number 65 bus goes over the river to West London, while numbers R68 and 391 go south to Richmond.

## Richmond (TW9/TW10)



Richmond itself is a lovely village, packed with old-world charm. As in Hampstead, Richmond's older buildings are well-preserved; giving you a sense of what life was like hundreds of years ago—even if the heavy traffic through town brings you back to the 21st century with a bump. Richmond Green has held tournaments and archery contests since the 16th century, and cricket has been played here since the mid-17th century. The village attracts a mix of young professionals and families with young children.

a street of terraced houses in Richmond Hill

## The Splendor of Hampton Court

© ALEX POSTOVSKI/123RF.COM

Without a doubt one of Surrey's most remarkable attractions has to be the magnificent Hampton Court Palace on the banks of the River Thames. Although there had been a grand manor in the village of Hampton since medieval times, the popularity of this area with Tudor royalty led to the establishment of Hampton Court as a royal palace.

In the early 1500s the manor at Hampton was owned by Cardinal Wolsey, who extended the building quite substantially, transforming it from a large manor into a palace fit for a cardinal bishop. Cardinal Wolsey was a close friend of Henry VIII, and so the palace extension included a few royal suites for when the king came to stay. Wolsey used Hampton Court as a flamboyant country house for entertaining and state diplomatic visits (after all, he was the Lord Chancellor then). Unfortunately, the cardinal fell from grace with Henry VIII when he was unable to get the king's marriage to Catherine of Aragon annulled. The cardinal knew that his ascendancy was coming to an end. In 1528 ownership of Hampton Court was gifted to Henry VIII, with the cardinal dying two years later. By 1534 Henry VIII had divorced Catherine, separated England from the Catholic Church, and created the Church of England with himself as the Supreme Head.

Once Hampton Court became his, Henry VIII undertook a massive rebuilding of the palace lasting more than 10 years. Hampton Court was his favorite home, and he lavished sumptuous decorations and furnishings upon it. Once the building work was finished the palace was one of the finest and most modern buildings in England. The king had installed tennis courts, bowling alleys, pleasure gardens, and, of course, a hunting park. The palace now had a beautiful chapel, the Great Hall for feasts, and indoor toilets and plumbing, with water running through lead pipes. Henry VIII's heirs also made use of Hampton Court as a magnificent country home. All three of his children used it during their reigns as a place of refuge from London politics and the confined quarters of St. James Palace (built in 1531-1536 by Henry VIII and still the official residency of the sovereign).

During the Stuarts' reign (1603-1714) the palace continued as a place for rural pursuits such as hunting and hosted court banquets for visiting dignitaries. Even Oliver Cromwell used the palace as a country retreat during his time as leader of the Commonwealth (1654-1658). When King William III and Queen Mary II came to the throne in 1689 they asked Sir Christopher Wren to update the royal apartments. Their heir, Queen Anne, ensured that at least the remodeling work for the King's Apartment was completed. However, it wasn't until the Hanoverian King George II and Queen Caroline financed more building work that the Queen's Apartments were finally finished. The last time that Hampton Court was used by the entire royal family was in 1737, during George II's reign. In 1838 the magnificent Hampton Court Palace was opened to the public for viewing by Queen Victoria and remains so to this day.

Properties consist of large family homes with ample gardens, though some of these have been converted into flats. The most desirable area is Richmond Hill. The nearby 2,500-acre Richmond Park offers open green spaces for walks and bike rides (and deer watching)—another reason why families love it here. The village center has wonderful shopping along George Street and Hill Street (and the surrounding streets) with a mix of national chains, a department store, and appealing independent shops. Down on the river's edge by Richmond Bridge, there are several good pubs, bars, and restaurants.

### GETTING AROUND

Richmond station is the last stop on one of the western branches of the Underground's District line; it takes at least 40 minutes to get to the West End. Commuters can also take a South West Train and reach Waterloo station in less than 30 minutes or take the Overground toward Stratford and change at Highbury & Islington to get to the city (via Whitechapel). As many as 13 different bus routes weave their way through Richmond village, with some going to Kingston upon Thames (numbers 371 and 65) while others head over the river to Hammersmith in West London, including numbers 33 and 391. The number 490 heads out to terminals 4 and 5 at Heathrow Airport.

## Kingston Upon Thames (KT5)



South along the river past Richmond is the borough of Kingston upon Thames, just on the fringes of London, before you hit the rural suburbs in the surrounding counties. The area known as Kingston (which the borough is named after) is a good-sized market town situated on the banks of the River Thames around 12 miles (19 kilometers) southwest of the center of London. Kingston is deep into London's suburbs, yet still part of the capital—offering the best of both worlds. The town boasts superb shopping, with a large shopping precinct in the center of town offering both high street chains and independent boutiques. Here you'll find well-preserved timber-framed Tudor buildings next to modern store fronts—an unusual mix of architecture to say the least! Property here is a mix of flats and mainly semi-detached houses (a plus for families), though much of it is owner-occupied. These houses can be from the mid-20th century (or newer), although there are also some older properties in Kingston. In 2015, rent for a one-bedroom flat started at around £240 per week, with a two-bedroom averaging around £420 a week; rent for a nice family house tended to be £700 per week, though more desirable parts of town cost substantially more. There is a large student population from the nearby University of Kingston, so you will also find lower-priced student rentals. In 2015, the average price for a one-bedroom flat in Kingston was just under £300,000, with a two-bedroom flat around £450,000. Of course, a house costs much more and could be several million, with most going for around £1.2 million. The council tax rates in 2014-2015 ranged £1,119-3,356.

### GETTING AROUND

There is no Underground service this far out from central London, but there is a large train station. Trains from here go to Waterloo station, although you can change at Clapham Junction for Victoria station. The station also links with trains from the south, southeast, and southwest of England heading into London. Kingston town center has more than 40 different bus routes with several servicing the suburbs in Surrey

## It's Football, but Not as We Know It

Although its near neighbor American football is probably the most popular game in the United States, the game of rugby hasn't really taken off there—perhaps because there are too many similarities between the two games. Both games are contact sports and involve two teams lining up opposite each other while using brute force to drive the ball forward or to stop it if you are on defense. Points are given for taking the ball into the end zone or "making a try." Kicking the ball through the uprights will get you a few points, with the added bonus that you can get a conversion after a try or touchdown. But that is where the similarities end.

### THE EVOLUTION OF RUGBY

It's thought that rugby started at the private elite boarding school that bears its name. Supposedly, in 1823 William Webb Ellis (a pupil at Rugby) caught the ball while playing soccer and ran toward the opposition's goal, thus creating the game of rugby. While this story is now thought to be apocryphal, the school of Rugby was instrumental in establishing the rules of the game. For more than a century now, there have been two versions of rugby played in Britain and other rugby-playing nations: Rugby Union and Rugby League. In 1895 an argument developed over whether players should be allowed to become professional and be paid, with the result that those in favor of payments created Rugby League and those in favor of the status quo played Rugby Union. In time the rules of Rugby League developed to make the game more entertaining for spectators.

Rugby League is closer to American football than Rugby Union, as it also concentrates on making downs within a limited number of tackles. However, one major difference between the two games is forward passing. This is allowed in American football, and quarterbacks are required to be able to throw the ball some distance—accurately. In rugby, however, forward passing is not allowed unless the pass is a kick and the receiver is behind the ball (so they must run forward to catch it before it lands). It is thought that American football evolved from Canadian football, which was developed from Rugby League, all of which helps to explain the origins of the different games.

### RUGBY UNION, THE PURIST'S GAME

Although the rules of Rugby Union have changed slightly (mainly to make the game safer for participants), it is considered to be closer to the original game. The Rugby Football Union (RFU) was formed as early as 1871, and it standardized the rules of the game and created a league where different teams could compete against each other. As many of the original teams came from southwest of London (areas such as Richmond, Blackheath, and Wimbledon), it somehow seems natural that the modern day home of Rugby Union would settle in this part of London. Today, the home of Rugby Union (at least in England) is in Twickenham, in the borough of Richmond. The stadium there (owned and operated by the RFU) is where the England team plays its home games, be it in the Six Nation tournament of European sides or matches against squads from the southern hemisphere. If you are a big American football fan and wouldn't mind seeing something a little bit different, you may want to go to an England Rugby Union home game in Twickenham or even watch one of the London teams (maybe Harlequins or Wasps) to see the origins of American football.

and the rest of the borough, as well as numbers 285 and 111 out to Heathrow. The number 85 goes to Putney Bridge station (District line) in Fulham, while the number 65 goes to Richmond and on through west London.

### Chiswick (W4)

If you like the idea of being near the Thames in southwest London but don't want to be south of the river, you should consider the equally fashionable neighborhood of Chiswick (pronounced "CHIZ-ick") in the borough of Hounslow (with part of the area in the boroughs of Ealing and Hammersmith and Fulham). Nestled between the Barnes and Kew meanders in the River Thames, Chiswick is a great area (especially for young families) with good local shopping and a slightly more suburban feel than more centrally located neighborhoods. That said, you can easily take the Underground and be in the West End in around 20 minutes. The homes near Chiswick High Street are mainly two-story Victorian cottages and large Edwardian terraced and semi-detached houses (some converted into flats), with a few apartment buildings. Down by the river you'll find some lovely modern developments as well as Chiswick Mall, with its elegant 17th- and 18th-century houses overlooking the Thames. To rent a one-bedroom apartment in Chiswick, expect to pay around £375 per week and at least £500 per week for a nice two-bedroom place. Chiswick has a few two- or three-bedroom cottages, which start at around £700 per week, though you should expect to pay more than £1,000 per week for a five-bedroom house. Those thinking of buying should expect to pay at least £450,000 for a one-bedroom flat and more than £600,000 for a two-bedroom apartment. Houses run around £900,000 for a small cottage to £2 million (or more) for a large five-bedroom house. State primary schools are on the decline in Chiswick, though it does have some good private ones, and there is an international school in nearby Gunnersbury. You will need to look elsewhere for a secondary school. In 2014-2015, the council tax for the borough of Hounslow ranged £934-2,801.



#### GETTING AROUND

Both Turnham Green and Chiswick Park stations (District line) are in the area, and the Overground line goes to nearby South Acton station. The Piccadilly line also stops at Turnham Green station before 6:30am and from midnight until 1:20am, as the District line doesn't run during these times. Ten bus routes run along Chiswick High Road. As you are so far west in Chiswick, you may feel that you'll need a car, but at least parking for residents shouldn't be a problem.

## Daily Life

Richmond does tend to attract the international community, including quite a few Americans. However, it doesn't have the same level of support network for Americans that you would get in Westminster, Camden, or Kensington and Chelsea. Yet the area does have a vibrant shopping precinct in Richmond, which the locals are keen to preserve. The River Thames seems to be a big attraction for many residents in the borough of Richmond—be it the spectacular views of the river or simply rowing past Richmond Bridge.

## SCHOOLS

Quite a few of Richmond's 44 primary state schools are very well regarded, and as a consequence are oversubscribed. However, there are also more than 15 private primary schools, which reflect this area's affluence. There are nine state secondary schools and eight private secondary schools. There are more private schools on the north side of the river, which many residents travel to each weekday. If you're after an international/American school, ACS Cobham operates a bus service to most of the borough.

## SHOPPING

The main focus for shopping in the borough must be Richmond itself, which tends to dominate. It offers a good mix of independent retailers, well-known British chains along with some smaller boutiques, and the odd antiques shop. The smaller villages in Richmond have a smattering of shops (both chains and independents), but most people head to Richmond or Wandsworth—or over the river—for some retail therapy.

## LEISURE

If you are a theater buff but don't really want to go into town to see a play, Richmond Theatre often previews shows before they start in the West End. Richmond's other theater—the Orange Tree—is a popular venue for fringe theater. There are three cinemas in Richmond if you fancy a movie. On the other side of the river from Richmond Village is the area known as Twickenham—the home of English rugby. Other sporting activities include bike rides or walks through the wild landscape of Richmond Park. You can even enjoy the company of the numerous deer that roam in the park. Of course, one of the best ways to spend a sunny afternoon is wandering around the Royal Botanic Gardens in Kew, though young children may prefer the birdlife in the Wildfowl and Wetlands Trust Center in Barnes.

## GETTING AROUND

As seems to be the norm for boroughs south of the Thames, Underground stations are at a premium. In fact, there are just two Underground stations in the borough of Richmond: Kew Bridge and Richmond, both on the District line's Richmond arm. This means most residents have to rely on the railroad service to get in and out of central London. Although the trains can be crowded during rush hour, it is usually less than a 30-minute trip to Waterloo or Victoria station. There are of course buses, some of which take you north of the river, though many of the buses going through the borough head to Kingston upon Thames or Surrey. Unless you are living in Richmond itself, you will probably want to have a car. The borough has nearly 40 different residential parking permit zones, and the prices vary between the different controlled parking zones.

# OUTSIDE OF LONDON

Life in a big city isn't to everyone's liking. Those who prefer a more sedate suburban, or even rural, lifestyle may want to consider the counties west of London, such as Surrey or Buckinghamshire. North of London, there are some lovely suburban towns in Hertfordshire, such as St. Albans or Harpenden or around Rickmansworth just beyond the northwest border of London. On the other side of London, there is Essex to the northeast and Kent to the southeast (although these areas aren't particularly popular with Americans). It is usually the case that you get more for your money outside the capital, so many Londoners head out of town once they start a family. However, property prices across the southeast of England are high and are predicted to outstrip the rate of increase in the capital in the next five years.

If you decide that suburban living suits you best, bear in mind that the homes in the towns and villages outside of London are owner-occupied, so finding appropriate rental property can be a challenge in certain areas. Of course, popular expat living locations, such as those near an international school, will have a decent number of options; look for properties in summer, toward the end of the school year when families are most likely to relocate.

Those heading off to work in London will have a tiring two- or three-stage commute (driving to the station, taking the train, and then making their way across London).

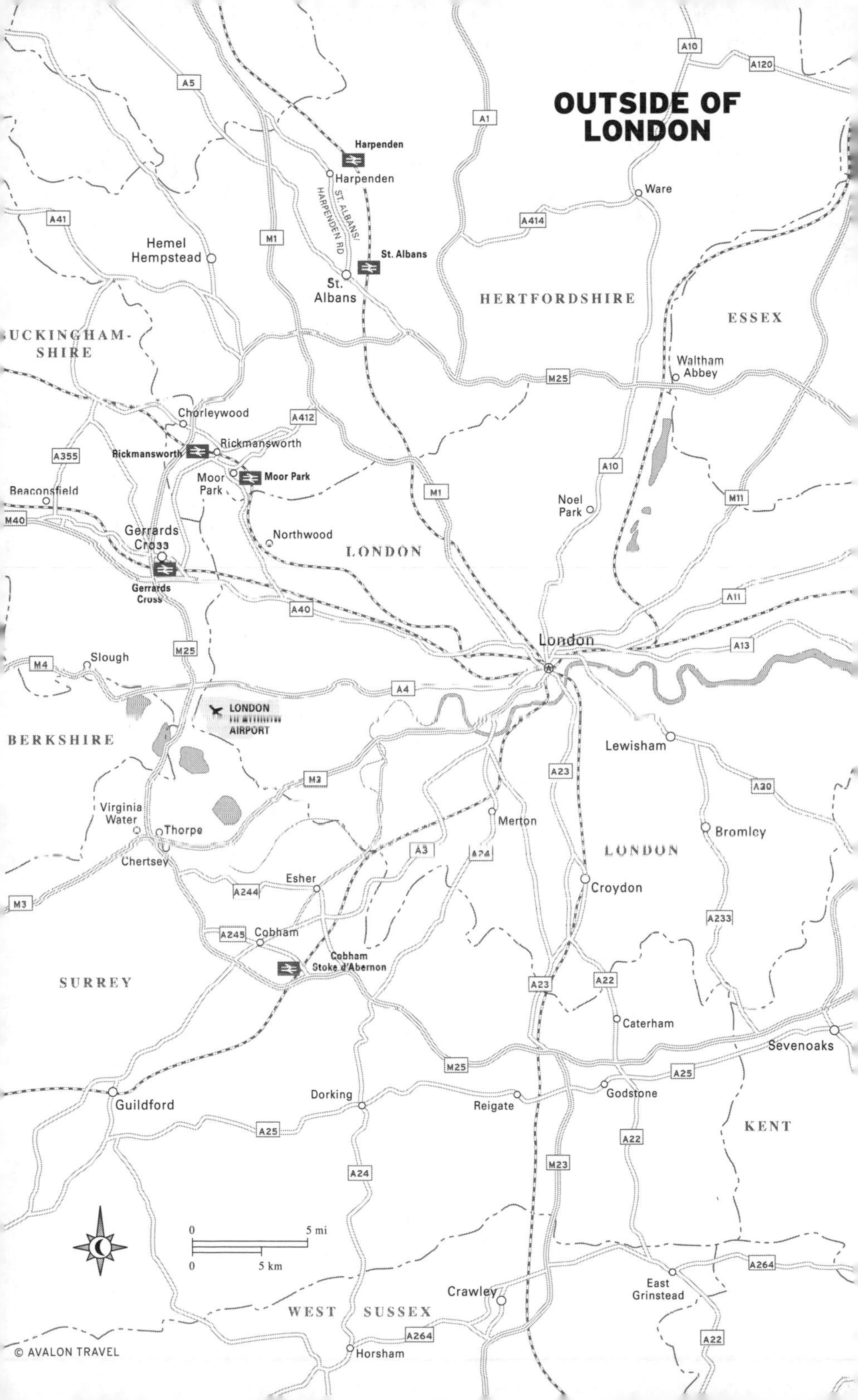
OUTSIDE OF LONDON
A10
A120
A5
A1
Harpenden
Harpenden
ST. ALBANS/ HARPENDEN RD
Ware
A41
A414
M1
Hemel Hempstead
St. Albans
St. Albans
HERTFORDSHIRE
ESSEX
BUCKINGHAMSHIRE
Waltham Abbey
M25
Chorleywood
A412
Rickmansworth
Rickmansworth
A355
Moor Park
Moor Park
A10
M1
Beaconsfield
Noel Park
M11
M40
Gerrards Cross
Northwood
LONDON
Gerrards Cross
A11
A40
M25
London
M4
Slough
A13
A4
LONDON AIRPORT
BERKSHIRE
Lewisham
A23
M3
A20
Virginia Water
Merton
Thorpe
Bromley
Chertsey
A3
A24
LONDON
Esher
Croydon
A244
M3
A233
A245
Cobham
Cobham Stoke d'Abernon
SURREY
A23
A22
Caterham
Sevenoaks
M25
A25
Guildford
Dorking
Reigate
Godstone
KENT
A25
A22
A24
M23
0
5 mi
0
5 km
A264
East Grinstead
Crawley
WEST SUSSEX
A264
A22
Horsham

In addition, there are fewer leisure activities in the suburbs, rural towns, and villages, with fewer places for a special occasion meal or evening out. There will be a smaller range of shops locally, though if you are shopping for a special occasion you may want to head to the West End for some serious retail therapy.

# Surrey

Surrey is one of England's more affluent counties and is considered part of the "stockbroker belt" for good reason. It offers a good blend of rural-village or small-town life with direct access to London, making it a desirable place to live for those longing to wake up to a rural idyll but be at work in around an hour. The county is very close to London: In fact, some of its traditional regions have been lost to Greater London. In 1965 both Kingston upon Thames and Richmond upon Thames were absorbed into Greater London and became two of the capital's 33 boroughs. There are large built-up areas in the north of the county, which is nearest London—a sign of the county's increasing popularity—although there are still some small rural villages and market towns offering a more tranquil lifestyle. In 2014-2015, the bands for council tax in Elmbridge borough in Surrey (which covers Esher and Cobham) ranged £1,074-3,221, with rates for Runnymede borough (covering Virginia Water, Thorpe, and Chertsey) slightly less.

## WHERE TO LIVE

Generally, Americans live near the American or international schools in Surrey, favoring small towns such as Cobham and Esher. These are what the British would call "market towns," and are one step up from a village. The nearby villages of Virginia Water, Thorpe, and Chertsey are also very popular. Both these areas have easy road access to the international and American schools and railroad stations into London. To rent a large detached family home in these areas of Surrey, expect to pay at least £750-1,000 per week, although prices can be as up to three times more for very desirable homes. To buy a similar property, expect to pay at least £1 million—maybe several million for something special.

### The Lay of the Land

Surrey lies to the southwest of London, bordering the counties of Berkshire, Kent, East Sussex, West Sussex, and Hampshire, as well as Greater London. The River Thames meanders through the northern part of the county. Its largest town is Guildford (some 30 miles/50 kilometers from the center of London), and the county has been subdivided into 11 smaller boroughs. Many of the major highways in southeast England cut across Surrey, including London's orbital motorway (the M25) and the M3 and A3 corridors, which head into London. The county is divided by the North Downs, a small chalk ridge that cuts across the southeastern tip of England, starting in the east in Kent through to Farnham in Surrey. On the summit of the North Downs in Surrey is Box Hill, which has some of the oldest natural woodland in Europe.

### Cobham/Esher

It's no real surprise that these areas are popular with Americans expats, as they offer the right schooling, lovely countryside, large detached homes, and simple access to London from either Cobham and Stoke d'Abernon or Esher station into Waterloo station in London. Property in these two small market towns is a mix of older terraced homes and much larger (and grander) recently built detached houses, often on private streets. The rental market is much smaller here, so you may find that your choices are limited (especially outside of the summer months). The shopping in both places is fairly good, with large grocery stores and several independent shops and boutiques selling everything from household goods to fashion and gifts, as well as a few upmarket national chains. The nearby River Mole also makes for a nice place for an afternoon stroll past some of the town's historical stately homes, or you could try the 18th-century landscaped garden at Painshill Park. Both towns have some acceptable national restaurant chains, as well as a few independently owned options. A few lovely pubs in both places keep you entertained in the evening, and in Esher you'll find a cinema.

### Virginia Water/Thorpe/Chertsey

Another area of Surrey worth considering is in the north of the county near to Runnymede, which is where in 1215 King John was forced to sign the Magna Carta, laying the foundations for our legal system and establishing the rights of men. Often, Americans decide to live in and around the villages of Chertsey, Thorpe, and Virginia Water—with just four miles (six kilometers) between them all. Again there are international and American schools nearby, which is one of the main attractions of the area for expats, though the general affluence of the area is another. These villages are close to some of Surrey's best golf courses, including the world-famous Wentworth Golf Club in Virginia Water. Here you'll find a mix of old and new housing, combining a few cottages and Victorian houses with 1930s and post-war modern homes, often on private roads. Recently, a few gated communities joined the property scene in Virginia Water. The shopping in Virginia Water and Thorpe will be mainly functional. However, the historic town of Chertsey offers more in the way of amenities and shopping, including a supermarket. For a night out you'll have to rely on the local pubs or a nearby restaurant.

## DAILY LIFE

The American expat community is particularly strong in the aforementioned areas of Surrey, mainly due to the proximity of the international schools. The American Women of Surrey club is based in Cobham and can help newcomers settle in to their new life in Surrey. It also performs philanthropic work for the local community. There is also an American Women of Berkshire & Surrey (AWBS) club based in Virginia Water. Of course, the international schools don't attract just Americans. Other nationalities will be drawn to the area because of the schools, giving these communities a slight international feel, which is unusual for the suburbs outside of London.

### Schools

One of the main reasons why Americans choose to live in Surrey is so that their children can continue their education at an American-style school—and this county has

## The Highs and Lows of Commuting by Train

While living in the rural suburbs around London and commuting to London for work may seem like the obvious solution to balancing the budget, meeting the needs of a growing family and working in London, it has to be said that commuting by train to the capital day after day can be challenging at times.

**SARDINE TIME**

High gas prices and a lack of parking have pushed many suburban commuters onto the railroad network. The result is that some lines into London suffer from overcrowding on their peak hour trains. These poor commuters then have to face crowded Underground trains. The whole experience of traveling to and from work may make the suburban commuter feel more like a sardine in a can than a traveler. Nearly 900,000 people commute into London each weekday by the rail network. This number is growing all the time as high property and rental prices push workers out of central London and into the suburbs and beyond. In peak rush hour times some lines are bursting at the seams they are so overcrowded. The worst railroad is thought to be the 7:32am train from Woking in Surrey to London's Waterloo station, which is more than 150 percent overloaded. True, the government and the train operators are trying to do something about the overcrowding. Crossrail, a new cross-London railroad, is being built to link rail services for the counties west of London with those east of the capital, with a tunnel going underground through central London. But major infrastructure improvements take time, and Crossrail isn't expected to be fully operational until 2018, though some part of the above-ground service east of London will commence service in 2015. There are also plans for High Speed 2 (or HS2, as it is more commonly known), which would provide a high-speed service between the Midlands (middle of England) and London's Euston station, though this won't be up and running until around 2025. In the meantime, commuters into London will have no choice but to endure the overcrowding.

**DELAYS ON THE LINE**

London's commuter trains have a reputation for being a bit unreliable. All too often trains are delayed or canceled with little or no notice (for problems as minor as leaves

three of them. There are several other independent schools in Surrey, some of which offer boarding. Surrey is home to the American School in England, as well as two other international schools (ACS Cobham and ACS Egham). As for state education, there are around 180 state infant/junior or primary schools across Surrey and 54 state secondary schools. More importantly, Surrey's state schools are among the best performing in the country. As the state schools are so much better than those in London, often families in London will cash out and move to Surrey, especially once the children reach school age. However, the best school may be oversubscribed, so you can't guarantee that you'll get a place at the state school of your choice, even if you are within the catchment area and living within a stone's throw of the school.

### Shopping

The largest town in Surrey is Guildford, and there are several other largish towns (such as Staines, Woking, and Leatherhead, among others) where you'll find the usual range of high street stores and national chains. Kingston upon Thames (with its large mall) isn't that far away from some of the county, while access to central London is

or dew on the lines), though more serious problems such as points failures also happen. The fact is, the network is old and creaking, and the upgrades can't come fast enough. In the meantime London's suburban commuters need to have bucket loads of patience and a good fallback travel plan (such as getting to a station on another line) in case their usual line is out of action.

**SPIRALING PRICES**

For decades Britain's rail network suffered from underinvestment. As a consequence, action has only recently been undertaken to improve the rail infrastructure and provide better reliability and more capacity. Unfortunately, these improvements don't come cheaply, and as the group who will benefit the most from an improved service, rail passengers are being asked to pick up much of the tab. The government now regulates annual price increases on around half of the railroad lines, which for the moment are linked to the rate of inflation. Nevertheless, rail season tickets are expensive; in 2015, an annual season ticket between Cobham in Surrey and London cost around £2,500, which doesn't include fares for the London Underground, adding another £1,284.

You may think that you'll still be ahead of the game because your rent or mortgage will be less than in London. However, property analysts have suggested that to make a significant savings on a mortgage someone needs to be at least an hour's train journey away from London or farther. Prices can be lower in the suburbs, but this depends on the area. Popular affluent areas that are a short commute away are more or less in line with prices in London. However, what you do get for your money is a traditional family home and garden. Nevertheless, you also need to add into the equation the costs of owning and running a car. If you live more centrally, you may not need a car, whereas if you live in the suburbs you'll probably feel that a car is essential.

The decision of whether or not you should live out of town depends very much on your priorities and budget. If you live in the suburbs in the United States and enjoy access to a city without the hustle and bustle of city life on your doorstep, then London's suburban counties may suit you. Just be aware of what you are taking on in terms of costs, time, and personal comfort.

straightforward for those wanting a major day out shopping in London's West End. In very small rural villages the shopping may be limited and require you to drive to a larger town for groceries.

## Leisure

Larger towns in Surrey have movie theaters and small shopping malls, as well as restaurants and pubs. Sporting activities include Epson Race Course, Wentworth Golf Club, and the Surrey Cricket Club. There are 29 sports and leisure centers across the county, most centered in the larger towns. Perhaps the best way to spend time in Surrey is on one of the nature trails along the North Downs or at some of the historical stately homes, such as Loseley Park and Sutton Place.

## Getting Around

Your best (if not only) option for getting around in Surrey is by car. It has to said, though, that the main commuting roads—such as the M25 orbital motorway, the M3 (London to Southampton) and A3 (London to Portsmouth), as well as A24 (to the south

## Teeing Off in Surrey

While London is full of cultural activities to keep you occupied on the weekends, if your hobby happens to be playing golf, then you may be a bit disappointed with city life. Although the capital does have numerous parks, golf courses are a bit thin on the ground, and those that we do have tend to be in out-of-the-way neighborhoods in the outer boroughs. For avid golfers, one advantage to living in the suburbs would be that they wouldn't have so far to travel to get to a decent golf course. The question is, which suburb is best for golfers?

Now, if you were to ask most British people what they associate with the county of Surrey they'd probably reply "stockbrokers and golf courses." As well as being a confirmed member of the stockbroker belt, Surrey is also known for its numerous golf courses, including the championship venues of Wentworth, Walton Heath, and Sunningdale. In fact, it has one of the highest concentrations of golf clubs in England, with more than 140 golf courses spread right across the county. The diversity of landscapes in Surrey—from heathland to downs and common land—provides a rich assortment of playing conditions for golfers, and goes some way in explaining why there is such a high concentration of golf courses here. With so many courses to choose from it is clear that Surrey is an obvious choice for keen golfers (and learners) alike.

Probably the best-known golf club in Surrey is Wentworth Club in Virginia Water. Having hosted Ryder Cups, World Match Play tournaments, and PGA Championships, Wentworth has an impressive tournament pedigree. The course dates from the late 1920s, and the original 1924 design used the area's mixture of woodland and open heathland to give players different challenges at each hole. In the 21st century the club's West Course (one of three) has been updated and improved by the professional South African golfer Ernie Els. His redesign brought the courses at Wentworth bang up to date by lengthening some of the holes and refashioning a few bunkers so that even today's modern golfers face a significant challenge at Wentworth.

If you think that Wentworth may be a bit beyond your league, don't worry because there are many other golf courses in Surrey that might suit you better. These range in difficulty and expense. You could be lucky enough to get a game at one of Surrey's more exclusive golf courses, or maybe you'd feel more at home at one of the more moderate venues aimed at the growing number of people who have taken up this sport. Whether you are looking for a membership at one of the more selective clubs or are just after a place to play the odd 18 holes, you'll probably find the right golf course for you somewhere in Surrey.

For more information on golf courses in Surrey, see the website www.surreygolfguide.com.

coast) and M23/A23 (London to Brighton) in the south of the county—can all be subject to very heavy traffic. Those who are planning to commute to central London will find the train service into Waterloo, Victoria, and London Bridge stations in London (via National Rail) fairly swift. For example, it should take around 30 minutes to travel by train from Esher to Waterloo. The county lies between both of London's major international airports—Heathrow and Gatwick—so getting away on vacation or traveling overseas for work is a breeze here compared to other counties around London.

# Buckinghamshire

Like Surrey to the south, Buckinghamshire (its nickname is "Bucks") has beautiful countryside, including the Chiltern Hills, considered to be an area of outstanding beauty, and the River Thames. It attracts high-earning professionals—including some Americans—working in London who want a more suburban or rural environment in which to raise their children. The commute from Buckinghamshire is a 30-minute train ride to Marylebone station in Central London. The towns of Gerrards Cross and Beaconsfield tend to be popular with Americans, as they can provide easy access to nearby international schools as well as London. The local state and private schools in this part of Buckinghamshire are also worth considering. The council tax charges vary depending on which town you live in, but in the South Buckinghamshire District they ranged £1,000-3,010 in 2014-2015.

## WHERE TO LIVE

If you prefer to live in a small and well-to-do village community around 30 miles outside of London, consider the area around Gerrards Cross and Beaconsfield. Here you will find lovely large detached homes with massive gardens, all set in the leafy green surroundings of the Chiltern Hills. Although this is a predominantly rural area, it offers a relatively easy commute into London, and so attracts wealthy city-types. In the latter half of the 20th century many British celebrities lived in Gerrards Cross because of its surroundings and lovely homes, as well as its proximity to Pinewood Studios.

### The Lay of the Land

As you head northwest out of London you come to the county of Buckinghamshire, bordering Bedfordshire and Hertfordshire to the northeast, Oxfordshire to the west, and Berkshire in the south. Aylesbury, Milton Keynes, and High Wycombe are its largest towns. The main geographical feature of Buckinghamshire is the beautiful Chiltern Hills, which cut through the county. The southeastern tip of the county borders Greater London, and even some of London's Underground networks terminate in the county.

### Gerrards Cross and Beaconsfield

The villages of Gerrards Cross and Beaconsfield are two small towns in the Chilterns, yet it takes only just over an hour to get to the City of London or West End from one of these towns' railroad stations. This combination of natural beauty and good commuter lines means that property in this part of Buckinghamshire is quite desirable. The town center of Beaconsfield has a small but thriving shopping center, while Gerrards Cross has good local shopping and a great common with a playground that is popular with dog walkers and footballers. You can find some elegant large Arts and Crafts homes here, as well as more recently built property. Unfortunately, most properties are owner-occupied, so it can be difficult at times to find a rental. To rent a large detached family home, you will pay upwards of £925 per week, while it will cost between £900,000 and several million to buy a similar house. In Beaconsfield the prices are

a supermarket in Gerrards Cross

© KAREN WHITE

slightly higher both to rent and buy. There are a few independent schools in Gerrards Cross and Beaconsfield, mainly for primary school ages, and it is a commutable distance to the international school in Hillingdon. In the evening you could take in a movie or visit your local pub. Both towns are near the M25 motorway, which encircles London, and the M40, which runs between London and Birmingham.

## DAILY LIFE

Although perhaps not as large as in Surrey, nonetheless there is a sizable international and American community in this part of Buckinghamshire, with the very active Chilterns American Women's Club based in Gerrards Cross. Becoming a member of an expat organization is a good way to meet other long-term expats who can pass on their insider knowledge of life in Buckinghamshire and the United Kingdom.

### Schools

The state schools in Buckinghamshire have a good reputation and perform well above the national average. It is one of the few areas in England that still has grammar schools (academically selective secondary schools), which provide a more stimulating academic environment than the standard secondary schools in Britain (known as "comprehensives" or as "secondary modern schools" in Buckinghamshire). There are some 181 infant/junior or primary schools and around 38 secondary schools (including the 13 grammar schools). The county also has some private schools for both primary and secondary school ages, with a few going straight through from age 4 up to 18. Some of these offer boarding as well.

### Shopping

You'll find shopping malls in the larger towns in Buckinghamshire, offering the usual range of British high street stores, with larger supermarkets outside Buckinghamshire's larger towns. Of course there are a few small shops and boutiques in the towns throughout the county, as well as a few farmers markets. With London less than an hour away, the occasional sojourn to the West End for a day's shopping shouldn't be out of the question.

### Leisure

The county offers a few sport centers (mainly in the larger towns), and more affluent areas have private health clubs or golf clubs. The Chiltern Hills are a wonderful place for a hike through the woods. If you are in one of the more rural communities (or can drive to one), you may be able to do a bit of horse riding at a local stable.

### Getting Around

Your main transportation option in Buckinghamshire will be the car, though there are some local bus services in the larger towns, such as Aylesbury or Milton Keynes. The county lies between two main motorways, the M1 and M40, with the popular A41 (Oxfordshire to Watford) and A413 (toward London) in the southern part of the county. Commuters can use the Chiltern Railway from Gerrards Cross or Beaconsfield to get to Marylebone station in London. London Underground's Metropolitan line has termini in Amersham and Chesham, in the southern part of Buckinghamshire.

## Hertfordshire

Just 10 or so miles (16 kilometers) north of central London is the southern border of the county of Hertfordshire, and again good transportation links make much of this county popular with London commuters. However, it isn't swarming with Americans, though a few have settled out this way, wanting more house and garden for their money. Generally, Hertfordshire is more industrialized than either Surrey or Buckinghamshire, which have a more rural, small village feel about them. This isn't to say that you don't get small rural villages here or that Surrey and Bucks don't have sizable towns with thriving industries. It's just that Hertfordshire industrial parks and business centers seem to be attracting more and more businesses, especially in the service industries. Certainly Hertfordshire transportation links are an advantage, as the M25, M1, and A1 highways all go through the county, and it has good train links either south to London or north to the rest of the United Kingdom. This has prompted many of the United Kingdom's larger corporations to make Hertfordshire their home, including GlaxoSmithKline, Kodak, and Roche. Approximately 1.14 million people live in Hertfordshire, with the south of the county (the bit nearest London) the most urban. The amount of council tax payable each year varies depending on where you live in Hertfordshire, but in 2014-2015 it typically ranged £965-2,950.

## Consider Kent

If you work in Docklands (and don't need to worry about maintaining your children's American education) yet want to live outside of London, consider the county of Kent, which is southeast of London. Commuter trains from Kent go to several stations in the City of London, including Blackfriars and Cannon Street, before heading up to St. Pancreas. They also go to London Bridge and Waterloo in South London, as well as Charing Cross and Victoria stations in Westminster.

Although a popular commuter belt, Kent doesn't have a substantial American expat community to match those in London or Surrey. As a starting point in Kent, look around the town of Sevenoaks. Set among Kent's North Downs hills, Sevenoaks is a firm favorite with commuters, as it's an easy 30 minutes by train to Waterloo station. Again you find traditional recently built family homes and fairly good shopping facilities offering the usual British retail chains. In 2015, the council tax for the Sevenoaks district ranged £1,040-3,120. Major road links for Sevenoaks include the M25 (the London orbital motorway) and the M2, which is the motorway to Dover and ferries to the Continent. To rent a large detached family house, expect to pay upwards of £650 per week, and expect to spend at least £650,000 to buy a comparable house, though really nice houses are well over £1 million.

## WHERE TO LIVE

For true suburban living with detached houses and sizable gardens you could try around Rickmansworth or the nearby towns of Chorleywood and Moor Park. These are just on the edges of London and are still served by the Underground. Farther from London there are the larger towns of St. Albans and Harpenden, which both offer fast rail service into London and are near the M1 and A1 highways. Once again you may find it difficult to find the right rental property, as most people own their own homes out here in the suburbs, so if a rental becomes available grab it quickly. To rent a large detached family house in these parts of Hertfordshire, expect to pay around £650-1,100 per week (or more), and to buy a similar place would cost between £700,000 and £3 million (and more for something special). These may be relatively new homes and so lack the dimensions and architectural features that you get with period property.

### The Lay of the Land

Hertfordshire is just north of London and has the county of Essex to its east and Buckinghamshire to the west, with Bedfordshire and Cambridgeshire to its north. Most of the county's population is in the towns along the M1 and A1 corridors, especially where they link with the M25 orbital motorway in Watford and Potters Bar.

### Chorleywood, Rickmansworth, and Moor Park

These small "Metro-land" towns are classic examples of suburban London living. These towns are all on the London Underground's Metropolitan line (and there are National Rail services to Marylebone station), and you could argue that they were essentially developed for London's commuter. There is only around five miles (eight kilometers) between the three neighborhoods, all of which offer traditional large detached houses with ample gardens, and the prices are very slightly lower than those in the suburban

© KAREN WHITE
a street in Rickmansworth

counties to the south and west. The area is also close to the M25 motorway, providing easy access to Heathrow airport. Supermarkets and other essential shopping can be done in Rickmansworth, which lies between the other two towns. Gerrards Cross, in Buckinghamshire, is just a few miles away. The nearby international school in Hillingdon offers a bus service to these towns.

### St. Albans and Harpenden

Those wanting to be farther away from London may prefer the commuter towns of St. Albans and Harpenden. Both of these towns are serviced by Thameslink trains, giving commuters easy access to the West End and the City. St. Albans was once a Roman town, and continued to be an important market town for centuries. In the 20th century better commuter links with London pushed the town into prime commuter-belt territory. Around five miles (eight kilometers) north of St. Albans you find Harpenden, which has an exclusive village feel and all the conveniences of a town. As a rule, most of the houses in both areas will be newly built and architecturally uninspiring, but serviceable. When it comes to schooling in this area you must rely on local British schools, be they state or private.

## DAILY LIFE

There isn't a large international community up this way, although if your children are attending the ACS school in Hillingdon you may meet a few fellow expats through school. There is also an American Club of Hertfordshire based out of Welwyn City Garden, which is less than 10 miles (16 kilometers) to the east of Harpenden and St. Albans on the A1 highway. Like many Londoners, you may decide to start your career in London by living in town, and then move out to the suburbs when it becomes clear that you will be living in the United Kingdom longer term. This way you will have already established friendships and so may not feel so isolated in the suburbs.

## Schools

The state schools in Hertfordshire do not have quite the same reputation as those in either Surrey or Buckinghamshire (mainly because they don't offer grammar schools), but they are generally pretty good. Nevertheless, there is also a large choice of private schools (both day and boarding) for all ages in Hertfordshire. The far south of the county (by Rickmansworth, Moor Park, and Chorleywood) is within easy reach of the ACS American-oriented international school in Hillingdon.

## Shopping

In the south of the county Watford is the main shopping precinct, with its large mall and out-of-town supermarkets. However, as Hertfordshire is very populated, other large towns (such as Harpenden, Stevenage, and Letchworth) have good amenities and shopping, even if they are limited to mainly national British brands and chains. St. Albans also has good shopping in the center of town.

## Leisure

As a rule, cultural activities in the southeast of England are limited to London, with Hertfordshire's residents expected to come to town to see the museums, galleries, and theater here. Of course you'll find movie theaters, small local drama productions, and restaurants and pubs for evening entertainment. During the day you can make use of local sport centers and private gyms and clubs (golf, tennis, and the like) to keep you fit or try biking and walks on countryside trails.

## Getting Around

Easy transportation links to London are the main advantage of Hertfordshire, especially in the south where there is access to the Metropolitan line or Thameslink trains. Various train lines run from Hertfordshire to London, including services to Euston, St. Pancras/King's Cross, London Bridge, and Liverpool Street stations—so reaching London is easy from many parts of the county. The M25 orbital motorway and the M1 and A1 all go through the county. Two of London's airports (Luton and Stansted) are in Hertfordshire—though they do not service flights to and from the United States.

# RESOURCES

© SUNG KUK KIM/123RF.COM

# Embassies and Consulates

## IN THE UNITED STATES

### BRITISH EMBASSY

3100 Massachusetts Ave. NW
Washington, DC 20008
tel. 202/588-6500
www.gov.uk/government/world/usa
Jurisdiction: Delaware, Maryland, Virginia, Washington DC, and West Virginia

### ATLANTA

British Consulate-General
Georgia Pacific Center
133 Peachtree St. NE, Ste. 3400
Atlanta, GA 30303
tel. 404/954-7700
www.gov.uk/government/world/organisations/british-consulate-general-atlanta
Jurisdiction: Alabama, Georgia, Mississippi, North Carolina, South Carolina, and Tennessee

### BOSTON

British Consulate-General
1 Broadway
Cambridge, MA 02142
tel. 617/245-4500
www.gov.uk/government/world/organisations/british-consulate-general-boston
Jurisdiction: Connecticut, Maine, Massachusetts, New Hampshire, Rhode Island, and Vermont

### CHICAGO

British Consulate-General
625 N. Michigan Ave., Ste. 2200
Chicago, IL 60611
tel. 312/970-3800
www.gov.uk/government/world/organisations/british-consulate-general-chicago
Jurisdiction: Illinois, Indiana, Iowa, Kansas, Kentucky, Michigan, Minnesota, Missouri, Ohio, Nebraska, North Dakota, South Dakota, and Wisconsin

### DENVER

British Consulate-General
World Trade Center Tower
1675 Broadway, Ste. 720
Denver, CO 80202
tel. 303/592-5200
www.gov.uk/government/world/organisations/british-consulate-general-denver
Jurisdiction: Colorado, New Mexico, and Wyoming

### HOUSTON

British Consulate-General
Wells Fargo Plaza
1000 Louisiana, Ste. 1900
Houston, TX 77002
tel. 713/659-6270
www.gov.uk/government/world/organisations/british-consulate-general-houston
Jurisdiction: Arkansas, Louisiana, Oklahoma, and Texas

**LOS ANGELES**
British Consulate-General
2029 Century Park East, Ste. 1350
Los Angeles, CA 90067
tel. 310/789-0031
www.gov.uk/government/world/organisations/british-consulate-general-los-angeles
Jurisdiction: American Samoa, Arizona, Guam, Hawaii, Nevada, Southern California, and Utah

**MIAMI**
British Consulate-General
1001 Brickell Bay Dr., Ste. 2800
Miami, FL 33131
tel. 305/400-6400
www.gov.uk/government/world/organisations/british-consulate-general-miami
Jurisdiction: Florida, Puerto Rico, and the US Virgin Islands

**NEW YORK**
British Consulate-General
845 3rd Ave.
New York, NY 10022
tel. 212/745-0200
www.gov.uk/government/world/organisations/british-consulate-general-new-york
Jurisdiction: Connecticut (Fairfield County only), New Jersey, New York, and Pennsylvania

**SAN FRANCISCO**
British Consulate-General
1 Sansome St., Ste. 850
San Francisco, CA 94104
tel. 415/617-1300
www.gov.uk/government/world/organisations/british-consulate-general-san-francisco
Jurisdiction: Alaska, Idaho, Montana, Northern California, Oregon, Washington

## IN THE UNITED KINGDOM

The American embassy is located in London, and more information on the consular services can be found on its website.

**US EMBASSY**
24 Grosvenor Square
London W1A 2LQ
tel. 020/7499 9000
http://london.usembassy.gov



# Planning Your Fact-Finding Trip

The official visitor organization for London is Visit London, and its website is www.visitlondon.com. The official tourist website for England is www.visitengland.com, with www.visitbritain.com covering the rest of Britain.

Here are some privately run websites you may find useful:
www.timeout.com/london
www.tourist-information-uk.com

## TOURIST INFORMATION

### Royal Borough of Kensington and Chelsea

Kensington & Chelsea Tourism Sites
www.kcts.com

### City of Westminster

City of Westminster Tourist Information
www.london-tourist-guide.com/en/areas/westminster-london.html

### Borough of Camden
Love Camden
www.lovecamden.org

### Borough of Islington
Islington Tourist Information Centre
Discover Islington Visitor Centre
www.islington.gov.uk/islington

### City of London
City of London Information Centre
www.cityoflondon.gov.uk/

### Borough of Hackney
Destination Hackney
http://home.destinationhackney.co.uk

### Borough of Tower Hamlets
Tower Hamlets Tourist Information Centre
18 Lamb St.
London E1 6EA
tel. 020/7375 2539

### Borough of Wandsworth (Merton)
Wimbledon Library Visitor Information Centre
35 Wimbledon Hill Rd.
London SW19 7NB
tel. 020/8274 5757

### Borough of Richmond Upon Thames
Visit Richmond
www.visitrichmond.co.uk

### Suburban Counties

#### SURREY
Visit Surrey
www.visitsurrey.com

#### BUCKINGHAMSHIRE
Visit Buckinghamshire
www.visitbuckinghamshire.org

#### HERTFORDSHIRE
Hertfordshire.com
www.hertfordshire.com

#### KENT
Visit Kent
www.visitkent.co.uk

## SIGHTSEEING

### Guided Bus Tours of London
For a hop-on hop-off guided bus tour, try The Original Tour Bus company (www.theoriginaltour.com) or the Big Bus Tour Company (www.bigbustours.com/eng/london). For something a bit more unusual try London Duck Tours (www.londonducktours.co.uk), which uses amphibious buses to provide tours both in and out of the River Thames.

## DINING
Comprehensive reviews of restaurants in the capital by type of cuisine and location.

#### SQUARE MEAL
www.squaremeal.co.uk

#### TIME OUT
www.timeout.com

#### ZAGAT
www.zagat.com/london

# Making the Move

## IMMIGRATION AND VISAS

Before moving to London, you must apply for a visa to live, study, or work in the United Kingdom through the UK government's Visas and Immigration Department's online visa application at www.gov.uk/apply-uk-visa. The United Kingdom's visa requirements are subject to change, and you will find the latest information on the UK Visas and Immigration website (www.gov.uk/government/organisations/uk-visas-and-immigration).

The Tier 2 Shortage Occupation List can be seen at www.gov.uk/government/publications/tier-2-shortage-occupation-list-from-6-april-2013. For information about visas and studying in the United Kingdom, visit www.gov.uk/tier-4-general-visa. For information regarding residency, nationality, citizenship, leave to remain in the United Kingdom, or immigration, visit www.workpermit.com/uk/uk.htm. Another useful site for information regarding UK visas is www.ukvisas.co.uk.

### Companies Offering Immigration Services

www.escapeartist.com
www.globalvisas.com
www.1stcontact.co.uk
www.bic-immigration.com
www.internationalworkpermits.com

### Shipping Options

For information on International Federation of International Removals members, go to www.fidi.com. To find an international shipper that services your part of the United States and ships to London, go to International Movers at www.intlmovers.com, where you can use its online quote facility to find shipping companies that will help with your move to London, and ask for a quote. Or you can find out more about international movers at the International Association of Movers website (www.iamovers.org).

### UK Customs

For the latest customs information see the UK government's website www.hmrc.gov.uk/customs/arriving/moving.htm. For information on the current duty free limits, go to www.gov.uk/duty-free-goods.

## MOVING WITH PETS

For detailed information on traveling to the United Kingdom with pets and the Pet Passport, as well as quarantine facilities (if needed), see the Department for Environment, Food, and Rural Affairs (DEFRA) website (www.gov.uk/bringing-food-animals-plants-into-uk).

## MEETING OTHER EXPATS

**AMERICAN WOMEN'S CLUB**
68 Old Brompton Rd.
London SW7 3LQ
tel. 020/7823 8292
www.awclondon.org

**HAMPSTEAD WOMEN'S CLUB**
http://hwcinlondon.co.uk

**KENSINGTON CHELSEA WOMEN'S CLUB**
www.kcwc.org.uk

**ST. JOHN'S WOOD WOMEN'S CLUB**
www.sjwwc.org.uk

**AMERICAN WOMEN OF SURREY (AWS)**
P.O. Box 170
Cobham, Surrey KT11 3YJ
www.awsurrey.org

**CHILTERNS AMERICAN WOMEN'S CLUB**
P.O. Box 445
Gerrards Cross, Buckinghamshire SL9 8YU
tel. 07789/076238
www.cawc.co.uk

**AMERICAN CLUB OF HERTFORDSHIRE**
63/65 New Rd.
Welwyn, Hertfordshire AL6 0AL
tel. 01438/714846
AmClubHerts@aol.com

### Expat Websites and Forums

www.canuckabroad.com/forums/canadians-in-the-uk-vf10.html
www.easyexpat.com/en/guides/united-kingdom/london.htm
www.expatfocus.com/expatriate-uk
www.focus-info.org
http://london.usembassy.gov
www.uk-yankee.com

### Meet-Up Groups and Clubs

www.citysocializer.com (search for American Expat Group)
www.facebook.com/americansabroad
www.meetup.com/americansabroad
www.meetup.com/American-Professional-Women-London

# Housing

## PROPERTY WEBSITES AND ESTATE AGENTS

### Nationwide Property Websites

Estate agents use these web portals to advertise property. They are not always up to date, but are a good starting point for a property search.

**MY PROPERTY GUIDE**
www.mypropertyguide.co.uk

**ON THE MARKET**
www.onthemarket.com

**PRIMELOCATION**
www.primelocation.com

**RIGHTMOVE**
www.rightmove.co.uk

**ZOOPLA**
www.zoopla.co.uk

### Regulated Residential Agencies

To find a regulated letting or estate agency, see these organizations and use the "find a member" function to locate a good agency in your selected living location.

**ASSOCIATION OF RESIDENTIAL LETTING AGENCIES**
www.arla.co.uk

**NATIONAL APPROVED LETTING SCHEME**
www.nalscheme.co.uk

**NATIONAL ASSOCIATION OF ESTATE AGENCIES**
www.naea.co.uk

**THE PROPERTY OMBUDSMAN**
www.tpos.co.uk

**ROYAL INSTITUTION OF CHARTERED SURVEYORS**
www.rics.org/uk

### London-Wide Estate Agents

Here are just a few of the realtors who cover London and are used to dealing with expats. There are other local specialists; to find one in your selected living location go to the website of a regulated residential agency (listed above).

**BARNARD MARCUS**
www.barnardmarcus.co.uk

**CHESTERTONS**
www.chestertons.com

**FELICITY J LORD**
www.fjlord.co.uk

**FOXTONS**
www.foxtons.co.uk
Their area guides include information on the average prices for particular neighborhoods and on the types of property available.

**GREEN & CO**
www.green-property.com

**JOHN D WOOD**
www.johndwood.co.uk

**KINLEIGH FOLKARD & HAYWARD**
www.kfh.co.uk

**MARSH AND PARSONS**
www.marshandparsons.co.uk

**WINKWORTH**
www.winkworth.co.uk

### East and Central London Estate Agents

**CARTER JONAS**
www.carterjonas.co.uk

**CURRELL**
www.currell.com

**HURFORD SALVI CARR**
www.hurford-salvi-carr.co.uk

**STIRLING ACKROYD**
www.stirlingackroyd.com

### UK-Wide Estate Agents

**CLUTTONS**
www.cluttons.com

**HAMPTONS INTERNATIONAL**
www.hamptons.co.uk

**JACKSON-STOPS & STAFF**
www.jackson-stops.co.uk

**KNIGHT FRANK**
knightfrank.com

## LONDON BOROUGHS AND NEARBY COUNTIES

On these websites you can find information about schools, council taxes, libraries, and leisure centers, as well as recycling and garbage collection.

**ROYAL BOROUGH OF KENSINGTON AND CHELSEA**
www.rbkc.gov.uk

**BOROUGH OF HAMMERSMITH AND FULHAM**
www.lbhf.gov.uk

**CITY OF WESTMINSTER**
www.westminster.gov.uk

**BOROUGH OF CAMDEN**
www.camden.gov.uk

**BOROUGH OF ISLINGTON**
www.islington.gov.uk

**CITY OF LONDON**
www.cityoflondon.gov.uk

**BOROUGH OF SOUTHWARK**
www.southwark.gov.uk

**BOROUGH OF HACKNEY**
www.hackney.gov.uk

**BOROUGH OF TOWER HAMLETS**
www.towerhamlets.gov.uk

**BOROUGH OF WANDSWORTH**
www.wandsworth.gov.uk

**BOROUGH OF MERTON**
www.merton.gov.uk

**BOROUGH OF LAMBETH**
www.lambeth.gov.uk

**BOROUGH OF RICHMOND UPON THAMES**
www.richmond.gov.uk

**BOROUGH OF HOUNSLOW**
www.hounslow.gov.uk

**SURREY COUNTY COUNCIL**
www.surreycc.gov.uk

**BUCKINGHAMSHIRE COUNTY COUNCIL**
www.buckscc.gov.uk

**HERTFORDSHIRE COUNTY COUNCIL**
www.hertsdirect.org

**KENT COUNTY COUNCIL**
www.kent.gov.uk

## STUDENT ACCOMMODATIONS

Here are some online property portals for students.
www.accommodationforstudents.com
http://housing.london.ac.uk/cms
www.spareroom.co.uk
www.studenthousing.lon.ac.uk

This is a forum and resource center for students.
www.thestudentroom.co.uk

# Education

## AMERICAN/ INTERNATIONAL SCHOOLS

### ACS INTERNATIONAL SCHOOL COBHAM CAMPUS

Portsmouth Rd.
Cobham, Surrey KT11 1BL
tel. 01932/869744
www.acs-schools.com/acs-cobham-home

### ACS INTERNATIONAL SCHOOL EGHAM CAMPUS

London Rd.
Egham, Surrey TW20 0HS
tel. 01784/430800
www.acs-schools.com/acs-egham-home

### ACS INTERNATIONAL SCHOOL HILLINGDON CAMPUS

108 Vine Ln.
Hillingdon, Middlesex UB10 0BE
tel. 01895/259771
www.acs-schools.com/acs-hillingdon-home

### AMERICAN SCHOOL IN LONDON

1 Waverley Place
London, NW8 0NP
tel. 020/7449 1200
www.asl.org

### INTERNATIONAL SCHOOL OF LONDON

139 Gunnersbury Ave.
London W3 8LG
tel. 020/8992 5823
www.islschools.org/london

### MARYMOUNT INTERNATIONAL SCHOOL

George Rd.
Kingston upon Thames, Surrey KT2 7PE
tel. 020/8949 0571
www.marymountlondon.com

### SOUTHBANK INTERNATIONAL SCHOOL IN LONDON

36-38 Kensington Park Rd. (3-11 years)
London W11 3BU
tel. 020/7229 3230

16 Netherhall Gdns. (3-11 years)
London NW3 5TH
tel. 020/7431 1200

17 Conway St. (11-16 years)
London W1T 6BN
tel. 020/7631 2600

63-65 Portland Place (16-19 years)
London W1B 1QR
tel. 020/7631 2600
www.southbank.org

### TASIS ENGLAND AMERICAN SCHOOL

Coldharbour Ln.
Thorpe, Surrey TW20 8TE
tel. 01932/565252
http://england.tasis.com

## BRITISH SCHOOL RESOURCES

### ANGELS AND URCHINS SCHOOL GUIDE

www.angelsandurchins.co.uk/lifestyle/schools

**GABBITAS EDUCATIONAL CONSULTANTS**
www.gabbitas.co.uk

**THE GOOD SCHOOLS GUIDE**
www.goodschoolsguide.co.uk

**THE GUARDIAN SCHOOL GUIDE**
www.theguardian.com/education/primary-schools

**INDEPENDENT SCHOOLS COUNCIL**
tel. 020/7766 7070
www.isc.co.uk

**OFSTED**
www.ofsted.gov.uk
The official UK government's inspectorate of schools, including state and some private schools. You can find its reports online.

**SCHOOLSNET**
www.schoolsnet.com

**SCHOOLS WEB DIRECTORY UK**
tel. 01603/477619
www.schoolswebdirectory.co.uk

**WHICH LONDON SCHOOL GUIDE**
www.schoolsearch.co.uk

## UNIVERSITIES IN LONDON

### University of London

The University of London is one of the oldest universities in the United Kingdom and comprises 19 different colleges and institutes. You can find out more about these colleges on the University of London website, and here you'll find contact details for the most popular of these institutions.

**HEADQUARTERS**
Senate House
Malet St.
London WC1E 7HU
tel. 020/7862 8000
www.london.ac.uk

**COURTAULD INSTITUTE OF ART**
Somerset House
Strand
London WC2 0RN
tel. 020/7872 0220
www.courtauld.ac.uk

**KINGS COLLEGE LONDON**
Strand
London WC2R 2LS
tel. 020/7836 5454
www.kcl.ac.uk

**LONDON BUSINESS SCHOOL**
Regent's Park
London NW1 4SA
tel. 020/7000 7000
www.london.edu

**LONDON SCHOOL OF ECONOMICS AND POLITICAL SCIENCE**
Houghton St.
London WC2A 2AE
tel. 020/7955 7686
www.lse.ac.uk

**ROYAL ACADEMY OF MUSIC**
Marylebone Rd.
London NW1 5HT
tel. 020/7873 7373
www.ram.ac.uk

**UNIVERSITY COLLEGE LONDON**
Gower St.
London WC1E 6BT
tel. 020/7679 2000
www.ucl.ac.uk

## Other Universities

**CITY UNIVERSITY LONDON**
Northampton Square
London EC1V 0HB
tel. 020/7040 5060
www.city.ac.uk

**IMPERIAL COLLEGE LONDON**
South Kensington Campus
London SW7 2AZ
tel. 020/7589 5111
www.imperial.ac.uk

**LONDON SOUTH BANK UNIVERSITY**
103 Borough Rd.
London SE1 0AA
tel. 020/7815 7815
www.lsbu.ac.uk

**UNIVERSITY OF THE ARTS LONDON**
272 High Holborn
London WC1V 7EY
tel. 020/7514 6000
www.arts.ac.uk

The university includes the following colleges: Central St. Martins College of Art and Design; Chelsea College of Art and Design; London College of Fashion; Wimbledon College of Art; Camberwell College of Arts; and London College of Communication.

## American Universities and Colleges in London

For more information on American universities with an exchange program or London campus, see the US Embassy website (http://london.usembassy.gov/us_universities_in_uk.html).

**AMERICAN INSTITUTE FOR FOREIGN STUDY**
37 Queen's Gate
London SW7 5HR
tel. 020/7581 7300
www.aifs.com

**AMERICAN INTERCONTINENTAL UNIVERSITY**
(part of Regent's University London)
110 Marylebone High Street
London W1U 4RY
tel. 020/7487 7505
toll-free US tel. 877/701-3800
www.regents.ac.uk/aiul

**AMERICAN INTERNATIONAL UNIVERSITY**
Queen's Rd.
Richmond, Surrey TW10 6JP
tel. 020/8332 8200
www.richmond.ac.uk

**AMERICAN UNIVERSITY**
97-101 Seven Sisters Rd.
London N7 7QP
tel. 020/7263 2986
www.aul.edu

**NEW YORK UNIVERSITY**
6 Bedford Square
London WC1B 3RA
tel. 020/7907 3200
tel. 212/998-4433 (New York)
www.nyu.edu/global/london

# Health

## UK HEALTH SERVICE INFORMATION

### DEPARTMENT OF HEALTH

www.gov.uk/government/organisations/department-of-health

### NATIONAL HEALTH SERVICE

www.nhs.uk/NHSEngland

## PRIVATE HEALTH INSURANCE

For information on the types of health insurance available and what's covered, see www.privatehealth.co.uk, or check out the findings from the United Kingdom's consumer association reviews at www.which.co.uk.

The US Embassy has a list of private healthcare professionals at http://london.usembassy.gov/cons_new/acs/medical.html.

### AVIVA

www.aviva.co.uk

### AXA PPP

www.axappphealthcare.co.uk

### BUPA

www.bupa.co.uk



## HOSPITALS WITH EMERGENCY (A&E) WARDS

### Central London

#### ST. MARY'S HOSPITAL

Praed St.
London W2 1NY
tel. 020/3312 6666
www.imperial.nhs.uk/stmarys
Includes special children's A&E unit.

#### ST. THOMAS' HOSPITAL

Westminster Bridge Rd.
London SE1 7EH
tel. 020/7188 7188
www.guysandstthomas.nhs.uk

#### UNIVERSITY COLLEGE HOSPITAL

235 Euston Rd.
London NW1 2BU
tel. 0845/155 5000
www.uclh.nhs.uk

### North and Northwest London

#### ROYAL FREE HOSPITAL

Pond St.
London NW3 2QG
tel. 020/7794 0500
www.royalfree.nhs.uk

#### THE WHITTINGTON HOSPITAL

Magdala Ave.
London N19 5NF
tel. 020/7272 3070
www.whittington.nhs.uk

### West-Central and West London

#### CHARING CROSS HOSPITAL

Fulham Palace Rd.
London W6 8RF
tel. 020/3311 1234
www.imperial.nhs.uk/charingcross

#### CHELSEA AND WESTMINSTER HOSPITAL

369 Fulham Rd.
London SW10 9NH
tel. 020/3315 8000
www.chelwest.nhs.uk
Includes children's A&E.

## East London

**HOMERTON UNIVERSITY HOSPITAL**

Homerton Row
London, E9 6SR
tel. 020/8510 5555
www.homerton.nhs.uk
Includes children's A&E.

**THE ROYAL LONDON HOSPITAL**

Whitechapel Road
London E1 1BB
tel. 020/7377 7000
www.bartshealth.nhs.uk

## South London

**UNIVERSITY HOSPITAL LEWISHAM**

Lewisham High St.
London SE13 6LH
tel. 020/8333 3000
www.lewishamandgreenwich.nhs.uk

## South and Southwest London

**KINGSTON HOSPITAL**

Galsworthy Rd.
Kingston upon Thames, Surrey KT2 7QB
tel. 020/8546 7711
www.kingstonhospital.nhs.uk

**ST. GEORGE'S HOSPITAL (TOOTING)**

Blackshaw Rd.
London SW17 0QT
tel. 020/8672 1255
www.stgeorges.nhs.uk

**WEST MIDDLESEX UNIVERSITY HOSPITAL**

Twickenham Rd.
Isleworth, Middlesex TW7 6AF
tel. 020/8560 2121
www.west-middlesex-hospital.nhs.uk

# EYE HOSPITALS

**MOORFIELDS EYE HOSPITAL (CITY ROAD)**

162 City Rd.
London EC1V 2PD
tel. 020/7253 3411 or tel. 020/7566 2345
(help line available 9am-4:30pm Mon.-Fri.)
www.moorfields.nhs.uk

**WESTERN EYE HOSPITAL**

Marylebone Rd.
London NW1 5QH
tel. 020/3312 6666
www.imperial.nhs.uk/westerneye

# MINOR INJURY UNITS

## Central London

**ST. BARTHOLOMEW'S HOSPITAL**

West Smithfield
London EC1A 7BE
tel. 020/7377 7000
www.bartshealth.nhs.uk

## West-Central London

**ST. CHARLES CENTRE FOR HEALTH AND WELLBEING**

Exmoor St.
London W10 6DZ
tel. 020/8962 4656
www.clch.nhs.uk/locations/st-charles-centre-for-health-and-wellbeing.aspx

## Southwest London

**QUEEN MARY'S HOSPITAL**

Roehampton Ln.
London SW15 5PN
tel. 020/8487 6000
www.stgeorges.nhs.uk

## South London

**GUY'S HOSPITAL**

Great Maze Pond
London SE1 9RT
tel. 020/7188 7188
www.guysandstthomas.nhs.uk

## CENTRAL LONDON WALK-IN CENTERS

### AMS WALK-IN CENTRE

Ritchie Street Group Practice
34 Ritchie St.
London N1 0DG
tel. 020/7537 1663
www.angelgp.co.uk/walkin.html

### SOHO NHS WALK-IN CENTRE

1 Frith St.
London W1D 3HZ
tel. 020/7534 6500
www.clch.nhs.uk/locations/soho-nhs-walk-in-centre.aspx

### WHITECHAPEL NHS WALK-IN CENTRE

174 Whitechapel Rd.
London E1 1BZ
tel. 020/7943 1333
www.bartshealth.nhs.uk/our-hospitals/the-royal-london-hospital

## LATE-NIGHT PHARMACIES (CHEMISTS)

### BLISS CHEMISTS

50-56 Willesden Ln.
London NW6 7SX
tel. 020/7624 8000
www.blisschemist.co.uk
Open 9am-11pm daily.

### BLISS CHEMISTS

5-6 Marble Arch
London W1H 7EL
tel. 020/7723 6116
Open 9am-midnight daily.

### WARMAN FREED

45 Golders Green
London NW11 8EL
tel. 020/8455 4351
Open 8:30am-midnight daily.

### ZAFASH

233-235 Old Brompton Rd.
London SW5 0EA
tel. 020/7370 7538
www.zafashpharmacy.co.uk
Open 24 hours daily.

## ALTERNATIVE THERAPIES

### COMPLEMENTARY MEDICINE ASSOCIATION

www.the-cma.org.uk

## FITNESS

### Private Gyms and Health Clubs

#### DAVID LLOYD

www.davidlloyd.co.uk

#### FITNESS FIRST

www.fitnessfirst.co.uk

#### LA FITNESS

www.lafitness.co.uk

#### VIRGIN ACTIVE

www.virginactive.co.uk

## ACCESS FOR PEOPLE WITH DISABILITIES

You can get information about using public transport on the Transport for London's website (www.tfl.gov.uk/transport-accessibility). The official visitor organization for London (Visit London) also provides information on accessibility on its website (www.visitlondon.com). Access in London (www.accessinlondon.org) has a guide listing facilities for persons with disabilities.

# Employment

## JOB SEARCHING SUPPORT

### THE AMERICAN CHAMBER OF COMMERCE (UNITED KINGDOM)

75 Brook St.
London W1K 4AD
tel. 020/7290 9888
www.babinc.org

The American Chamber of Commerce (United Kingdom) publishes the *Anglo-American Trade Directory,* which lists American companies with a subsidiary or agent in the United Kingdom.

### FOCUS INFORMATION SERVICES

13 Prince of Wales Terrace
London W8 5PG
tel. 020/7937 7799
www.focus-info.org

FOCUS Information Services provides services and resources for the international community in London, including job searching support.

## ONLINE JOB SITES

There are numerous online job sites where you can look for employment, including the following:

www.efinancialcareers.co.uk
www.fish4.co.uk
http://jobs.theguardian.com
www.jobserve.co.uk
www.jobsite.co.uk
www.monster.co.uk
www.reed.co.uk
www.topjobs.co.uk
www.totaljobs.com
http://uk.linkedin.com/job/jobs-in-london

## STUDENT EMPLOYMENT

### BRITISH UNIVERSITIES NORTH AMERICA CLUB

www.bunac.org

This organization helps young graduates to get temporary work or volunteer overseas. The American program offers help in getting a six-month internship in the United Kingdom.

### EMPLOYMENT 4 STUDENTS

www.e4s.co.uk/docs/student-jobs-search.htm

### UK COUNCIL FOR INTERNATIONAL STUDENT AFFAIRS

www.ukcisa.org.uk

## VOLUNTEERING

Volunteering for an organization can be a good alternative to work and may lead to some paid employment. It will certainly look good on your résumé. Here are some organizations that help people find volunteer positions.

### DO IT

www.do-it.org.uk

### TIMEBANK

Royal London House
22-25 Finsbury Square
London EC2A 1DX
tel. 020/3111 0700
www.timebank.org.uk

### VOLUNTEERING ENGLAND

Society Building
8 All Saints St.
London N1 9RL
tel. 020/7713 6161
www.volunteering.org.uk

## STARTING A BUSINESS

You can find more information about starting a business and freelancing from these organizations.

**THE ASSOCIATION OF INDEPENDENT PROFESSIONALS AND THE SELF-EMPLOYED (IPSE)**
Heron House
10 Dean Farrar St.
London SW1H 0DX
tel. 020/8897 9970
www.ipse.co.uk

**BUSINESS LINK**
www.gov.uk/browse/business
The UK Government's online link for businesses.

**THE CITIZENS ADVICE BUREAU**
www.citizensadvice.org.uk

**COMPANIES HOUSE**
Crown Way
Cardiff CF14 3UZ
tel. 0303/1234 500

**COMPANIES HOUSE, LONDON OFFICE**
Companies House Executive Agency
4 Abbey Orchard St.
London SW1P 2HT
tel. 0303/1234 500
www.companieshouse.gov.uk

**SMALLBUSINESS.CO.UK**
www.smallbusiness.co.uk/starting-a-business/

# Finance

## COST OF LIVING COMPARISONS

**EXPATISTAN**
www.expatistan.com

**NUMBEO**
www.numbeo.com/cost-of-living
Provides comprehensive information on international cost of living.

**XPATULATOR**
www.xpatulator.com

## SAFE DEPOSIT BOX FIRMS

**CHANCERY LANE SAFE DEPOSIT COMPANY**
www.chancerylanesafedeposit.com

**METRO BANK**
www.metrobankonline.co.uk/Commercial/More-Convenient-Services/Safe-Deposit-Boxes/

**METROPOLITAN SAFES**
www.metrosafe.co.uk

## LEADING UK BANKS

Some British banks have branches in the United States, which you may want to visit to find out about opening a British account before your move. These banks all offer mobile and Internet banking.

**BARCLAYS BANK**
tel. 0345/605 2345 (UK)
tel. 02476/842091 (overseas)
www.barclays.co.uk

**HSBC**
tel. 03456/040626
www.hsbc.co.uk

**LLOYDS**
tel. 0845/3000 000
www.lloydsbank.com

**NATWEST**
tel. 03457/888444
www.natwest.com

## UK TAXES

**HER MAJESTY'S REVENUE AND CUSTOMS (HMRC)**
www.hmrc.gov.uk/incometax/tax-arrive-uk.htm (Income Tax)
www.hmrc.gov.uk/migrantworkers/working.htm (Workers)

## Accountants

**BUZZACOTT LLP**
130 Wood St.
London EC2V 6DL
tel. 020/7556 1200
www.buzzacott.co.uk

**MACINTYRE HUDSON**
New Bridge Street House
30-34 New Bridge St.
London EC4V 6BJ
tel. 020/7429 4100
www.macintyrehudson.co.uk

## US TAXES

There is an IRS office at the US Embassy in London, and the US Embassy website lists a number of CPAs who specialize in US taxes for Americans living abroad (http://london.usembassy.gov).

## LEGAL MATTERS

The consular services page on the US Embassy website provides a list of US lawyers (http://london.usembassy.gov). The embassy also offers a notary service.

# Communications

## TELEPHONE, INTERNET, AND TV COMPANIES

You can compare Internet/TV/telephone packages at:
www.cable.co.uk
www.simplifydigital.co.uk
www.uswitch.com
www.broadbandchoices.co.uk

**BRITISH TELECOM (BT)**
tel. 0800/800150
http://home.bt.com

**BT WI-FI**
www.btwifi.co.uk
BT Wi-Fi is available on a daily or hourly basis, and there is no contract to sign.

**PLUSNET**
tel. 0800/432 0080
www.plus.net

**SKY**
tel. 0844/241 1653
www.sky.com

**TALK TALK**
tel. 0800/049 1424
www.talktalk.co.uk
Just voice and Internet.

**VIRGIN MEDIA**
tel. 0845/840 7777
www.virginmedia.com

## TV LICENSE

You should register for a TV license online at www.tvlicensing.co.uk. If you are watching TV in the United Kingdom you must have a TV license.

**PAYPOINT**
www.paypoint.co.uk

## POSTAL AND COURIER SERVICES

### PARCEL FORCE

www.parcelforce.com

### POST OFFICE

www.postoffice.co.uk

### ROYAL MAIL

www.royalmail.com

## COMMUNITY SERVICE

Many of the American Women's Clubs in and around London are very involved in fundraising for the community, as is the Junior League.

### JUNIOR LEAGUE OF LONDON

CAN Mezzanine
49-51 East Rd.
London, N1 6AH
tel. 020/7250 8104
www.jll.org.uk

# Travel and Transportation

## PUBLIC TRANSPORTATION

### BARCLAY CYCLE HIRE

www.tfl.gov.uk/modes/cycling/barclays-cycle-hire

### TRANSPORT FOR LONDON

www.tfl.gov.uk

## RIVER BOATS

### THAMES CLIPPERS

Unit 12, The Riverside Building
Trinity Buoy Wharf
64 Orchard Place
London E14 0JY
tel. 020/7001 2200
www.thamesclippers.com

## TAXIS

### Black Cabs

### CALL-A-CAB

Fleet Services Centre
Advantage House, Unit 7-8
Mitre Bridge Industrial Park
Mitre Way
London W10 6AU
tel. 020/8901 4444
www.callacab.com

### COMPUTER CABS

CityFleet Networks Limited
7 Woodfield Road
London W9 2BA
tel. 020/7432 1432 (credit card bookings)
tel. 020/7908 0207 (cash bookings)
www.comcablondon.com

### DIAL-A-CAB

Dial-a-Cab House
39-47 East Rd.
London N1 6AH
tel. 020/7426 3420 (credit card booking)
tel. 020/7253 5000 (cash booking)
www.dialacab.co.uk

### LONDON BLACK CABS

tel. 07779/336612
tel. 07468/466588 (airport service)
www.londonblackcabs.co.uk

### Minicabs

You can use the Cabwise text messaging service offered by Transport for London to get information on the two nearest licensed minicab firms. See www.tfl.gov.uk/campaign/be-cabwise for details.

**ADDISON LEE**
35-37 William Rd.
London NW1 3ER
tel. 020/7409 9000
www.addisonlee.com

**AIRPORT CARS**
562 Rayners Ln.
Pinner, Middlesex HA5 5DJ
tel. 0800/783 7280
www.airportscars.co.uk

**MEADWAY RADIO CARS**
1019-1021 Finchley Rd.
London NW11 7ES
tel. 0845/456 8000
www.meadway.com

**MINICABS IN LONDON**
214-216 Preston Rd.
London HA9 8PB
tel. 020/8900 5555
tel. 0800/052 4360
www.minicabsinlondon.com

**UBER**
www.uber.com/cities/london

## PUBLIC TRANSPORTATION APPLICATIONS

**LONDON BUS COUNTDOWN**
http://countdown.tfl.gov.uk or http://buschecker.com
Includes bus departures from designated stops and a map with all nearby stops and buses.

**CITYMAPPER**
http://citymapper.com/london/apps
Includes departures for overground trains, the Underground, bus and cycle hire, walking routes, and cab price comparisons.

**NATIONAL RAIL**
http://www.nationalrail.co.uk
Includes travel routes, live trains, service alerts, and ticket purchases.

**TUBE MAP (ANDROID)/ TUBE DELUXE (IOS)**
http://mxapps.co.uk
Includes Tube maps, route planning, service updates, departures, and further travel information.

## DRIVING

Information about driving in the United Kingdom can be found on the Department for Transport website (www.gov.uk/government/organisations/department-for-transport) and The Driving Standards Agency website (www.gov.uk/government/organisations/driving-standards-agency). For information on the rules of the road see www.gov.uk/highway-code.

**NATIONAL CAR PARKS (NCP)**
www.ncp.co.uk

### Congestion Charge

Congestion charge can be paid online at www.tfl.gov.uk or by calling 0343/222 2222.

### Driving Schools

**AUTOMOBILE ASSOCIATION**
www.theaa.com/driving-school/index.html

**BRITISH SCHOOL OF MOTORING**
www.bsm.co.uk

### Car Road Tax

**TAX DISC**
www.gov.uk/tax-disc

### Car Clubs

**CITY CAR CLUB LIMITED**
Matthew Murray House
97 Water Ln.
Leeds LS11 5QN
tel. 0845/330 1234
www.citycarclub.co.uk

### ZIPCAR/STREETCAR LONDON
Melbury House
51 Wimbledon Hill Rd.
London SW19 7QW
tel. 0333/240 9000
www.zipcar.co.uk

## Car Rental Companies
### AVIS RENT A CAR
tel. 0808/284 0014
www.avis.co.uk

### BUDGET CAR HIRE AND VAN RENTAL
tel. 0808/284 4444
tel. 01344/484100 (outside UK)
www.budget.co.uk

### ENTERPRISE RENT-A-CAR
tel. 0800/800227
www.enterprise.co.uk

### EUROPCAR
tel. 0871/384 1087
www.europcar.co.uk

### HERTZ CAR HIRE
tel. 0843/309 3099
www.hertz.co.uk

### THRIFTY CAR AND VAN RENTAL
tel. 0203/468 7686
www.thrifty.co.uk

## AIRPORTS
### BAA HEATHROW AIRPORT
tel. 0844/335 1801
www.heathrowairport.com

### BAA STANSTED AIRPORT
tel. 0844/335 1803
www.stanstedairport.com

### GATWICK AIRPORT
tel. 0844/892 0322
www.gatwickairport.com

### LONDON CITY AIRPORT
tel. 020/7646 0088
www.londoncityairport.com

### LONDON LUTON AIRPORT
tel. 01582/405100
www.london-luton.co.uk

## TRAINS
### CHILTERN RAILWAYS
www.chilternrailways.co.uk

### EAST COAST TRAINS
tel. 03457/225333
www.eastcoast.co.uk

### EUROSTAR
tel. 03432/186186 (within UK)
tel. 01233/617575 (outside UK)
www.eurostar.com

### FIRST CAPITAL CONNECT
tel. 0345/026 4700
www.firstcapitalconnect.co.uk

### LONDON MIDLAND
tel. 0344/811 0133
tel. 0121/634 2040 (from a cell phone)
www.londonmidland.com

### NATIONAL RAIL
tel. 08457/484950
www.nationalrail.co.uk

### RAILCARDS
tel. 0345/3000 250
www.railcard.co.uk

### SOUTHEASTERN RAILWAY
tel. 0845/000 2222
www.southeasternrailway.co.uk

### SOUTH WEST TRAINS
tel. 0345/6000 650
www.southwesttrains.co.uk

### COACH COMPANIES

**GREEN LINE COACHES (PART OF THE ARRIVA GROUP)**
tel. 0844/801 7261
www.greenline.co.uk

**NATIONAL EXPRESS**
tel. 08717/818181
www.nationalexpress.com

**PREMIUM TOURS**
tel. 020/7713 1311
www.premiumtours.co.uk

## Useful Shopping Information

### STANDARD STORE OPENING HOURS

Stores are usually open Monday to Saturday 9am or 10am to 6pm or 8pm, Sunday noon to 6pm.

### ONLINE GROCERY SHOPPING

Ordering groceries and having them delivered to your door is a great service for busy people and those without a car. Here is a list of the companies offering this service.

**OCADO**
www.ocado.com

**SAINSBURYS**
www.sainsburys.co.uk

**TESCO**
www.tesco.com

**WAITROSE**
www.waitrose.com

### AMERICAN FOOD

A few places stock American food.

**AMERICAN FOOD STORE**
2 Ladbroke Grove
London W11 3BG
tel. 020/7221 4563
www.usafoodstore.co.uk

**COSTCO WATFORD**
Hartspring Ln.
Watford, Hertsfordshire WD25 8JS
tel. 01923/699800
If you have a Costco membership, you can use it in the United Kingdom.

**PANZER'S DELI**
13-19 Circus Rd.
London NW8 6PB
tel. 020/7722 8596
www.panzers.co.uk

**PARTRIDGES GLOUCESTER ROAD**
17-21 Gloucester Rd.
London SW7 4PL
tel. 020/7581 0535
www.partridges.co.uk

**PARTRIDGES SLOANE SQUARE**
2-5 Duke of York Square
London SW3 4LY
tel. 020/7730 0651

**SELFRIDGES FOOD HALL**
400 Oxford St.
London W1A 1AB
tel. 0800/123400
www.selfridges.com

**SKYCO INTERNATIONAL FOOD CLUB (UK)**
Unit F10/11 The Mayford Centre
Woking, Surrey GU22 0PP
tel. 01483/776444
www.skyco.uk.com

**WHOLE FOODS MARKET CAMDEN**
49 Parkway
London NW1 7PN
tel. 020/7428 7575
www.wholefoodsmarket.com/stores/camden

**WHOLE FOODS MARKET CLAPHAM JUNCTION**
305-311 Lavender Hill
London SW11 1LN
tel. 020/7585 1488
www.wholefoodsmarket.com/stores/clapham

**WHOLE FOODS MARKET FULHAM**
2-6 Fulham Broadway
London, SW6 1AA
tel. 020/7386 4350
www.wholefoodsmarket.com/stores/fulham

**WHOLE FOODS MARKET KENSINGTON**
63-97 Kensington High Street
The Barkers Building
London W8 5SE
tel. 020/7368 4500
www.wholefoodsmarket.com/stores/kensington

**WHOLE FOODS MARKET PICCADILLY CIRCUS**
20 Glasshouse St.
London W1B 5AR
tel. 020/7406 3100
www.wholefoodsmarket.com/stores/piccadilly

**WHOLE FOODS MARKET RICHMOND**
1-3 George St.
London, TW9 1AB
tel. 020/8334 4130
www.wholefoodsmarket.com/stores/richmond

## CLOTHING AND SHOE SIZES

### Women's Clothing

| US | 6 | 8 | 10 | 12 | 14 | 16 | 18 | 20 |
|---|---|---|---|---|---|---|---|---|
| UK | 10 | 12 | 14 | 16 | 18 | 20 | 22 | 24 |

### Women's Shoe Sizes

Shoes are often labeled by their European size, so you'll need to be familiar with these.

| US | 4.5 | 5 | 5.5 | 6 | 6.5 | 7 | 7.5 | 8 | 8.5 | 9 | 9.5 | 10 | 10.5 |
|---|---|---|---|---|---|---|---|---|---|---|---|---|---|
| UK | 2 | 2.5 | 3 | 3.5 | 4 | 4.5 | 5 | 5.5 | 6 | 6.5 | 7 | 7.5 | 8 |
| European | 34 | 35 | 35.5 | 36 | 37 | 37.5 | 38 | 38.5 | 39 | 39.5 | 40 | 41 | 42 |

### Men's Clothing

US and UK sizes for men, including shirts, are the same usually.

### Men's Shoe Sizes

| US | 5.5 | 6 | 6.5 | 7 | 7.5 | 8 | 8.5 | 9 | 9.5 | 10 | 10.5 | 11 | 11.5 |
|---|---|---|---|---|---|---|---|---|---|---|---|---|---|
| UK | 4.5 | 5 | 5.5 | 6 | 6.5 | 7 | 7.5 | 8 | 8.5 | 9 | 9.5 | 10 | 10.5 |
| European | 37.5 | 38 | 38.5 | 39 | 40 | 41 | 41.5 | 42 | 42.5 | 43 | 43.5 | 44 | 45 |

### Children's Clothing

Children's clothes sizes in the United Kingdom are usually age based and/or by height (in centimeters).

### Children's Shoe Sizes

| US Boy | 7 | 8 | 9 | 10 | 11 | 12 | 13 | 1 | 2 | 3 | 4 | 5 |
|---|---|---|---|---|---|---|---|---|---|---|---|---|
| US Girl | 8 | 9 | 10 | 11 | 12 | 13 | 1 | 2 | 3 | 4 | 5 | 6 |
| UK | 6 | 7 | 8 | 9 | 10 | 11 | 12 | 13 | 1 | 2 | 3 | 4 |
| European | 23.5 | 24.5 | 25.5 | 26.5 | 27.5 | 28.5 | 30 | 32 | 33 | 34 | 36 | 37 |

# Glossary

**anti-clockwise:** counterclockwise
**articulated lorry:** a large truck made of a cab and a trailer
**aubergine:** eggplant
**banger:** sausage (and anything else that goes bang, such as an old backfiring car)
**beef mince:** ground beef
**berk:** jerk
**biscuit:** cookie (a savory biscuit is a cracker)
**blag:** to lie or exaggerate
**bobby:** police constable (as in "bobby on the beat")
**Bob's yer uncle (. . . Fanny's yer aunt):** used here like "hey presto" or "voilà"; usually only the first half of the phrase is said these days
**brackets:** parentheses
**car park:** parking lot
**chemist:** drugstore, pharmacy
**chuffed:** an adjective expressing happiness or satisfaction
**coriander:** cilantro
**courgette:** zucchini
**crumpet:** similar to an English muffin, but fluffier
**dishy:** term used to describe attractive men
**dodgy:** not quite right or illegal
**fag:** a cigarette
**fire:** a source of heating, often used to refer to electric and gas heaters
**flapjack:** oat and golden syrup cereal bar
**fringe:** bangs
**git:** annoying person
**gobsmacked:** utterly speechless; used when someone is very surprised and amazed
**go pear-shaped:** go all wrong; the phrase "go tits up" is also used
**gutted:** upset that something didn't turn out the way you wanted
**hard shoulder:** verge
**Heath Robinson:** adjective for something that is over-engineered and absurdly complex
**ice lolly:** popsicle
**indicators:** blinkers
**inside lane:** the lane nearest the verge; the "outside lane" is the passing lane
**jammy:** lucky (as in "jammy git")
**jelly:** Jell-O
**jimmy:** to urinate (as in "Jimmy Riddle")
**jumper:** a heavy sweater that you pull over your head
**just the job:** a perfect fix or the solution to a problem
**kerfuffle:** a fight or disturbance
**knackered:** very, very tired
**lift:** elevator
**loo:** toilet or bathroom
**lorry:** truck
**lurgy:** a flu-like virus
**minger:** someone who is unattractive
**motorway:** highway
**naff:** tacky or poor quality
**nick:** to steal
**nil/nought:** zero (especially with soccer scores)
**pancake:** French crepe
**paracetamol:** acetaminophen
**parky:** cold
**PC:** police constable
**pissed:** drunk; "on the piss" is a night out drinking
**plait:** braid
**plimsoll:** canvas shoes with rubber soles (such as Converse)
**plonker:** a fool
**porridge:** oatmeal
**pram:** a stroller for a baby
**prawn:** shrimp (for the British, shrimp are very small prawns)
**PTO:** stands for "please turn over," usually on the bottom of a page or letter
**pudding:** dessert or a flour-based cake that is usually steamed, not baked
**pull:** means someone is looking for or found a one-night stand (as in "on the pull" or he "pulled last night")
**pushchair:** stroller (also called buggy)
**rocket:** arugula
**rubber:** eraser
**scrummy:** delicious, as in scrumptious
**shattered:** tired
**sixes and sevens:** muddled up
**skew-whiff:** uneven
**skinfull:** drunk
**skint:** broke (in London people may say "boracic" for boracic lint, which rhymes with skint)
**skive:** avoid
**slag/slapper:** an insult that means a woman of "loose virtue"

**spanner:** wrench
**stone:** 14 pounds; people are sometimes measured in stones, but usually it is in kilos these days
**stonking:** huge
**suss:** to figure something out
**swede:** rutabaga
**swimming costume:** swimming suit
**take the Mickey/Mick/piss:** to tease or mock and can be derogatory to the Irish if used with Mick
**throw a spanner in the works:** to upset or ruin a plan
**tosser/tosspot:** a jerk
**totty:** an attractive/sexy woman
**WAG:** "wives and girlfriends"
**wally:** an idiot
**WC:** water closet (toilet)
**whinge:** to moan
**white coffee:** coffee with milk
**wireless:** radio
**wonky:** not straight or correct

# Suggested Reading

## GUIDEBOOKS

Avalon Travel. *Moon Metro London* (3rd edition). Berkeley, California: Avalon Travel, 2009. A useful guide to visiting London covering accommodation, dining, popular sights, and other activities.

Steves, Rick, and Gene Openshaw. *Rick Steves' Pocket London.* Berkeley, California: Avalon Travel, 2011. A pocket-size guidebook with useful information about London, its sights, and getting around town.

## MAKING THE MOVE

Chesters, Graeme, and David Hampshire. *Living and Working in London* (5th edition). London: Survival Books Limited, 2010. Aimed at the British as well as the international community, this book gives you a practical overview of all of London and the settling-in process.

Junior League. *Living in London: A Practical Guide* (11th edition). Available from the Junior League e-store (www.jll.org.uk) and online booksellers. An indispensable guide, filled with useful information and resources to help you settle in London.

Lyall, Sarah. *A Field Guide to the British.* London: Quercus, 2008. This is a funny and informative look at life as an American expat in London.

Willis, Janetta. *Newcomer's Handbook for Moving to and Living in London.* Portland, Oregon: First Book Inc., 2008. This is a valuable guide to help you set up home in London.

## HOUSING CONSIDERATIONS

Hampshire, David, and Sue Harris. *Buying or Renting a Home in London.* London: Survival Books Limited, 2006. This book guides you through the rental and housing-buying process in the United Kingdom.

## TRAVEL AND TRANSPORTATION

McGhie, Caroline. *The Telegraph Guide to Commuter-land.* London: Aurum Press Limited, 2009. This is a practical guide to commuting to and from London's suburbs.

# Index

## I



## JKL



## M



## NO



## P

## QR



## S



## T

## UV



## WXYZ

## Also Available

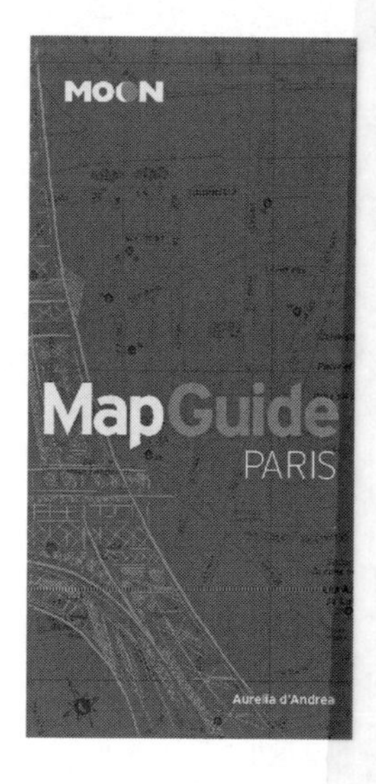

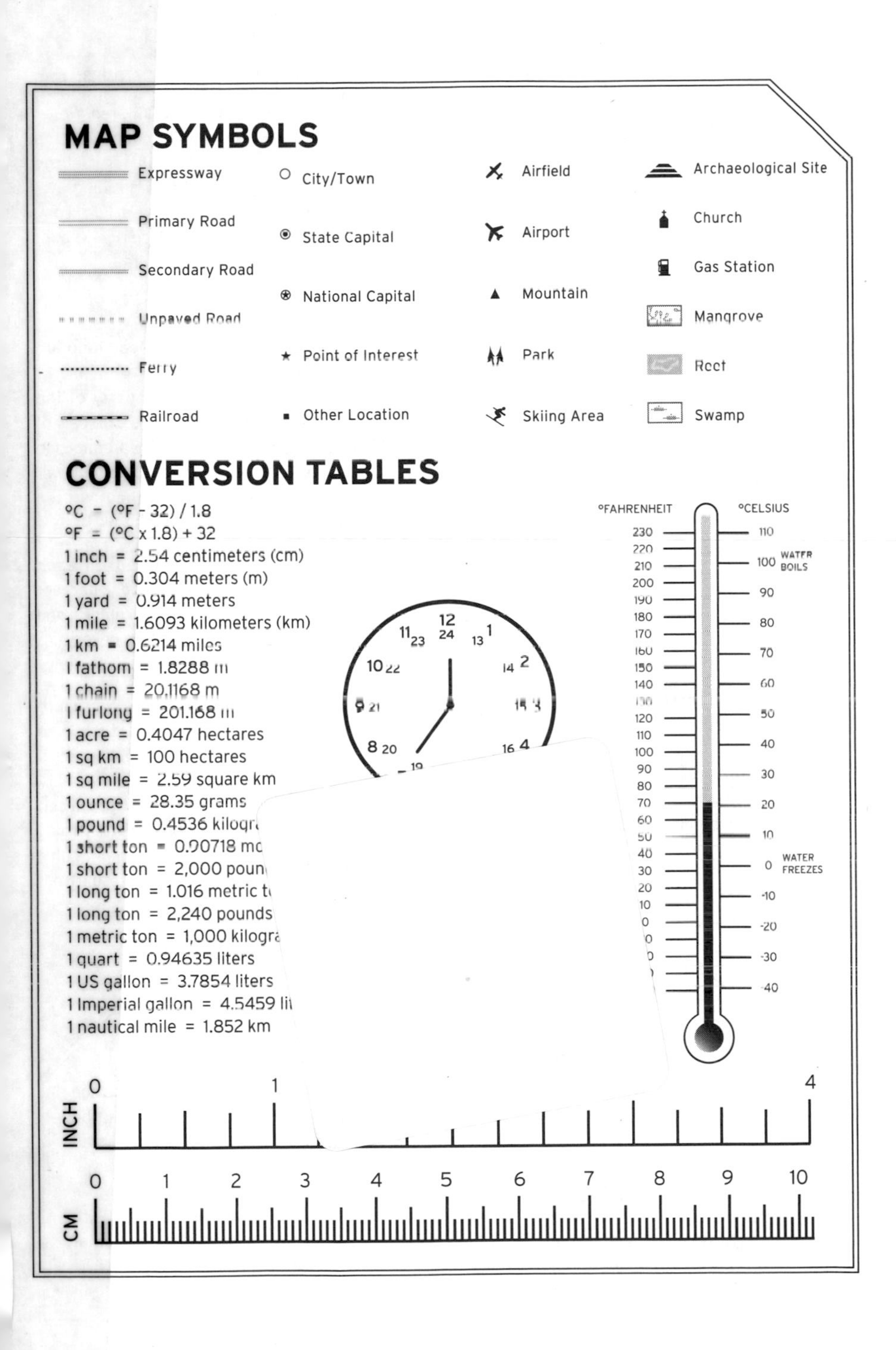

# MAP SYMBOLS

- Expressway
- Primary Road
- Secondary Road
- Unpaved Road
- Ferry
- Railroad
- City/Town
- State Capital
- National Capital
- Point of Interest
- Other Location
- Airfield
- Airport
- Mountain
- Park
- Skiing Area
- Archaeological Site
- Church
- Gas Station
- Mangrove
- Reef
- Swamp

# CONVERSION TABLES

°C = (°F - 32) / 1.8
°F = (°C x 1.8) + 32
1 inch = 2.54 centimeters (cm)
1 foot = 0.304 meters (m)
1 yard = 0.914 meters
1 mile = 1.6093 kilometers (km)
1 km = 0.6214 miles
1 fathom = 1.8288 m
1 chain = 20.1168 m
1 furlong = 201.168 m
1 acre = 0.4047 hectares
1 sq km = 100 hectares
1 sq mile = 2.59 square km
1 ounce = 28.35 grams
1 pound = 0.4536 kilogr
1 short ton = 0.90718 mo
1 short ton = 2,000 poun
1 long ton = 1.016 metric t
1 long ton = 2,240 pounds
1 metric ton = 1,000 kilogr
1 quart = 0.94635 liters
1 US gallon = 3.7854 liters
1 Imperial gallon = 4.5459 li
1 nautical mile = 1.852 km

**MOON LIVING ABROAD LONDON**
Avalon Travel
a member of the Perseus Books Group
1700 Fourth Street
Berkeley, CA 94710, USA
www.moon.com

Editor: Sabrina Young
Copy Editor: Deana Shields
Production and Graphics Coordinator: Elizabeth Jang
Cover Designer: Elizabeth Jang
Map Editor: Kat Bennett
Cartographers: Brian Shotwell, Chris Henrick
Indexer: Greg Jewett

ISBN-13: 978-1-63121-161-4
ISSN: 2165-2244

Printing History
1st Edition — 2012
2nd Edition — November 2015
5 4 3 2 1



Front cover photo: traffic on London's Regent Street © Alan Copson/Exactostock-1672

Title page photo: © alessandro0770/123rf.com

Interior color photos: p. 4-5 © Karen White; p. 6 © Thomas Dutour/123rf.com; p. 7 (top left) © Karen White, (top right) © George Redgrave, (bottom left) © George Redgrave, (bottom right) © Tamara Kulikova/123rf.com; p. 8 (top left) © Karen White, (top right) Laura Smithson, (bottom) © Karen White

Printed in Canada by Friesens



## KEEPING CURRENT

Although we strive to produce the most up-to-date guidebook that we possibly can, change is unavoidable. Between the time this book goes to print and the time you read it, the cost of goods and services may have increased, and a handful of the businesses noted in these pages will undoubtedly move, alter their prices, or close their doors forever. Exchange rates fluctuate—sometimes dramatically—on a daily basis. Federal and local legal requirements and restrictions are also subject to change, so be sure to check with the appropriate authorities before making the move. If you see anything in this book that needs updating, clarification, or correction, please drop us a line. Send your comments via email to feedback@moon.com, or use the address above.